ALSO BY JIM RASENBERGER

The Brilliant Disaster: JFK, Castro,
and America's Doomed Invasion of Cuba's Bay of Pigs

America, 1908: The Dawn of Flight, the Race to the Pole,
the Invention of the Model T, and the Making of a Modern Nation

High Steel: The Daring Men Who Built the World's Greatest Skyline

REVOLVER

SAM COLT
AND THE
SIX-SHOOTER THAT
CHANGED AMERICA

JIM RASENBERGER

SCRIBNER
New York   London   Toronto   Sydney   New Delhi

Scribner
An Imprint of Simon & Schuster, Inc.
1230 Avenue of the Americas
New York, NY 10020

First Scribner hardcover edition May 2020

Interior design by Kyle Kabel

Manufactured in the United States of America

3   5   7   9   10   8   6   4

Library of Congress Cataloging-in-Publication Data is available.

ISBN 978-1-5011-6638-9
ISBN 978-1-5011-6640-2 (ebook)

For Ann

A broadside from the 1850s featuring scenes engraved on the cylinders of Colt's revolvers.

Contents

A Taste for Distasteful Truths

I

In 1831, somewhere in the middle of the Atlantic Ocean, aboard a ship called the *Corvo*, a sixteen-year-old American boy named Sam Colt was struck by an extraordinary idea. Exactly where he got the idea remains an open question. The common story is that he was inspired by observations he made aboard the *Corvo*, either of the ship's wheel or, more likely, its windlass, the barrel-shaped crank that sailors turned to hoist the anchor. Others have suggested that he stole the idea from an inventor whose work he'd seen while abroad in India. Either version is plausible: Colt was certainly brazen enough to steal, but he was also ingenious enough to come up with a brilliant creation on his own. It's also possible that the entire episode never happened and Colt made it up. He was capable of that, too.

In any event—as the story goes—Colt found a quiet moment on a glassy sea and pulled out the small knife a family friend had given him before the start of his voyage. He whittled at a few pieces of scrap wood to create a model of what he had in mind. When he was done, the thing in his hand resembled a small wooden pistol—a child's toy—except that Colt's creation, with its fist-shaped bulge above the trigger, would have appeared ridiculous to people who knew what a pistol looked like in 1831. He had carved an object that would expand the notion of how a gun was supposed to operate. In doing so, he had solved, or at least started to solve, one of the great technological challenges of the early nineteenth century: how to make a gun shoot multiple bullets without reloading.

For more than two decades after he returned home from Calcutta, Sam Colt would strive to perfect and market his "revolving gun" and wait for the world to catch up to his idea. In the meantime, he lived in perpetual motion—"centrifugal chaos," one biographer has called it. At seventeen, he

1

began touring the country as a traveling showman, selling hits of nitrous oxide to audiences in dire need of amusement. (The country was suffering a cholera epidemic at the time.) At eighteen, he went up the Mississippi and Ohio Rivers in a steamboat, and, at nineteen, down the Erie Canal on a canalboat. He was rich by the time he was twenty-one, poor at thirty-one, then rich again at forty-one. He may have had a secret marriage and almost certainly had a son he pretended was his nephew. His brother John committed an infamous murder that could have been lifted straight out of an Edgar Allan Poe story—though in fact it went the other way; Poe lifted a story from *it*—and while John was waiting to be hanged in New York City, Sam invented a method of blowing up ships in the harbor with underwater electrified cables. In 1849, he visited the palace of St. Cloud near Paris and the Dolmabahçe Palace in Constantinople. In 1851, he went to the Crystal Palace in London (not really a palace, but enchanting nonetheless), and in 1854 to the Winter Palace in St. Petersburg. In 1855, he built his own palace, Armsmear, on a hill above his personal empire, called Coltsville, in Connecticut. Coltsville included homes for workers, churches, a music hall and library, schools, a dairy farm, a deer park, greenhouses fragrant with flowers and fruits in all seasons, a beer garden (for German employees), and, at the center of it all, the most advanced factory in the world. While Colt did not single-handedly develop the so-called American System of mass production—using machines to make uniform and interchangeable parts—he was a pioneer of the technological revolution of the 1850s that had nearly as much impact on the world as the American political revolution of the 1770s.

The life of Sam Colt is a tale that embraces many events and facets of American history in the years between the War of 1812 and the Civil War. But it is also—trigger warning—the story of a gun.

The broad thesis of this book is that we cannot make sense of the United States in the nineteenth century, or the twenty-first for that matter, without taking into account Colt and his revolver. Combined in the flesh of the one and the steel of the other were the forces that shaped what the country became: an industrial powerhouse rising in the east, a violent frontier expanding to the west. In no American object did these two forces of economic and demographic change converge as dynamically and completely as in Colt's revolver. Compared to other great innovations of the era, such as Cyrus McCormick's reaper, Charles Goodyear's vulcanized rubber, and Samuel Morse's telegraph—in which Colt played a small but significant part—Colt's gun, a few pounds in the hand, was a featherweight. But it did as much as, if not more than, those others to make the world that was coming.

II

Before we can understand the significance of Colt's revolvers, we need to know what guns were before he came along. The first firearms, in the thirteenth century, were simple barrels or tubes of metal (though the Chinese may have used bamboo) filled with combustible powder and a projectile. When the powder was lit, it exploded in a high-pressure burst of gases—nitrogen and carbon dioxide—that forced the projectile out of the barrel and into flight. Besides perfecting the recipe for gunpowder, the earliest gun innovators focused on barrels and stocks, making guns safer and easier to hold and aim. They then turned their attention to the mechanism, called the lock, which ignited the gunpowder. Originally, a shooter simply held a burning ember to a hole near the back of the barrel. The so-called *matchlock* added a serpentine, or finger lever, that lowered a burning wick to the powder. That lever evolved into a trigger, and the firing mechanism evolved into the *wheel lock* and the more enduring *flintlock*, both of which created sparks from friction and dispensed with the inconvenience of keeping a lit match on hand. In 1807, seven years before Colt's birth, a Scottish clergyman named Alexander John Forsyth devised an important improvement called the *caplock* or *percussion lock*: a small self-enclosed capsule or "pill" of mercury fulminate ignited when sharply hit by the spring-loaded hammer of the gun.

Attempts to increase "celerity of fire," the rate at which projectiles could be discharged from a gun, went back nearly as far as guns themselves. A number of methods had been tried. One obvious solution was to add barrels to the gun—two barrels, four barrels, even six or more, bundled in a sheaf, laid side by side like organ pipes, or fanned out like the toes of a duck. Leonardo da Vinci conceived (though does not seem to have ever built) a giant duck-footed gun with ten splayed barrels. In 1718, James Puckle took a significant leap when he invented a large gun on a tripod with a single barrel and a revolving centerpiece with numerous chambers, but Puckle's gun never advanced beyond the prototype stage. Other attempts to use revolving cylinders had been made over the years. Colt later swore that he knew of none of them until after he invented his own. He may have been lying, as many of his rivals suggested, but his claim is not implausible. All these earlier guns were ultimately discarded and forgotten. They were too unwieldy, too heavy, too complicated, too impractical.

In short, while firearms were easier to use and more dependable at the start of the nineteenth century, the guns of 1830 were essentially what they had been in 1430: single metal tubes or barrels stuffed with combustible powder and projectiles. After every shot, the shooter had to carry out a minimum of three steps: pour powder into the barrel; add a projectile (cannonball, lead ball, or later bullet); then ignite the gunpowder and send the projectile on its way. Even the best rifles in the most experienced of hands required at least twenty seconds, and more likely thirty, to load between shots.

Such guns were most effective when deployed by vast armies—think Frederick the Great and his highly trained, flintlock-armed Prussians—in which hundreds or thousands of men, organized in ranks, loading and shooting in synchronized volleys, created a multishot or machine-gun effect. Of course, the critical element in this machine was the men who were its cogs. As long as guns were primarily used by armies on battlefields, and as long as living men could be supplied to replace the dead and wounded, the advantage went to whoever possessed more guns.

Which brings us back to the significance of Colt's gun. One place where single-shot firearms were *not* effective was in the American west before the Civil War. Western pioneers were usually small in number, facing unfamiliar terrain and Native Americans who resented their presence. When Indian warriors swept across the grasslands on horseback, firing arrows at a rate of one every two or three seconds, even the best-armed Americans—military personnel with Kentucky rifles—were sitting ducks. Not only did their rifles have to be reloaded after every shot; they had to be fired from the dismount, on the ground. An Indian warrior could get off as many as twenty arrows for every bullet, all the while galloping at thirty miles per hour toward the pinned and doomed rifleman.

Colt's revolvers and repeating rifles (which used similar technology) were to become the weapons of choice in engagements with Indians. They were brandished against the Comanche in Texas, the Apache in Arizona, the Cheyenne in Kansas, the Sioux of the Northern Plains, the Nez Perce in the Pacific Northwest, and nearly every other tribe west of the Missouri River. Colts also played a small but important role in the Mexican War in the late 1840s—the war put Colt on the path to riches—and accompanied gold rushers to California in 1849, becoming as indispensable to western sojourners and settlers as shovels, picks, and boots. Next to a Bible, a Colt revolver was the best travel insurance available. As such, it emboldened Americans contemplating a western journey. The west would have been settled sooner or later, but *how* it was settled and *when* it was settled owed a great deal to Colt's gun.

A sense of what the revolver meant in the antebellum west can be gleaned from an article published in a newspaper in Independence, Missouri, in the summer of 1850, describing the guard that would accompany a wagon train delivering passengers and mail to California:

> Each man has at his side, strapped up in the stage, one of Colt's revolving rifles; in a holster, below, one of Colt's long revolving pistols, and in his belt a small Colt revolver, besides a hunting knife—so that these eight men are prepared in case of attack to discharge one hundred and thirty six shots without stopping to reload! This is equal to a small army, armed as in olden times, and from the courageous appearance of this escort, prepared as they are, either for offence or the defensive warfare with the savages, we have no apprehension for the safety of the mails.

III

To contemporary ears, talk of warfare with "savages" sounds more like genocide and imperialism than triumph, but in the age of Manifest Destiny—a term coined in 1845, a year after the Texas Rangers first fired their Colts at the Comanche—Americans embraced it as moral rhetoric supporting the noble cause of westward expansion. During Colt's forty-seven years of life, the country grew in territory by 1.3 million square miles and from less than 10 million to more than 30 million inhabitants. This growth brought out many of America's finest qualities and some of its most compelling history, but it came at a moral price. Born as a puritanical theocracy in the seventeenth century, then born again as an Enlightenment-era republic in the eighteenth, the United States emerged in the first half of the nineteenth century as a nation still nominally defined by religious and political ideals but animated by purely practical pursuits. The Age of Enlightenment became the Age of Expediency. "I know of no country, indeed, where the love of money has taken stronger hold on the affections of men," wrote Alexis de Tocqueville in 1835, the same year Sam Colt, at age twenty-one, began seeking patents for his new gun.

During this period the program to remove Native Americans from their lands became official US government policy, slavery became more entrenched, and America forcibly took from Mexico half a million square miles of that nation's territory, in large part to provide more land for slave plantations. The government became more ethically compromised, as patronage under President Jackson evolved into flagrant corruption under President Buchanan, and more politically divided. Americans became more pious but also more violent, and more modern but less civil. Colt and his revolver were deeply connected to all of these developments in ways both real and symbolic. In addition to telling the story of the man and the gun, then, this book will aim to shed light on the nation as it was in those dark ages of American history. The picture that emerges is not entirely pretty, and before wading in, we might do well to heed the advice of the writer Ambrose Bierce, who fought at the Battle of Shiloh in early April of 1862 and watched twenty-four thousand men fall in forty-eight hours: "Cultivate a taste for distasteful truths."

IV

Sam Colt adored the America of his time, and he embodied it. He was big, brash, voracious, imaginative, and possessed of preternatural drive and energy. He was a classic disruptor—the ur-disruptor—who not only invented a world-changing product but produced it and sold it in world-changing ways, and he became the prototype for hundreds of such disruptors to come, from Thomas Edison to Henry Ford, from Thomas Watson to Steve Jobs. Friends admired him for his generosity, his warmth, and his boldness; adversaries reviled him for his dishonesty and rapaciousness. He possessed all of these qualities, and above all, he was relentless—as relentless in his way as Ahab, the whaling-ship captain who arrived off the pen of Herman Melville at the very moment Sam Colt stepped onto the world stage. But while Ahab pursued one big whale, Colt had many fish to fry.

Because he was a man with his own distasteful truths, and heirs willing to hide them, Colt left behind rabbit holes—ellipses, traps—for his future biographers. The missing pages of a journal, for instance, that he kept when he was seventeen and that might have shed light on his experience aboard a slave ship to New Orleans. Or the letters of women with whom he shared his bed, which have mostly, though not entirely, been culled from his archives. One of his brothers once accused Colt of having "a wife in every port," but the exact nature of his amorous relations is mostly a matter of conjecture.

The problem has not been helped by several Colt biographies that blend verifiable fact with outright fiction, making little attempt to distinguish which is which. The best work on Colt has come from art monographs of his pistols (especially from curators at the Wadsworth Atheneum in Hartford, owners of a large collection of Colt firearms and other Colt artifacts) and several noteworthy articles and books by gun experts and scholars of American industry and western history. Colt gun collectors have added valuable information to the record, though it tends to skew to the interests of people who collect guns. With these exceptions, Colt has not been treated seriously by historians or biographers. We tend to be more comfortable in the company of historical figures who pulled the triggers (soldiers, desperadoes, psychopaths) than those who made the guns, perhaps because the business of manufacturing and selling weapons seems less compelling, and more clinical, than the business of using them. I hope Sam Colt's life will, if nothing else, defy that expectation.

Putting aside said rabbit holes, the most significant questions raised by Colt and his guns are as alive now as they were during his life—even more so, because not even Colt could have guessed how sophisticated and lethal multishot firearms would become. How such guns matter to us as a country today is a question so vital and polarizing that it may be difficult to address events from two centuries ago without inciting strong and reflexive responses. But I hope not impossible. The past is the one place in American life where we can lower our weapons and consider our common heritage, much as Union and Confederate troops did one evening in Stones River, Tennessee, in late December of 1862, on the eve of one of the Civil War's bloodiest battles, when both sides put down their muskets and revolvers and joined across the battlefield in singing "Home, Sweet Home."

The composer of that famous song, John Howard Payne, was a friend of Colt's, and we will meet him in these pages, along with many other interesting folk. For the moment, I will simply add that what follows is a work of fact, for better and for worse, with no agenda other than to honestly tell what happened to Sam Colt, his gun, and America in the years 1814 to 1862.

PART I

BEFORE THE MAST

1814–33

Thou sea-mark! thou high and mighty Pilot! thou tellest me truly where I am—but canst thou cast the least hint where I shall be?

—Herman Melville,
Moby-Dick; or, The Whale,
1851

I am an American. I was born and reared in Hartford, in the State of Connecticut—anyway, just over the river, in the country. So I am A Yankee of the Yankees—and practical; yes, and nearly barren of sentiment, I suppose—or poetry, in other words.

—Mark Twain,
A Connecticut Yankee in King Arthur's Court,
1889

CHAPTER ONE

Lord's Hill

1814–29

The home of Lydia H. Sigourney on Lord's Hill.

I

In the spring of 1815, a twenty-three-year-old schoolteacher named Lydia Huntley left her home in Norwich, Connecticut, to travel inland to the small city of Hartford. An only child in a family of modest means—her father was the gardener of a wealthy widow—Huntley was intelligent and attractive but still unmarried, having turned down several suitors to devote her full affection and attention to her aging parents. She had intended to live out her days in Norwich as a teacher of local girls, an anonymous writer of verse, and, above all, a good and loving daughter. But then came the invitation from Daniel Wadsworth.

Wadsworth was one of the richest men in Connecticut and the de facto arbiter elegantiae, as one scholar has put it, of Hartford. In keeping with his high position, he was a patron and benefactor of many civic and philanthropic causes, including a savings bank, a school for the deaf, and—some

11

years later—an art museum. Now, in 1815, he wanted to open a school for girls. It was not to be just any school, but an exclusive academy with fifteen or so pupils to be selected by Wadsworth himself to ensure that all came from a "similarity of station and attainment." To operate such a school he needed an exceptional teacher. He found one in Lydia Huntley. He summoned her to Hartford, and she, her vow to her aging parents notwithstanding, came.

It was there at her little school that Lydia Huntley first came to know the Colt family. Two of the Colt daughters were her pupils. The older daughter, Margaret, born in 1806, was vivacious and thrived under "the sunshine of joy," as Huntley wrote. Sarah Ann, two years younger, was more bookish and more serious, but many years later Huntley vividly recalled "her profuse flaxen hair, clear, blue eye, and sweet smile, as she lingered by the side of her elder sister."

Other than Huntley's own description of it, all that remains of the school is a notebook kept by Sarah Ann Colt in 1819, when she was eleven. The pages are filled with carefully executed calligraphy and colorful drawings. A geography of the earth ("Though called globe it is not perfectly such; its diameter from east to west is 34 miles longer than from north to south") is followed by an account of the seasons ("They are 4 without the tropics . . . and two within"). Then come beautifully illustrated descriptions of the Ptolemaic system and the theories of Danish astronomer Tycho Brahe.

Finally, Sarah Ann describes the revolutionary views of Copernicus, the sixteenth-century astronomer who profoundly disrupted Europeans' understanding of the universe by observing that the sun does not revolve around the earth but rather the earth around the sun. "This System supposes the sun to be the centre of the System," Sarah Ann wrote in her impeccable script, "and that all the planets move round him."

In the summer of 1819, Lydia Huntley married a wealthy Hartford widower named Charles Sigourney. Her marriage meant the end of the little school, but it also brought Lydia Huntley Sigourney, as she was now known, closer to the Colt family. She moved with her new husband to an estate on Lord's Hill, an enclave of mansions on a verdant rise west of the center of Hartford, "the most beautiful eminence about the city," as a newspaper described it at the time. The Colts lived just across the lane, in a large house surrounded by barns, orchards, gardens, and pasture. "Roses of every hue and variety cast their perfume upon the air," Lydia Sigourney wrote of her new surroundings; "the clematis threw over the piazzas its rich masses of cerulean blue."

From her new vantage, Lydia Sigourney enjoyed watching the large young family across the way. "How often from my window," she wrote of Margaret Colt, "have I seen her traversing the pleasant grounds and shaded retreats of her home, or heard the glad tones of her voice, welcoming some approaching guest." In addition to the two daughters, Sigourney came to know the four spirited Colt sons. John was the eldest at nine, followed by Christopher Jr., seven. The youngest, James, was three.

The one who caught Sigourney's eye was the third son, Samuel, or Sammy, who turned five in the summer of 1819. She often saw him in the pack of neighborhood boys who ran through the fields and woods around Lord's Hill and into the halls of her house to visit her stepson, Charles. Curly haired and rambunctious, Sammy Colt was "a beautiful boy," she later wrote, "uniting sprightliness with a thoughtful temperament."

The parents of this large brood were "our handsomest couple." Sarah Colt, known as Sally, was the "model of dignified beauty" and the daughter of Major John Caldwell, an esteemed veteran of the Revolution and a prosperous merchant. Christopher Colt was "a gentleman of fine form and countenance, and amiable manners." He did not come from great wealth, but his family had roots in southern New England that traced back to the arrival of the Colt family, or *Coult* as they sometimes spelled it, from England in 1633. Christopher's father, Benjamin Colt, had been a respectable farmer in Hadley, Massachusetts. One of Christopher's uncles, Peter Colt, had been a close acquaintance of Alexander Hamilton's and an early textile manufacturer in New Jersey and Connecticut. Several of Christopher's first cousins had also achieved distinction, among them Judah Colt, a pioneer of western Pennsylvania, and Roswell Colt, son of Peter, who had married into a rich Baltimore family and accumulated great wealth and important friends.

A story had it that when young Christopher arrived in Hartford around 1800, he was so lacking in funds that the citizens decided to expel him, as New England towns sometimes did to impecunious young men who showed up on their doorstep like stray cats. That seems unlikely given the prominence of Christopher's relations, and in any case, he stayed. In 1802, he opened a store on Main Street and began placing advertisements in the *Hartford Courant* offering "CROCKERY, GLASS WARE, CHINA and LOOKING GLASSES." After marrying Sally in 1805, he branched out into wider markets, buying cargo on consignment from ships that came from all over the world and sailed up the Connecticut River to Hartford or nearby Middletown: rum from Antigua, brandy from Barcelona, gin from Holland, tea from China, chocolate from Mexico, indigo from India.

In 1807, he advertised for a ship carpenter who could build him a 200-ton ship and a 140-ton brig.

By 1814, the year Sammy was born, Christopher was no longer a mere storekeeper but an international merchant. As he grew wealthy, he joined the boards of various civic organizations in Hartford. He became a director of the Connecticut Asylum for the Education and Instruction of Deaf and Dumb Persons (founded by Daniel Wadsworth) in 1817, treasurer of the Agricultural Society in 1819, and trustee of the Society for Savings later that same year. Christopher was not just respected but genuinely liked and admired, enjoying, as one friend put it, "the higher confidence and esteem of our citizens." He was also said to be "fond, very fond of his children."

Christopher and Sally Colt.

II

At the time she was getting to know the Colt family, Lydia Sigourney was embarking on a literary career that would make her one of the most celebrated writers in the United States. "The Sweet Singer of Hartford," as she came to be known, would produce a body of work that included more than two thousand published poems and hundreds of articles and essays in magazines and journals, many of which would be recycled into more than sixty books under her name. Beyond her much-beloved poetry, she specialized in advice books for girls and young women. She presented an idealized view of American families in all of her writing. Every daughter was pure and sweet, every son dutiful and respectful, every husband noble, and every wife selflessly devoted to her family, "like the sun behind the cloud," as she put it, "giving life & warmth & comfort to all around, itself unseen." There is some irony in this, as Sigourney's own husband accused her of being more interested in her literary career than in her family, but she was not so much hypocritical as aspirational. She described American life not as it was but as she believed it should be. This was precisely what made her work so popular. "When account shall be made of the various agencies, moral and intellectual, that have moulded the American mind and heart during the first half of the nineteenth century," an 1852 anthology of her work predicted, "few names will be honoured with a larger credit than that of Lydia H. Sigourney."

That prediction turned out to be wrong. Lydia Sigourney is almost entirely forgotten now, and when she is remembered, it is mainly to marvel at the awfulness of her poetry. As a teacher, she had encouraged rigor and lucidity, but as a poet, she favored treacle: full moons, dewy lawns, and tremulous sighs. Her biographer, Gordon Haight, began his 1930 account of her life with the admission that he could find no justification for the reputation she had once enjoyed.

But if Sigourney's verse was bad, it was arguably bad for good reasons. The foamy gauze she cast over American life was meant to make ugly things pretty and unbearable things bearable. Life in early nineteenth-century America could be very cruel. The young nation's economy was unstable and reversals of fortune were common. Businesses dried up, investments soured, and one of five households became insolvent—"embarrassed," they called it then—at least once. Even if wealth could be sustained, life itself was easily snatched away. Infectious diseases were rampant and devastating. One early nineteenth-century study of mortality conducted in New York City over several decades, while not entirely applicable to the smaller city of Hartford, gives a sense of life's tenuousness. The city's health inspector found an average life span of thirty years in 1815, which fell to twenty-two years by 1837. The greatest number of deaths was in young children—40 percent would not make it to age five—but adults between twenty and forty filled more than a quarter of the city's coffins. No family was spared. For Lydia Sigourney, who lost several children of her own, the solution was poetry—*lots* of poetry: an infinite profusion of soothing words.

III

The trouble began soon after Sigourney moved to Lord's Hill. It arrived suddenly and unexpectedly, following several years of prosperity under Presidents Madison and Monroe. The Panic of 1819, as the cataclysm would come to be known, was a financial meltdown triggered mainly by an abrupt tightening of credit. Many Americans were ruined by it, and Christopher Colt was one of them. Exactly how he was exposed is not clear, but a man who buys on consignment and builds ships is generally a man with debts. Later, Sam would recall seeing his mother get the news that his father had gone bankrupt. He was playing under the piano in the drawing room. Sarah clasped her hands and cried out, "My poor little children!"

In June of 1819, Sarah gave birth to another girl, Mary. In May of 1821, she gave birth to a boy, Norman. A month later, in the middle of June, shortly before Sam's seventh birthday, she died of consumption—pulmonary tuberculosis. Christopher Colt was now forty-one, in debt, and the father of eight motherless children. That number was reduced to seven when the infant boy, Norman, died in the spring of 1822.

The Colts' turn in fortunes is almost palpable in Sarah Ann's mottled notebook, the same in which she had a few years earlier drawn her beautiful flowers and summarized Copernican astronomy. Sarah Ann is now thirteen. She has flipped over the notebook and started anew, upside down and backward, a kind of Copernican revolution in miniature. The inside cover, from this end, is dated 1821. A small burgundy maple leaf, relic of some long-ago autumn day (placed there, apparently, by Sarah Ann herself) is pressed between the pages. Rather than elegant calligraphy and bright pictures of flowers, these pages are filled with moody poems, all copied in Sarah Ann's neat hand.

> I love to muse, when none are nigh,
> Where yew branches wave
> And hear the winds, with softest sigh,
> Swept o'er the grassy grave

begins one poem, entitled "The Grave," by Bernard Barton. Another is called "Death of an Affectionate Mother." Several are by Sarah Ann's former teacher Mrs. L. H. Sigourney, who was already developing a kind of specialty in sentimental death poetry. Sigourney's poems stand out from the others as particularly tender views of death; no one in a Sigourney poem dies without a soft smile on her face. Sigourney would pen hundreds of rhyming eulogies during her lifetime, so many that after she died in 1865, Timothy Dwight V—later president of Yale University—would joke that prominent Americans, "beset by a kind of perpetual fear that she might survive them," were privately relieved they no longer had the threat of a Sigourney poem hanging over them.

In March of 1823, Christopher Colt remarried. His new wife was thirty-five-year-old Olivia Sargeant, from Hartford. As Olivia and Christopher added two children—a boy named William and a girl named Olive—Christopher worked to maintain the family's status, placing bets on various enterprises and schemes. In September of 1823, he solicited "subscriptions" (stock purchases) for the Connecticut River Steamboat Company, to operate between Hartford and New York. On at least two occasions in 1824 he imported and sold large shipments of salt. His most serious venture was a textile mill called the Union Manufacturing Company, an attempt to follow his uncle Peter Colt on the path from merchant to manufacturer.

None of these attempts were profitable enough to allow the family to remain on Lord's Hill. In early 1824, when Sam was nine, Christopher sold the house, along with five acres of orchard and meadow—"a desirable situation for a gentleman's residence," as he advertised in the papers—and moved his family to a house on Church Street, near the center of town.

In some accounts, to save money Sammy was sent to live with a family on a farm in Glastonbury, Connecticut, across the river from Hartford. There are anecdotes, naturally, involving guns. One has young Sammy sitting under a tree, taking apart a pistol given to him by his grandfather, then putting it back together into perfect working order. In another, a Colt relative comes upon the boy one afternoon standing on a wooden bridge over the Connecticut River, shooting into the water.

Beyond these few slim stories, it's hard to gauge Colt's exposure to firearms as a boy. Guns were common household items at the time, though exactly how common is a contentious subject even today. (One attempt to count firearms in early America ended up with the scholar who conducted it accused of academic fraud.) It seems clear enough, though, that many if not most American households had at least a rudimentary firearm, with a greater prevalence in the south and west than in the north. America's frontier history promoted a "gun culture," as the historian Richard Hofstadter has put it, because pioneers needed guns to feed themselves and protect themselves against wild animals and Indians. The Revolutionary War, too, had placed a premium on gun ownership. By the time Colt was born in Hartford, though, the need for guns had greatly been reduced in New England and along most of the Eastern Seaboard. They were mainly tools for hunting and fowling, to add food to the table or for an afternoon of sport or, in Colt's case, for shooting fish.

Regarding his future as a gunmaker, probably the most significant fact of Colt's youth is where he grew up. Though a small city, with a population of just seven or eight thousand during Colt's childhood, Hartford was nonetheless a significant inland port. The Connecticut River ran along its eastern flank, linking the towns of northern New England to Long Island Sound and New York City, while the Boston Post Road passed south through Hartford to New Haven and New York. Partly due to its location as a transportation hub, Hartford gave rise to banking, shipping, and insurance companies, as the Connecticut River Valley became the central artery through which the materials and products of America's industrial revolution flowed. Up and down the valley companies formed to produce textiles, clocks, axes, swords, and—above all—guns.

The most important gun manufacturer in the nation during Colt's youth was the US Armory in Springfield, Massachusetts, thirty miles upriver from Hartford. Another federal armory had been founded in Harpers Ferry, Virginia, but the combination of government funding and Yankee ingenuity made Springfield not only the most important supplier of arms to the United States but the most influential factory in the country during Colt's youth. Nearly as important as Springfield was a private armory twenty miles downriver from Hartford, at Middletown, owned by Simeon North. Another private armory, belonging to Eli Whitney, was not strictly in the Connecticut River Valley—it was in New Haven—but it added to the state's industrial luster and know-how. Guns were still largely crafted by hand, but all of these armories, and many smaller gun mills and shops between, were making the production of firearms simpler and cheaper by the use of machinery. In doing so, they were becoming the cradles of an industrial revolution that would transform the United States in the nineteenth century. The Connecticut River Valley has been described as the Silicon Valley of its day, and while the comparison may be a bit glib, it captures the synergy of concentrated talent and technology that surrounded Sam Colt in Hartford.

Colt would eventually build his own oversize cradle of industry, but the important fact of his youth is that he was not exposed to guns in the usual way that many American boys were—as hunting weapons, as tools, as heirlooms—but as products to be manufactured and sold and, not least, improved.

IV

Little is certain about these years in Colt's life except that they were regularly visited by grief. Margaret, the eldest Colt child and cherished pupil at Miss Huntley's school, died at the age of nineteen, "with the early light of a cloudless summer morning," in July of 1825, snatched by consumption. According to one dubious story, recounted in a newspaper years later, she "had a quarrel with her step-mother, and in a fit of frenzy rushed out the house, in the midst of a tremendous storm of hail, snow and rain . . . and caught a violent cold, which caused her death of quick consumption." Lydia Sigourney visited Margaret a few days before the young woman's death and describes a more plausible, albeit highly sentimentalized, course of tuberculosis: "Months of suffering, mingled with the knell of the consumptive cough." Less convincing is Sigourney's depiction of Margaret at the end: "Yet on her pure brow, was the smile of one, from whom the bitterness of death had been taken away."

Sigourney wrote a long poem about Margaret's funeral. It begins at her graveside, her friends "with their brows of bloom, and shining tresses," her family and fiancé weeping as she is lowered into the ground. It ends with an assurance that all of this is for the best:

> Cold reasoners! be convinced. And when ye stand
> Where that fair brow, and those unfrosted locks
> Return to dust, where the young sleeper waits
> The resurrection morn, oh! lift the heart
> In praise of Him who have the victory.

Less than a year after Margaret's death, in March of 1826, another of the daughters born to Sarah, Mary, died. Then, in 1827, came a different kind of loss. John, the eldest Colt son, ran away. The supposed villain, again, was Olivia, the stepmother John blamed for his discontent. This was the first in a number of episodes featuring John that would become more troubling as the years passed.

Sometime in the winter of 1829, as the country celebrated—or lamented, as many did—the election of Andrew Jackson to the presidency, a bit of good news came the Colts' way. Christopher was offered the position of mill agent at a company in the town of Ware, Massachusetts. This was a respectable job and a reprieve from the financial distress that had dogged the family for the last decade. Before the Colts could move to Ware, though, they had to endure one more trial.

Sarah Ann, the flaxen-haired, blue-eyed sister who had drawn such pretty pictures as a girl and transcribed such mournful poetry as a teenager, was now twenty-one. She had followed Lydia Sigourney into education. She was one of seven teachers at the prestigious Hartford Female Seminary, a school for girls founded in 1823 by Catharine Beecher, daughter of the famous Congregationalist minister Lyman Beecher. Another of the new young teachers was Catharine Beecher's seventeen-year-old sister, Harriet, who would become famous many years later as the author of *Uncle Tom's Cabin*.

On March 26, 1829, Sarah Ann committed suicide by swallowing arsenic. Why she killed herself is not clear. Lydia Sigourney suggested that Sarah Ann never got over the death of her sister. Others attributed the suicide to unrequited love. One of her brothers, James, blamed it on too much time spent reading books. Blame would fall, too, on Olivia, the captious stepmother. But the simplest explanation may be a streak of emotional instability that ran through the Colt family, along with dark currents harder to specify. In time, every Colt sibling would experience depressions, rages, and dependencies. Meanwhile, not even Lydia Sigourney's talents could make poisoning by arsenic—unquenchable thirst, diarrhea, frequent vomiting of blood—sound sweet. While Margaret got her death poem, Sarah Ann never did.

Sam Colt eventually got his. It would be read on a winter day, as war raged to the south—a war in which Colt's guns would play a significant part and by which his factory would profit enormously. Sigourney's eulogy for Colt would be filled with pretty sentiments ("That stately form,—that noble face / Shall we no more behold?") that may have given solace to some of the mourners gathered at his grave but had no bearing on the life he had just lived. The truth is, Sam Colt never had much use for poetry.

CHAPTER TWO

His Name Was Colt

JULY 4, 1829–JULY 4, 1830

Ware Cottage.

I

The Colts arrived in Ware sometime in the early spring of 1829. There were seven of them, including the two young children of Christopher and Olivia. John, the eldest son, remained absent. Sarah Ann had recently been buried in Hartford, near her mother and sisters.

Assuming they came directly from Hartford, fifty miles by road, they took an early-morning stage north to Springfield, Massachusetts, switching to the noon stage that ran east every Tuesday and Thursday through central Massachusetts. This brought them to the outskirts of Ware just before 4:00 p.m., after nearly ten hours on roads hard with winter frost or dissolved into mud by springtime thaw or—most likely at that season—frozen, then thawed, then refrozen into bone-rattling humps and ruts. Compared to the

21

budding Connecticut River Valley, this country, already falling into evening shadow, was bleak. The hills of Ware had been burned over regularly by Native Americans, and what remained of trees had been cut by farmers, and the land was now as bald as the moon. Even so, the hills might have been described as gentle were it not for the giant boulders scattered over them, looking as if they had just been dropped from the sky and might begin to roll at any moment.

The last miles of the Colts' journey scrolled by like one of the enormous panoramas of historical chronologies popular at the time in the museums of Boston and New York: *A History of New England in Two Scenes*, this one might have been titled. First, the coach passed through Ware Center, the original village, incorporated in 1761. Both the town hall and the Congregational church were housed inside a simple white clapboard meetinghouse. In front of the meetinghouse was the town green. On one side of this green stood a blacksmith shop, on the other side a tavern, and clustered nearby were plain saltbox houses—altogether a settlement that would not have appeared out of place at the time of the Revolution.

Two miles farther down the road, they came upon the other, newer Ware. They probably heard it before they saw it, a thrum rising above the clatter of horse hooves and carriage wheels, clarifying into a heavy bass thump under a soprano squeal. Moments later, the Colts were riding east down Front Street. No building here was older than five or six years. There was a small bank with oversize Grecian columns, a few shops, an apothecary, and a hotel, recently built for a fortune of $10,000 and boasting "several hot and cold baths." At the far end of Front Street, on the banks of the Ware River, rose the pulsing heart of the place, the reason for its existence, and the source of all the racket: a large brick textile mill, nearly three hundred feet long and fifty feet high, with a high-pitched roof capped by a cupola.

Ware Factory Village was one of dozens of towns that sprang up from the hard ground of New England in the 1820s, transforming quiet and barren landscapes into hives of industry. The man indirectly responsible for this was Francis Cabot Lowell, a Bostonian who had opened his first cotton mill in Waltham, Massachusetts, in 1814, the year of Sam Colt's birth. Lowell died in 1817, but in 1823 his former partners opened a new factory on the Merrimack River and honored Lowell by naming the town after him. Investors in the Lowell mills saw an annual return of 17 percent in early years, spinning, as one historian writes, "cotton into gold."

Textile mills thrived in New England rather than in, say, Virginia or Ohio, for many good reasons. Some credit goes to the famous Yankee "go-ahead" industriousness and inventiveness that propelled New England into the nineteenth century. But mills were also born of economic necessity. New England's soil, never much good to begin with and now depleted by generations of poor farming techniques, was so unsuited to growing that Yankees needed to branch out from agriculture if they hoped to prosper. The same geological features that made New England poor farmland made it ideal for mills. Mills wanted steady precipitation and steep grades—water + gravity was the formula for hydropower—and the corrugated landscape of New England was perfectly formed to supply this. Out west, waterways such as the mighty Ohio River averaged just six inches of fall per mile, and southern waterways averaged between three and six feet per mile. The rivers and streams of New England averaged five to ten feet of fall, with enough rain and snow to keep rivers full and fast year-round.

At Ware, the drop was an extraordinary seventy feet in a quarter of a mile. The river hurtled down from the north, then plunged and turned sharply in a series of cataracts before burbling off to the west, where it eventually drained into the Connecticut River. In 1822, the Ware Manufacturing Company, a group of Boston investors, raised the vast sum of $600,000 to turn the falls into a mill site. First, the falls were dammed and the river rerouted, a Herculean project of trench digging and earthmoving. The river filled in behind the dam and became a large reservoir, to be called Ware Pond. Narrow channels, or *raceways*, sucked water from the pond into swift flumes, where it met the buckets of the giant wooden waterwheels that powered the mill. The raceways and mill were completed by 1824, and by 1825 Ware Factory Village had an iron foundry, a machine shop, stores, homes, and a new church. As early histories of Ware put it, "a desolate wilderness" had been transformed into a prosperous village "as by enchantment."

That exaggerated matters a little. The site was not a wilderness before it became a mill town. Local Indians had lived or visited there for generations to fish in the weirs (hence the name). As for prosperity, that would eventually come to Ware, but so far it had proved elusive. At the start of 1829, Ware Manufacturing Company had gone bankrupt and sold its property to a new venture, the Hampshire Manufacturing Company. It was this new company that brought in Christopher Colt to run its operations.

II

The stage stopped in front of the hotel. Passengers continuing east to Boston would spend the night, then resume their journeys the next morning. The Colts probably transferred to a cart or wagon to carry them the rest of the way to their new home, down Front Street then a sharp right, over the narrow bridge that crossed the river, and up the hill. Perched on the slope above the mill, shaded by a grove of spruce trees and surrounded by a picket fence, the house, known as Ware Cottage, was considered one of the prettiest in town.

As he looked down from the veranda at the back of Ware Cottage, Sam Colt's first impressions of the town were probably mixed at best. To a worldly boy raised in the metropolis of Hartford, with a bustling population now close to ten thousand, and with shops of every variety and ships from every port, Ware, claiming just two thousand souls between the old town and the new, must have seemed close to nowhere. Until recently, the place had been "remarkable only for the meanness of its soil, and the large number of stones it raised to the acre"—a place "so discreditable," according to one of its own inhabitants, that people were ashamed to admit they lived there. The last time anything worth reporting had happened in Ware was the previous summer, when a man named Thomas McClentick accidentally stepped on the handle of a scythe in the village store and the blade had jumped up and sliced his neck, "making a deep cut and completely severing the jugular vein," as one newspaper put it.

More intriguing to Colt might have been the story of the unfortunate inventor Fordyce Ruggles. The previous winter, Ruggles had been showing off his newly patented pistol at a local tavern when a friend picked it up to examine it. The friend accidentally discharged the gun and shot Ruggles in the chest, killing the inventor with his own invention.

But if Colt encountered Ware as a provincial backwater with little to offer beyond coarse cotton and portentous ironies, it's likely that he also understood, because he was a young man with a mechanical bent and an eye on the future, that the mill deserved his attention. Textile mills were still a new phenomenon in New England, but they were transforming the region, by nineteenth-century terms, at breakneck speed. Dependent on topography and weather—they needed rain to operate—these early mills still had one foot in the agrarian culture of the early nineteenth century, but they were the laboratories where the machinery of the late nineteenth century was developed, and where the young men who would invent and perfect the tools of the industrial revolution learned their trade. When Colt descended into the thunderous substructure of the mill—it's impossible to believe he did not—he got a free education in modern technology, circa 1830.

The most striking fact of the early industrial revolution was that it was revolutionary in a literal sense: everything *turned*, starting with those giant wooden wheels in the mill races, sluggishly rotating under the pressure of falling water. This motion was carried through an axle to a series of beveled and ever smaller—and faster—cast-iron gears, their respective cog-teeth biting into one another. From the cogs the motion was transferred into rods and shafts and belts. Thus, the energy of falling water ran through the power train into the working floors above, where it was finally conveyed, just seconds after the river met the wheel, to the machinery—carding, drawing, roving, winding, and spinning—that turned raw cotton into yarn and yarn into cloth. In later years, when energy began to secrete through cables and wires, the most advanced technologies would be invisible to the human eye. In the early nineteenth century, though, the mechanics of energy could be studied like the guts of a Brobdingnagian's watch cracked open for repair. A young man with a mechanical bent could learn a great deal simply by watching: how things connected, how they turned, how they revolved.

III

Other than a few letters written by Samuel's stepmother and a large leather ledger kept by Christopher Colt at the mill—which now gathers dust in the attic of the Young Men's Library Association, down the street from where the old mill once stood—little remains of the Colts' time in Ware. But three anecdotes have found their way into histories of the Colt family. In the first of these, a lovestruck Sarah Ann leaps suicidally into the Ware River from a high rock (known to this day as Lover's Leap). That story is apocryphal; Sarah Ann died in Hartford, and the Colts did not arrive in Ware until the spring after her death.

The second story features John Colt. Since fleeing home a second time, John had been living in Baltimore, employed as a mathematics teacher at a school for girls, and then in Wilkes-Barre, Pennsylvania, working on a canal. After learning of Sarah Ann's suicide, John, bereft and adrift, decided to join the Marines. No sooner did he enlist in the summer of 1829 than he realized that military life was not for him. He tried to withdraw, but the corps would not let him go. So John forged a note from his "father," a farmer in Massachusetts whom John named George Hamilton. John mailed the note in an envelope to his youngest brother, asking James to post it from Ware and send it back to Norfolk, to the commander of the Marines. In the note, George Hamilton pleaded with the commander to release the young man who called himself Colt but was in fact Hamilton's underage son; the foolish lad had lied about his name and age to join the corps and had broken the hearts of his father and mother, and please would the commander take pity and send him home at once? This elaborate and absurd ruse worked. John Colt was released from the Marine Corps. Unlike his fictional self, though, he had no intention of returning home and never did.

The third Colt story, also from that summer of 1829, features Sam. The setting is Ware Pond. The date is July 4.

As usually told, the story makes no mention of the weather, which was rainy and blustery. The entire East Coast, from the Carolinas to New England, was wet. In Raleigh, North Carolina, the Independence Day concert on the State House Grove had to be postponed. In Washington City—as the nation's capital was then known—President Jackson skipped an event to mark the opening of a section of the Chesapeake and Ohio Canal in favor of staying dry. Numerous celebrations and marches were canceled in New York, though outdoor concession stands remained open and did a brisk business from patrons who "love rum better than rain." In Boston, a young journalist named William Lloyd Garrison was seen striding through a cold drizzle on his way to Park Street Church to give a speech that would be remembered as the clarion call of the abolitionist movement.

Compared to Garrison's speech, or even Jackson's decision to stay indoors, Colt's performance that day hardly constitutes a monumental occasion in American history. But it was a kind of declaration in its own right. And unlike some other anecdotes of Colt's youth, this one seems to be based in fact.

The details of the day are sparse, but many can be reasonably surmised, starting with Colt's path from Ware Cottage, where he began his day, to Ware Pond, where it almost ended. Descending the muddy hill above the mill, he would have crossed the bridge to Front Street, into the center of the village. Because he was new here and son of the mill agent, villagers probably took notice as he approached. He was hard to miss. At fourteen, soon to turn fifteen—his birthday was July 19—Colt was tall for his age, on his way to six feet, and considered handsome. Curls of light brown hair spilled out from his hat, and beneath the brim his eyes were a lively pale blue. His chin was probably covered in the first wisps of the beard he would keep his whole life. As a man, he would put on flesh in the way prosperous men in the nineteenth century tended to do, but he was still slender. He probably wore a brightly colored swallowtail coat and calf boots to fend off the rain and mud. As someone once wrote of Colt, his biggest idea was "making the world aware that he was in it," so his outfit may have been enhanced by few shiny trinkets and buttons. Such accessories were common, and Sam Colt was not the kind of young man to eschew them.

Even if he had been physically unassuming and plainly attired, he would have been conspicuous on this day because of the heavy load he carried. He probably had a coil of black cable hung around his neck or rakishly draped from a shoulder, and a satchel in his hands. Everyone knew where he was going with this load because he had advertised his intentions on a bill posted around town:

SAM COLT WILL BLOW UP A RAFT ON WARE POND

He turned upriver toward the mill and the dam. Front Street was surely crowded with mill workers. Usually rain meant good water power, but the mill was closed for the holiday. Because this Fourth of July fell on a Saturday, the workers were enjoying that rarest of pleasures, a two-day rest from their usual six-days-a-week, twelve-hours-a-day toil. No drizzle was likely to dampen the mood, but if it did, a hogshead of rum from the village store could lift it. Men in stovepipe hats would be gathered under the eaves of stores, smoking and chewing tobacco, spitting the juice into the muddy ruts on the road. Girls not much older than Colt would be strolling Front Street. Mills in towns such as Ware hired girls and young women to run some of the machines, paying them less than men, but also giving them an independence rarely available to unmarried females, including the freedom to walk the streets when and with whom they pleased. Somewhere, probably, a fiddler played a patriotic tune. Toasts were raised to Presidents Adams and Jefferson—both of whom had died, by extraordinary coincidence, exactly three years earlier *to the day*—and more toasts to the new president, Andrew Jackson, a man so adored by some and reviled by others that it's safe to assume oaths were uttered and fists thrown when his name came up. "The stir, the gossip, the animation, the regularity of a manufacturing place," is how one contemporary described Ware's social life. It was a "population so much thrown together in their daily employment as to favor the rapid spread of evil or of good."

As Colt passed the dam, he might have heard a voice thundering in the distance. Up the hill from the pond, inside the East Evangelical Church, the Reverend Parsons Cooke was delivering a fiery Fourth of July sermon on the dangers of "ardent spirits," as alcoholic beverages were known. "Ours is the cause of God!" Cooke exclaimed from his pulpit. "And if those bought with the blood of Christ will stand aloof, when the world declares neutrality as an enemy, methinks angels will weep over your ingratitude and folly!"

Parsons Cooke had been installed in the new church by a wealthy and exceedingly pious mill agent named Sampson Wilder, one of Christopher Colt's predecessors. Wilder was the sort of Calvinist who equated pleasure with sin. When a group of young people had tried to launch a dance school in Ware, he'd been pleased to note that both the dance instructor and his best pupil immediately caught cold and died—God's way, believed Wilder, of clarifying His position on dance.

Worse than dancing to Calvinists such as Wilder and Cooke was drinking. They had good reason for concern. Americans in the early nineteenth century consumed stupendous quantities of liquor—an average of seven gallons of hard alcohol per capita per year, according to one estimate—and the villagers of Ware did their part to boost the national average. One historian of Ware estimated that a group of two hundred or so mill workers easily drained a hogshead of rum every working day (a hogshead being about sixty gallons). What particularly galled Wilder during his tenure in Ware were the many young men and women who enjoyed Sundays by rowing a mile or two up the river and "having at a groggery what they called a jollification," thus "desecrating the Sabbath."

That groggery was probably getting heavy traffic this day. On no occasion did Americans drink more than on the Fourth of July. Many ministers had made the holiday an occasion to mount their pulpits and preach the gospel of temperance, but few could match Parsons Cooke's intensity as he tied alcohol consumption to broader moral threats. The industrial revolution was changing not only New England's demographics and physical landscape, believed Cooke, but its moral terrain. "Rather than journeying to the wilds of Ohio, or, farther yet, to the Sandwich Islands to convert the heathen," the scholar Philip F. Gura has written, "Cooke and others chose as their missionary field these communities where the millworking population threatened the older agricultural order with unorthodox opinions and lax moral standards." The people of Ware had lost their way, and Parsons Cooke's job was to shepherd them back to righteousness.

Colt stopped at the edge of the pond and put down his load. A slow current ran toward the dam. Raindrops pecked the rippled water. Colt never left a record of how he carried out his demonstration, so his exact materials are not certain, but he had at least three items with him: a long copper wire, waterproofed with cloth and tar and probably spliced in the middle with a strip of filament; a waterproofed container packed with gunpowder; and an instrument to produce an electrical charge, most likely a simple Leyden jar, a glass vessel covered in foil and filled with water, which stored enough static electricity to generate a spark.

Colt was not the first person to try to blow up something with electricity. Ben Franklin had used "electric flame" to ignite gunpowder as far back as 1751. Underwater explosives were not new, either. Colt was no doubt familiar with the story of a Yale graduate named David Bushnell who in 1776 created a small hand-propelled submersible to sneak up on enemy vessels and attach keg mines to their keels. (Bushnell's *Turtle* managed to nuzzle under the flagship of the British fleet in New York Harbor, but the keg mine failed to attach and the operation was aborted.) From the perspective of the twenty-first century, when naval mines are commonplace and airborne military drones can be piloted by operators thousands of miles away, triggering an explosive in the middle of a pond remotely with an invisible "fluid" called electricity may not seem remarkable. But in 1829 it remained more in the realm of magic than reality. That a fourteen-year-old boy was proposing to do it made it preposterous, and therefore not to be missed.

"It had been noised around that a youngster—one Sam Colt—would blow up a raft on the pond that day, and so I with other apprentices of the neighborhood walked some way to see the sight," Elisha Root, then a twenty-one-year-old machine shop worker, recalled many years later. Root's words and Colt's own brief description, plus a few accounts by early biographers, are the only record we have of that day at Ware Pond, so there is a lot we do not know about it. One reasonable assumption, though, is that the crowd that gathered to watch Sam Colt blow up a raft was not the same crowd that attended Parson Cooke's temperance sermon up the hill. Many were well into their grog, and the mood was rowdy. They might have been interested in the bourgeoning science of electricity. More likely, they came to see something blow up.

Colt stood among the reeds at the edge of the pond. The raft drifted in the wind. He waited for it to arrive where he wanted it, then he joined the end of his wire to the Leyden jar, closing the circuit and sending an electric current to the explosive under the boat. With a thick *whoosh* the pond water heaved up. Dogs were probably barking, waterfowl flapping into the air, stunned fish floating to the surface. A little wave swept downriver and lapped over the dam. But the raft just drifted on, a little faster, chased by the wake but unscathed. "An explosion was produced," Elisha Root recalled, "but the raft was by no means blown sky-high."

What went into the sky was a plume of brown water, and when it came back down, much of it fell over the spectators. They were already wet from rain, but now they were wetter, and muddier, and probably a few drams beyond reason. "In wrath they converged on Sam swearing vengeance" is how one account tells it, to administer a "sound birching." Before they could grab Colt, Elisha Root intervened. "He wiped the muddy water from his face, grinned reassuringly, and led Sam to safety." Root later recalled that his curiosity about "the boy's explosive contrivance," rather than human-itarian concern, led him to take Colt under his protection. He wanted to know how Sam did it.

IV

"We received your letter today and we all feel gratified that you have located yourself where you can acquire a suitable knowledge of Navigation. I hope you will sedulously improve all your time, save what is necessary for exercise & relaxation, that you may prosecute your studies with renewed energy & vigour."

The letter from Olivia Colt was dated Ware Cottage, June 15, 1830, and addressed to Samuel Colt, Amherst, Massachusetts. Nearly a year had passed since Colt's experiment on Ware Pond. Presumably Sam had spent the year in Ware with his family, prosecuting his studies—to judge from the tone of his stepmother's letter—less than sedulously. Now, in June of 1830, he had traveled twenty miles west to attend Amherst Academy.

At the time, Amherst Academy was one of the finer preparatory schools in New England, "without doubt, the leading academical institution in Massachusetts," as one history of the town of Amherst put it. The academy had been founded in 1814, the year of Sam's birth, originally as a coedu-cational school. By the time he attended, the academy was all-boys, but it would admit girls—again—after he left. Among its future graduates would be the poet Emily Dickinson, whose family lived just down the street and who would be born a few months after Colt attended. Already the place was practically an extension of the Dickinson family. One of its founders was Emily's grandfather Samuel Fowler Dickinson, who later cofounded another school up the hill, known today as Amherst College. During the brief time that Colt attended the academy, at least four of his ninety or so schoolmates were Dickinsons.

Aside from the school's life span—1814–61—which would almost precisely match his own, Amherst Academy was a poor fit for Colt. He was too restless for the quiet discipline of scholarship. As Olivia's letter indicates, he was only biding his time there. He had another ambition in the summer of 1830: he wanted to go to sea. Olivia wrote him now to give him news. A family friend named Samuel Lawrence was seeking a position for Sam on a ship and "has seen the Captain & had conversations with him favorable to your obtaining your wishes, provided you qualify yourself."

Olivia seemed to be under the impression that Sam was at Amherst Academy to prepare for a career as a ship's captain. If so, he was in the wrong place. The nearest ocean was seventy-five miles away. While brochures for the school advertised a broad curriculum, navigation and seamanship were not on it. "It is strictly a classical Institution being devoted, almost exclusively, to instruction in those studies, which are preparatory to admission in New-England Colleges."

Classes met in the academy's "spacious and commodious building" on Amity Street. The building contained one large schoolroom, two "recitation rooms," a kitchen and cellar, and sixteen dorm rooms on its upper floors. Many students boarded in the homes of faculty and neighbors, but Colt lived at the academy with about thirty-five other students, watched over by two "principals," as faculty were called. "The Principals will affectionately endeavor in their intercourse with the pupils to cultivate their manners, minds and morals. The government will be of kind, paternal character, and no member of the school will be allowed to remain who refuses to yield a cheerful obedience to its reasonable regulations."

These regulations were straightforward. Religious services were mandatory; students were confined to rooms after 9:00 p.m.; drinking of ardent spirits was forbidden; and, most important, no firearms were to be discharged "either in shooting at game or at mark, or for amusement in any manner."

Though Olivia Colt would later be cast in the unflattering role of cold-hearted stepmother, her letters to Sam that summer express concerned affection as she tries to steer him to a life of diligence and piety. "You see then Samuel, that self-application is necessary to the gratification of your inclination in your favorite pursuit and a thorough knowledge of Navigation will be a great advantage to you in a voyage upon the Seas," she gently admonishes. She is clearly concerned that Sam is at risk of transgression, but her tone is more beseeching than scolding.

> You stand as it were upon an eminence, a given point of time for you
> to take your stand. Look around—on the one side you see the abodes of
> Wisdom and virtue—enter in thru her gates. On the other that of vice

and folly—her habitation looks to misery and wretchedness—pass not
by her gates—turn away, pass by on the other side.

Sam clearly considered Olivia's letter worth saving; it is one of few
papers he kept from his early life. He also held on to a short letter Olivia
wrote a week later, accompanying a package she sent to him containing
a dictionary, a ruler, and an umbrella, "as I think you will have use for it,
we have so much rain." Before closing this second letter, she mentioned
that Sam's father had just taken tea with his friend Mr. Lawrence, who had
spoken on Sam's behalf to the owner of a ship bound for Calcutta. "He
speaks highly of the situation," wrote Olivia, "to be absent ten months."
Colt's biographers have generally assumed that he got himself kicked out
of Amherst Academy with bad behavior, but Olivia's letters make it clear
that he *wanted* to leave. He just wanted to do it with a bang.

He did exactly that in the predawn hours of July 4, 1830, when he
broke several academy rules at once. He was out of his room well after 9:00
p.m.; ardent spirits were most likely involved; and while there was nothing
pertaining to cannons in the prohibition against firearms, that is probably
because no one had ever imagined a circumstance in which a student would
fire a cannon near the center of town.

Colt was not alone that night. One of his companions is said to have
been Alphonso Taft, future secretary of war and attorney general of the
United States and father of President William Howard Taft. Actually, Taft's
participation is doubtful—it seems he had already graduated and gone off
to Yale by the summer of 1830. Another companion was Robert Purvis.
Four years Colt's senior, Purvis was a striking young man from an unusual
background. His wealthy father was white and Christian, his mother African
and Jewish. Rather than pass as white, as many mixed-race Americans did,
Purvis would embrace his complex identity and use his inherited wealth to
assist the cause of abolition, and go on to live an altogether distinguished
and serious life. On that summer night in 1830, though, he somehow fell
into the company of Sam Colt.

In all of the several versions of the tale Colt was the ringleader of an
operation to acquire a cannon. In one version, the purloined cannon came
all the way from South Hadley; in another it belonged to an Amherst man
named Ebenezer Mattoon, a local politician and veteran of the Revolutionary
War. Even before the cannon came into play, the night had been a rowdy
one in Amherst. One local resident would later complain of the "gang of
ungovernable, disorderly, ragamuffin boys" who disturbed the peace that
night, "firing and huzzaing, at the expense of rest to all the citizens of the

centre." The following year, in anticipation of the return of the holiday, an Amherst College student named J. A. Cary would write that July 4, 1830, would "long stand recorded in the annals of Hell." Cary especially recalled "the roar of artillery" and how "the cheers & shouts of the ungodly were echoing and reechoing from the dark caverns below."

Unlike the previous Fourth in 1829, when it rained all day, this one was dawning as a beauty. The sky was clear and the moon nearly full. Colt and his companions must have struggled mightily to roll the cannon up the long hill, to the flat top where a cluster of brick college buildings stood. Catching their breath, perhaps they paused to take in the view of the moonlit town below. Then Colt used a match to light the fuse.

After the cannon fired, Colt and his companions loaded more gunpowder, then Colt showed Purvis how to light off another round. There is no record of how many blasts were fired, but based on Cary's description, it was enough to give the impression of a bombardment. The thunder of the cannon would have carried for miles around, rattling windows and rousing the people of Amherst from their beds, including the family of Emily Dickinson at the bottom of the hill.

Many years later, Edward Dickinson, Emily's father, recalled the story of the cannon in a letter to Henry Barnard, Colt's first biographer. "I well recollect the main incidents of the celebration enquired about," Dickinson wrote in 1864. "A young wild fellow of the name of Colt, of Ware, was a member of our Academy & joined with other boys of Academy Lodge, on College Hill, in firing cannon, early in morning of 4th July. Some of the officers of College interfered & tried to stop the noise." When a professor named John Fiske—one of the school's trustees—marched up the hill and demanded that Colt cease fire, Colt "swung his match, & cried out, 'a gun for Prof. Fiske,' & touched it off.

"The Prof. enquired his name—& he replied, 'his name was Colt, & he could Kick like Hell' "

The story of Colt and the cannon had often been repeated in Amherst over the years, Dickinson informed Barnard, but until the biographer's inquiry Dickinson had never realized that "the celebrated Hartford Sam Colt, was the hero of that occasion." In any event, wrote Dickinson, "He soon left town, for good."

CHAPTER THREE

The Voyage of the *Corvo*

AUGUST 2, 1830–JULY 4, 1831

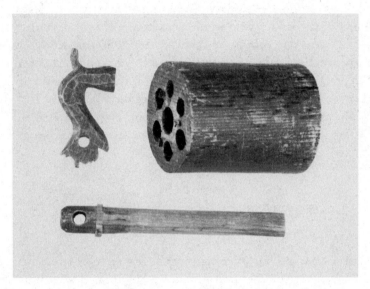

Parts of the wooden model Sam Colt supposedly carved on his voyage to Calcutta.

I

A month after his hasty exit from Amherst, Sam Colt stood on the deck of the ship *Corvo*. It was a hot and windless morning in Boston, and he was dressed in a newly purchased sailor's outfit of canvas duck trousers, checkered shirt, and wide-brimmed hat. In a few hours, he was to embark on a seventeen-thousand-mile voyage across the Atlantic, around the horn of Africa, through the Indian Ocean and Bay of Bengal, and up the Hooghly River to the city of Calcutta. First, though, he had to endure the beating sun and a thousand or so Bostonians crowding the deck of the ship and the docks of India Wharf.

The throng had come to bid farewell to a group of missionaries who would be sailing aboard the *Corvo* to become "a Christian herald to the

35

heathen," in the words of a Baptist publication that had sent a correspondent to cover their departure. That same magazine remarked approvingly of the "stillness and decorum" of the ceremony at India Wharf. As Colt and his fellow sailors watched in respectful silence, the four missionaries and their wives stood under an awning the captain had raised on the deck to shield them from the sun. All but one of the missionaries were under thirty. Three were Presbyterians, not long out of Princeton Theological Seminary, headed for Bombay; the fourth was a Baptist recently graduated from seminary in Andover, Massachusetts, whose final destination was Burma. Their summers had passed in a blitz of ordinations, blessings, and weddings to the brides who would accompany them on their missions. None had been married longer than six weeks, so this voyage was, in a sense, their collective honeymoon—though *honeymoon* was not quite the word to describe a seventeen-thousand-mile voyage to Calcutta in 1830.

After a prayer, the Christians began to sing "Blest Be the Tie That Binds." One of the Presbyterian missionaries, William Hervey, later recalled how sweetly the "multitude of voices" carried over the calm water of Boston Harbor.

> From sorrow, toil, and pain,
> And sin, we shall be free;
> And perfect love and friendship reign
> Through all eternity.

To a sixteen-year-old boy impatient for the sea, eternity was a hymn of six verses followed by another prayer, followed by more devout murmuring, as he poached under the sun in stiff new clothes. The warm air smelled of spices, incense, turpentine, and the excrement of the frightened animals that had been hustled aboard the ship to be slaughtered and eaten along the way. The shadows on the ship's deck shortened and Boston's church bells rang ten times.

When the singing and praying finally ended, the crowd of well-wishers filed off the *Corvo*. The first mate barked orders, and the sailors climbed up the masts and onto the yards to unfurl the sails. The ship began to drift listlessly into the harbor, a slow fade into a summer haze.

Several of the captain's friends remained on board for an hour or so before boarding a small vessel and returning to Boston. Among this group would have been Samuel Lawrence, the friend of Christopher Colt's who had delivered Sam to the *Corvo*. In a letter to Christopher later that day—August 2, 1830—Lawrence reported that Sam was in good spirits on his departure and painted a swashbuckling image:

That last time I saw Sam he was in tarpaulin, check shirt and check trousers, on the fore topsail yard loosing the topsail. This was famous at first going-off . . . He is a manly fellow, and I have no doubt he will do credit to all concerned.

With that, the *Corvo* sailed away, slowly, around the curled tip of Cape Cod and into the Atlantic Ocean, her holds filled with copper, flour, and spirits of turpentine, her decks and cabins populated by a small ark's worth of living creatures: one goat, two dogs, eight sheep, dozens of ducks and chickens, twenty-eight pigs, and twenty-seven humans, including the four missionaries and their four wives and one Sam Colt, who was probably already starting to wonder whether this new wardrobe—this whole voyage—had been a colossal mistake.

II

Beyond the fact that Colt is supposed to have invented his gun aboard the *Corvo*, little attention has been given to the voyage. This is mainly because Colt left no record of it and none was known to exist. In fact, records do exist, though some of these have been hidden away since the 1830s. They make it clear that this was a deeply affecting year in Colt's life, one that almost certainly left him with scars, figurative and literal, and propelled him toward his future.

One chronicle useful to understanding Colt's experience on the *Corvo* has not been hidden at all. This is Richard Henry Dana's classic memoir of his own voyage out of Boston four years after Colt's, when Dana was nineteen and on leave from Harvard. *Two Years Before the Mast* was one of the bestselling books of the nineteenth century. Dana's experience did not fully parallel Colt's—he sailed around Cape Horn to the Pacific, while Colt rounded the Cape of Good Hope into the Indian Ocean, and was aboard a brig (two masts) rather than a ship (three masts)—but his book gives as clear an account as exists of the life of a sailor on a merchant vessel in the 1830s. Had the book come out a few years earlier, it might have warned Colt away from the sea. "Yet a sailor's life is at best, but a mixture of a little good with much evil," Dana would write, "and a little pleasure with much pain."

More particular to Colt's voyage are the long-buried letters and journals of the missionaries who accompanied him. The most illuminating of these is an account by William Hervey, composed as a kind of epistolary journal addressed to his parents. A graduate of Williams College and seminary in

Princeton, Hervey—the oldest of the missionaries at thirty-two—was a keen observer and vivid writer. His work not only opens a window on life aboard a ship in the age of sail, it offers a striking glimpse of Sam Colt at the age of sixteen.

The *Corvo* voyage has been described by some biographers as a punishment meted out by Colt's father to instill discipline in the boy following his expulsion from Amherst Academy. While sea voyages *were* considered a sensible method by some nineteenth-century fathers to reform wayward sons, especially—curiously—after Dana's grueling depiction was published in 1840, this was not true in Sam Colt's case. He *wanted* to go to sea; the voyage was *his* idea. To later generations of young American men, adventure meant going west into the untamed lands beyond the Mississippi, but to Colt's generation—including Dana and Herman Melville among others—the sea was the glimmering vastness that called to them. "There is witchery in the sea," wrote Dana, "and many are the boys, in every seaport, who are drawn away, as by an almost irresistible attraction, from their work and schools, and hang about the decks and yards of vessels, with a fondness which, it is plain, will have its way."

Colt knew something about ships before he embarked on the *Corvo*. He had seen them at anchor on the Connecticut River and probably boarded a few with his father. He had seen bowlegged sailors swaggering—and often staggering—down the streets of Hartford, filled with salty tales and liquor. Probably he had read *The Pilot* and *The Red Rover*, high-seas adventures by James Fenimore Cooper, books that fired the imaginations of American boys at the time. But many boys admired ships and sailors and read sea tales yet did not attempt to act on their fantasies. Colt did.

He went to sea in a relatively coddled position. Not only did he go by choice, rather than of economic necessity, but he took with him a sea chest befitting a Venetian prince. Samuel Lawrence had spent $90 outfitting the boy. That was a minor fortune when experienced sailors aboard the *Corvo* were earning about $10 a month. In addition to the sailor's outfit, Lawrence had bought Colt a compass, a quadrant, and a seaman's almanac, none of which an ordinary seaman required. Forwarding the bill to Ware, Lawrence assured Christopher Colt that "in a first fitting out there are a great many things necessary which need not be replaced for years." That would have made sense had Sam amortized the costs over a lifetime at sea, but for a single voyage it was exorbitant. Other than the notable exception of a $1 jackknife—this would come in handy—Lawrence did the boy no favors by indulging him. It marked him from the start as soft and spoiled.

Colt's efforts to emulate a jack-tar were doomed in any case. "But it is impossible to deceive the practiced eye in these matters," Dana wrote in *Two Years Before the Mast*. "A sailor has a peculiar cut to his clothes, and a way of wearing them, which a green hand can never get." Nor could a green hand hide his smooth (soon to be blistered) palms and his pale (soon to be sunburned) skin. He could not fake the able seaman's rolling gait, which came from years of walking on ship decks, or the disproportionately developed muscles of the chest and shoulders, formed by hauling and climbing ropes. Least of all could he fake the comprehension and skill necessary to execute orders barked at high volume and speed by the first mate. "There is not so helpless and pitiable an object in the world as a landsman beginning a sailor's life," wrote Dana.

Along with the new sailor's challenge of learning the ropes,* Colt had to handle himself among some of the most hardened and profane men on earth. Sailors were famous for drinking, swearing, whoring, and fighting. Probably not by chance had Sam's father and stepmother consented to this voyage in particular. The presence of the missionaries on the *Corvo* would encourage decency and decorum. It might add some life insurance, too, on the perilous sea. Surely God would spare this good vessel from harm.

He did not spare Colt and the missionaries from seasickness, though. It hit them before the sun set on that first day. The water was calm, but the ship's combined motions—bobbing up and down, yawing side to side, pitching fore and aft—brought on that special hell reserved for novices of sea voyages. "The stomach is thrown into disorder," scribbled William Hervey between bouts of illness, "the head becomes dizzy and frequently aches, nausea at the stomach is produced, and soon vomiting succeeds."

Colt was every bit as ill as the missionaries, but while they could suffer belowdecks in their cabins, he was expected to be on his feet, working. Seasoned sailors had no sympathy for the seasick and no tolerance for "sogering,"† or lying about. Work for a sailor often meant climbing high into the rigging of the ship, where every roll and dive was compounded. A seasick sailor was a desperate creature, grasping ropes with blistered hands so as to not be flung off the rigging and into the sea, while trying to retain the contents of his stomach and some semblance of his dignity. Dana later

---

* Quite literally; the expression has been handed down from sailing ships, which were largely controlled by dozens of ropes, each with a name that had to be learned.

† The term is derived from *soldiering*, an occupation mariners held in low regard.

recalled his own first night at sea, when he was sent aloft to reef a topsail while "making wild vomits into the black night, to leeward." That last bit—*to leeward*—was critical; the only thing more pathetic than a seasick greenhorn was one who forgot to vomit to the lee.

For those well enough to notice, the weather was balmy and pleasant in the early days of the voyage. After leaving Cape Cod behind, the *Corvo* cut southeast across the Gulf Stream. The sea turned bluer, then warmer. Sharks slipped by. A school of porpoises accompanied the ship for a while. The captain threw a harpoon at one or two but missed. When an eighteen-inch sea turtle was found floating on the calm water, a jolly boat was dispatched to capture it. "The cook, who seems to know all the tribes of the ocean, calls it a 'logger head turtle,' " William Hervey wrote. "We expect he will have it forthcoming on the table in a day or two."

At first, Hervey was too under the weather to enjoy the voyage, much less stewed turtle, but after a couple of weeks his stomach settled. He began to record details of life on the *Corvo*, starting with a description of the vessel itself, "large and commodious" at 110 feet, its main cabin divided into small chambers for the comfort and privacy of the missionary couples.

From the ship, Hervey turned his attention to the captain. "He appears to be a generous, moral, and very respectable man—treats us with much attention and kindness." Hervey also had a few good words for John James Dixwell, the supercargo, or business agent, who was accompanying the *Corvo* to handle the selling and buying of goods in Calcutta; although Dixwell was of Universalist leanings, Hervey counted him as "quite a gentleman." The first mate, named Congdon, was a "rough sort of fellow, who seems to care but little about religion in any form," and the second mate, Mahoney, was Irish Catholic. The cook was a sixty-year-old Cherokee Indian, "kind and accommodating"; the steward was a black man, "rather surly and morose."

Of the ten regular sailors, Hervey had little to say, with a single exception. One fully captured his attention. Hervey wrote far more about this pitiable young sailor—"a raw hand, a boy 17 years old"—than any other person on the ship. Had he realized that Sam Colt had just turned sixteen, not seventeen, he might have been even more sympathetic.

> His parents live in Ware, Mass. His father is overseer of the factories in that place—a pious and respectable man. Young Colt was brought up with much indulgence and tenderness. He might have remained at home, attended school and had every advantage for becoming a useful man. But he conceived a passion for sea life; and to sea he would go, notwithstanding the remonstrances and tears of his friends.

Hervey's interest in Colt's plight was stirred by concern for his own younger brother, who had expressed longings for the sea. "I am persuaded he would abandon that notion forever, if he could be in Colt's situation one week."

> But the poor fellow now bitterly repents his folly. He is kicked about without mercy by the mates and sailors. . . . He would give more than "all his old shoes" to be at home. He says that if he ever reaches America, he shall never be caught at sea again—his first voyage shall be his last.

By nearly every measure, as Hervey saw it, Colt's life was morally hazardous—a ship being "almost a perfect school of vice"—and physically perilous, subjecting him to constant exposure to the elements and requiring him "to climb 100 feet or more on the ropes and rigging, where he is shaken hither and thither by the wind, and is in constant danger of falling on deck, or into the sea." Worst of all, wrote Hervey, a young sailor such as Colt "has none to pity him when sick, or to care for him when dead."

Hervey's personal and religious views may have amplified his concern, but he did not exaggerate the challenges and privations Colt faced. Other than for a few hours of relaxation on Sundays, a sailor's labors were unrelenting. He was never given more than four hours of sleep between watches, and hours on watch were spent in constant maintenance of the ship, "tarring, greasing, oiling, varnishing, painting, scraping, and scrubbing," as Dana put it. When not engaged in such housekeeping chores, he was lowering and raising the ship's fifteen or so sails—"reefing, furling, bracing, making and setting sail, and pulling, hauling, and climbing in every direction"—which required agility and balance, not to mention a strong stomach.

The most onerous part for Colt would have been that all of this was done under strict and constant supervision and directed by an officer whose orders were absolute. A ship at sea was the opposite of a democracy. At best, it was a benign dictatorship, in which all power and rights emanated from a wise and just captain; at worst, it was a prison ruled by a petty tyrant, as was the case on Dana's ship. Colt's future suggests he did not object to rank or even absolute rule on principle, but he bridled at being under any authority other than his own. Insofar as he would ever express a dogma, it was the gospel of self-determination. "It is better to be at the head of a louse than the tail of a lion," he would write in a letter fourteen years after the *Corvo* voyage, repeating an aphorism he first heard as a child from his mother. "Its sentiment took deep root in my heart and too has been the mark which has and shall control my destiny."

But there was no controlling his destiny on the *Corvo*. A voyage before the mast required a sacrifice of autonomy—and of pride, too. While the officers and missionaries slept on soft cots in semiprivate quarters, the sailors made do with the forecastle deck or, if they were lucky, a hammock. While the officers and their passengers dined at table on fresh meat, poultry, and fish—those pigs, ducks, and chickens that had been loaded aboard in Boston, with the occasional bonito or tuna taken from the sea—Colt and his fellow crewmen gathered on the deck to gnaw the standard sailor's rations of salt beef and biscuit.

III

By September, drudgery and tedium had settled over the ship like a heavy fog. The chief diversions were the hapless creatures who arrived now and then by water or by air or, sometimes, by both, such as the hundreds of small winged fish that leaped from the waves one day, scattering like "an immense flock of birds scared up from the ground" and landing on the deck. The *Corvo* was also visited by Cape hens, snow petrels, and a small bird known as a Mother Carey's chicken. When several large white birds called boobies flew over the ship, the captain grabbed his musket and shot one out of the sky, and it landed on the deck with a plump thud. The captain also shot three giant albatross, which fell into the sea. Hauled up to the deck, the birds measured ten feet wing to wing. "They are good for nothing to eat," wrote Hervey, "though the pigs seem to relish them." The quills were more useful than the flesh. Hervey told his parents that he was using one as a pen to write the very words they were reading.

Some days the *Corvo* managed eight knots and occasionally it made ten, but other days the wind died and the ship stalled. Between the fast days and the slow, the *Corvo*'s seventeen-thousand-mile voyage would stretch out to 145 days, for an average of about 120 miles per day, or 5 miles per hour.

If too little wind was bad, too much was worse. All at once, tedium was replaced by blinding fear. That happened off the western coast of Africa, due west of the Cape of Good Hope, on Sunday, October 3. Until this moment, the weather had been mostly placid, with occasional harmless squalls. Now, two months into the journey, the *Corvo* intersected with the path of "a gale as severe, perhaps, as is often witnessed at sea," wrote Hervey.

The storm had introduced itself on Saturday night with rising seas. It picked up through the night, and by 3:00 a.m. was in a full rage. Waves lifted and dropped the *Corvo*. Inside the cabins, any item not bolted down reacted violently. Trunks, boxes, and chairs tumbled across the decks. Bottles and jars shattered against walls. Several dozen barrels stowed at the front of the main cabin—beef, pork, fish, vinegar, raisins—came loose and began rolling back and forth across the cabin floor with every lurch and pitch. The missionaries had to dodge them as best they could.

Compared to the sailors, the missionaries were comfortable and safe. Hervey could hear the commotion above. Peeking up from the hatch several times, he was awed by "the sublimity and terror of the scene." As the ship lurched violently, the sailors—Colt included—were high in the rigging, attempting to lower the sails. The captain and mates bellowed orders into speaking trumpets.

> The wind howled round the ship, and whistled through the rigging in a most dismal manner—the rain and hail poured down in sweeping torrents, pelting the poor sailors most piteously—the waves ran like rolling mountains, while the Corvo, which before had seemed to bid defiance to their fury, was now tossed by them in every direction, like a feather in the bosom of a whirlwind.

Every wave that crashed across the deck might wash Colt or one of his fellow sailors over the edge; every heave might launch him from the rigging. The risk of falling into the sea was extremely high in such storms, and a man who went overboard was beyond rescue.

For more than twelve hours the storm battered the *Corvo*, and when it ended that afternoon and the sun peeked through the clouds, the ship was in disarray. Cargo and furniture were strewn about the cabins; rain and ocean had sprayed through newly opened crevices in the hull, and an ankle-deep brew of water, wine, and fruit preserves sloshed over cabin floors. Incredibly, the only person injured was Reverend Jones, the Baptist missionary, who had been thrown against an iron brace, "by which he was bereft of reason for a few hours."

The weather improved after the storm, and on October 15, the *Corvo* "doubled" the horn of Africa and entered the Indian Ocean. "So farewell to the sea whose waters wash the shores of my native America!" wrote William Hervey in his journal. "I may never sail on your deep bosom, or gaze on your clear blue waters more; but long shall I remember the dear land, and the dearer friends beyond your heaving floods."

Five days later, on October 20, Hervey recorded another significant incident in his journal.

This morning one of the sailors was convicted of theft, and received as part of his punishment two dozen lashes from a raw hide. He had stolen raisins, sugar, molasses, jelly, &c.&. As many as eight or ten pounds of raisins, and twelve or fifteen pounds of sugar, were found in his possession, and the jar which had contained the jelly, and which belonged to Mrs. Jones.

Other than storms, floggings were the most unnerving experiences on ships, not just for those who received them but for all aboard. In *Two Years Before the Mast*, Dana recorded his response to seeing two fellow sailors flogged: "I could look on no longer. Disgusted, sick, and horror-struck, I turned away and leaned over the rail, and looked down into the water." Years later, the very mention of the word *flog* still provoked in him a revulsion "which I can hardly control."

Flogging was already controversial by 1830, and over the next two decades—with a boost from Dana's book—reformers and politicians would call for an end to the practice, which was finally outlawed on US Navy vessels in 1850. To some northerners, the cruelty of shipboard flogging evoked the evils of southern slavery, for the only two classes of humans routinely and lawfully flogged in America were sailors and slaves. "You see your condition!" bellowed the captain on Dana's ship as he whipped one of his men for a minor infraction. "You see where I've got you all, and you know what to expect. . . . You've got a driver over you! Yes, a slave-driver—a negro-driver! I'll see who'll tell me he isn't a negro slave!"

Captain Spalding of the *Corvo* was not cruel or a slave driver, but stealing food was a serious offense on a ship in 1830, and flogging was the automatic punishment. Unlike Dana's sadistic captain on the *Pilgrim*, Spalding did not administer the flogging himself. He gave the task to Mahoney, the Irish second mate.

In the established ritual, all hands were called to the deck to bear witness. The thief's shirt was stripped off. He was bound to the rigging, prone and spread-eagled so his back could receive the whip. Then it began. A single lash on a bare back was excruciating, as the leather bit into skin and instantly raised a welt. Every lash that followed was worse. "The man writhed under the pain, until he could endure it no longer," wrote Dana of one of the sailors he saw flogged. Another former sailor, Jacob Hazen, who had been flogged as a young man, later recalled the "rushing sound" just before the whip landed. Then "a heavy blow descended on my back, suspending my breath, and penetrating every fiber of my body with a pain more excruciating than if molten metal had been poured upon me, seething and scorching my flesh to the very marrow."

Both William Hervey and a fellow missionary named William Ramsey wrote of the flogging that occurred on the *Corvo*. Hervey had shown a great capacity for pity earlier in his journal, but he seemed to consider the flogging fair punishment for the raisins and sugar that had gone missing. He recorded no details of it. Ramsey was short on details, too, but he expressed more compassion in his journal: "Poor fellow from my heart, I pitied him. . . . He now finds sin is a bitter thing. I hope it may prevent him from worse crime & punishment."

Unlike Hervey, Ramsey gave the name of the flogged sailor in his journal. He scribbled it at the top of the page, then wrote it again in the entry itself. It was Colt.

IV

Two more gales and a few minor squalls rattled the *Corvo* in the Indian Ocean, but nothing like the storm of early October came again. For the most part, progress was slow, day after day, wrote Hervey, of "the same floating, rolling, plunging prison beneath us."

For Colt, these days must have passed painfully. The welts on his back would have made sleep difficult and work almost unbearable. The worst part of a flogging, sailors agreed, was not the physical pain but the humiliation. To be publicly stripped and whipped was degrading. Even an unjustly whipped sailor was utterly humiliated, and no one on the *Corvo* would have considered Colt's whipping unjust.

William Ramsey added a curious addendum to Colt's whipping. Two days later, the ship's black steward was found to have stolen food, too. He protested his innocence vehemently but received four dozen lashes, more than twice as many as Colt. "Poor fellow, he hollered <u>murder, murder</u> with a loud voice," recorded Ramsey, "but there was no one to relieve him till he had received the full number." Did this mean that both Colt and the steward had stolen? Did it mean that Colt was not guilty after all—that he had been punished for another man's crimes? Or was the steward paying in some way for Colt's?

If we accept the findings of Captain Spalding and take Colt's guilt at face value, the whole episode raises at least two questions regarding his character, neither of which can be answered definitively. First, how much weight should be given to his thievery? Should it be viewed as a foolish but forgivable transgression by a miserable sixteen-year-old boy looking for treats to soothe himself? Or did it indicate a larger moral flaw? Not knowing all the facts, the best course might be to give young Sam the benefit of the doubt, for the same reason that most legal systems purge the misdemeanors of minors: we recognize that youths should not be held to the same standards as adults. We give him a pass, in other words, and rule his crime inadmissible in our estimation of him as a man. Of course, that is more easily said than done. Once we know Colt stole, we cannot unknow it.

If the first question is whether Colt's actions reflect some essential flaw in his character, a second question is what effect the episode had on him. Dana portrayed the men whipped aboard the *Pilgrim* as profoundly damaged, skulking about afterward like shadows of their former selves. That does not seem to have happened to Colt. On the contrary, he seems to have drawn power from the experience, fortifying his resolve to serve no master but himself.

The flogging was never mentioned by Colt. It was obliterated from all records of his life. The only document naming him as a thief who was flogged was a single page of a missionary's journal that would end up in the archives of the Presbyterian Church in Philadelphia. Surely at some moments, though, Colt removed his shirt in the company of another person—the woman he married, for example—and revealed the faint pink stripes on his back. The scars of flogging lasted a long time.

V

On the morning of December 19, the crew and passengers of the *Corvo* saw land for the first time since leaving Cape Cod behind in early August. By afternoon they were peering through a telescope at "an immense and desolate jungle, inhabited only by tigers, jackalls, and other wild animals," in the words of John T. Jones, the Baptist missionary aboard the *Corvo*. As the ship entered the mouth of the Hooghly, a local pilot boarded the ship to direct it the rest of the way.

The passage up the river was slow. Villages lined the shore. Small boats approached the *Corvo* and fishermen in loincloths offered their catch for sale. Then dead bodies began to appear, floating down the river "in different states of putrefaction," as William Ramsey recorded. Cholera was raging in Calcutta. Fifteen hundred people were dying every week. The bodies of the upper-caste dead were placed on pyres that could be seen burning onshore, but the lower caste and the casteless were simply thrown into the river for the vultures and fish.

The *Corvo* took six days to sail from the mouth of the Hooghly to Calcutta. She arrived on December 25, 1830. Christmas Day.

Perhaps a letter is tucked away in a box in an attic somewhere in which sixteen-year-old Sam Colt regales his family with his impressions of Calcutta. No such letter has ever surfaced. But if he wrote it, it must have been crowded with impressions to the point of bursting. Calcutta had a staggering population, somewhere between 500,000 and 900,000, according to estimates made at the time of Colt's visit. It dwarfed both Boston, the largest city Colt had ever seen, with a population of 60,000, and New York, at 185,000; Calcutta was larger than the five largest cities in America combined. It was also, with the possible exception of London, the most cosmopolitan city on earth, bringing together an extraordinary array of Armenians, Portuguese, Greeks, Persians, Arabs, and Chinese, as well as the English bureaucrats who governed India, and the largest contingent of all, the Indians, mainly Bengalis, who lived and worked in it. The city was divided along stark racial lines into "white town," featuring wide avenues paved with pressed brick, stately government buildings of white marble, and Christian churches; and "black town," composed of narrow muddy alleys, bamboo huts, and mosques and pagodas. The disparities of wealth, status, and religious faith would have been striking to a boy of New England.

For all of its poverty and death, Calcutta was a beautiful city, especially in winter, when the temperature seldom climbed above eighty degrees during the day or dropped below fifty-five at night. The sky remained cloudless for weeks at a time over the steeples and domes, and beyond the city was the thick green of rice plantations and fields of tamarind and cocoa and poppies, "the whole illumined by a flood of dazzling light from a blue and cloudless sky," according to a contemporary description.

What a young man of Colt's temperament experienced in Calcutta can only be imagined. In the company of fellow sailors, no longer under the eye of missionaries, it seems likely that he was exposed to the temptations for which Calcutta was famous among sailors, such as prostitution and opium dens. If someone was looking for an education in illicit pursuits, Calcutta was a good place to get it.

The most serious question about Colt's seven weeks in Calcutta, still pondered by arms historians to this day, is what guns he saw there; specifically, whether he ever saw a flintlock pistol made by an American named Elisha Collier.

In 1813, Collier, of Boston, had invented a gun with a rotating cylinder of six chambers that could be brought, one by one, into alignment with the barrel—a kind of revolver. He had sold a number of his guns to the British government, which sent them to army units posted in India. Colt's detractors would later assert that Colt pilfered the idea for his revolver during his stay in Calcutta, after seeing British troops armed with Collier guns.

Given Colt's sticky-fingered escapade on the *Corvo*, he might indeed have stolen his idea. But Collier himself later admitted in a patent trial that he made only "thirty or forty" guns that operated similarly to Colt's— with cylinders that rotated when cocked—before he abandoned the idea. Not all of those guns ended up in Calcutta, no more than "a dozen or twenty" by Collier's admission, and who knows if any that did were still in use in 1830. It's not clear Colt could have seen one in Calcutta even if he wanted to.

The *Corvo* left Calcutta on February 18, 1831. The ship was loaded with $25,000 worth of indigo, cow hides, goat skins, shellac, and saltpeter, among other products to be sold upon its return to Boston. No missionaries were on board this time. They were gone to Burma and Bombay to convert the heathen and to meet their respective fates. William Hervey had often entertained the idea that he and his wife might never again see America, and his premonition proved to be accurate. The *Corvo* was still sailing back to Boston when Hervey's wife, Elizabeth, died after giving birth to a son. Hervey himself died the following spring.

Sometime on that return voyage, according to what would become the central creation myth of his gun, Sam Colt gathered a few pieces of scrap wood and pulled out the $1 jackknife that Samuel Lawrence had given him in Boston. It would have been a Sabbath afternoon, his chores complete and no missionaries to pester him with their sermons and religious tracts. He found a quiet corner of the ship and began to whittle. His inspiration, as the story goes, was either the wheel that steered the *Corvo* or, more likely, the ship's windlass.

Colt never explained why the gun came into his mind in the first place. But it's not hard to imagine that a young man who had suffered as he had would have weapons on his mind, every cut of the jackknife an act of quiet vengeance not only against those who had flogged him but against the nameless forces that had snatched away his childhood with financial ruin and death. What better way to retaliate than to create an instrument that beat death at its own game and could make him rich in the bargain? Perhaps such thoughts went through Colt's head as he sailed home. Or perhaps not. We can speculate, but nothing can adequately explain why this angry young man came to invent a new kind of gun, while countless other angry young men invented nothing.

*   *   *

The *Corvo* sailed into Boston Harbor on July 4, 1831. It was a busy day in Boston as Colt stepped onto terra firma. At the Park Street Church that morning, a children's choir gave the first-ever performance of a new song entitled "America," with lyrics that would soon become familiar to children across the nation ("My country, 'tis of thee / Sweet land of liberty / of thee I sing"). At noon, a parade left the statehouse and wended its noisy way through town to Quincy Hall. The George Washington Society convened to read the Declaration of Independence, and a band played that evening on Boston Common.

Also on that day, exactly five years after the almost simultaneous deaths of John Adams and Thomas Jefferson, James Monroe, fifth president of the United States, passed away at the age of seventy-three. That three of the first five American presidents died on the anniversary of the nation's founding was the kind of extraordinary coincidence that confirmed what many Americans already believed about their country, that it was blessed with divinity. On the other hand, lest anyone start taking the holiday too seriously, the most popular attraction in Boston that day was an eighteen-month-old female orangutan dressed up to look like a little American girl. She was on view near Tremont House, all day, twenty-five cents admission.

CHAPTER FOUR

The Nitrous Oxide Tour

1831–33

Sam Colt, circa 1832.

I

One event that did not occur the day Sam Colt returned to Boston was the most notorious slave rebellion in American history. As originally planned, Nat Turner's attack on white slaveholders in Southampton County, Virginia, was set for July 4, 1831. The date had come to Turner months earlier during a solar eclipse, in what he took to be a divinely inspired vision. Timing the attack to coincide with Independence Day would underscore the terrible hypocrisy of a holiday meant to celebrate freedom in a nation that permitted slavery. ("What, to the Slave," Frederick Douglass would rhetorically ask twenty years later, "is the Fourth of July?") Turner became too ill to proceed in July, though, and was forced to postpone. Not until late August did he and his cohorts commence "the work of death," as Turner called it. What they lost in symbolic value they made up for in blood. Before it was over, more than fifty whites would be slaughtered.

Some years later, a story would circulate that Colt invented his gun in response to Nat Turner's revolt. By giving slaveholders rapid-fire guns, went the logic, he would give them a greater chance to defend themselves against vengeful slaves. Of course, if those same slaves got their hands on revolvers, more, not fewer, whites would die, so perhaps it was just as well for slaveholders that guns made poor tools for massacres in 1831. (Turner put a few muskets to use, but axes and fence posts did most of the killing.) In any event, if the story of the *Corvo* is true, Colt did not invent his gun in response to Nat Turner because he had already invented it.

That both the *Corvo* story and the Nat Turner story almost certainly came from Colt's own lips says something about the challenge of sifting fact from fiction in his early years. Add to this the allegation, promulgated by his future competitors, that his real inspiration was a Collier gun in Calcutta, and the origin story becomes almost impossibly murky. But each of Colt's stories served a purpose. The first cast him as a sympathetic popular hero, a Yankee boy who changed the world with nothing but a whittling knife and ingenuity. The second appealed to a southern market, which Colt hoped to court. In all likelihood, neither story was entirely true nor entirely false. At some point Colt *did* whittle out the pieces of his gun; these are now preserved at the Wadsworth Atheneum in Hartford. At some other point he realized the possible application of repeating firearms to rebellious slaves.

By the time Nat Turner was hanged in Virginia in November of 1831, Colt was back with his family in Ware, Massachusetts, his wooden model presumably stashed somewhere out of sight if not out of mind. Having recently turned seventeen, he seemed determined that autumn to devote himself to learning a practical trade. He took employment in the dying and bleaching department of the Hampshire Manufacturing Company, working under the supervision of a chemist at the mill, William Smith. Surrounded by scales, vials, and retorts—long-beaked vases used to distill liquids—and probably perched by a high window to gain as much natural light as possible from the waning autumn sky, he produced chemicals to bleach finished cloth. A notebook left behind by Colt (now preserved at Yale University) shows him at work, recording formulas for dyes and solvents. In contrast to the sloppy penmanship of his later years, his words here are cleanly drawn on lined paper, though many are misspelled—*vegetable* is "vigitable," *colors* is "colurs." Even in an age of improvisational spelling, Colt would stand out for his. Included are recipes to produce common potash, carbonated soda, and sulfate of soda. On October 28, he described a preparation for "Nitrate of Soda"—sodium nitrate—a chemical compound that could be used for explosives but was also a common solvent. "Took a solution of Carbonate of Soda & saturated it with nitric acid, I evaporated untill a pillicle appeared on its surface, filtered it while warm, on cooling obtained clusters of nitrate of soda." (A pellicle is a thin membrane.) On November 12, Colt considered the "Mode of Assertaining the differences of chlorite gas in different samples of Chlorine of Lime," and on December 1, he wrote out directions for producing nitric acid. This was practical chemistry on a fairly sophisticated level, and Colt might have enjoyed a fine and respectable career as a chemist in the textile industry had he been so inclined. Instead, on December 4, in the middle of a recipe "To Prepare Sulphurick Eoither," he stopped writing, midsentence.

So ended Colt's pursuit of the practical applications of chemistry to textiles. More broadly, it ended his attempt to follow anything like a conventional occupation. Sometime that December, he left Ware to journey back to his hometown of Hartford. In his luggage was the wooden model of his gun.

II

The gunsmith Anson Chase recalled meeting Sam Colt in late spring or summer of 1831, but he must have been mistaken. They could not have met until fall or winter, after Colt returned from Calcutta. As Chase would recount twenty years later, he had recently moved to Hartford from Enfield, Massachusetts, to open a gun shop. He leased a store on the east side of Main Street, near the old statehouse, in a building known to locals as the north Schenevard shop. His primary occupation was repairing guns, but in his spare time he made new ones.

"He had something of a model and was trying to perfect something of a repeating arm," Chase recalled of the day Colt entered. "It was a wooden cylinder with holes bored in it; he brought a drawing also." Colt later suggested, and gun experts who have studied it confirm, that the wooden model was not a revolver but a pepperbox. So called because they resemble old-fashioned spice grinders, pepperboxes are made of multiple barrels forged together in a kind of bundle, like a fistful of straws. Pepperboxes would later become popular as a way for gunmakers to sell repeating firearms without infringing on Colt's patent—a sort of poor man's revolver—but as Colt himself quickly concluded, a gun with multiple barrels is heavy, lumpy, and impractical. That he ever entertained a multibarrel design robs his eureka moment on the *Corvo* of some of its epiphanic glory, but it also bolsters his claim that he did not filch his idea from Collier. Why would he have started with a pepperbox if he'd already seen a revolver?

Colt came into the north Schenevard shop every day or two that December to work with Chase and an assistant named William Rowe. After quickly abandoning the pepperbox design, they were soon working to make a device more like a true revolver—"a rotating cylinder containing several chambers," as Colt put it, "and to discharge through one barrel."

A multichambered cylinder combined with a single barrel was an elegant solution, but it was not Colt's most original contribution. Where he distinguished himself was in figuring out how to rotate the cylinder: how to turn it from chamber to chamber; how to index a chamber so that it lined up in perfect sync with the barrel in front and the hammer behind; and how to lock the chamber tightly so the shot would get off cleanly and safely.

To turn his cylinder Colt used a tiny gear-like disk called a ratchet. Unlike the vertical teeth of a normal gear, the teeth of a ratchet are angled or sheered in one direction, such that the wheel can only turn in the opposite direction. According to the *Corvo* story, Colt had spent time on the ship studying the windlass, which employed a ratchet to hoist the anchor. The ratchet in Colt's guns was minuscule by comparison to a windlass's ratchet, but it worked more or less the same way. To engage the ratchet and advance the cylinder, the shooter had only to cock the hammer with his thumb. Drawing back the hammer prepared it for firing while simultaneously engaging a small hand, or pawl, that acted on the ratchet to turn the cylinder from one chamber to the next. Simultaneously, a small spring-activated pin, or arbor, clicked into a divot on the outside of the cylinder and held it firm until the hammer was cocked again.

In retrospect, using a pawl to push a ratchet—to turn a cylinder to fire a gun—sounds like fairly basic applied mechanics. In 1831, it was nothing less than revolutionary.

In the second week of January of 1832, while Sam was in Hartford with Anson Chase, Christopher Colt wrote from Ware to a whale ship captain named Abner Bassett, in Norwich. Captain Bassett was a family relation, married to Olivia Colt's cousin. By his wife's description, Bassett was a "whale crazy" man, home briefly before his next voyage around Cape Horn to the hunting grounds of the Pacific. Christopher hoped the captain might recommend a position for Sam aboard one of the whaling vessels sailing out of New London.

Christopher's letter does not survive but Bassett's reply does, and a lot can be inferred from it, starting with the fact that Sam was evidently considering a return to sea. This is surprising given the hardship and disgrace he'd experienced on the *Corvo*. Bassett's letter also makes clear that Christopher had inquired specifically about opportunities for Sam to sail as an officer, an audacious request on behalf of a boy who would not turn eighteen for another six months and whose previous conduct as a sailor had been less than exemplary. Bassett politely disabused Christopher: "Your son could get a whaling voyage all most any time in a months notice and some times immediately, but he would have to go before the mast one voyage before he could be an officer as it is required that the officers should have some experience in the business." Bassett offered Sam a position as a sailor on his own ship, scheduled to leave New London in April for a two- or three-year voyage to the Pacific, but he recommended that Sam take a shorter voyage, to the South Atlantic or along the coast of Brazil. That way, Sam could quickly gain some of the required whaling experience, then apply for a longer voyage as an officer.

Had Colt followed Captain Bassett's advice, his next few years would have unfolded very differently than they did. Whaling was gritty and grimy work, more dangerous than merchant shipping, and performed in some of the harshest environments on earth. Even barring extraordinary circumstances or injury, a whaling voyage was a commitment that would have removed Colt from any other pursuit for at least two years. How seriously did he consider it? Seriously enough to send his sea chest to Captain Bassett, presumably in preparation for a voyage. We know he sent the chest because some weeks later Captain Bassett wrote to say that he was sending it back. Colt had decided he would not go to sea after all.

He went, instead, it seems, to Washington. Arriving in the nation's capital in mid-February of 1832, he had a model of his gun with him and apparently hoped to get a patent for it. The only record of this trip is a letter to Christopher Colt from Henry L. Ellsworth, a friend of the Colts' who would later, as the US patent commissioner, become an important mentor to Sam. Ellsworth was not yet commissioner in 1832, but he must have been in Washington on other business and agreed to look after his friend's son. "Samuel is now here getting along very well with his new invention," Ellsworth wrote to Christopher on February 20. "Scientific men & the great folks speak highly of the thing. I hope he will be rewarded well for his labors."

Colt did not get a patent on that visit to Washington. He may have been advised to hold off until he'd improved his gun and could file a more fine-tuned application. In any event, his ambitions were still inchoate, or at least undeclared, that winter. This is suggested by a letter Christopher wrote to Sam on March 30, 1832. A moving expression of paternal hopes and fears, it's a version of the address generations of fathers have delivered to countless departing sons. "You are once more on the move to seek your fortune," Christopher begins, "and must remember that your future prospects and welfare depend on your own exertions. Do not despond, my son, but be resolute and go forward.

> It matters but little what employ you embark in, if it is but an honest one and well followed up, with determination to excel in whatever you undertake. This will enable you to obtain a good living and to command respect. Whether you go into a store, or go to sea, or join in any kind of manufacturing, I deem it of but little consequence, provided you devote yourself to your employ with habits of close application; and all leisure time you can have, devote to study and sober meditation, always looking to that kind Providence which gave you existence, to be by Him directed in the path of virtue and usefulness.
>
> When you get located, write me. In the meantime, remember, I have more anxiety for your welfare than can be expressed.

III

Colt never did get located, not then and not for many years to come. Instead, he embarked on a journey that would last far longer than his voyage to Calcutta, longer even than a whaling voyage to the Pacific—a tour of thousands of miles that would take him to nearly every city in the nation, and many parts between, as he joined a great human tide of itinerant peddlers and tinkers, traveling dentists and fly-by-night medicine men, fleet-footed lottery salesmen and footloose dance instructors and roaming preachers and nomadic portrait painters—and many, many more. Along with the legions of occupational travelers were those Americans simply moving in pursuit of better lives, venturing with loaded wagons into vaguely defined futures. Americans were a kinetic people by nature, "infected with the mania of rambling and gambling," as Thomas Jefferson had disapprovingly put it, and this peripatetic tendency had been encouraged by a recently improved infrastructure of roads, canals, and steamboat routes. Americans still moved at glacial speeds by twenty-first-century standards, but by their own terms they were in a collective dash, propelled by the fortune they hoped awaited them over the next hill or around the next bend, anxious they might miss out if they did not hurry. "There were always the rewards that others might grab if you were not there before them," wrote the historian Daniel Boorstin of the wanderlusting Americans of these years. "Perhaps America really was the land of the future, but for the transients it seemed to be the land of now-or-never."

We don't know exactly where Colt went on his journey because he left no clear record of it. But he did drop enough clues—a receipt here, a newspaper notice there—to let us form a picture not just of his life but of the America he saw: a nation brimming with industry and ingenuity and hope, and with anxiety, fear, and brutality.

His travels began in early 1832, when he was still seventeen. Colt's first biographer would call what followed "a brief and sportive episode" and "a specimen of that lowliness which is young ambition's ladder." But the author of those words was a friend of the family's and was soft-pedaling the truth. The "lowliness" in Colt's case was selling hits of nitrous oxide gas to fund the development of his gun. The "sportive episode" lasted nearly three years.

Sam Colt was not the first to traffic in nitrous oxide. There had been public exhibitions of the "exhilarating gas" (or laughing gas, as it is more commonly known) since the great British chemist Sir Humphry Davy began dosing himself and friends (such as poet Samuel Taylor Coleridge) with it at the end of the previous century. Colt had probably learned how to make nitrous oxide from William Smith, the chemist at the mill in Ware. The gas was produced by gently heating crystals of ammonium nitrate over a flame or stove. It was then passed through a chamber of water to filter out impurities and to cool it—as in a water pipe, for example—and captured in a bag or, in Colt's case, an urn-like device called a gasometer. From this, the nitrous oxide could be inhaled through a wooden mouthpiece. As anyone who has ever taken laughing gas in a dental chair knows, the effect can be instant pleasure. Humphry Davy observed in 1800 that the gas was "capable of destroying physical pain" and might make a good anesthetic, but such use would not become common until after the Civil War. For the moment, in the 1830s, its value was primarily in entertainment.

Nitrous oxide had a lot to recommend it as a road-friendly elixir. Besides the relative transportability of the equipment required to make it, the gas combined the self-improving appeal of science (Colt often began his demonstration with a serious-sounding lecture on chemistry) with the allure of spectacle. It came, too, with a whiff of scandal. Some women were said to lose inhibitions and become sexually aroused on nitrous oxide. The great Davy himself, according to rumors, had "gained admittance" to several women under the gas's influence, which was not true but probably did not hurt ticket sales. "Those Ladies who may be anxious of witnessing the Exhibition," Colt wrote in one early newspaper ad, "may be assured, that . . . not a shadow of impropriety attends the Exhibition to shock the most modest." The very denial of impropriety suggested its tantalizing possibility.

He probably started his tour in small venues around New England, moving town to town, renting performance spaces—public halls, hotel drawing rooms—then posting bills and publishing advertisements to attract crowds. That spring he began spelling *Colt* as *Coult*, as some of his ancestors had done, inserting the more European *u* to give himself a cosmopolitan provenance. The first published notice of *S. Coult* appeared in several Boston papers in the early summer of 1832. "The subscriber respectfully informs the Ladies and Gentlemen of Boston and vicinity, that he will administer the Exhilarating or Nitrous Oxide Gas Tomorrow Evening, the 8th inst. at the Basement Hall of the Masonic Temple, the exhibition to commence at 7¾ o'clock, precisely." The advertisement mentioned the work of Sir Humphry Davy, thereby establishing Colt's scientific bona fides, then previewed the effects of nitrous oxide on those who inhaled it, including "innumerable fantastic feats" of singing and dancing. "As the subscriber is a practical chemist, no fears need be entertained of inhaling an impure gas," Colt assured potential audiences, "and he is willing to submit his preparations to the inspection of any scientific gentlemen."

IV

After several successful weeks in Boston, Colt started for New York. He could not have picked a worse time to visit. The same cholera epidemic he'd witnessed in the winter of 1830–31 in Calcutta had since blazed across Asia into Russia and Poland, then into western Europe. North America was its next target, and New York, with its dense population of two hundred thousand—the largest by far in the country—was the bull's-eye.

Cholera had been around for centuries in Asia and India, originating in the mangrove swamps of Bangladesh, but it was virtually unknown in the United States before 1831. The symptoms were diarrhea, intense thirst, and cramping, followed by, in at least half of the cases, death. It struck with stunning swiftness. A victim might appear perfectly healthy at breakfast, start

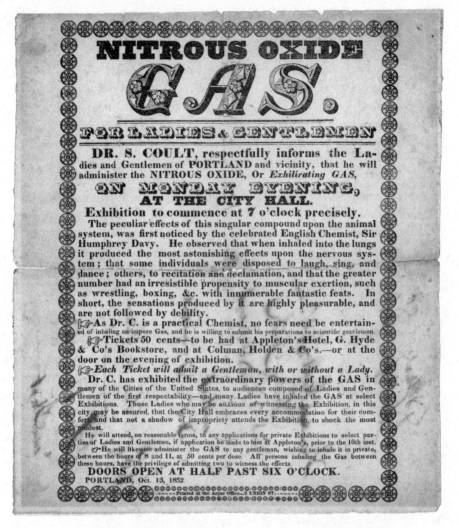

*A bill from one of Dr. Coult's "lectures," this one in Portland, Maine,
in October of 1832. At eighteen, Colt already showed a flair for salesmanship,
combining the respectability of scientific inquiry with pure spectacle.*

vomiting at lunch, and be dead by dinner. The Reverend William Hervey,
the missionary on the *Corvo* who had written so sympathetically of Colt's
miseries, was a case in point. Hervey contracted cholera in Ahmednagar, in
western India, in March of 1832. As one of his fellow missionaries described
his death in a letter to Hervey's parents, their son appeared perfectly well at
two in the afternoon but by seven in the evening had taken to his bed, his vis-
age "already marked with death." He uttered his last words later that night.

Colt was still in Boston when cholera landed in Quebec on June 15, 1832, introduced by a ship carrying immigrants from either France or Ireland. Over the next several days, the bacterium moved south, hitching rides inside the intestinal tracts of unsuspecting (though soon to be violently ill) hosts, down shipping routes on Lake Champlain and the Hudson River. The mayor of New York imposed a strict quarantine. Vessels were not permitted within three hundred miles of the city. All carriages and wagons were stopped a mile and a half out of town.

It came anyway. The first case was confirmed in New York on June 26. By Monday, July 2, there were nine cases, eight of them fatal. The following day, Tuesday, July 3, the terrified populace began its exodus. The *New York Evening Post* described the scene: "The roads, in all directions, were lined with well-filled stage coaches, livery coaches, private vehicles and equestrians, all panic struck, fleeing from the city, as we may suppose the inhabitants of Pompeii or Reggio fled from those devoted places, when the red lava showered down upon their houses." Many of the evacuees simply walked, carrying what they could. Some clambered aboard the Hudson steamboats offering passage upriver to the countryside.

Colt arrived in New York at the very moment others were fleeing. He entered on or about the Fourth of July. As neither vessels nor carriages were permitted into the city, he must have come by foot, slipping across one of the several bridges that connected the north end of Manhattan to the mainland. More perplexing than how he penetrated the quarantine is what possessed him to do so. Perhaps having avoided the cholera in India he felt immune to it. Or it could be that in the last weeks of his boyhood—he would turn eighteen later in the month—he had a young man's confidence in his immortality. Or maybe he just saw an opportunity to make money. Those who remained in the city were in want of escape and entertainment, and for the moment they still had a few coins to spare.

Independence Day was subdued, quieter even than the sodden holiday three years earlier. Broadway, usually pulsing with life, was eerily hushed. Churches were open for prayer but pews were empty. Now and then a firecracker popped, boys being boys even in plagues. Colt's first stop was probably the office of the *Commercial Advertiser*, at 46 Pine Street, to place his advertisement for the next day's paper. This notice was virtually identical to the one he had published in Boston, with one difference: he added an honorific to his name and was now *Dr. S. Coult*. He had not earned his title by any diploma or certification, but neither had most Americans earned theirs. As the English actress Fanny Kemble wryly noted, Americans, for all of their pretensions to democracy, were "as title-sick as a banker's wife."

Colt rented out the Masonic Temple on Broadway, "the finest edifice in the city of New York (excepting the City Hall)," according to one nineteenth-century history of the city. On the second floor was the Long Room, a "grand Gothic saloon" ninety feet end to end and nearly fifty feet wide. On the evening of Saturday, July 7, Colt took the stage. The spelling is his:

> Ladies & Gentlemen
>   If you will give me your attention for a few minuits, I will commence the evening entertainment with a few intraductary remarks.

He started every show with a talk, probably delivered as he heated and purified the ammonium nitrate to create the gas. After briefly relating the history of the gas, from its discovery by Joseph Priestley in 1772 to the experiments of Humphry Davy in 1799, Colt told his audience what to expect.

> It effects upon some people are truly ludicrus, producing involuntary muscular motion, & propensity for leaping & Running. In other involuntary fits of laughter & in all high spirrits & the most exquisately pleashourable sensations, without any subsequent feeling of debillity.
>   Agreable to my usual custum, I wil enhale the first dose of Gas myself, in order to show you that it is purfectly pure, & and that there need be no fear of inhaling it—I woulde observe to all pursons who inten taking the Gas, this evening, to duspose of their nives, or other weppins, preavous to there taking it, in order to gard against an accident, altho I do not apprehend any danger for I have never had an accident hapin.

By now the windows would be dimming in the summer twilight. It was impossible to ignore the epidemic spreading outside the hall, or within. The audience may have taken solace in the proximity of New York Hospital, just across Broadway to the west, where birds were settling in the trees of the garden; somewhat less solace, though, if they knew the hospital had just decided to refuse admission to anyone with cholera. Behind the Masonic hall, a few hundred yards to the east, was the Five Points. Many of the thirty-five hundred New Yorkers who would die over the summer would come from these crooked and impoverished streets, confirming (to those who liked to believe it) that the poor Irish immigrants and free blacks who lived there brought the scourge upon themselves. Tonight the streets of the Five Points were quiet, except for the pigs who roamed them day and night, the stray dogs who barked at the pigs, and the boys lighting firecrackers.

Inside the hall, Colt took his dose. Then the willing began to file up for theirs. Some inhaled, while others got their enjoyment from simply watching the "ludicrus" behavior of their fellow humans. The hall filled with laughter, the last time that sound was probably heard in New York for many weeks.

Colt remained in the northeast of the country through the summer and fall of 1832. From New York he went to Newark, New Jersey, then to Portland, Maine, and Providence, Rhode Island. He was one step ahead of cholera outbreaks or one step behind. At the end of the year, he was back in Hartford, paying Anson Chase to make improvements to his gun. A receipt from Chase for $64.25 is dated December 30, 1832. The following day, Colt was in New Haven, and then it was 1833.

Early that winter, Colt wrote to his family from Baltimore. His letter is gone but we know of it from the response of his sixteen-year-old brother, James, which survives. In part, James's letter, dated March 6, 1833, is a breezy, meandering account of life at home. Christopher Colt had parted ways with the Hampshire Manufacturing Company and the Colts were back in Hartford, renting a large house in the center of town, on Prospect Street, owned by Christopher's friend Henry Ellsworth. James and Chris Jr. were at home, along with their half-siblings, William and Olive. Also visiting for a time were two fetching young women from Norwich, relations of Olivia's, a Miss Fitch and a Miss Spalding. The latter, no relation to Captain Spalding of the *Corvo*, was the daughter of a prominent family in Norwich. She was also, James intimates, Sam's sweetheart—"yourn," as he puts it.

The main subject of James's letter was not news of family or gossip about pretty girls. It was the revelation that Sam had evidently made in *his*. "Your letter containing the project of your last years study was received some time since & more cordially than I forethought it would," wrote James. "Uppon its arrival mother opened it (as father was away from home), read it aloud to Miss Fitch & Miss Spalding. . . . I unfortunately was out and therefore cannot tell you whether it was spurned at by her (Mother) (as most natural it would be) or welcome as nature's God would wish it to be. The ladyes of corce spoke well of it."

Exactly what Sam shared is not stated by James, but it was evidently some kind of declaration regarding his gun, and it caused considerable excitement. According to James, no one was more excited than their older brother Chris Jr. "He says your fortune is made if it proves as you say and was minty pleased about it . . . was aggrinning and singing all the morning, undoubtedly thinking that some part of the fruits reped from it might at some future time be beneficial to him."

James's letter is as intriguing for what it leaves out as for what it includes. Nowhere does he refer to Sam's plan to embark on a long voyage to the west. This suggests that Sam failed to mention his travel plans in his letter, either because he had no definite itinerary when he wrote or because he decided, for some reason, to keep it to himself. In either case, it's a curious omission from a young man about to embark on a long journey to a part of the country he had never been and where he knew no one.

V

He used the same notebook he had opened in the fall of 1831 to record his chemistry recipes in Ware. As his sister Sarah Ann had done with her old school notebook, he simply flipped his over and started anew from the other side. The title page, apparently inscribed by Colt himself, is greatly damaged. But held up to the light of the window of the archive at Yale University where it's stored, its pages begin to reveal, palimpsest-like, where he went in 1833:

JOURNAL

OF A PASSAGE

FROM

NORFOLK

TO

NEW ORLEANS

VIA

ALEXANDRIA

IN THE BRIG AERAL, MASTER JOHN SMITH

The facing page is dated February 27, 1833. Then—nothing. Just the stubs of eight or nine torn-out pages. Why were these pages removed? Perhaps they were scribbled with details so mundane that Colt or one of his heirs got rid of them. More likely, they were too interesting.

Although the content is expurgated, the title of Colt's journal of his voyage from Norfolk to New Orleans—*via Alexandria*, a significant detail in itself—is packed with information, starting with the vessel on which he sailed. Colt spells the name of the brig as *Aeral*, but the correct spelling was *Ariel*. A classified advertisement published in Washington that winter gives February 25 as the date of the *Ariel*'s departure for New Orleans and offers cabin or steerage passage on this "splendid Packet." The advertisement ends with "apply to FRANKLIN & ARMFIELD."

Those names mean little now, but they meant a great deal then. The firm of Franklin & Armfield was the largest slave-selling operation in the country. Isaac Franklin and John Armfield bought slaves mainly in Virginia, then sold them at great profit to cotton and sugar plantations in the Deep South. An act passed by Congress in 1807 had made importing slaves from abroad illegal in the United States, but the domestic slave trade was booming in the 1830s, and Franklin, a native of Tennessee, and Armfield, of North Carolina, were its undisputed leaders. Operating out of a complex of buildings in Alexandria—part of Washington at the time—they ran one of the largest businesses in the American south, selling, as Franklin would boast in 1833, "more negroes than all the traders together." The firm owned a fleet of several ships to carry slaves south. The *Ariel* was one of these.

Incredibly, a fragment of a receipt for seventeen of the slaves who were aboard the *Ariel* with Colt survives in an archive at Harvard University. Dated February 21, 1833, it was written by Bernard Raux, himself a slave trader of French Creole origin. Raux had subcontracted with Franklin & Armfield, paying a freight charge of $17 for each slave ten years or older and half that for each under ten. The left side of this receipt is jaggedly sheared and many of the names are difficult to make out, but some are clearly visible, and so are their ages. Most are very young; only three of the seventeen are older than Colt; four are under ten. The remaining ten are mostly in their early or mid-teens. There is a twelve-year-old named John, a fifteen-year-old named Ben, and a sixteen-year-old named James. They had all possessed last names in Virginia, but last names did not follow slaves to the Deep South. Nor did families—none of these children were likely to see their parents or siblings again. As hard as their lives had been in Virginia, they were about to become worse. The boys and young men were destined for the cotton or sugarcane fields of Louisiana and Mississippi, where a high price would be paid for them, and where their work would be backbreaking and their living conditions miserable. The girls, too, were destined for the fields, unless they were light skinned, in which case they might become a "fancy maid," which could mean what it sounded like—a domestic servant—or what it was often a euphemism for: a concubine of a white male slave owner.

That the *Ariel* was to sail north to Alexandria before it went south to New Orleans tells us that it was to pick up slaves at Franklin & Armfield's headquarters. Along with Raux's slaves, the firm was shipping its own. Altogether, the *Ariel* would leave Alexandria with over a hundred slaves crammed into its small hold. The only thing that made the voyage remotely humane was how it compared to the firm's other method of transporting slaves, which was to walk them in coffles, chained and shackled, from Alexandria to the Mississippi River, an eight-week overland journey of nearly a thousand miles.

The elaborate frontispiece of Colt's journal suggests that he looked forward to the voyage to New Orleans as an epic adventure on which he might someday reflect proudly. The absent pages suggest things did not go quite as planned. Did he tear them out because he was ashamed of them? It is impossible to know, just as it is impossible to know his response to living on a slave ship for nearly a month. This was Colt's first close contact with slaves and slave traders, and it must have made a deep impression on him. What that impression was we can only guess.

VI

Even a worldly young American such as Colt, who had seen Boston, New York, and Calcutta, had to be amazed by New Orleans. With a population of fifty thousand, it was the fifth-largest city in the county, but its shipping traffic and trade made it second only to New York as America's busiest port. When it came to iniquity, it had no rival. "This Babel of all Babels," one writer called New Orleans around the time of Colt's visit, "this Sodom of all Sodoms."

The city was its most vibrant and alluring in April, when the air was scented with flowers, the population swelled, and all manner of temptation beckoned. The flatboats arrived from up the Mississippi River, hundreds of them, after the ice had cleared in the north and the water flowed high and fast. They came from Ohio and Indiana, from Kentucky and Missouri, laden with corn and fruit and whiskey, among other staples. They also brought the young men who steered them down the river. In theory, these fellows were there to sell their cargo, hawk their flatboats as scrap or firewood, then find cheap passage on the nearest steamboat and return straightaway to whatever farm, forest, or town from which they hailed. In practice, most of them stayed awhile. The city opened its doors to cater to their desires, and the young men returned the favor by opening their pockets. Liquor flowed, roulette wheels spun, and prostitutes whispered in their ears.

For true iniquity, no place competed with Hewlett's Exchange, a two-story brick building with an arched entrance and tile roof on the corner of St. Louis Street and Chartres Street. Hewlett's was "the soul of New Orleans," as one contemporary put it, and the center of the city's slave trade. Like most visitors to New Orleans, Colt probably stood in the crowd at Hewlett's and watched a slave auction or two. "Purchasers are in the habit of examining the mouth and the limbs, in the same way that a horse is subjected to the scrutinising touch of the buyer," wrote an Englishman of the scene at Hewlett's. "The joints are tried, and turned, to see if they are strong and supple. Should the back, or shoulders, or any other part of the body, exhibit marks of frequent or severe flogging, the 'animal' is set aside, as rebellious and refractory."

The only trace of Colt's time in New Orleans is a single torn receipt, for $70, dated April 20, 1833. Whatever it was for, the receipt tells us that Colt was there at least a month. To pay his bills he probably performed his nitrous oxide show, though there are no records to prove this. We do know that in late April he boarded a steamboat and started up the Mississippi River. The evidence for this is circumstantial but persuasive: he ended up in Cincinnati that summer, and the only practical route from New Orleans to Cincinnati in 1833 was via the Mississippi and Ohio Rivers.

There is evidence, too, that Colt made it as far as Natchez, on the eastern bank of the river, by May 3. A notice in a local newspaper that day advised "fellow citizens not acquainted with the qualities of Nitrous Oxide or the Exhilarating Gas" to visit Mr. Parker's hotel for a demonstration. "They cannot fail of being amused, many may be instructed by it." The newspaper did not include the name of the person administering the gas, but almost certainly it was Dr. Coult.

As Colt would have learned soon after his arrival, he had been beaten to Natchez by the slaves of the *Ariel*. In an incident that local papers were calling "The Excitement," the bodies of several young slaves had been found in gullies and shallow graves around the city. Apparently they were victims of cholera and had hastily been disposed of, under cover of night, to hide that they carried disease. Upon discovering that these slaves were among a group recently arrived from New Orleans, the editors of the *Mississippi Free Trader* identified the culprit. "It seems a Mr. Franklin"—Isaac Franklin, owner of the *Ariel*—"who for many years past has brought slaves into this state and Louisiana for sale, had shipped from Alexandria (District of Columbia) upwards of an hundred slaves for this place,—that they had been stowed during the voyage in the hole of a small vessel, and on their arrival at New Orleans were placed on the deck of a steam boat and greatly exposed to the weather which was cold and tempestuous, and that immediately after their arrival here several of them took sick with the Cholera and died." The newspaper concluded that "the secret and midnight burial rests upon Mr. Franklin."

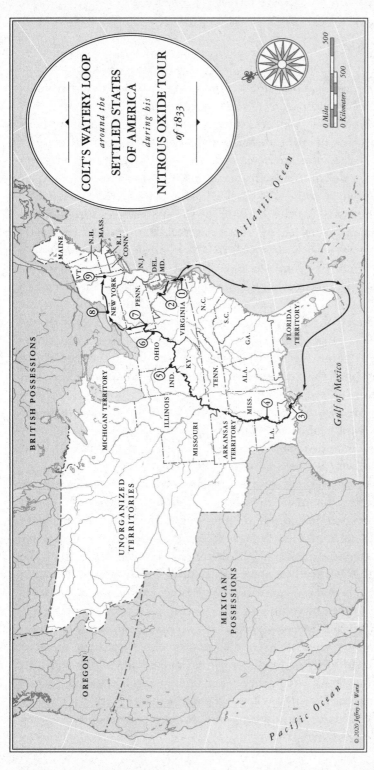

COLT'S WATERY LOOP
around the
SETTLED STATES
OF AMERICA
during his
NITROUS OXIDE TOUR
of 1833

Atlantic Ocean

Gulf of Mexico

Pacific Ocean

BRITISH POSSESSIONS

MEXICAN POSSESSIONS

OREGON

UNORGANIZED TERRITORIES

MICHIGAN TERRITORY

ARKANSAS TERRITORY

MISSOURI

ILLINOIS

IND.

OHIO

KY.

TENN.

ALA.

GA.

MISS.

LA.

FLORIDA TERRITORY

S.C.

N.C.

VIRGINIA

MD.
DEL.

PENN.

NEW YORK

N.J.

CONN.
R.I.

MASS.

N.H.

VT.

MAINE

0 Miles   500
0 Kilometers   500

© 2020 Jeffrey L. Ward

In late February 1833, Colt, then eighteen, embarked on the *Ariel* from (1) Norfolk. The ship first sailed up the Potomac River to (2) Alexandria to pick up slaves from Franklin & Armfield, then turned south, arriving in (3) New Orleans in late March. Sometime after April 20, Colt proceeded up the Mississippi River by steamboat, appearing in (4) Natchez—where the slaves of the *Ariel* had been delivered—on May 3. At Cairo, Illinois, he turned into the Ohio River and arrived in (5) Cincinnati in July 1833. On August 7, Colt, now nineteen, performed in (6) Wheeling, then continued up the Ohio to (7) Pittsburgh. Leaving that city on or shortly after August 22, he (most likely) traveled by land across northwestern Pennsylvania to Lake Erie, steamed to Buffalo, and started east in a canal boat on the Erie Canal. He passed through (8) Rochester on September 19 and arrived in (9) Albany in mid-October.

VII

For Europeans traveling on steamboats in western America, the most interesting and challenging part were the people accompanying them. From fast-talking "go-ahead" Yankees, such as Sam Colt, to refined southern gentry sipping mint juleps at the bar, to roughneck "Kaintocks" (Kentuckians) heading back home after escapades in New Orleans, the collection of Americans on steamboats fascinated, amused, and repelled the Europeans. Steamboat voyages offered a quick education in American democracy, one that left many Europeans longing for the aristocracies they'd left at home. "Let no one who wishes to receive agreeable impressions of American manners, commence their travels in a Mississippi steam-boat," wrote the English memoirist Fanny Trollope; "for myself, it is with all sincerity I declare, that I would infinitely prefer sharing the apartment of a party of well conditioned pigs." The worst offense to Trollope was the constant spitting of tobacco juice by American men of all classes, "so deeply repugnant to English feelings." The eating habits, too, of shipboard Americans raised Trollope's gorge: "the voracious rapidity with which the viands were seized and devoured, the strange uncouth phrases and pronunciation . . . the frightful manner of feeding with their knifes, till the whole blade seemed to enter into the mouth." Everyone agreed that it was dangerous to get between an American and food. "The table was cleared in an amazing short space of time," recorded another English passenger of a shipboard meal, "and food was *bolted* as I have never seen before."

The journey upriver was slow but steady. Steamboats working against the current averaged no more than a hundred miles in twenty-four hours, about what the *Corvo* had achieved on its way to India. Yet the nine days it now took to get from New Orleans to Louisville was a good deal faster than the nine months the journey had required a decade earlier, when the only way north was a keelboat and a pole to push it. "Distance is no longer thought of in this region," exclaimed one western guidebook in 1831; "it is almost annihilated by steam!"

The first 160 miles gave passengers a view of riverside sugar plantations— cane fields, manor houses, clustered slave cabins—before the cultivated land was replaced by dense forests of white oak and cedar. Now and then a flatboat drifted south late in the season, or a lone Indian paddled across the river in a canoe. The forest occasionally opened up to reveal the clearing of a woodcutter, and the steamboat pulled to shore to take on fuel for the boiler. The ships stopped two or three times a day at these lots, where the

Kentuckians earned part of their passage by helping load the ship with wood. At night, the woodcutters lit great bonfires onshore so the ships could find them.

Victuals and juleps alleviated some of the tedium of the journey, but the ever-looming chance of catastrophe was what kept passengers on their toes. The kinks of high-pressure steam engines had yet to be worked out, and ship boilers exploded frequently and devastatingly. At least 150 steamboats would suffer major disasters between 1825 and 1850, and at least fourteen hundred people would be killed by flying metal, scalding steam, and drowning. "We ran a hundred times more risk on steamboats" than in crossing the Atlantic, wrote Alexis de Tocqueville in 1832. "Thirty of them exploded or sank during the first six weeks we were in the United States."

Perhaps the most stirring part of the voyage took place in the imaginations of those passengers drawn to the portside deck. Surely Colt passed some time there, leaning against the railing and gazing across the water, wondering what lay beyond. To the immediate west was Arkansas, still a territory in 1833, and, farther upriver, Missouri, a state since 1821. What lay west of that remained a mystery to most Americans in 1833. Lewis and Clark had reconnoitered the vastness of the Louisiana Purchase in 1804 and gotten all the way to the Pacific by way of the Missouri and Columbia Rivers, but their expedition had covered only a narrow strip of the nearly 2 million square miles west of the Mississippi. Other white men, and a few African Americans, had ventured into the far west since then, but these were mostly trappers and mountain men working for the American Fur Company or one of its rivals, and they tended to stick to themselves.

At the very moment Colt was steaming up the Mississippi, several hundred such men were scattered across the plains and mountains of the west, including future legends such as Kit Carson, who was trapping and hunting somewhere in the Northern Rockies that spring, and William Sublette, who was preparing to push off from Lexington, Missouri, with a hundred kegs of liquor in his boats, headed to the annual fur traders' rendezvous in Wyoming. Later that summer, after the rendezvous, a mountain man named Joe Walker would lead a group of half-starved trappers to the edge of Yosemite, the first time whites ever set eyes on the magnificent valley. These early pioneers traveled "in the geography of fable," as the historian Bernard DeVoto put it. If not quite terra incognita, the harsh land they passed through—the Great American Desert, mapmakers had named it—was still more mythical than real to most Americans. They heard accurate reports of a great salt lake somewhere beyond the mountains, but believed, less accurately, that it emptied into a giant whirlpool and flowed through underground rivers to the Pacific Ocean. They believed that a broad navigable river, called the Buenaventura, crossed from the western end of the Great Lakes to the Pacific, and that the Rockies were too high to penetrate. Of the mountains beyond the Rockies, the Sierra Nevadas, most Americans had only the vaguest idea. And of the indigenous people who occupied this land—some quarter of a million in 1833—the great majority of Americans were entirely ignorant.

VIII

A single brief anecdote from Colt's steamboat voyage survives. It comes in several versions in early biographies of Colt, but in all he is summoned to attend a passenger who has come down with cholera. Dr. Coult protests that he is not in fact a medical doctor but finally agrees to try his gas. Nitrous oxide was useless as a cure for cholera, but so were most other medical treatments of the time, such as bleeding and purging. At least Colt's gas caused no harm, and perhaps it even gave a few moments of pleasure to a sick passenger before he took his last breath.

Colt probably got off along the way to perform in river towns such as Vicksburg and Memphis, spending a night or two entertaining the locals, then boarding the next ship north. In his luggage, and always in his thoughts, he carried the guns Anson Chase had made for him, and perhaps he pulled these out now and then, devising improvements, tinkering, or just shooting at fish in the river. At Cairo, Illinois, he turned east into the mouth of the Ohio River and was soon passing Louisville. A hundred miles later, on the northern bank of the river, embraced by a proscenium of lush hills, rose Cincinnati.

Cincinnati had been a city for less time than Sam Colt had been alive, but already its population was close to thirty thousand, having doubled in just a decade. It boasted two colleges, ten bookstores, a printing house, and scores of churches. Many visitors praised its beautiful location and vibrant culture, but Fanny Trollope, for one, begged to differ. Arriving in 1828, she'd found Cincinnati grubby, swine infested, and filled with dreary buildings and drearier people—"this triste little town," she called it.

The oasis for Trollope during her two-year stay in Cincinnati had been the Western Museum. This was one of the many American entertainment venues that brought together an odd assortment of fine arts (painting, sculpture), scientific displays (fossils, stuffed birds), and just about any attraction lurid or novel enough to sell tickets. The Western Museum had been created by a Frenchman named Joseph Dorfeuille but day-to-day management fell to a struggling but gifted young artist named Hiram Powers. Trollope and Powers became friends and fell into a happy collaboration. Based on Trollope's intimate knowledge of the *Divine Comedy*, they created a kind of horror-house display of Dante's Inferno.

By the time Colt arrived in Cincinnati in the summer of 1833, Trollope was long gone, back in England, where she had just published a bestselling book about the foul habits and ridiculous behavior of Americans. Hiram Powers was still at the Western Museum, though, and he hired Colt to perform.

Years later, when both men were wealthy and world-famous, Colt for his guns, Powers for his sculptures, Powers would recall the performances Colt gave that summer. "I shall never forget the gas—at the old Museum, nor your sly glances at the ropes stretched around the columns, when about to snatch the gas bag from the huge blacksmith, who glowered so threateningly at you, while his steam was getting up—nor his grab at your coat tail as, frog like, you leaped between the ropes."

As Powers's letter suggests, Colt's performances had become more unruly and sensationalistic, as if infected with some of the wildness of the regions through which he had passed. The decorum and scientific pretense that his ads pledged back east no longer applied. According to a newspaper description of his act at the Western Museum, Colt was now making his demonstration "peculiarly attractive" to audiences by giving the gas to a "curiously deformed black man."

Colt remained in Cincinnati for several weeks, then returned to the Ohio River and continued eastward. On August 7, he stopped in Wheeling, Virginia (now West Virginia). By mid-August, he was performing at a museum in Pittsburgh. Probably because he was giving audiences high doses of nitrous oxide, his shows were now positively anarchic. "The scenes that ensued from inhaling [the gas] during the exhibition, beggars all description," a local newspaper reported. "Some danced and jumped, others cut up singularly fantastic tricks, but the greater portion of those who inhaled it became extremely pugnacious. Some of these, though placed within a strong enclosure, managed to escape from it, and attacked and beat unmercifully the audience. One strong fellow, who became on taking it as furious as an enraged lion, sprang over the enclosure, and drove every soul out of the room into the street, beating two or three very severely."

A week after arriving in Pittsburgh, Colt came into conflict with a prominent figure named William McKnight, an iron merchant, bank director, and alderman. What passed between them can only be surmised. McKnight may have found the shows objectionable and demanded that

Colt desist. On August 22, Colt placed a notice in the local paper. "Dr. S. Coult respectfully informs his patrons, and the public in general, that, in consequence of the great annoyance that his Exhibition has been to Mr. Wm. M'Knight, his Exhibition will be postponed until further notice." Colt soon left Pittsburgh, never to return. For the moment, his watery loop, thirty-six hundred continuous miles since Alexandria, had come to its end.

PART II

EXERTIONS AND ENTERPRISE

1833–38

Providence had meditated better things for me than I could possibly imagine for myself.

—Nathaniel Hawthorne,
1850

CHAPTER FIVE

The Anatomical Cabinet

OCTOBER 1833–APRIL 1835

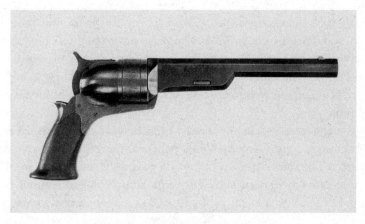

An early Colt revolver, made by John Pearson.

We never beheld such an anxiety as there has been during the past week, to witness the astonishing effects of Dr. Coult's gas. The museum was crowded to excess every evening; and so intense the interest which was manifested, that the doctor has been compelled to give two exhibitions almost every evening.

—*Albany Microscope*, October 26, 1833

I

The proprietor of the Albany Museum, Henry Meech, later recalled meeting the young man who introduced himself as Dr. Coult and carried a gasometer with him. Meech hesitated before making an engagement, "not sure it would be proper" to exhibit nitrous oxide at the museum. Finally he agreed to give the gas a chance. He was not disappointed. Putting behind him the violent antics of Cincinnati and Pittsburgh, Colt gave a more subdued exhibition, and Albany audiences responded favorably. The show was a hit.

Colt had arrived in Albany in mid-October, after traveling north by land from Pittsburgh to Lake Erie—a 130-mile portage that took him through territory settled by Judah Colt, one of his father's cousins—then boarding a canalboat for the eastbound journey down the Erie Canal, 360 miles of tedium. "I was inclined to be poetical about the Grand Canal," the author Nathaniel Hawthorne would write of his own expectations prior to setting off on a canalboat in 1835, but reality was more prosaic: "an interminable mud-puddle" that passed through "dismal swamps and unimpressive scenery." Colt took his time on the canal, stopping in towns along the way to perform, and when he got to Albany he was ready to put his proceeds to use.

"I always called him Doctor," Meech would recall of his acquaintance with Colt. "He had a rotary gun with him at that time; I saw it, and think I worked it." During performances Colt asked Meech to hold the gun for safekeeping.

Colt spent three weeks in Albany. Nights went to nitrous oxide, days to improving his gun. Among Colt's papers are receipts from two Albany gunmakers. These are dated 1832, but they are almost certainly from 1833. One, from November 3, is signed by a gunsmith named Samuel Gibson. "Received of Dr. Samuel Coult the sum of $11.00 for marking on repeating pistol in full." The next, dated November 5, is signed by the firm of True & Davis, also for $11.00, for "forging work for Pistols." In addition to the above, Colt paid a whopping $60 to a gunsmith for producing a "Six Chambered Shot Gon." Altogether, he spent $82 in Albany.

Henry Meech accompanied Colt to the gunsmiths on several occasions. He remembered seeing one of Colt's guns fired. Colt asked Meech whether he was interested in going into the business of manufacturing the guns, but Meech declined, as he had no real knowledge of firearms. He only used one now and then, he later explained, to shoot birds for the taxidermy display in his museum. "I used to be very fond of doing that."

In 1836, when Colt sat down to make a full tally of the expenses he had accrued in developing his gun, he would start with his payments in Albany that November of 1833. Apparently he did not consider money spent on the earlier models by Anson Chase worth recording. Albany was where Colt's efforts became intense and focused, for a few possible reasons. He had saved enough on his travels to afford to spend large sums, and the city had a number of accomplished gunsmiths who could carry out the kind of sophisticated detail work he required. A further incentive may have been an introduction to the work of an Albany inventor named Reuben Ellis, who happened to be a good friend of Henry Meech's. Some years earlier, Ellis had sold some repeating guns to the state of New York. His gun operated with a "sliding lock," whereby three or four loads of gunpowder and projectiles were jammed into the gun, one behind the other, then fired in succession—assuming they did not all go off at once. Like most attempts at repeating firearms before Colt's, the Ellis gun was as likely to be lethal to the shooter as to the target. If anything, it was a lesson in how not to make a repeater, and assurance to Colt that his revolving chamber was the superior solution. But it also reminded him that other inventors were in the hunt and there was no time to lose.

If Colt left Albany on the day of his last payment to a gunsmith—November 5, 1833—the earliest he could have arrived by stagecoach in Hartford was the evening of November 6. This would have given him a night with his family at the Ellsworth house on Prospect Street. The following day, November 7, he was back in the Main Street shop of Anson Chase. He began recording payments to Chase that same day.

Colt remained in Hartford and worked with Anson Chase and William Rowe through the rest of the year. Some days Colt and Rowe went to the outskirts of the city to test the guns. During one of these shooting sessions an accident occurred that could have cost Colt a few fingers. His pistol misfired. This was the first indication of a serious defect in Colt's firearms, one that would return to haunt him in years to come. While not as dangerous as the stacked charges of Reuben Ellis's rifle, a gun with multiple chambers always carried the risk that a detonation in one chamber would leak over into adjacent chambers and ignite their powder, potentially setting off a chain reaction that would leave the gun—and the shooter—in pieces.

Recalling the accident later, Chase placed it in 1832, but a promissory note in Colt's files suggests it occurred in late 1833. "On Demand I promise to pay Anson Chase the Sum of Twenty Six Dollars (or thereabouts) . . . for making a repeating pistol with the extry expenses for damage done by me to the same after Said pistol is furnished in good stile. I agree to pay all reasonable demands for his extry trouble." The "extry" trouble must have been repairing the damage from the misfire.

Though not yet nationally observed, Thanksgiving was a significant holiday in New England in the 1830s, more ardently celebrated than the Fourth of July or Christmas. Then, as now, it was a time for homecomings, for gathering around a table near the fire and feasting on autumn's bounty. Turkey was a staple, though chicken and goose were also commonly served, and it all ended, inevitably, with pie. "One dish, that wakens memory's longing sigh," an 1830 poem declared, was the "genuine far famed Yankee pumpkin pie." Olivia Colt would look back on that Thanksgiving of 1833 as "so lively and cheerful." The big Ellsworth house on Prospect Street filled with Colt family and friends. Sam sang a ballad, to the delight of his little half sister, Olive. His old sweetheart Eliza Spalding came visiting from Norwich.

Whatever feelings Colt may have once possessed for Eliza, the true object of his devotion now was his gun. Two days after Thanksgiving, he recorded a payment of $123.85 for "Work on Pistol & Rifle." This brought his total gun expenses to $205.85. Translating money values over centuries is inexact, but one way to grasp the value of $205.85 in 1833 is that it would take more than a hundred twelve-hour workdays for a skilled craftsman to earn it. Colt was discovering that bringing his invention to fruition was going to be very expensive.

At the start of 1834, Colt left Hartford, taking the finished guns with him but leaving behind two pistols and the wooden pieces he supposedly carved on the *Corvo*. Anson Chase rolled these up in some paper and put them in a box. Chase later explained that he did not consider the guns to be of any practical use but figured the model might be interesting someday, as a curiosity if nothing else. "I did not place any great value upon them, but thought I was the one who made the first and that I would preserve them."

Chase left Hartford and moved to New London soon after that. He did not see Colt again until many years later, when, in a gun shop in New York City, a man of prosperous girth and evident wealth entered after Chase. Someone whispered to him that the man was Samuel Colt, famed inventor of the revolving pistol.

II

Colt never explained his decision to make Baltimore his base of operations. But back to that city he went in early 1834, and there he more or less settled, insofar as he settled anywhere, for the next two years. With a fast-growing population of about eighty-five thousand, making it the nation's second-largest city after New York, Baltimore had much to recommend it. It may have lacked the Connecticut River Valley's deep pool of firearms expertise, but the city could claim plenty of talented craftsmen, and its location, tucked into a harbor of the Chesapeake Bay between Maine and Georgia, made it ideal for coastwise travel. The fact that Baltimore was near Washington City added another important convenience, as Colt hoped to secure a patent and, eventually, government patronage. Finally, and this would not have escaped his attention, Baltimore was the primary residence of Roswell L. Colt, his father's cousin. More on him later.

One day in the late winter of 1834, Colt entered the shop of Arthur T. Baxter, on Pratt Street in Baltimore. Colt was flush with money from a recent nitrous oxide performance in Winchester, Virginia, and he had a gun that needed work. Baxter, recently widowed and with two young children, had his hands full, so he turned the job over to a thirty-one-year-old gunsmith in his shop, John Pearson.

Pearson was a native of Nottinghamshire, England. He had arrived in the United States in 1832, settling immediately in Baltimore. A photograph taken of Pearson later in life shows a man with a massive head, vast brow, deep-set eyes, and a chin that looks as if it could deflect any fist that came near it. Appearances to the contrary, Pearson was "a very quiet, unassuming man," as his obituary would put it many years later, "beloved and respected by all who knew him." He was one of those humble geniuses seldom celebrated in history who do much of the hard pushing toward progress by sheer mechanical acumen and long hours of trial and error. Colt knew several such men over his life and owed them a large debt. In Pearson's case, he never acknowledged it.

A record of the first transactions between Colt and Pearson, with Baxter as middleman, is scribbled on the interior pages of Colt's notebook—the same notebook in which he'd set down chemistry recipes in 1831 and the expurgated journal of his voyage to New Orleans in 1833. Pearson began working for Colt in mid-February of 1834, at $2 per day. On March 1, Colt paid Baxter "Twenty Eight Dollars for work of Mr. Pearson on Repeting Rifle & Two Dollars for forging the same." On March 17, he paid $25 for twelve more days of Pearson's work, then paid another $13 on March 22.

Colt had spent $68 on his guns since arriving in Baltimore in February and was now in need of funds. Leaving behind a set of instructions and a promise to return soon, he boarded a packet boat for Charleston.

The vessel that carried Colt south, the *General Sumter*, was named after Thomas Sumter, the Carolinian hero of the American Revolution. Sumter was also the eponym of the US military fort in Charleston Harbor that would receive the first offensive fire of the Civil War in April of 1861—but that was nearly three decades in the future. For the moment, in the more or less peaceful springtime of 1834, Charleston was intoxicating. "To a person who arrives . . . on a moonlight evening in March or April, it seems he has never seen or imagined so delicious a place," wrote one visitor. Unlike much of the United States, which appeared to Europeans as if it had been thrown up a week before their arrival, Charleston struck foreign visitors as charmingly steeped in history and culture. The aristocratic planter class was almost European in its unhurried gentility and courtly manners.

It all appeared very civilized until you realized that the wealth that made it possible came entirely from the labor of slaves. White South Carolinians excused the barbarity of slavery by telling themselves that the practice was not merely morally justified but positively beneficent. In the words of men such as John Calhoun, their brilliant longtime senator, liberty was "a reward to be earned" and slavery provided "the most safe and stable basis for free institutions in the world." As soothing as Calhoun's sophistry may have been to the consciences of whites, it did not alter the fact that nearly three-quarters of the people in the state might decide to claim their liberty, as Nat Turner had done in 1831, rather than earn it. All of this created a decadent, fragile society. "Nothing could be gayer than the external aspect of these entertainments," wrote the English visitor Harriet Martineau after attending an elegant debutante ball in Charleston, "but it is impossible for the stranger to avoid being struck with the anxiety which shows itself through it all."

Whatever else could be said of Charleston in the spring of 1834, the city enjoyed nitrous oxide. Arriving on March 31, Colt soon began performing at Seyles' Long Room, on King Street. He was back to pledging rollicking lowbrow entertainment, absent any pretensions of scholastic benefit. "To make the Exhibition of more than ordinary attraction," one of his advertisements informed Charlestonians, "the Gas will be administered to SIX INDIANS of the Catawba Nation." The Catawba had once ruled the borderland between South Carolina and North Carolina; now they were an impoverished tribe of about a hundred people, six of whom found employment that spring with Sam Colt.

Colt had promised Baxter to hurry back to Baltimore with cash to pay Pearson. But the days passed and Colt did not return. In mid-April, he sent a small advance, but this hardly sufficed. Baxter was now paying Pearson out of his own pocket and was "much disapointed," as he wrote to Colt on April 21, "at your not returning at the time agreed on."

By the time Baxter's letter arrived in Charleston, Colt was long gone. Rather than return to Baltimore, he'd moved on to Augusta, Georgia, and then to Savannah, where Baxter's letter finally caught up to him. Colt offered no apology. Instead, he scolded Baxter for failing to update him on Pearson's progress. "You may be inshured that I was not a little supprised to see it was from you & that you have not said anything about how you are giting along with my pistols & Rifles. However since this is the case it can't be helped & there is no use in my saying anything more about it." He expected his guns to be complete when he arrived back in Baltimore and saw no reason to send money in the meantime. "As I should probably be in Baltimore in a few days after you reseve this, I doo not deem it expedient."

Colt was nineteen years old; Pearson and Baxter were both a decade or so older, established and serious family men whom Colt had failed to pay as promised. Yet Colt's response was to tell them to keep working, and by the way, be sure the task was completed to his satisfaction before he returned. He had stunning confidence, if not impudence, for his age. He was right, others were wrong. For the rest of his life he would encounter the world on these terms. This would be one of his greatest assets as he pushed his way through seemingly insurmountable challenges, but also one of his most costly flaws.

He did eventually return to Baltimore, in late May, to pay Baxter $117 for a month's work by Pearson. Baxter had seen enough of Colt's habits to decide he wanted out of the arrangement. The gunsmith would henceforth work directly for Colt—or almost directly.

Before leaving town again, Colt befriended a colorful and hapless figure by the name of Joseph E. Walker. Walker's role in Colt's life would be brief but histrionic, like a scenery-chewing cameo by an actor before his hasty exit into the wings.

In the winter of 1834, Walker was running a museum on the corner of Calvert and Baltimore Streets. Founded in 1814 by Rembrandt Peale, this outfit was much like the Western Museum in Cincinnati and Meech's museum in Albany, not to mention other Peale family properties in Philadelphia and New York. The museums of the remarkable Peale family—which included the painter Charles Willson Peale and his four sons, Raphael, Rembrandt, Titian, and Rubens (the first three notable American painters in their own right)—were the very models and progenitors of such museums, including, eventually, the one P. T. Barnum would open in New York in 1842. Walker had been at the helm of the operation in Baltimore since at least 1831, when it was still known as Peale's Museum and Gallery of Fine Arts. The museum had since gone bankrupt and changed names. It was now simply the Baltimore Museum.

According to a nineteenth-century history of Baltimore, Walker was "an untiring and able caterer for the amusement of the public." He followed the usual recipe for American museums of the time, mixing art (painting, sculpture) and natural history (animals, both live and stuffed) with lowbrow entertainments such as ventriloquists, magicians, and a man who weighed 515 pounds ("the living mammoth," as the newspaper ads called him). Somewhere in the cultural space between high and low were the nude wax figures on the fifth floor, complete with human parts so anatomically correct that gentlemen and ladies were admitted at separate times to avoid embarrassment.

Despite Walker's best efforts, the museum struggled to stay afloat. In February of 1833, a year before Colt moved to Baltimore, a fire had broken out in the upper floors and caused grave damage, worst of all to the "anatomical cabinet," which melted to a puddle of wax. Still, Walker pushed on. "The Manager respectfully informs the citizens, strangers and his friends, that come when they may, he expects always to be prepared with some novelty to please them," he wrote in a series of ads that were by turns ingratiating and desperate. "Exertions will not cease nor expense spared to make it a pleasing and fashionable place of resort."

Strangely, one novelty Walker seems never to have featured is Dr. Coult. The name never appears in the museum's advertisements. Perhaps nitrous oxide was too edgy for a family museum; or perhaps Walker chose for some reason not to mention it in printed ads. (Or possibly Dr. Coult *was* mentioned in some papers but those papers have since disintegrated or disappeared.) Whatever the case, the two men became fast friends, and Colt decided to bring Walker into his dealings with Pearson. As Colt continued touring to make money, Walker would act as overseer and go-between. Colt would send money to Walker, Walker would pay Pearson, and Pearson would make Colt's guns.

III

Leaving matters in Walker's hands, Colt escaped the thick heat settling over Baltimore and went north. He returned to Albany at the end of June, giving an encore performance at Henry Meech's museum, then continued up Lake Champlain, that deep slice of fresh water between the Adirondacks and the Green Mountains. He was in Montreal in mid-July, keeping audiences "in a state of almost continual merriment," according to a notice that appeared in the *Montreal Vindicator* on July 18. The next day, he celebrated his twentieth birthday by moving east with the current of the St. Lawrence River, to Quebec City. His usual advertisement now translated into French ("Amusement Scientifique"), he performed in Quebec from August 4 through August 6, then returned to the St. Lawrence, sailing into the great mouth of the river. A brutal wind from the sea held the ship in the Gulf of St. Lawrence for many days, and not until late September did Colt land in Saint John, New Brunswick. From here he curled west around the coast to St. Andrews, then across the Bay of Fundy and east again to Halifax, Nova Scotia. The weather now, in late October, was cold, and heavy mists were rolling in. "I must have been farther east than the yanky was when he said he saw the sun rise to the westward of him," he wrote to his father, "for I never saw it rise at all owing in a meashur to tremendous fogs in that Fish Country."

Colt found a letter awaiting him in Halifax, from Olivia, in response to one Sam had mailed from Saint John. Olivia sent mixed news from Hartford. Christopher Colt's factory at Dutch Point had failed. Money was tight and the family had taken in several boarders over the summer. More propitiously, Sam's brothers Chris and James had both found clerking positions in Savannah and planned to live together to save their earnings. The long-absent John had sent word that he was on the Erie Canal, heading west. And Miss Eliza Spalding—seldom did a letter from Olivia fail to mention her—was in better health than when Sam last saw her and "inquires after you with some interest."

Olivia ended by expressing her own desire to know more of Sam's peregrinations. "I have thought much of you the summer past. I think you have seen as much of our own country as most young men of your age. . . . I hope you will ere long be rewarded for your exertions & enterprise."

In December, Colt returned to Baltimore. He found a mess when he got there. Joseph Walker, the museum proprietor who was supposed to be overseeing Pearson, had left the city and moved to Richmond, Virginia. Pearson had stopped working on Colt's guns months earlier, when Walker stopped paying him. Of the $150 that Colt had sent to Walker in three installments during Colt's travels—well, it took Walker to explain, as he did in his inimitable fashion.

Dear Sir,

I read your letter date 25th instant and haist to answer it. I must inform you that the cause of your work not been done was not my fault as I stated

to you in my letter to you at St. Johns in answer to you after you had sent
the $75—that I had been forced to petition for the act of insolvency and
in consequence of that and my being forced previous to leave the museum
was the cause on my part of not being able to keep Pearson at work.

Walker's words raced out in a medley of explanations and excuses. The
upshot was that Pearson, after receiving from Walker an initial payment
of $50—money Colt had sent in late July—had worked for several weeks,
then stopped when no more money arrived. Walker could not pay Pearson
out of his own pocket because he had gone bankrupt. When Colt sent more
money, Walker—this according to Walker—went back to pay Pearson but
the gunsmith refused to return to work, suspecting that he would be left in
the lurch again. "Finding him not in any way disposed to work after calling
on him three or four times," explained Walker, "I determined not to pay
him." Of the entire $150 sent by Colt, then, only the first part had gone to
Pearson. An additional $14.25 had gone to other gun-related expenses. "I
owe you $85.75," Walker calculated magnanimously. "Which sum I will
send you in sixteen days from this day positively."

In effect, Walker had given himself an interest-free loan out of funds
meant for Pearson. Before letting this uncomfortable truth sink in too
deeply, he turned to a matter likely to be more pleasing to Colt. Walker
was now coproprietor of the Richmond Museum and would be delighted
to have Colt perform there at his earliest convenience. He would give Colt
half the receipts of the house, taking just $5 a day himself for expenses.

It might seem that Colt would resist putting himself back into the hands
of someone who had bungled his affairs, but he needed the money and he
took the offer. Before leaving Baltimore, though, he had to put things right
with Pearson. He clearly recognized Pearson's ability and did not want to
lose him. Why would Pearson continue working for Colt, who had proved
himself completely unreliable as an employer? The answer may again have
been simple financial need. But Colt also had a gift for convincing others
to do as he pleased, even after it had become obvious it was not in their
interest to do so.

Pearson moved out of Baxter's gun shop and rented a rifle bench in the
shop of a Mr. O'Brien. He agreed to work almost exclusively for Colt. These
arrangements made, and promising to send money soon, Colt headed south.

Walker had not misled Colt about his prospects in Richmond. Soon after
arriving there in mid-January of 1835, Colt was performing at the museum

and making money. On January 23, he sent Pearson a draft for $50. Enclosed with this was a long list of instructions: "Make, if you have not, all the tools necessary for taking to peaseis and pooting together the repeating shot gun. When you have obtained all the nesessaries belonging to the gun, go to a good cabinate maker & agree with him to make a handsome case." In another letter he directed Pearson to "Excercise your best judgement in pooting the works of the rifle together."

Having no better way to communicate than by written word, with several weeks' delay in any communication, Colt had to leave some decisions to the gunsmith's discretion. Nonetheless, Colt's letters show attention to detail, not only regarding the mechanics of the gun but its decorative accoutrements. "I forgot I wished you to have the ornament on the stock ingraved," he wrote in one letter. "Take it to the ingraver under the museum or some other good ingraver & have him ingrave the Colts heads in the center of which I want my name as (S. Colt P.B.) engraved." Having gone by *Coult* for several years, Colt was returning to his given name. And it would be not just his name now. It would be his brand.

He ended the letter by promising to pay Pearson $9 per six-day week. If the gunsmith was willing to work twelve hours per day, instead of ten, Colt would raise this to $10.

It is easy to imagine Pearson reading Colt's letter as he sat at his rifle bench in Baltimore on an icy afternoon in late January, the furrows in his large brow deepening with each sentence. It was not the many tasks Colt assigned that made him so vexing. Rather, it was his total failure to grasp that every one of these cost money. Fifty dollars was nowhere near sufficient to cover the gunsmith's wages *and* pay for materials and other expenses. Pearson wrote back, the first of many attempts to set Colt straight.

> The money you sent won't pay all your bill and you order me to buy a barrel & files &c. and pay for forging and all these things which will take a great part of it. I think it nothing but just and right that you pay me my money that is due and advance money to buy all these other things.

Colt's salary offer did not please Pearson, either.

> And for my service I will have 9.50 per week to the 1 of April and after the 1 of April 10 dollars per week for 10 hours each day. And for

your offer of $10 for twelve hours each day I take as an insult for you to offer me.

"Don't be alarmed about your wages," Colt wrote back. "Nothing shall be wrong on my part, but do well for me and you should fare well."

IV

Colt gave his final performance as Dr. Coult in Lynchburg, Virginia, in early April. In Lynchburg, too, he received his last letter from Joseph Walker.

The museum proprietor—or former proprietor, as matters now stood—was once more in financial distress. He had lost about $300 on various investments and had no means to pay it back. Consequently, he was lying low in Richmond, preparing to take flight for Baltimore. From that city he intended to abscond to New York, where he believed he could hide out from his creditors. He was desperate for money and asked Colt to send him some. His pleas rolled off his pen in a stream-of-consciousness jumble that would not have been out of place in the work of James Joyce a century later.

> Oh god is it possible, can I yes I can, depend on my friend, in all things, small as the sum is that you are indebted to me is a gods blessing to me if complied with as I expect and trust it will be, no doubt shall overshadow my mind as to my request of you should it I am <u>undone</u>.

Walker begged Colt to send him at once $20 or $30, care of Peale's Museum in New York, where he would pick it up when he arrived in that city.

> Secrecy I require of you. . . . If when you arrive in Richmond do not know anything about me where I am or anything whatever, nor in Baltimore as they might find me out before I would be ready to meet them or their demands as I have got myself in much debt and no one to assist me and their laws are so severe I think my best plan is to be off—and meet them when I am prepared which I shall do if God saves me. . . . I am almost deranged.

Whether Colt ever sent the money is not known. If there were further letters from Walker, Colt did not save them. Walker's name appeared once more in newspapers when his coproprietor at the Richmond Museum placed a notice publicly dissolving their partnership. After that, it seems, he simply vanished.

Perhaps Walker's hysterical last flight focused Colt's mind on his own trajectory. Now twenty, he had been traveling and performing for three years, living much of the time hand to mouth, moving almost daily. Sometime that spring he decided that the moment had come to put down his gasometer. Returning to Baltimore in mid-April, he rented a room for himself, paying $8 in advance for two months. He possessed several working models of his repeating firearms, both pistols and shotguns. By his reckoning he had paid out $605.53 since the fall of 1833 to create these prototypes. He had achieved a great deal, but to bring his ambition to fruition, he would need more money. A lot more money.

Fortunately, he knew someone nearby—right around the corner—who had some. And his name was Colt.

CHAPTER SIX

On the Verge

1835

The unfinished US Capitol in the 1830s, rising over Washington City like "a general without an army," in the words of one unimpressed foreign visitor.

I

On the first Saturday in May, Sam sent a note to "R. Colt, Esq" at number 10 Gay Street in Baltimore. He had probably seen Roswell Colt in Baltimore before this, but the note makes clear that his relationship with his father's cousin was still formal and distant. The note also suggests that Sam had never before mentioned his firearms to Roswell. "I take this method to beg of you the favour of a personal interview at a time & place of convenience to yourself," he wrote, "insofar as to make known some facts that I think will excite your interest." Later that same day, a note came back from Roswell: he would gladly receive Sam.

Until this moment, Colt's progress had depended mostly on his own savvy and drive. Now the luck of his birth—his lineage, his background, his blood—became critical to his ambitions.

Americans had long operated under the myth of the self-made man, with
Benjamin Franklin the ever-ready example of the humbly born tradesman
who by dint of ingenuity and hard work rose to worldly success. But in
truth, family mattered enormously in the first half of the nineteenth century, especially to a young entrepreneur such as Colt. Today, someone in his
position might convince a bank or venture capitalist to provide financing
largely on the merits of a smart idea and a sound business plan. Not so in
1835. Part of the problem was that lenders had no way of ensuring they
could collect money from people they hardly knew. They had the law on
their side, but reprobate debtors had geography on theirs. The technological
and legal infrastructure that now allows creditors to track and collect from
debtors did not exist, and little prevented a defaulter from absconding, as
Joseph Walker had done, into the vastness of the country. This is where family came in. Family provided a network of ties that helped ensure trust and
guarantee loans. While by no means a perfect guarantee—as a few of Sam's
relatives would soon discover—it made lending a reasonable proposition.

After he became rich, Colt would often claim that he had paddled his
own canoe to get where he was. That phrase—"paddled my own canoe"—
became one of the tenets of his oft-repeated success story. But it was not
entirely accurate. Colt paddled his canoe, but plenty of others were paddling,
too, to get him where he wanted to go. One of these was Roswell Colt.

Roswell L. Colt was a different kind of Colt from that other celebrated
cousin, Judah. While Judah was carving his name into the Pennsylvania
frontier as a rough-and-tumble pioneer, Roswell had made his way to New
York City, where he launched his career in the counting house of Herman
LeRoy—father-in-law of Daniel Webster—and became the beau ideal of
polished urbanity. A portrait of Roswell as a young man, painted by Thomas
Sully, shows him in full neoclassical glory. His shoulders are narrow as a
snake's and cloaked in a black frock, his neck is long as a swan's and wrapped
in a white linen stock, and his head is round as a plum and crowned by
wisps of tousled hair. In the middle of all this is a handsome face, with lips
slightly turned up in a half smile that manages to be both mirthful and sly.

Roswell was fifty-five years old in the spring of 1835, and fabulously, if
erratically, wealthy. He had benefited in his own way from family connections. His father, Peter, had been a successful manufacturer and landowner.
After marrying in 1811, Roswell had taken up residence near his extremely
rich (and recently deceased) father-in-law, Robert Oliver, in Baltimore.

Baltimore may have been his home, but Roswell was a New Yorker at heart.
A year after Sam's first visit, he would separate from his wife and move back
to New York to live in a manner more suited to his tastes. His friends were

numerous and eminent and included such men as former New York mayor Philip Hone, former president John Quincy Adams, and Daniel Webster. "No man enjoyed social life with a keener relish," wrote another of his famous friends, Thurlow Weed, the New York newspaper publisher and leader of the Whig Party. Roswell made his reputation as one of the city's great hosts not only with his splendid conviviality but with his excellent collection of Madeira wines. At one of his famous dinner parties, according to a story told by Weed, Roswell brought out fourteen of his finest bottles. John Quincy Adams amazed his fellow guests by identifying eleven of them by taste alone.

If all of this made Roswell sound like a mere bon vivant, he was also a shrewd businessman, "widely known, highly enterprising, and universally respected," as Weed wrote. Others have put it less generously. According to one history of the Colt family, Roswell was "adept at using his friends and family to secure money, position, and power."

Among Roswell's closest and most useful friends was Nicholas Biddle, the brilliant president of the Second Bank of the United States and one of the most powerful men in the country, despite the best efforts of President Jackson to destroy him and his bank. Jackson disliked banks in general and "Biddle's Bank" in particular, condemning it as a "mammoth of power and corruption." Jackson had crippled the bank by vetoing legislation to recharter it and by withdrawing federal deposits, but for the moment the bank remained solvent and Nicholas Biddle remained a good friend to have.

With advice and tips from Biddle, Roswell placed bets on an array of investments, from railroads to canals to western real estate. Roswell's fingers were in every pot of gold—or fool's gold, as often turned out to be the case in those days of unfettered speculation. By 1835, his wife had apparently tired of his risk-taking, if not his Madeira drinking. His marriage was breaking up, and his wife's brothers were suing him for unpaid debts. Altogether, Roswell, as Sam found him that spring, was a complicated man and contradictory, "a scoundrel and swindler" to some, "the greatest of all the Colts" to others.

Sam probably brought along a couple of his repeating guns to their meeting that Saturday in May, demonstrating how the cylinders turned and locked with clocklike precision. Perhaps they traveled to the edge of town so Roswell could experience the nerve-tingling novelty of firing half a dozen lead balls in quick succession, then galloped back to Gay Street, ears ringing and hair smelling of black powder, to celebrate over a dram of Madeira. (Sam developed a taste for the beverage around the same time he met his cousin.) Roswell had no expertise in guns, but he was a gambler by nature and saw a bet worth taking. A week after their meeting, he gave Sam a loan for $100, to which he soon added $200 more.

This initial $300 was critical seed money. But more important than Roswell's money would be the contacts he helped Sam cultivate in coming months; and more important still would be the encouragement Roswell gave to the young entrepreneur. Like Sam, Roswell did not let scruples and sentiment get in the way of pleasure and profit. Perhaps this made him morally corrupt by some lights, but it also meant he would not pass judgment on Sam when nearly everyone else did.

II

Sam now turned his attention to another relation, a New York attorney named Dudley Selden. The son of Christopher Colt's oldest surviving sister, Ethelinda, Dudley was Sam's first cousin, albeit twenty years his senior. The two shared blood and ambition but little else. Whereas Roswell recognized Sam by animal smell, Selden tolerated his cousin by holding his nose.

No record of Colt's first conversation with Selden survives, other than a few receipts establishing that Sam visited New York in July of 1835 ("Sundary Expenses to New York & back $35.00"). They may have met at Selden's home near Washington Square, or perhaps in his office at 69 Cedar Street. This was Sam's first extended visit to New York since his nitrous oxide performance three years earlier. The cholera was gone but New York was experiencing a strange and turbulent summer. A sultry haze had settled over the city, the air so thick, a visiting Yankee remarked, that you could drive a peg through it and hang your hat. The cause was meteorological—a stalled weather system—but in that age of miasmas and portents the haze seemed to bode an ill wind. There was real reason to worry. The previous July, a wave of extraordinarily violent anti-abolitionist race riots had broken out in New York, as working-class whites tormented blacks and any whites suspected of abolitionist sympathies. Now, in the midsummer of 1835, the mood was turning rank again.

Some of New York's malice that July was directed at Dudley Selden, who had recently returned to the city after a brief and prickly tenure in the US House of Representatives. Selden had gone to Washington as a Jacksonian but soon resigned his seat in opposition to Jackson's crusade to destroy Biddle's Bank. The pro-Jackson press, especially William Leggett of the *New York Evening Post*, denounced him as a "treacherous and thick-witted apostate" guilty of "political mendacity and knavery." But the merchant class of New York greeted him as a hero who had courageously defended the interests of common sense and sound fiscal policy against the stupid tyranny of a despotic president. In March of 1834, Philip Hone, the former mayor of New York, had stood in front of the Merchants' Exchange on Wall Street and led a crowd of more than five thousand in a rousing cheer for Selden.

Selden was putting all that behind him now, though, settling into a career of law and a life of sober business and good society. Like Roswell Colt, he was well-connected and clubbable; as Roswell would be a founding member of the Hone Club, Dudley would be a founder of the Kent Club—the city's two most select men's clubs at the time. But Selden had neither the epicurean tastes nor the ethical casualness of Roswell. He was priggish and irascible and suffered fools badly, and he would come to suffer Sam worst of all. That he got involved with his young cousin in the first place suggests that he was not immune to the speculation fever that gripped his fellow New Yorkers that summer, nor to Colt's persuasive powers.

Selden would have many opportunities to regret the day he and Colt made their pact. But for Colt, to have the support of a man of Selden's stature and connections was an extraordinary achievement. Approaching his twenty-first birthday that July, he had money in his pocket and at least two prominent relations lending their names and money to his enterprise.

III

One more critical step had to be taken before Colt could proceed: he needed a patent. When he had directed John Pearson to engrave a rifle stock with the words *S. Colt P.B.*, the *P.B.* stood for "patent bearer"—but that was Colt getting ahead of himself. He had no patent, and until he did, nothing prevented another inventor from coming along and claiming Colt's design as his own.

As if on cue, a third important family connection—not a blood relation but an old friend—entered the picture. This was Henry Leavitt Ellsworth, who had escorted Sam around Washington in 1832. Having recently served President Jackson as an Indian commissioner in the trans-Mississippi west (traveling in a party that included Washington Irving), Ellsworth was back in the capital to run the US Patent Office.

By the time he became commissioner of patents, Henry Ellsworth was forty-three years old and in the middle of a distinguished career. Born into one of the most illustrious families in Connecticut, he had been blessed by distinction from the start. The Ellsworths may not have been as wealthy as, say, the Wadsworths, but they were more intellectually accomplished.

Henry's father, Oliver, had represented Connecticut at the Constitutional Convention in 1787 then later served as the state's US senator. Oliver had been a favorite of George Washington's, and Washington once visited the family's home during his presidency. According to Ellsworth lore, the president put little Henry on one knee and his twin brother, William, on the other and sang an off-color song, "The Darby Ram" ("The man that owned the ram, Sir, I think is very rich. . . . And the boy who wrote this song, Sir, is a lying son of a bitch"). Washington then appointed Oliver Ellsworth as chief justice of the US Supreme Court.

After graduating from Yale, Henry had gone west to inspect family-owned properties in the Western Reserve of Connecticut (now northeastern Ohio) and written a book about his travels. He studied law at Tapping Reeve's law school in Litchfield, Connecticut—the first law school in the country—then became president of the Aetna Insurance Company and mayor of Hartford. For all his privileges and high position, Ellsworth was a man, according to Washington Irving, "in whom a course of legal practice and political life had not been able to vitiate an innate simplicity and benevolence of heart."

It's not clear how or when the friendship between Christopher Colt and Henry Ellsworth began. It may have been in 1823, when both joined a consortium to found a steamboat line between Hartford and New York. Christopher had also served on the board of directors of the Hartford Insurance Company with Oliver's twin, William, now a US congressman (and later governor of Connecticut); and for the last several years the Colts had lived in Ellsworth's house on Prospect Street in Hartford. But the best indication of the warmth between the two families is the attention that Ellsworth gave to Sam. His first day on the job at the Patent Office was July 8, 1835. Colt arrived in Washington less than two weeks later.

Colt lodged at the National Hotel on Pennsylvania Avenue and Sixth Street. Commonly known as Gadsby's, after its proprietor John Gadsby, the hotel was a favorite of the capital's elite. President Jackson had stayed at Gadsby's before his first inauguration. Senator Henry Clay resided there when Congress was in session. Much of the dealmaking in Washington occurred in the hotel's halls over cigars and whiskey.

The Patent Office was a few blocks away from Gadsby's, in a four-story pile on Eighth and E Streets known as Blodgett's Hotel. Twenty years earlier, Blodgett's had temporarily housed Congress after British troops burned the Capitol. Now it was old and sagging under the weight of the mostly useless and forgotten contraptions that had been sent in over the decades by hopeful inventors. Soon, Blodgett's would do the honorable thing and burn down. Ellsworth would then move the Patent Office to a much larger headquarters and transform it from a satellite concern of the US government into a beacon of American progress and prestige.

Ellsworth saw his job as encompassing far greater responsibilities than applying stamps and signatures to documents. He was there to promote a culture of American innovation and technology. He began by creating a better system to index existing patents, so that inventors could more easily find prior inventions that might be similar to their own. He also pushed for higher standards for patent applications and better laws to protect those patents that were approved. This would spur American inventors to greater originality while assuring them that they could avoid the fate, for example, of Eli Whitney, who saw the design of his cotton gin stolen from under his nose.

Ellsworth's efforts to improve the Patent Office would make him one of the most significant forces behind the extraordinary burst of new technology in America in the mid-nineteenth century. During his decade-long tenure, he would usher through his offices the first great wave of American inventors, including Charles Goodyear, Cyrus McCormick, and his old Yale classmate Samuel F. B. Morse. Ellsworth began, though, by championing the project of Sam Colt and his gun. As one historian of the American patent system has put it, Colt was to be "a poster child to validate his vision."

With letters of introduction from Ellsworth, Colt ventured into the swelter of summertime Washington. The nation's capital remained a city more in theory than in fact. The avenues that looked so grand and stately in the drawings of the city's designer, Pierre L'Enfant, were desolate. Few buildings lined them and few people trafficked them, especially in July, when Congress was in recess and pigs outnumbered politicians. As one visiting Englishman would write in 1838, the Capitol surrounded by so much emptiness gave the appearance of "a general without an army."

From the front of Gadsby's, Colt headed not east toward the Capitol but west, along the wide avenue lined by poplar trees, to a cluster of buildings on the opposite end. These five buildings housed nearly the entire executive branch of the federal government. At the center was the President's House (the term *White House* came later), and at each of its corners was a two-story brick building containing one of the major departments of the government: on the east side were State and Treasury, on the west side War and Navy. It was to these latter buildings that Colt made his way that July morning.

"The bearer of this, Mr. Colt of Connecticut, has invented a new kind of fire arms which invention if successful is deeply interesting to the Army and Navy," wrote Ellsworth in a letter of introduction. "Will it be convenient for you to direct any examination of his invention by those scientific gentlemen connected with your department."

Colt left one of his guns at the navy building for inspection. The following day, an officer wrote to tell him that the navy did not feel "competent to form a satisfactory opinion upon the merits of your invention" and advised him to try the Ordnance Department of the army, which handled most of the weapons procurement for the government. Colt visited the army building and received another quick reply: as soon as he provided models and drawings, the officers would be pleased to test his new pistol and rifle.

With advice from Ellsworth, Colt settled on a bold strategy for securing his patents. He would first get patents in Europe and only then submit an application in America. Despite the risk in waiting for a US patent, the greater risk was that England and France would refuse to issue patents for an invention already patented in the United States. British law, especially, made it difficult to receive a patent for any previously patented invention. Though it was never stated, Colt had the assurance of knowing that Ellsworth might quash any competing application that came in during his absence.

Ellsworth revealed the plan in a letter to Christopher Colt on July 24. Acknowledging that it would cost a good deal of money to obtain European patents, including travel expenses and legal fees, Ellsworth suggested that Sam sell a portion of his patent right for $1,500 or $2,000. That was a lot of money but a bargain, suggested Ellsworth, for any investor. "As to the value of the invention if it succeeds (and the officers here think favorably of it without a trial) our govt. would not offer less than $100,000 for it for the Army and Navy so I think. In England and France it might be worth as much."

By Ellsworth's estimate, then, Sam's invention might have a value of $200,000 outright, a staggering sum in 1835. Ellsworth told Christopher he would gladly put up money for a share of Sam's patent himself if his position as head of the Patent Office did not make this "honorably if not sensibly" impossible.

"I hope Samuel will do well and if there is anything to be made I hope it will be made in the family." With this encouragement from Ellsworth, Colt left Washington and hurried home to Hartford, a most vulnerable and infectious figure—a young man on the verge of great fortune.

IV

Hartford was less a homecoming for Colt than a set of hasty transactions. No doubt Ellsworth, even as he urged Sam to go to Europe before he secured his US patent, urged him to *hurry*. The air was filled with rumors of other repeating guns on both sides of the Atlantic, and every day lost was possibly lost forever. Sam huddled with his father to come up with a plan to raise money.

Because Christopher Colt did not have the financial or professional resources of Roswell Colt, Dudley Selden, or Henry Ellsworth, his role in promoting his son is easy to overlook. In fact, no one mattered more to Sam in these years. Christopher was Sam's chief adviser, his most tireless advocate, and one of his earliest stakeholders. All of this would eventually make the relationship between father and son problematic. For the moment, though, Sam depended heavily on his father.

Due to ongoing business woes, Christopher did not have the money Sam needed. He worried that attempting to raise it in Hartford risked sharing the invention too widely before a patent secured it. On July 30, with Sam at his side, Christopher wrote a letter to Roswell Colt: "He informs me you are acquainted with his invention, and that you have been very very kind in availing him." After repeating Ellsworth's conviction that the invention stood to earn a great deal of money, Christopher broached the occasion for his letter. Sam needed $2,000 to go to Europe. Might Roswell be interested in putting up the money in return for a premium on the investment? "You will I think excuse me from intruding myself upon you in this manner, knowing as I trust you do the anxious feelings of a father for the welfare of his children."

Sam took the letter to Baltimore to deliver it by hand. Either he received an unfavorable response or found Roswell out of town or indisposed. He was back in Hartford by Friday, August 7, a journey of nearly but not quite impossible speed in 1835. In his absence, a new source of funding had appeared. Dudley Selden's father, Joseph Selden, was in Hartford with Aunt Ethelinda, visiting from Troy, New York. Joseph Selden was not rich by Roswell Colt's standards, but he had money to spare and was looking to invest it well for his retirement years.

That Friday, Sam signed a contract with his father. Christopher agreed to buy one-eighth of the "rights and benefits arising" from Sam's patent for $1,000. Because Christopher did not have $1,000 on hand, he had to borrow it from Joseph Selden. After endorsing Christopher's note, Joseph gave Sam another $1,000 in exchange for his own one-eighth interest in the patent, which he would share, fifty-fifty, with his son Dudley. In total, Sam had sold a quarter of the value of his patent to his father and uncle. But he now had $2,000 to go to Europe.

V

Still requiring passports to travel, as well as letters of introduction from Ellsworth, Colt returned to Washington once more that summer. He arrived at an extraordinary moment. Violence was breaking out across the country, nearly all of it perpetrated by white mobs against abolitionists and free blacks. The immediate pretext for the uproar was a campaign by the American Anti-Slavery Society to spread its message to the south using the US postal system. The organization had already sent tens of thousands of copies of abolitionist pamphlets to southern cities. In some of these cities, the mails were intercepted by angry citizens to prevent the distribution of the pamphlets. In Charleston, a mob broke into the post office, seized mailbags, and tossed them onto a bonfire. A mob in Mississippi lynched nine black men and one white man on the suspicion that they were planning a slave insurrection. In Boston, William Lloyd Garrison was attacked and dragged through the streets by a rope. In New York, where the miasma of July had thickened in August heat, the abolitionist merchant Arthur Tappan was threatened with assassination and the property of free blacks destroyed. Between July and October of 1835 the country saw no fewer than a hundred anti-abolition riots. One of the worst of these occurred in Washington.

The Snow Riot, as the episode would come to be known, had been triggered on the night of August 4, 1835, when an inebriated eighteen-year-old slave named Arthur Bowen picked up an ax and entered the bedroom of his owner, a wealthy widow named Anna Maria Thornton. The widow's deceased husband, William Thornton, had been the architect of the Capitol. He had also once held the office, years before Henry Ellsworth, of US patent commissioner. But none of that had any bearing on what happened that August in Washington.

What Bowen intended to do with the ax is not exactly clear, but before he committed any harm, his mother, herself a slave in the Thornton household, stopped him. Anna Thornton quickly forgave the young man, but word of the attempted attack got out and Bowen was arrested. At once, a mob of whites swept through the city, demanding the young man's death. Like other mobs that summer, the Washingtonians spewed their fury not only upon blacks but on any whites suspected of abolitionist leanings.

With President Jackson out of town that August, Francis Scott Key took responsibility for restoring order. Best recalled today for his lyrics to "The Star-Spangled Banner," Key was the district attorney of Washington, a federal position to which he had been appointed by Jackson. Key's strategy for calming the mob was mainly to agree with it. He determined to have Arthur Bowen tried and executed with all possible dispatch.

When Colt arrived in Washington on August 11 to see about his plans for Europe, he entered a city essentially under mob rule. Failing in its efforts to break into the jail and lynch Bowen and a white Connecticut abolitionist named Reuben Crandall, the mob had turned its rage on a free black man, Beverly Snow, who owned a popular restaurant on the corner of Pennsylvania Avenue and Sixth Street (near Gadsby's hotel). Snow escaped with his life, but the mob destroyed his restaurant and the riot came to bear his name.

Henry Ellsworth captured the city's menacing atmosphere in a letter he wrote to Christopher Colt on August 12. The ostensible purpose of the letter was to apprise Christopher of Sam's progress, but Ellsworth could not hide how rattled he was by the mob outside his window: "The streets are full of people . . . and certain persons are marked out." Under the circumstances, simply being identified as a Connecticut Yankee was dangerous. "The fury of a mob is terrible. I fear for tonight but hope for the best."

Eventually, no thanks to Francis Scott Key, calm was restored. Arthur Bowen would be saved from the gallows by a plea from Anna Thornton to President Jackson. Key would prosecute Reuben Crandall for "publishing malicious and wicked libels," but the young abolitionist would be acquitted. What Colt thought of the whole affair is impossible to know. If he was like most white northerners at the time, he had no fondness for slavery but even less for abolitionists. He wanted the issue of slavery to be resolved peacefully, without economic disruption and turmoil. Then again, it might have occurred to him that turmoil was not all bad for the inventor of a new gun.

Colt took one more trip to Baltimore before leaving for Europe. He paid John Pearson $90.62 and issued the gunsmith three checks, of $50 each, to cover wages and expenses in his absence. Then he raced to New York to catch his ship. "I hope Samuel will have a safe voyage and that kind Providence should preserve him on his way across the mighty ocean," wrote Henry Ellsworth to Christopher Colt, "and return him again in safety to his native land."

CHAPTER SEVEN

Fire

AUTUMN 1835–SUMMER 1836

New York's Great Fire of 1835. The city that rose from the ashes was an exciting place for an ambitious twenty-one-year-old with money to burn.

I

In the autumn of 1835, while Sam Colt was in London securing his English patent, a little war broke out in a region of Mexico north of the Rio Grande called Texas. Tensions had been simmering there for years, practically since Mexico won its independence from Spain in 1821 and began inviting Americans to settle in its vast northern territory. Drawn by empresarios such as Stephen Austin—whose father, a Connecticut Yankee named Moses Austin, had brought him to Texas as a boy—they dribbled in at first, the Americans, mainly from the southern states, then in increasing numbers and from greater distances. The Mexicans had a self-serving interest in

101

welcoming these settlers. They wanted a buffer against the Comanche Indians who roamed Texas on horseback and raided deep into Mexico, stealing, torturing, raping, and killing. The Americans were to be the flypaper that kept the Indians occupied. What the Mexicans failed to anticipate was that the sort of people willing to brave Comanche were not the sort likely to behave themselves as settlers. The Texians, as the Americans came to be called, were nearly as wild and violence-prone as the Indians. Realizing too late its mistake, Mexico tried to halt American immigration in 1830. By that point, twenty thousand Americans were in Texas. Five years later, there were thirty thousand.

The precipitating event to armed conflict that autumn of 1835 was an attempt by the Mexican army to retrieve a brass cannon from the Texas town of Gonzales. Some years earlier, the Mexicans had loaned the cannon to the American settlers to keep Indians at bay. Now they wanted it back. The Texians not only refused to return the cannon, they attacked the Mexican detachment that came to retrieve it. In the ensuing skirmish on October 2, 1835, two Mexicans were killed and one Texian was injured when he fell off his horse. This was enough to spark what followed. Before the year ended, the Texians had declared their independence from Mexico and raised an army, headed by a feisty former Tennessean named Sam Houston, to fight for it.

Given the slow passage of news, Colt could not have known any of this as it happened. Nor could he have known how much the events in Texas would come to mean to him. He'd have to wait nearly a decade to find out.

II

Colt arrived in London on September 18 and remained there through October. On the advice of John Colt, Roswell Colt's well-traveled brother, he hired an attorney named John Isaac Hawkins to help him secure his patent. As time allowed, he probably toured London. With nearly 2 million inhabitants, the city was almost ungraspable in its enormity, especially as it was often obscured by the smoke of millions of coal fires. The city behind the smoke was just then being illuminated by the pen of a twenty-three-year-old journalist named Charles Dickens, who had recently started to publish a series of vivid urban sketches, under the pseudonym Boz. Drawn from his endless walks through the teeming metropolis, Dickens's descriptions revealed London as a marvel of human multiplicity and sensation, smelly, dirty, loud, but never dull.

We do not know much about where Colt went or what he did in London. He left no description of his visit there, just a few receipts for payments associated with securing an English patent ($676.50), and his fee for John Isaac Hawkins ($50). Such tallies make for a dry recitation of what must have been an exciting time for a twenty-one-year-old on his first sojourn in Europe.

At least one biographer has depicted Colt's time abroad as very exciting indeed. According to William B. Edwards's generally accurate though often florid and sometimes frankly baffling account, Colt, after receiving his patent in London in the fall of 1835, traveled to Edinburgh to apply for a Scottish patent. There he fell in love with a sixteen-year-old German named Caroline Henshaw, "honey-blonde with flashing black eyes, a strikingly beautiful girl," as Edwards describes her. At once, Sam and Caroline secretly married, then Caroline accompanied Sam to Paris to share in the pleasures of that city as he pursued his French patents. "He was mercurial in temperament . . . and frequently with his emotion running away from him, he did things which in sober reflection he repented," Edwards explained. "What tender circumstances, what passionate justification occurred, may never be known."

Edwards's tale is not only scintillating but somewhat plausible, given events that came later in Colt's life. Unfortunately, Edwards provides no evidence of this Scottish interlude and none seems to exist. All available evidence suggests that Colt did *not* go to Scotland in the fall of 1835 nor, it follows, get married there. Rather, on November 3, he paid $20 to cross the English Channel and travel directly by *diligence* to Paris *tout seul*—in the French version of a stagecoach, that is, by himself.

As soon as Colt arrived in Paris, he purchased a whopper of a guidebook. The seventeenth edition of Galignani's *New Paris Guide*, published in 1830, included "detailed and accurate Descriptions of all the Public Edifices," a history of Paris, advice on where to lodge and how to order a bottle of wine, and "A Plan for Viewing Paris in a Week." The copy Colt carried with him survives today, his name signed in pencil on the frontispiece and dated—*Nov. 7th 1835*.

The application of patents required a good deal of waiting around for the Gallic bureaucracy to grind its gears, so Colt had plenty of time to put his Galignani to use. Many features of the city he encountered in 1835 would be familiar to twenty-first-century tourists, including the Tuileries, the Louvre, Luxembourg Palace, Notre Dame, the Place Vendôme, and the innumerable cafés filled with people who "lounge away nearly the whole day." On the whole, though, Paris of the 1830s would have been more recognizable to a traveler from the fourteenth century than one from the twenty-first. Not until several decades after Colt's visit would the city be leveled and reconceived under the direction of Napoléon III. In 1835, Paris was more medieval than modern, its many narrow lanes forming a malodorous maze seldom penetrated by sunlight or travel writers. Galignani's editors could only warn tourists to beware. "In the Palais-Royal and its vicinity there are subterranean haunts where the stranger, if he ventures to enter, should be upon his guard against the designs of the courtesan and the pick pocket."

Even holding on to his wallet, Colt managed to spend another $120 or so in expenses and nearly $200 for his patent.

On December 3, in Le Havre, Colt boarded the ship *Albany* to return home. According to William Edwards, Caroline was with him, and the two of them sailed across the Atlantic in each other's arms. "The thirty-four day trip seemed as short as minutes to Sam and Caroline, young though they were, life never had enough time. But the future was all coming true and he was on top of the world." The future may have been coming true, but, alas for Colt, there was no Caroline aboard the *Albany*. The manifest of the ship shows Colt and five other passengers, all male.

If Colt did not have a sweetheart to quicken the winter passage, he did have a fellow passenger whose presence on the *Albany* was nearly as stirring. His name was Thomas Pennant Barton. A portrait of Barton, painted in Europe shortly before the *Albany* sailed, shows a wasp-waisted, cock-hipped young man with a droll expression. Today, Barton is known among bibliophiles as the first serious American collector of Shakespeare, a passion he had only recently acquired when Colt met him. Likely stowed in the cargo hold of the *Albany* were a number of now priceless seventeenth-century folios, the earliest publications of Shakespeare's plays. But this is not what made Barton's presence on the *Albany* interesting to Colt. Rather, it was the fact that Barton was the American chargé d'affaires to France—or *had been* until a short while ago, when President Jackson abruptly and angrily recalled him home.

Barton's recall from France was the latest and most significant step in a now forgotten diplomatic crisis that fixated both sides of the Atlantic in the late months of 1835. A dispute had arisen between the United States and France regarding indemnity payments owed by the French for damages inflicted on America during the Napoleonic Wars several decades earlier. France's delay in paying was perceived by Jackson as an insult to the American people. The contretemps had become an *affaire d'honnuer* between Jackson, who had fought several duels over personal slights, and the French, for whom taking umbrage was a national pastime. The French refused recompense until Jackson retracted his insults; Jackson would retract nothing until the French paid up. In the meantime, he threatened to direct the American Navy to seize French ships.

Jackson's political rivals cast his handling of the French debt question as proof of his imprudence, while supporters applauded it as a demonstration of Old Hickory's resolve. To Colt, it smelled of opportunity. Even before the recall, Congress had considered appropriating money for war. Now, with Barton's hurried exit from France and tempers flaring on both sides of the Atlantic, an appropriation for military expansion seemed all but certain. When Sam arrived in New York on the morning of Thursday, January 7, 1836, he bore glad tidings: war was near!

III

It must have been a measure of Colt's excitement that he failed to notice the extraordinary scene that greeted him in New York. Disembarking the *Albany*, he entered a city barely recognizable as the one he'd left in August. Three weeks before his return, on the intensely cold and windy night of December 16, 1835, a fire had engulfed much of lower Manhattan. The flames burned so brightly that people as far away as Poughkeepsie and New Haven thought their own towns were on fire. By the time the flames died down, seven hundred buildings had been destroyed, including the supposedly fireproof Merchants' Exchange, and the cost of damages was three times greater than the money spent to build the Erie Canal. As Colt traveled north up Broadway, virtually everything to the east—his right—was gone.

The most remarkable thing about Colt's reaction to these ruins is that he had none. "I have this morning arrived in the packet ship *Albany* from Havre," he wrote to his father that afternoon. "I succeeded with my business in Europe to the most sanguine of any expectations (considering the short allowance of money I were on) & am now ready to make arrangements for the introduction of my patent invention in this Country." Not a word about the charred stumps of buildings. This was strange but not out of character. At times, Colt had a focus so narrow as to almost literally obscure his peripheral vision. He had arrived back in America piping with ambition, and all his attention went to this. "I shall call on Mr. Selden this evening to advise with him," he wrote to his father. "Please write as soon as possible. I am anxious to improve every minute."

Colt had two pressing messages for his father. The first was that war was coming, and the second was that he needed money. So depleted were his resources that he'd been able to pay only half the fee for his French patent and had been forced to borrow from the captain of the *Albany* to afford his passage home. Listing his debts and expenses, including the $300 he still owed to Roswell Colt and $200 for the balance on the French patent, Colt told his father that he was in immediate want of $1,500.

Nearly every letter Colt wrote for the next year—indeed, for the rest of his life—mentioned money, either money owed to him or by him, money to be made, money to be spent, or money that had somehow to be found. Given that money is at the core of commerce, and commerce was at the core of Colt's life, this is perhaps not surprising. But if it can be explained by the nature of his work, it also owes something to the nature of the man. Colt's appetite for money would be insatiable, and his inability to hold on to it would be almost pathological.

The very evening he arrived back in New York, Colt visited Dudley Selden on Washington Square. Selden had lost some property in the fire but, like most New Yorkers, was moving on as fast as possible.

Now that Colt had secured foreign patents, and before he applied for his American patent, important questions had to be resolved. First among these was how his guns would get made. A gunsmith crafting bespoke firearms in a small shop might be suitable for models and prototypes, but scaling up the operation for government contracts and sales—for the many hundreds, then thousands, of weapons Colt intended to produce—would require sophisticated machines, water to power these machines, and men to operate them. It would require great quantities of money. The kind of money that could only be raised by forming a corporation.

Today corporations are so common as to require little explanation, but they were relatively new devices for private enterprise in America in 1836. In the eighteenth century, corporations had typically been formed to finance expensive endeavors in the public interest, such as turnpikes, canals, and banks. The new capital-intensive industries of the nineteenth century brought corporate financing into the private sector. While traditional arrangements of sole proprietorships or partnerships remained viable and common, especially for merchants and professional services, they were not suited to large industries with high start-up costs—the kinds of industries that emerged during the industrial revolution. Only corporations allowed numerous individuals to pool their money and share in a business's profits while limiting the liability of any single shareholder. Later in the century, corporations would develop into capitalist behemoths in the hands of tycoons such as Carnegie, Morgan, and Rockefeller, with power and financial resources great enough to challenge the US government itself. For the moment, though, they generally comprised small numbers of shareholders and were tightly controlled by the state legislatures that chartered them.

It may have been at Colt's meeting with Selden on January 7, or at another soon after, that the plan was fixed to locate their corporation in New Jersey, in the small city of Paterson, but in any case it was done early and seemingly with little discussion. None was really required. Paterson was an obvious choice. The town had exceptional water power, was close to New York City, and, not least, was owned and operated by Colts.

Borrowing $50 from Selden for travel expenses, Colt left New York the day after his arrival. There was no time to waste. He wanted to be in Washington with a display of his weapons when Congress met to consider appropriations for war with France. Colt intended to sell orders of his guns to the army and the navy, "who I am more than ever sure will introduce it to the States service, especially since a war is so like to take place," as he wrote to his father. First, though, Colt had to get back to Baltimore and retrieve the prototypes that Pearson had been preparing in his absence.

The weather did not cooperate. The winter of 1835–36 was shaping up to be long and severe. Harbors on the Eastern Seaboard were icing over, making water travel impossible. As he left New York, Colt ran into one of the worst winter storms to hit the east in years. He spent the next several days in a hard slog through heavy snow. At least part of the way he traveled by a newly built railroad, probably on the recently opened tracks of the Camden & Amboy line, from New York to Philadelphia, then transferred to the tracks of the Philadelphia, Wilmington & Baltimore Railroad. "I arrived last night," he finally wrote to his father on January 12, "after spending several days on the road in consequences of the large quantities of snow that have accumulated in the deep cuts."

He found matters in Baltimore more or less as expected, at least as far as Pearson's work went. A man hired to assist Pearson had been "neglecting and sporting his work during my absence" and Colt fired him at once. He figured it would take a month to get the guns ready for Washington, but by January 23, after less than two weeks in Baltimore, he informed his father that he expected to leave within a few days for New York City.

A return trip to New York was a roundabout way to get from Baltimore to Washington, especially in the depths of a harsh winter, but Colt considered the detour necessary. For one thing, he needed to get his guns stocked and engraved. He might have done this in Baltimore but apparently sought the finer skills of a New York artisan. More important, he needed Selden's money to pay for the work. Lastly, he came to fetch from Selden eight letters of introduction to influential men in Washington, including John C. Calhoun, the senator from South Carolina. These, plus a few more letters from Roswell Colt, would be his tickets for entry into the offices of the powerful.

IV

Colt's first objective in Washington that winter was to file his US patent application. On February 17, 1836, with a standard fee of $30, he submitted drawings of his gun, a description of its parts and operation, and one of the prototypes Pearson had made for him. Although Colt would go on to install his rotating chamber on many long guns—rifles, shotguns, carbines—his pistols would be what made him famous, so it's fitting that the drawings for his first and most important patent featured a handgun.

"Be it known that I, Samuel Colt, of Hartford, in the county of Hartford and State of Connecticut, have invented a new and useful Improvement in Fire-Arms; and I hereby declare that the following, with the accompanying drawings, is a full and exact description of the construction and operation of the said improvements invented by me." Describing a mechanism that had never before been described was not easy. The language of Colt's application, as of most patent applications, was numbing: "The key which holds the cylinder is hung at the fulcrum b. The lifter that works the ratchet has a working connection with the hammer on the left side at c. The arm d of the lifter works into the teeth of the ratchet on the left. . . ." In none of the two thousand words did Colt claim to have invented the rotating cylinder. However familiar he was or was not with Collier's gun in 1831, he knew by 1836 that others had come up with rotating repeaters before and since. Nonetheless, his application did include eight claims of originality. The first two pertained to the fitting of percussion caps onto his gun. So-called nipples were placed at the back of each chamber in the cylinder; the percussion caps were to be placed over these.

Colt also claimed that he had discovered how to isolate the chambers from each other to prevent the firing of one chamber from accidentally setting off the other chambers, as had occurred during his test-firing with Rowe in Hartford. This claim—number 3 on the patent application—would turn out to be dubious at best, but that was a problem for Colt's future.

The most important claims in the patent application were numbers 5 to 7, all of which pertained to Colt's method of turning and locking the cylinder.

5. The application of the shackle to connect the cylinder with the ratchet.
6. The principle of locking and turning the cylinder.
7. The principle of uniting the barrel with the cylinder by means of the arbor running through the plate and the projection under the barrel.

With Henry Ellsworth at the helm of the Patent Office, approval of Colt's application was assured, but it still had to go through a formal process of review. While waiting for this to be completed, Colt "improved" his time by engaging in an activity unnamed at the time but at which he would come to excel: lobbying. He hoped to convince both the army's Ordnance Department and the navy to test his guns. With war coming, as Colt still believed it was, positive reports from the military would open the golden faucet of congressional appropriations.

On the same day he filed his patent, Colt went to the navy building, on Seventeenth Street. He'd been there once before, just prior to his voyage to Europe, but now he came armed not only with samples of his guns, but a letter of introduction from Roswell Colt to the secretary of the navy, Mahlon Dickerson. Both Mahlon and his brother Philemon, a congressman and future governor of New Jersey, were close friends of Roswell's. Colt also had the letters from Dudley Selden, including one to the secretary of war, Lewis Cass, whom Colt visited on February 18, and another to John Calhoun, the senator from South Carolina, whom Colt visited on February 19—and who then wrote a letter of introduction for Colt to Colonel George Bomford, chief of the army's Ordnance Department.

Neither Colt nor anyone around him seemed to entertain the possibility that his guns would not be embraced by the government. "With all the aid you have thru the introduction of your Cousin Selden and such friendly advice as you will receive of Mr. Ellsworth," Christopher Colt had written on February 11, "I have no doubt you will be able to realize all the funds you will require from the Government or from the Army & Navy departments." As an indication of his faith, Christopher gave Sam a draft for $300, a generous sum from a man who had little to spare.

Not everything was progressing according to plan, though. That war with France, for example—where had it gone? On February 22, after sending several fiery special messages down Pennsylvania Avenue to the Capitol, President Jackson informed Congress that Great Britain had stepped in to mediate the dispute and France had agreed to pay what it owed to the United States. All at once, talk of war ceased, and the dispute faded into a historical footnote.

This had to be disappointing to Colt but his mind was already attuned to new possibilities. The most promising of these came, as would so many in future years, from Texas. The Texians were deep into their fight for independence that winter. To have any chance of success against the Mexican army, they needed money, men, and guns. The Texas Republic had dispatched agents to the northeast to raise all three. In a letter, Christopher alerted Sam that one such agent, Samuel Whiting, a Texas newspaper publisher formerly of Connecticut, planned to visit Washington. "If he has cash," wrote Christopher, "he may wish to hand over some to you for Rifles & Pistols to be forwarded to him in Texas."

On February 23, 1836, an army of about 1,500 Mexican troops, commanded by General Santa Anna, laid siege to an old mission in San Antonio called the Alamo. Inside the mission were about 150 Americans, including the frontier legend Davy Crockett, who had recently arrived to lend his sharpshooting skills to the Texas army, and Jim Bowie, the namesake of the long-bladed knife with which he'd once killed a man. The Americans had vowed to defend the Alamo with their lives.

Two days later, on February 25, in Washington, Sam Colt was issued his patent, "for the term of fourteen years . . . the full and exclusive right and liberty of making, constructing, using and vending to others to be used, the said improvement."

On March 5, the state legislature of New Jersey awarded a charter to the Patent Arms Manufacturing Company, a "body corporate" devoted to the manufacture of Colt's repeating firearms. The next day, Sunday, March 6, the Alamo fell to Santa Anna's army. All Americans inside, including Crockett and Bowie, were killed.

V

The American Hotel stood five stories tall at the corner of Broadway and Barclay Street, across from City Hall Park in New York. The hotel was adjacent to former mayor Philip Hone's house and would purchase it that spring, for $60,000, to give itself room to grow. Later that spring, the 309-room Astor House, the grandest hotel yet built in New York, would open one block south of the American.

The extraordinary price paid by the American Hotel for Hone's house was just one indication of how New York was reacting to the great fire of 1835, which was ecstatically. After destroying much of what had remained of the eighteenth-century city, the fire seemed to unmoor Manhattan from bedrock and reason. As the ice on the river splintered, the city crackled with energy. Real estate values skyrocketed from $143 million to $233 million. Insurance companies had gone bankrupt, but everyone else in New York seemed to take the fire as an incentive to get rich. For a twenty-one-year-old with heady aspirations, there was no better place to be.

Colt spent nights at the American Hotel and days with Selden at his office at 69 Cedar Street, working out the terms of the corporation. Every few days Colt mailed a letter to Hartford to let his father know where matters stood. In part, these were the letters of a son boasting of his success, but also looking for confirmation and advice. "I have written today a letter and shall address it to the board of directors of the manufacturing company," Sam informed his father on March 8, "in which I have offered them the exclusive right to manufacture in the United States my guns of all descriptions on my principal." In return, he would receive half of any profits arising from sales of his guns. Against these profits he would be given an advance of $1,000 a month for the first six months of the corporation's life—$6,000 in total. "I shall reap my harvest," wrote Sam, "in proportion to the merits of my invention."

Stock for the Patent Arms Manufacturing Company (P.A.M.C.) went on sale on April 7, 1836. Selden set a goal of $230,000, to be raised from shares valued at $100 each. Fifteen hundred shares were immediately purchased by friends of Roswell Colt's and Dudley Selden's. Buyers included members of the powerful LeRoy clan, for whom Roswell had once worked (and who were related by marriage to Daniel Webster), a New York attorney named Thomas Emmet, and William Edgar, founder of the New York Yacht Club. Selden himself took the largest number of shares, at 240. Christopher Colt purchased 50. Sam, applying his advance from the company, also purchased 50, with an option to buy more out of future advances.

Because the P.A.M.C. was a corporation, Colt did not in any sense own it, nor would he manage it—that would be done by a board of directors, with Selden, as treasurer, holding the purse strings and effectively in charge. Colt was to be, as it were, a hired gun. Per his contract with the company, he agreed to "devote sufficient time . . . to organize, establish and set in operation, proper works for the Manufacturing of arms."

Expecting a twenty-one-year-old with no manufacturing experience to handle the challenges of building a large company from the bottom up, and to do this in months, sounds, in retrospect, like wishful thinking.

The unwritten and untested assumption was that Sam would cope with assistance from Dudley Selden, his father, and a man named Pliny Lawton.

VI

"On Thursday the 21st of May," wrote Colt, "my father & myself met Mr. Lorton at Springfield & agreed with him for his servacis for the P.A. Man. Co." In this first entry in the small pocket diary he carried with him that spring, Colt committed a few errors, beyond the usual tortured spellings. The man he met was not Mr. Lorton,* it was Mr. *Lawton*; and the date was not May 21 but April 21.

April 21, 1836, is recalled in American history as the day Sam Houston's forces of eight hundred men, with shouts of "Remember the Alamo!," routed a Mexican army of fifteen hundred men at San Jacinto, a victory that would pave the way for Texan independence. It was also the day Sam Colt commenced his study of American industry. He began it with a steamboat ride from New York to Hartford to meet his father. Sam and Christopher then continued north up the Connecticut River to meet Pliny Lawton in Springfield, Massachusetts.

For the next five years Pliny Lawton would be an important figure in Colt's life, but not a great deal is known of him. As a young man he had worked in the mills of Lowell, Massachusetts, where he developed an expertise in machinery. He later moved to Ware to oversee, under Christopher Colt, the machine shop of the Hampshire Manufacturing Company. It was Christopher who recommended Lawton to supervise the production of Colt's guns. To this first meeting Sam brought models of the guns so Lawton could understand what was required. Lawton knew machinery, but his expertise was in machines that spun and wove fabric in textile mills. Guns needed machines that could shape metal, which was a different thing.

---

* Colt's misspellings let us hear his spoken voice. When he persists in writing Lawton's name as *Lorton*, or "entirely" as *intially*—putting *r*'s where they do not belong and omitting them where they do—he is evidently spelling phonetically, as he heard and pronounced the letters. To give a sense of Colt's voice, some of his original spelling and punctuation has been preserved here, but in many cases, especially going forward, these have been standardized in the interest of readability. It should be noted that many of Colt's letters were copied and improved by a secretary before they were sent. Further, it should be noted that spelling and punctuation were fairly improvisational in mid-nineteenth-century personal correspondence, and Colt was hardly alone in his literary errors. Capitalization was erratic, question marks were scarce, and commas and periods were applied to sentences more or less interchangeably, if at all.

To study how machines could be used to make Colt's guns, Lawton and Colt went where guns—among many other products—were made. Nowhere on earth provided a better education on the subject than the stretch of the Connecticut River on which Colt had been born, those forty miles of valley roughly between Springfield, Massachusetts, and Middletown, Connecticut. As they embarked on their tour, Colt jotted down facts and impressions in a diary. His entries are brief, but they give a snapshot of the state of the art of American manufacturing in 1836.

"Visited Mr. Amesies sword factory," Colt wrote on April 22, referring to the Ames Manufacturing Company in the town of Chicopee, just north of Springfield. From its origins as a family blacksmith shop and cutlery maker, the Ames company had evolved from smithing knives to forging swords, putting themselves, quite literally, at the cutting edge of metal-working technology.

After a few hours in Chicopee, Colt and Lawton turned back to Spring-field, where they visited the US Armory. It is unlikely that they toured "all parts" of Springfield on that first visit, as Colt claimed in his diary. The armory was a sprawling complex of buildings spread over the eastern bank of the river. To Colt the most notable part of this visit was an interview with Elizur Bates, inspector of arms at the armory. "Showed him my invention & he gave it as his opinion that they could be made for a less price than the U.S. Musket and thought their advantage preeminent."

Whether Colt fully grasped the industrial significance of Springfield and the other armories he visited is unclear, but it is almost impossible to overstate it. Gun manufacturers were leading the country into adopting what would soon be called the American System, which would then evolve, much later, into the assembly line. How this happened is explained by a combination of causes, but it starts with the fact that the government, and only the government, had both the need and the means to order hundreds, even thousands, of the same product. The government might have had a similar compounding effect on, for example, the sewing machine industry or the clock industry had it required thousands of sewing machines and clocks. But the government was not in the business of sewing or telling time; it very much *was* in the business of preparing for war, even if there were no wars to be fought just then. As a result, guns were among the first, and by far the most important, mass-produced items in the United States. Because the government was the main buyer of guns, it dictated how the guns were made. And it had a deep interest in solving problems of gun manufacturing.

The thorniest of these was the problem of unique parts. Today, the expectation that the parts of man-made products will be identical to, and therefore interchangeable with, their counterparts in duplicates of the same item is so commonplace as to seem a law of nature. When a modern appliance breaks, the defective part can be removed and a new part easily procured and fitted congruously into the appliance, which then functions more or less as good as new. It was not always so. In the age of handmade tools, every product was unique, made of singular bits and pieces. The parts and products might have looked the same, but they had slight variations in shape and size. This mattered little in the case of simple products such as kettles and pots and tables, but it mattered a great deal in the case of guns. Parts broke frequently, and if parts of an eighteenth-century musket broke, the entire gun had to be sent to a gunsmith and repaired. This was inconvenient, especially in the middle of war, and it was costly.

The quest, then, was for *uniformity* of parts—parts that, if not precisely identical, fell within narrow enough tolerances to be interchangeable. This quest was the main impetus behind innovation in machinery. Uniformity did not in itself require machine manufacturing. A gang of blacksmiths or gunsmiths working carefully with gauges could come close to achieving interchangeable parts. But machines were better than humans at repeating the same task in exactly the same way. They also, incidentally but importantly, worked faster than humans and reduced costly human labor.

The man generally credited with bringing machines to gunmaking is Eli Whitney. Or it *was* Whitney until twentieth-century historians began to doubt he did any of the things he talked about doing. Today, Whitney is best remembered as the inventor of the cotton gin, itself a machine of enormous impact on American history. What history often overlooks about Whitney is that he devoted most of his life to making guns. In 1798, he contracted with the government to produce ten thousand muskets within two years, for which he was to be paid $134,000. Before he made a single gun, he told Congress, he would make the machines to make the guns. "One of my primary objectives is to form the tools so the tools themselves shall fashion the work and give to every part its just proportion—which when accomplished will give expedition, uniformity and exactness to the whole." Whitney missed his deadline by six years and never made the machines he talked about. He opened a door into the future, though, simply by talking about them.

Another Connecticut gunmaker, Simeon North, stepped through that door. North had started making guns in 1799 in a factory in Middletown, where he experimented with assembly-line production. "I find that by confining a workman to one particular limb of the pistol until he had made two thousand," he said in 1808, exactly one hundred years before Henry Ford made his first Model T, "I save at least one quarter of his labor."

Meanwhile, back at Springfield, the brilliant and immensely innovative Thomas Blanchard had invented a lathe that used a template, or model, to make gun stocks. As a tracing wheel moved across the template, the cutting wheel followed its motion exactly, passing over raw material and carving it into a perfect replica of the model. Blanchard's lathe could form exactly the same shape, again and again and again.

While Springfield did not always lead the way in innovation, it absorbed the best developments and then standardized and promulgated them. Over time, many of the innovations first devised at Springfield and other armories, from the machines themselves to the ways machines were used, would spread to other manufacturers. Ultimately, with Colt's help, they would lead to a new American industrial revolution.

Colt and Lawton spent several weeks that spring of 1836 touring factories in the Connecticut River Valley. Colt took a side trip of several days to meet with iron suppliers in northwestern Connecticut—considered the best source of wrought iron at the time—and on May 16, the two men rendezvoused in Springfield to take another look at the US Armory. Now Colt had time to stroll through the vast works and inspect them more closely. First came the forges, where anthracite was roasted to extreme heat by water-powered bellows and gun iron was warmed and softened. The next stop was the eighteen trip-hammers, each powered by its own dedicated waterwheel, rising and falling six hundred times a minute, pounding the skelps of iron into rough approximations of the shapes they would assume. The barrels were formed by working the skelps around a mandrel, making an "incessant and intolerable clangor and din," as one visitor recorded. From here, the iron parts were sent to milling machines, which cut them more precisely, and to lathes, which smoothed them.* Colt was impressed by the assortment of machines and believed that what he saw "may at grate advantage be adopted to the construction" of his own guns.

On May 18, Colt and Lawton made their way down the Connecticut to Middletown and Simeon North's armory, where they saw more "exelent

---

* Both lathing and milling remove raw material to create the desired object, but they do it in different ways. The general rule is that in lathing, the object being worked on moves (spins) while the cutting tool remains stationary. In milling, the object is stationary and the tool moves over it. In industrial manufacturing, both lathes and milling machines follow strict predetermined movements to replicate the same object again and again.

mashinary." Then they returned to the river to take the steamboat to New York. The time had come to build a factory of their own.

VII

The waterfall on the Passaic River was considered one of America's natural wonders. Though more modest in scale than Niagara Falls, it was a lot easier to get to, a mere twenty miles from lower Manhattan. It was a peculiar waterfall. Rather than tighten into a turbulent cataract in anticipation of a great plunge, the river opened into an almost glassy lake, 280 feet across, before sliding off the face of the earth into the churning chasm seventy-five feet below. For years the falls had drawn sightseers who gaped and gasped at it. Washington and Lafayette had camped near the falls during the Revolution and enjoyed wandering into a "grotto" at its bottom, where, it was said, they carved their names into the smooth rock. (A nineteenth-century history claimed their names were still visible.) When the architect Benjamin Latrobe came upon the waterfall on his honeymoon in 1800, he declared it one of nature's "sublimest landscapes" and hoped it might become the site for an academy of art.

Alas, one man's art academy is another man's industrial park; where romantics saw the sublime expression of nature's primordial power, others saw merely power—water power. Nine years before Latrobe's visit, the Great Falls had been chosen by Alexander Hamilton, secretary of the treasury, as home of the Society for Establishing Useful Manufacturers (S.U.M.). Hamilton believed, contra Thomas Jefferson's agrarian vision of America, that the future prosperity of the country depended on its embrace of industry; and he believed this waterfall on the Passaic was the ideal place to bring his vision to fruition. Hamilton drafted a charter for the S.U.M., which was signed by the governor of New Jersey, William Paterson, whose chief legacy would be the name he gave to the place his signature conjured into existence: Paterson.

In 1792, the S.U.M. purchased seven hundred acres of land surrounding the falls and hired Pierre L'Enfant, fresh from designing Washington City, to draw up plans. Despite Paterson's very different topography, L'Enfant envisioned a city similar to Washington, with broad avenues radiating from a central point near the falls. The main feature would be a multitiered system of raceways, or canals, that channeled fast-moving water from the top of the falls through town. The S.U.M. designated plots of land along these raceways as future sites for mills, leasing out some and keeping a few for itself.

For all the talent and money that went into developing Paterson, it got off to a shaky start. L'Enfant turned out to be a prima donna whose execution was as poor as his plan was lofty. In 1793, Peter Colt—father of Roswell, uncle of Christopher, and great-uncle of Sam—was invited to Paterson to salvage it. As superintendent, Peter Colt made significant changes to the raceway system, built a few cotton mills alongside it, and generally improved the town. Without enough capital to carry the S.U.M. forward, though, the mills closed in 1797.

Peter Colt left Paterson but did not put Paterson behind him. He believed that the future would catch up to Hamilton's vision, and he encouraged his sons, especially Roswell, to invest. Roswell had the good sense to listen. He began buying stock as early as 1808 and, by 1814, was a majority shareholder in the S.U.M. and governor of Paterson. His brother John Colt was deputy governor and a successful manufacturer of yarns and twine. A cousin named Samuel—most likely the son of Peter Colt's brother Joseph—also became an important town leader, as a deacon and elder of the First Presbyterian Church, until he was banished from the church in 1822 for "intemperate use of Ardent spirits and unchaste conduct."

The fortunes of the S.U.M. lurched along with the American economy, but over time mill activity increased, and by 1836 Paterson was a thriving city of nearly ten thousand citizens with no fewer than seventeen cotton mills, a clock factory, an iron factory, a flax factory, and assorted other industries. Between siblings and cousins, members of the Colt family controlled more than two-thirds of the stock in the S.U.M. Because the mills rented land and raceway rights from the Society, the greater the number of mills, the greater the profit to Roswell Colt and his fellow shareholders. Not entirely out of benevolence and kinship, then, did the Colts welcome another of their own to Paterson.

On May 19, accompanied by his father and Pliny Lawton, Sam stopped off in New York to meet Dudley Selden, then the four men crossed the Hudson River by ferry to Paulus Hook or, as it was becoming less picturesquely known, Jersey City. Conveniently, a train line had recently opened on the west side of the Hudson, departing from Jersey City four times daily to chug west over the Bergen Hills. Arriving in Paterson that afternoon, the men went at once to inspect the site on which Colt's gun mill was to rise— on the eastern bank of the Passaic, just downriver from the falls. Already standing on the site was an abandoned nail factory that had been owned by John Colt and several partners.

Over the next several days, after visiting neighboring factories to gather ideas, they settled on a design for the gun mill. It would be four stories high, 135 feet long and 45 feet wide, and built of locally quarried brownstone. "Our progress since you left here has been as great as could be expected," Sam wrote to his father at the end of May, when Christopher was back in Hartford attending to his silk factory. "We have engaged a gang of hands to commence taking down the old building now on the lot & when done will proceed without delay to level the ground & lay the foundation for our factory."

Sam told his father that he was leaving supervision of the construction to Lawton. He needed to make a final visit to Baltimore "for the purpose of settling up my business there & bringing what tools I have to this place."

VIII

Though neither Sam Colt nor John Pearson was in a position to appreciate the irony, the entire Patent Arms Manufacturing Company—its hundreds of thousands of dollars of capital, its large mill now rising in Paterson, its machines that would be purchased or built to shape the metal to make thousands of guns, and its dozens of employees who would operate those machines—all of this came down, at the moment, to a single gunsmith working with hand tools at a rifle bench in Baltimore. In the transaction between John Pearson and Sam Colt was the shift from an age of skilled tradesmen, operating alone or in small groups to build implements by hand, to an age in which practically everything made by man would be manufactured by machine. In the case of Pearson and Colt, it was not a smooth handoff.

Colt arrived in Baltimore on May 31, his first time back in three months. Pearson had continued to toil in his absence, but every week that Colt failed to send money or show up had put the gunsmith in a fouler mood. A series of letters from Pearson to Colt that spring of 1836 ranges in tone from beseeching to furious.

"Sir I received your letter yesterday," Pearson wrote on March 27, "and I was greatly disappointed after waiting 3 weeks for a letter and money." Colt had promised funds and parts for guns but sent neither. When he wrote, it was generally to impose additional demands on Pearson, much to the latter's dismay. "You make nothing of disappointing me but you do not like I should disappoint you," wrote Pearson. He reminded Colt to send "50 Dollars $$$ . . . Don't forget by G_d."

When that letter failed to move Colt, Pearson sent another. "I am sorry I am under necessity of writing to you for I have waited until my Patience and money is all gone," he wrote in April. "I worked night and day almost so I would not disappoint you, and what have I got for it—why vexation and trouble."

A final letter from Pearson was dated May 9. Colt had sent $100, but this barely covered expenses already incurred, to say nothing of Pearson's salary or future expenses. "How can you think I can lay out of my money in this way by God." He told Colt that he had completed two guns and had two more in the works, but he would not send a single one until he was fully and fairly compensated. "When you think good to give me some satisfaction and pay me my due, then you may expect the same from me as usual but until you do that you can expect nothing from me." Pearson closed by referring, once more, to Colt's maddening hypocrisy. "You are in a devil of a hurry but not to pay your men."

We can only imagine the choice words Pearson had for Colt when the latter finally walked into the shop in Baltimore. But at last Colt had come to get the guns Pearson had made for him, and he brought money. A final receipt is written out in Colt's journal—the journal Colt had first opened to record his chemistry formulas in Ware in 1831 and again to record his voyage to New Orleans in 1833:

Received Baltimore June 4 1836 of Samuel Colt the sum of $119.76. Which is in full of all demands for all services rendered in the Planning, Constructing, and Manufacturing sundry kinds and descriptions of repeating guns and services to be rendered up to the evening of the sixth instant.

Under this is another line, also dated June 4.

Received the sum of $25 as a gratuity for extry services and good faith.

The gratuity was the equivalent of more than two weeks' wages, Colt's way, perhaps, of expressing contrition. Though a generous sum, it was far less than Pearson deserved. Over the two years he had known Colt, he had faithfully executed his work, producing nine revolving rifles, one revolving shotgun, and sixteen revolving pistols—twenty-six guns in twenty-six months. He had endured, in return, an employer who seemed incapable of appreciation, respect, or common courtesy.

John Pearson owes his earthly afterlife to Sam Colt; his name has lived on by its attachment to the revolving guns he made for Colt. But Pearson did a lot more for Colt than Colt did for Pearson. Later, Pearson's family would claim that Colt owed Pearson a great deal indeed—that the gunsmith deserved credit for inventing Colt's revolver. No doubt some of the features of the gun were his. Left alone for weeks and months at a time to carry out Colt's instructions, Pearson relied on his own skill to solve problems of fabrication and mechanics. Does this constitute invention? As a practical matter, many of the great inventors whose names we remember relied on men and women whose names we have forgotten to put together the nuts and bolts and work out the kinks of their inventions. Fair or not.

That meeting in Baltimore seems to have been the last contact between Sam Colt and John Pearson. Colt returned to Paterson. Pearson remained in Baltimore another year, then moved west to Little Rock, Arkansas, then farther west to the frontier of western Arkansas. When he died at the age of eighty, a flattering obituary ran in the *Missouri Dental Journal*.

> Mr. Pearson invented an article upon which Samuel Colt procured a patent in his own name, and from which he realized an independent fortune. Being a very quiet, unassuming man, Mr. Pearson never pushed his claims to the invention, nor, except to his most intimate acquaintances ever mentioned the fact that he was in any way connected with it.

Why a gunsmith had his obituary in a dental journal is explained by the fact that the journal's editor was John Pearson's son. Clearly, the son was still bothered by how shabbily his father had been treated during those years in Baltimore, and how little appreciation he had received. As for Sam Colt, he never gave John Pearson another thought.

CHAPTER EIGHT

Burst

1836–38

The US Army's Second Dragoons attacking
Seminole Indians in the "fastnesses" of Florida.

I

After the long icebound winter, the summer of 1836 brought a blissful stretch of warm and luxuriant days. America had never seemed so fortunate, nor had Americans ever been so willing to bet on their country's future. Property values soared in the east and money grew on trees in the west— almost literally in the case of Michigan Territory, where a man could spend $1,000 on a plot of forested land in June and sell it for $2,000 in July. Up with the price of land went the price of commodities, and up with commodities went the price of slaves; by 1836, Isaac Franklin was selling young males for $1,500, twice what he'd sold them for in 1830. "On whatever side we turn our eyes," declared the newspaper editor Horace Greeley in

1836, "we are greeted by the gratifying evidences of universal prosperity." Greeley had a prophetic bent—it was he who would famously advise his fellow Americans to "go west, young man"—but he was quite wrong in this case. What appeared as prosperity was a bubble gassed by rampant speculation. "Yet nobody perceived the illusion," a nineteenth-century political economist would write of those days before the collapse. "The dream seemed reality for the time."

For Colt, who turned twenty-two on July 19, 1836, it was a good dream while it lasted. He divided his time between Paterson, where he watched his factory slowly rise from the banks of the Passaic River, and New York City, where he found ways to spend the money that now filled his pockets. Among his new indulgences were regular visits to a New York tailor by the name of Hatfield & Pearson. The Pearson in this case was no relation to the gunsmith lately in Colt's employ, but he, too, would soon know the special challenges of doing business with Sam Colt.

For the moment, Hatfield & Pearson were probably delighted to see the young dandy walk into their shop at 164 Broadway. On June 14, Colt bought a pair of "Ribb'd Dailly Pants" for $8. Four days later, he ordered two pairs of white pants, at $7 each, a plain pair of pants at $6.50, and a white satin vest for another $7. To this he soon added a couple of white linen jackets, a pair of suspenders, and, in mid-July, the pièce de résistance, a "Super Olive Coat" for $35. After less than a month of shopping, he owed nearly $90 to the tailor.

Colt spent like a young man who believed he was destined to be rich, and for a while there was no reason to doubt it. Powerful officials in Washington had expressed interest in his gun, and wealthy financiers in New York were so confident of its success that they had put up tens of thousands of dollars to achieve it. The Paterson factory was still rising from the ground, but Colt was already thinking of ways to expand. When his younger brother James came to visit in June, they sat over champagne and "seegars" and began laying plans for James—still just nineteen—to learn French and sail to Paris to open another Colt armory there. And why not? Colt's guns were already drawing serious attention from distant parts of the world. According to Henry Ellsworth, the revolver was such a popular attraction among both American and foreign visitors to the Patent Office that the models on display had been "completely worn out they had been handled and snapped so much."

The most sustained attention continued to come from Texas. A man named A. J. Yates had written in June seeking five hundred repeating rifles and five hundred revolvers for the Texan army—a thousand guns. Yates had then dashed off a letter to Stephen Austin to share news of this remarkable new invention: "I am inclined to think that 100 cavalry with Colts carbines, with spring bayonets, and pistols, will be a very powerful and efficient force. Colts carbines and pistols discharge 30 rounds in the same time that it takes to load 3 times."

A week after Yates wrote that letter, Sam Houston routed Santa Anna and led Texas to independence. The urgency for guns was lost. But Texas would want more arms in the future, and the symbiotic relationship between Texas and Colt was only just beginning.

II

As welcome as Yates's inquiries must have been, they highlighted an awkward reality. Simply put, Colt had no guns to sell and would have none for months to come. Production had to wait for the completion of the gun mill, but as Colt acknowledged in his response to Yates, construction was at least four months behind schedule. Because builders had failed to provide the necessary materials in a timely manner, "it will be as late as next May before we will be able to supply many orders now on hand or supply new ones for any considerable quantity." Not even samples—those guns John Pearson had made more or less by hand—were available. Having served as models to impress investors and buyers, they were now filling a more humble function, as templates to create machine-made replicas. What Colt did not share with Yates was that adapting machines to copy Pearson's guns was far more difficult than he or anyone else had anticipated.

Christopher Colt first became aware of potential problems at his son's company at the end of summer. He alluded to them in a letter on September 14, in which he responded to a request from Sam to borrow $300. That Sam needed to borrow money was cause for concern in itself. According to the terms of his contract with the P.A.M.C., he was receiving $1,000 a month in installments on his $6,000 advance. At a time when a skilled tradesman—John Pearson, for example—would do well to earn $600 in a year, $6,000 was an extraordinary sum for a young man with only himself to support. Some of this money went to pay for stock options in the P.A.M.C., but even a small portion of it would have made Colt wealthy by all normal standards. Where had his money gone?

The answer is hinted at in the expenses Colt continued to rack up through the summer and fall. For example: on September 14, the same day his father wrote to him, he received a bill from the Astor House. Since opening in June, the Astor House had joined the ranks of the country's finest and most expensive hotels, and it had become Colt's residence of choice in New York. On this bill, he owed $7 for board, $2 for a ham hock, and $1 for champagne—a drop in the ice bucket, but a suggestion of budding tastes for the finer things. Meanwhile, he continued to add to his bill at Hatfield & Pearson. On October 4, he bought a pair of "Super Blk Pants" for $16; on October 26, a "Superfine Suit" for $62; and on November 10, "Fancy Pants" for $16. That $62 Colt paid for his Superfine Suit was about what he'd paid John Pearson for six weeks of work.

Of course, there were plenty of ways a young man could part with money in New York that did not involve a decorous exchange of bills and receipts. The grisly and infamous murder of a prostitute named Helen Jewett earlier in the year had exposed the vast undercarriage of the city's economy. Young men were flooding into the city for work in the 1830s, and so were young women, some of whom had fallen into lives as courtesans and prostitutes. By one estimate, as many as ten thousand women in New York were prostitutes; that was surely an exaggeration, but it *felt* true to many New Yorkers. As for the number of men who visited these women, no one dared estimate, but economics suggest that there were more clients than prostitutes. There is no evidence that Sam Colt spent on such diversions, but it would be surprising if he did not. Frequenting prostitutes was a regular feature of the "sporting life" that young men pursued in the city in the 1830s, and nothing in Colt's character suggests he was more constrained by scruples than other young men of his time.

Whatever Colt was spending his money on, he was spending it at an alarming rate and somehow going broke. "Money is a trash I have looked down upon," he would write in a letter to his half brother some years later. That statement would seem preposterous from Colt except for the fact that he *did* seem to treat money as trash: whenever he had it, he found ways to throw it away as quickly as possible.

Christopher's concern for the moment was not Sam's profligacy but what this suggested about his focus. It had come to Christopher's attention that his son was not devoting all of his time to the gun mill. Sam's success had gone to his head, it seems, distracting him from his usual single-minded focus. He needed that focus now more than ever. Not only did his future depend on his efforts, so now did the fortunes of many others. "My dear Samuel when I consider the common consequences to you & to all concerned in the success of this undertaking I cannot but advise that you should lay aside every amusement & devote all your time and close attention to get forward the fire arms," wrote Christopher. "When once well under way, your arms in the market & profit realized it will then be time to take a little recreation."

III

Christopher had hoped for a little recreation of his own that fall of 1836. He was just back from a visit to Ballston Spa, a pretty New York resort town in the foothills of the Adirondacks, where he had gone to sip the mineral waters and breathe the fresh mountain air. He was fifty-six years old and had lived through enough grief to fill a lifetime. Business and money woes had pestered him relentlessly and were amplified by his anxiety for his sons. "If I knew that my four full grown sons were all well located and doing a business that afford fair prospects for a respectable living," he'd written to Sam a few years earlier, "I should not as much regret my own situation."

Now, at last, some good had come to the family. One of his sons had earned the respect and confidence of serious and wealthy men and was on the cusp of riches. Surely a father was entitled to bask in paternal pride and even enjoy some financial gain from his son's success. Alas, as Christopher knew by now, fortune and fairness have nothing to do with each other. Ballston had disappointed—"the spring water did not agree with my present state of health"—and Christopher had returned early to Hartford, to his own sputtering silk business and worrisome news about Sam and his guns.

Christopher's relations with Sam had become extremely complicated. He remained the father of a young man who still had some growing up to do, who needed advice, affection, support, and occasional scolding. But Christopher was also a shareholder who had sunk a good deal of personal honor and wealth into the P.A.M.C. He was invested in Sam's success in every way. While their letters might refer in passing to news from brothers and other family, business—Sam's business—would now and forever be the chief subject of communication between them. "How goes up your factory building," inquired Christopher in a typical letter that fall. "When will you have a few rifles & pistols in the market. How many do you expect to build annually say rifles and how many pistols."

Olivia Colt's letters, sometimes sharing the same sheet of paper on which her husband wrote his, likewise reflected the new dynamic between Sam and the family. Olivia believed that her role as a wife and stepmother was to keep the tone light, dispensing her "medley of domestic hay"—her term—while leaving business to the men. So she came to the subject in her own distaff fashion. "On this fine morning the first day of November your father hands me his letter he's been writing," she began one note to Sam. "I cannot proceed with the important subject of your patent arms but must turn your attention from that to the family circle, and we often wish that you for an evening could step in & make one of our number." Following a bit of news about Sam's brothers and friends, she digressed, as ever, to the love life she imagined for him. "I wish you would sometimes turn aside from business and to pleasure and address a long letter and tell us about the ladies of your village"—meaning Paterson, presumably—"and whether you have lost your heart for that pretty Mrs. Colt."

Through this palaver, Olivia eventually worked her way to Sam's business, which was now inseparable from family life. "We received a letter from Aunt Selden this week," she wrote in late November. "She wants to hear how you are progressing." More to the point, Aunt Selden wanted to know "whether they can safely purchase a house worth $5000, & if they can place any dependence on the arms." Even a slight anecdote about Sam's young half brother, William, touched on the fate of Sam's company. William had recently gone bird hunting with a friend. He had shot two birds, one on the wing. His success made him determined to get a gun of his own, but his father told him he must be patient and wait for one of his brother's guns to come to market. Until Sam's company began producing, William would have to go without.

Bad as it was to disappoint a little brother in want of a gun, it was worse to disappoint an adult brother in need of a job. James, now twenty, wrote to remind Sam of their discussions back in the summer. "With respect to my being connected with you, I wish to know something definite. That is, I wish to know whether you wish me to be a salary man or do you expect to give me a portion of your patent privilege for being connected with you." The best solution, thought James, was for Sam to give him a portion of one of the European patents. With a little help from their father, James was sure he could manage the construction and oversight of an armory in Europe.

Among the realities of Sam's gun business that James failed to comprehend was that its prospects were already dimming. A week before James sent his letter, in December of 1836, Christopher Colt had gotten some unsettling news from Dudley Selden, which he relayed to Sam in an envelope marked "Confidential." Selden had gone into debt to pay the second installment on his 240 shares of P.A.M.C. stock, while some other stockholders had failed to meet their obligations. The money problems Selden and the P.A.M.C. were experiencing that fall were a prelude to a much larger financial disaster starting to unfold in the country. In the meantime, the company was becoming an albatross to Selden before it produced its first gun. He did not assign blame in his letter to Christopher, but in the coming months he would begin to suspect that there was, in fact, a culprit.

IV

When Colt had returned from Europe in the winter of 1836, brimming with news of impending war, he had taken it for granted that his guns would soon be approved and purchased by the government. That had not happened. Finally, though, in the winter of 1837, he was presented an opportunity to demonstrate his invention to the government. Actually, it was less a demonstration than a competition, as several other gunmakers were also invited to attend. Colt received official notice of the event in mid-February of 1837, signed Colonel Bomford, chief of the Ordnance Department.

Colt arrived in Washington several days later. He checked in to the National, aka Gadsby's, the same hotel he'd lodged at the previous winter. He ordered a bottle of port and a fire in his room and awaited further instructions. These came on February 25. A note from the Ordnance Board requested Colt to appear with his guns at the Washington Arsenal the following morning.

The arsenal was a large brick building south of the Capitol, on Greenleaf Point (now Buzzard Point), where the Potomac River met the Anacostia River. Colt spent much of the next three weeks there as his arms and those of his competitors were subjected to a series of tests. All the firearms tested were long guns, that is, rifles and muskets. They were judged in eleven categories, including accuracy, durability, recoil, and "celerity of fire." The press followed the trials with great interest. Every newspaper seemed to have a particular favorite among the competitors.

Of the four guns chosen by Congress for testing, two were breach-loaders. Though they carried only a single shot, breechloaders (loaded from the back of the barrel) were an important development in firearms, for they could be loaded faster and more safely than muzzleloaders (loaded from the front). The best known of these breechloaders was the rifle of John H. Hall, a well-known inventor from Maine whose guns had already been in the service for a decade.* Baron Hackett, a shadowy figure from England or Ireland—it's not clear where exactly he originated—represented a French gun called a *fusil Robert*.

The third candidate was the gun that raised the most concern for Colt and his investors. A multifiring rifle invented by a New Yorker named John Webster Cochran, it was similar to Colt's in that it used a revolving cylinder to bring multiple chambers into alignment, one by one, with the barrel. It had one glaring difference, though. Rather than rotate on a horizontal axis,

---

* In addition to making guns, Hall was a key innovator in the manufacture of uniform and interchangeable parts.

like a wagon wheel—and like Colt's cylinder—it turned on a vertical axis, like a potter's wheel or, more aptly, a roulette wheel. Cochran thus avoided infringing on Colt's patent, but the saucer-sized disk that contained the chambers was unwieldy in the extreme. It was also extraordinarily dangerous to use. Whenever one of its chambers aligned with the barrel, the other chambers faced to the sides and, most problematically, to the rear, directly at the person aiming the gun. Multichambered guns were *always* at risk of misfiring—this was to become an escalating problem with Colt's gun—but at least in Colt's case all the chambers faced *forward* and *away* from the shooter.

Strangely, the absurd design did not register as a nonstarter to either Cochran's investors or the Ordnance Department. Cochran had received admiring attention in newspapers and was said to have raised $300,000 in financing—considerably more than Colt—to manufacture his guns. Some of Colt's investors seemed to worry they had backed the wrong horse, especially when rumors circulated that the army favored Cochran. "I have been satisfactorily informed that Cochran's friends have been making great efforts with the Government and they feel very confident of success," Charles Pond wrote to Colt from New York. A future governor of Connecticut, Pond was a Colt family friend and an investor in the P.A.M.C. "I have no doubt that they have intrigued to a considerable extent."

While Pond was vague about Cochran's intrigues, rumors of mischief and machinations flitted through Washington and New York as the trials proceeded. In a second letter to Colt, Pond revealed that Baron Hackett now had the inside track. Enclosing an article from a Georgetown newspaper that apparently backed Hackett, Pond suggested that the editor of the paper "deserves to have his __ kicked," leaving it to Sam to fill in the blank and for us to speculate about what the offending editor wrote.

The testing paused the first weekend in March for the inauguration of Martin Van Buren. The former vice president was sworn in on Saturday, March 4, 1837, to become the nation's eighth president. Colt may have been among the crowd of twenty thousand in front of the East Portico of the Capitol that Saturday. He was in any event back at the arsenal the following week and the next. Between appearances at the arsenal, he devoted his time to lubricating newly acquired friends in Washington. Colt's bills at Gadsby's included regular charges for port wine and other liquor. He forwarded the bills to Dudley Selden, who bristled at Colt's extravagance. "The application on your part for money comes very malapropos," wrote Selden. "It seems to me that you use money as if it were drawn from an inexhaustible mine."

That Colt was using this money to win over esteemed men who might help the P.A.M.C. did not justify the expense. "I have no belief in undertaking to raise the character of your gun by Old Madeira." Everything about his cousin was starting to get under Selden's skin, including the young man's atrocious spelling. "Buy a dictionary," he scolded after reading yet another of Colt's orthographic contortions.*

V

Sometime that March, during the gun trials in Washington, it began to dawn on Selden that his cousin was guilty of crimes more heinous than profligate spending and bad spelling. He became convinced that Colt had duped him.

The record is sketchy and the timing is vague, but it appears that a specific incident or revelation triggered Selden's suspicions. What this might have been is hinted at in William Edwards's biography of Colt, in which the author quotes at length a letter dated March 3, 1837, from Sam Colt in New York to Pliny Lawton in Paterson. As a historical document, the letter has a few problems, the first being that it is not (or, perhaps more accurately, is no longer) in the archives of the Connecticut Historical Society, where Edwards places it. The other problem is that Colt was almost certainly not in New York on March 3, 1837, as he was in Washington, in the middle of the gun trials. That said, Edwards is clearly quoting from *some* letter, written *sometime*, and he quotes at length. The letter may be dated incorrectly but its content fits into the time frame of late winter or early spring of 1837.

"This is to inform you that my interest with the Patent Arms Man'y Co has entially seased [entirely ceased] the reason for which you are no doubt better informed than myself," writes Colt. "You will therefore much oblige me by testefiing in a note directed to the American Hotel of this City for me that you hird (if you ded so) Dudely Selden say that my contract with the Patent Arms Man'y Co. was broken. Which remark was made"—here Colt

---

* Among these contortions was Selden's name. Once, in trying to explain why Colt may not have received materials sent from London, his English attorney, John Isaac Hawkins, wrote, "I shall direct this letter to the care of the Honorable Dudley Selden, because your last two letters has this spelling, but your first, from Paris had Dudley *Selding* and Dudley *Seting*, your second, from Havre, as appears by the Postmark, although you have given neither date nor place, has Dudley *Selding*, I therefore directed my previous letters with that spelling of the name."

comes to the crux of the matter—"in our office in Paterson on the Evening after we had the good fortune to birst one [of] our make Gons in his presants."

Apparently, Selden had witnessed a misfiring of one of Colt's guns. A "birst" gun was far from good fortune—Colt was being sarcastic—and this burst was particularly ill-timed, coming at the very moment Colt needed the confidence of the company behind him. The accident brought to Selden's attention a real and serious problem with Colt's gun, which was its tendency to spread "lateral fire," or *chain fire*, as the phenomenon is sometimes called, to chambers adjacent to one discharged. The result of a misfire from a Colt gun was not likely to be as suicidal as, say, a Cochran misfire, but a gun that regularly misfired was doomed to fail.

In mid-March, the Ordnance Board adjourned, planning to resume the gun trials later in the year at West Point. Colt used the interregnum to address the problem with his gun. Before leaving Washington, he paid a visit to Henry Ellsworth at the Patent Office to file a caveat describing his remedy. A caveat did not have the legal force of a patent, but it would help establish priority in the event of a challenge. Colt's caveat was for an "improvement in fire arms." By chamfering the mouths of the cylinders "in order to ascertain the desirable angular plain to turn way the fire," as he later described it in a letter to Ellsworth, he could limit, if not eliminate, the problem of lateral fire.

Colt could not so easily repair his relationship with his cousin. Dudley Selden remained convinced that Sam had deceived him about defects in the gun and cost him and his fellow investors a great deal of money. On April 6, 1837, Selden's father, Joseph, died suddenly at the age of seventy-three. Selden could not blame his father's death on Colt, but it underscored how much the Selden family had risked on the P.A.M.C. Joseph Selden had been nearly as heavily invested in the company as Dudley, owning a portion of the patent as well as stock. In the final weeks of his life, he had written to Sam to ask for an update and to express concerns about delays in manufacturing. It seems that Sam never got around to responding.

Dudley Selden buried his father in Troy on April 9. The following day, he came to New York for the day and met with Christopher Colt, who was in town on other business. The meeting was brief and unpleasant. "The deception which he accuses you of," Christopher wrote to Sam that afternoon, "is that you knew the fire arms which you exhibited had a defect in principal & could not have been used in other hands than your own, & that you kept the deception by privately *wetting* the end of the cylinder, until you found the remedy." Some biographers and gun historians read this as *seating* the end of the cylinder—meaning that Sam was placing the cylinder in such a way as to avoid misfires. If the word is *wetting*, this probably referred to the practice, later common, of spreading a substance such as grease or petroleum jelly over each chamber. However Colt was dampening or controlling lateral fire, he was doing it, according to Selden, on the sly.

Christopher was understandably shaken by this accusation against his son. "If you have deceived the company in this or any other point," he wrote to Sam, "it is wrong, notwithstanding you found a remedy." On the other hand,

> if it is not true that you have been in the habit of wetting [seating] the end of the cylinder to prevent more than one charge from going off at a time, you ought to inform Mr. Selden of the error he is in. . . . I am unwilling to believe you ever intended to deceive the company or Mr. Selden in any way & think the impression should be nipped in the bud.

It does not absolve Colt of his deception to point out that a modicum of due diligence by Selden and his fellow investors would have saved them a lot of grief. They would have discovered that the Achilles' heel of *all* multichambered weapons at the time was their vulnerability to chain fire. The truth seems to be that Colt withheld potentially damaging information about his gun for the same reason his investors failed to discover it: they were all impatient to get rich in the get-rich-quick environment of America in the 1830s. Nobody wanted to acknowledge that the gun might be flawed.

Then, just like that, it all burst.

VI

The financial collapse proclaimed itself with dramatic literalness. Early on the morning of Tuesday, March 14, 1837, a large granite building on the corner of Wall Street and Exchange Street, in lower Manhattan, fell to the ground, sending vibrations through the foundations of buildings up and down Wall Street. The implosion could be traced to poor construction, but it was impossible not to read larger meanings into it. The building had been the headquarters of an important banking firm, Joseph & Company, the New York representatives of the great House of Rothschild. Two days later, the firm announced that it was going out of business.

Today, historians and economists continue to unpack the causes of the Panic of 1837, a head-spinning pileup that reverberated through much of the world. The historian Daniel Walker Howe ties the economic collapse to the silver mining industry in Mexico, the opium trade in China, and a bad harvest in Britain, all of which combined to dry up credit in the United States. There were domestic causes, too. Most of these led back to President Jackson's decision to pull federal funds out of Nicholas Biddle's Second Bank of the United States and place them in smaller local banks. The local banks had few of the restraints in making loans that had guided the more conservative US Bank, and their loans inflamed the "speculating mania," as one paper had called it back in May of 1836. When credit suddenly tightened, the mania turned into hysteria.

The panic started in the south when several large cotton brokers went belly-up, then swept north. By April 8, 93 merchant firms in New York had closed their doors; by April 11, that number was 128. Incensed mobs, realizing the paper money they held was becoming worthless, stormed banks to cash in their bills for the gold or silver that (theoretically) backed it. The New York banks responded by stopping all payments and locking their doors. Philadelphia banks soon followed suit, then Baltimore banks. The stock market plummeted. Land in upper Manhattan that had gone for nearly $500 an acre the previous fall now barely fetched $50. Men who had been rich on paper a year ago found their worth halved—if they were lucky. "This volume commences at the most gloomy period which New York has ever known," wrote the former mayor Philip Hone on April 25, as he put his pen to the first page of a new diary. "The clouds which have been for six months hovering over us have become darker than ever, and no eye can perceive a ray of hope through their obscurity."

For the moment, the P.A.M.C. was somewhat insulated. Selden had orchestrated the stock subscription before the collapse began, so capital was in the company's coffers. But because stockholders did not put all of their money in at once—they paid in installments—the tightening market meant that many of them lacked the funds to meet installments at the very time the company was sucking up money to build its factory and machines. Nor did it help that money was suddenly tight in the consumer market; a decline in disposable income meant fewer customers for Colt's gun. Fortunately, the government still needed guns. With this hope, Colt went north to West Point.

VII

He probably went by steamship. That's how most young men made their way up the Hudson Valley to the Point, as the US Military Academy was informally known. The Hudson River was not only the easiest and fastest route, it offered the most picturesque approach. Fifty-five miles north of Manhattan, a rocky prow jutted into the river from the western bank of the Hudson. Rising from this, flanked by forested hills, stood the austere stone buildings of the academy. As the ship prepared to dock, a few nervous teenaged boys would be standing portside, gazing up at the place where some of them—those who could endure it—would spend the next four years of their lives. It was late June, the start of the new school year and time for the matriculation of the freshman class.

At the wharf, Colt and the plebes placed their baggage on a horse-drawn wagon, then followed it up a curling path to the 160-acre plateau in the center of campus known as the Plain. They were greeted by the extraordinary spectacle of the annual encampment. Every summer upperclassmen vacated the stone buildings and bivouacked on the Plain to simulate conditions they might someday face on a battlefield. They marched, drilled, prepared food on open fires, and slept in tents. Life was never less than regimented and rigorous at West Point, but summers brought a slight loosening of collars and release from the usual Spartan privations, grueling academics, and relentless discipline. Cadets were given a chance to swim in the river or walk in the nearby hills. They were also allowed, ever so briefly, to mingle with young women at a series of summer balls and dances.

Although their names meant nothing to Colt in the summer of 1837, some of the cadets on the Plain that June would go on to become the celebrated generals who would lead armies into battle in the Civil War, against each other in some cases. They included the future Confederate Army leaders Pierre Gustave Toutant-Beauregard, of Louisiana, class of 1838—who would command the first bombardment of the Civil War, at Fort Sumter, and lead Confederate troops into battle at Bull Run (Manassas)—as well as Richard S. Ewell and Bushrod Johnson. Future Union commanders on the Plain that summer included Henry Halleck, William Rosecrans, John Pope, Joseph Hooker, and John Sedgwick, who would die at the Battle of Spotsylvania. One cadet who may have been at the encampment—he was granted a brief leave sometime that summer but it's not clear when—was a seventeen-year-old from Ohio, William Tecumseh Sherman, who had come up the Hudson by steamship the previous June.

Colt stayed at the West Point Hotel, at the northern end of the Plain, with views of the river to the north and the encampment to the south. He was no doubt happy to be out of Paterson. The weeks leading up to this had been marred by testy exchanges with Dudley Selden, mainly regarding the number of guns Colt would be permitted to bring with him to West Point. After nearly a year of watching money drain out of the company and his own pocket, Selden was understandably reluctant to spend more money until some started coming in. "My mind is entirely made up as to the samples & the number must not exceed the above," he'd written on April 14. When Colt wrote back to object, Selden reminded him that his own actions were to blame for unanticipated delays and expenses. "Had you divulged to the Company all the defects in the original plans the state of its affairs would have been different from what they are now."

The new set of trials got underway on June 19. The previous spring, the Ordnance Board had tested Colt's small rifle; now it tested his revolving musket and longer rifle. To measure penetration, the guns were fired from various ranges into planks of seasoned white oak. Colt's gun pierced the oak to a depth of 3.00 inches, compared to less than 2.2 inches by Hall's rifle and a pathetic 1.65 inches by Cochran's gun.

A number of circumstances quickly turned the competition to Colt's advantage. For one thing, the enigmatic Baron Hackett did not show up. Or rather, he did show up and was asked to leave for mysterious reasons; newspapers covering the trials refer to his absence but do not elaborate. Colt got another helping of schadenfreude when one of Cochran's guns misfired on June 19. Several of the contiguous chambers ignited and sent balls spraying from the side of the gun, nearly killing a bystander. Cochran's turret revolvers were irredeemable after that, creating "such a degree of dread and apprehension of their dangerous qualities," as the Ordnance Board's report would put it, "as to render them unpopular, and consequently almost powerless, weapons of war." Before Colt could gloat too much, one of his own guns misfired, two chambers igniting at once. This was less dangerous and damning than Cochran's disaster, but it was unfortunate.

Unlike the spring trials, which had dragged on for weeks, the West Point trials lasted just three days. Colt felt confident that his gun had triumphed, and much of the press agreed. "The by-standers seemed to consider the Colt's as the favorite," reported the *New York Courier*. "He fired 18 charges in the incredible short space of 58 seconds, and the accuracy and penetration of the balls proved as good as the ordinary rifle; indeed the penetration is said to be better." Colt shared the good news with his father. "Our trial at West Point is finished and my guns have beaten every other in every particular."

The official report would not be issued until the end of summer, but several members of the board had already privately expressed their enthusiasm for Colt's guns. That the board had written to Colt to inquire how much his guns would cost to manufacture gave him more reason to think its opinion was going to be favorable.

Sanguine as he was, Colt must have been aware of dissenting views. An unsigned column, first published in the *New York Star* and reprinted in numerous other newspapers, aired some of these.

> It is pretty generally understood that the board who recently finished their examinations of these newly invented destructive implements ordered for their consideration, have promptly rejected the whole of them in toto. The chief objection is that the common soldier must not have placed in his hands an instrument of complicated structure, which is but little calculated for the excitement which exists in the heat of battle. It's not time then to be obliged to enter into mathematical reasonings on gunnery, and to study out the processes which the management of an intricate piece of workmanship requires.

Nearly seven weeks passed before the board delivered its verdict to Congress. The report was twenty-seven pages long, complete with tables and assessments for each gun in the eleven categories stipulated by Congress. Colt's gun had clearly outperformed others in many of the categories, and the report began on a positive, if muted, note:

> It is the opinion of the board that the arm of Colt, involving all the merits, and free from some of the objections to the former, may be very usefully applied in *special* cases; as, in fixed positions in defense of a breach; to cover boarders; in tops of ships; or for personal attack or defense; in a word, under any circumstances where the operation is of a special and brief character, and it be desirable to throw a mass of fire upon a particular point for a limited time. In such or similar situations the entire strength of this arm might be so controlled and managed, as to render it fully available and highly efficient.

The main problem with the gun, the board believed, was the kit of appurtenances required to load it—rods, screwdrivers, and other tools—which would make it difficult to use "in the field." Then came the stinger:

> The board is of the unanimous opinion that, from its complicated character, its liability to accidents (one having occurred in practice on the 21st of June) in the hands of soldiers, and other reasons which may be

found in this report, that this arm is entirely unsuited to the general purposes of the service.

There it was: *entirely unsuited to the general purpose of the service.* The best guns for the service, the board concluded, were those already in use, the standard US musket and Hall's rifles.

Colt would ever after think of ordnance boards as filled with pettifogging "grannies" too timid to adopt new technology. He had a point. Armies tended to be run by men of conservative temperament who were naturally averse to developments that challenged what they knew of war, which was, inevitably, war as it had been fought in the past. But the board's assessment made a good deal of sense given the peculiarities of Colt's gun. Some years later, Colt himself would acknowledge of his early guns that the board "very justly reported them to be complicated & liable to accident in the hands of the common soldier."

Because the board included reloading times in its measurements of "celerity of fire," it gave Colt only a minimal advantage. Had it tested a fully loaded Colt rifle, with eight charged chambers, against a loaded single-shot long gun of any description, and limited the test to, say, one minute, the board would have found that Colt's guns at least tripled or quadrupled the standard rate of fire. But the board started each trial with all guns unloaded, putting Colt's at a considerable and arguably irrelevant disadvantage. Nobody would ever walk into a fight with an unloaded Colt.

But, again, the board's test was not entirely unreasonable. A sustained battle by an army, lasting hours, not minutes, would see many reloadings of any gun, including a Colt after the initial rounds were fired. Every flurry of bullets would have to be followed by a pause of about two minutes (in ideal circumstances). Revolvers ran like the hare in Aesop's fable: a sprint, then a long rest, then another sprint. The single-shot US standard musket or rifle was a slower but steadier tortoise.

For a nineteenth-century army, tortoises made more sense. The reasons for this are circular: because armies were organized around single-shot firearms, single-shot firearms suited them best. For centuries, armies had achieved volley fire by forming columns of consecutive lines, or ranks, of men: each line fired, then retired to the rear to reload as the next rank fired, essentially turning columns of men into multishot weapons. An individual soldier could fire only two or three times per minute, but together, taking turns, an army could achieve rapid high-density fire. In the late sixteenth century, a Dutch nobleman, Maurice of Nassau, Prince of Orange, had broken down firing and reloading into forty-two discreet actions, each named and assigned a command. In effect, infantrymen were expected to act as parts of a well-oiled machine, and the column was a multibarreled machine gun.

The problem with such a machine was that it was prone to breaking down. Men in formation were easy to kill, and as they fell, formations had to be reassembled with new men. This required soldiers to suppress their individual wills to survive for the sake of the machine, all "stepping as one man—all forming a line," as William Tecumseh Sherman put it in a letter from West Point around the time of Colt's visit. Centuries of men with single-shot guns in ranks had created not just a way of fighting, but an entrenched military culture of total discipline, self-sacrifice, and submission of autonomy to the machine.

As suggested in the *New York Star* article after the West Point trials, a problem with Colt's guns from a nineteenth-century military perspective was that they threatened to disrupt discipline, and the very culture, of armies. An infantryman with eight loaded chambers was liable to spew them all at once in an effort to preserve his individual life. At the very least, this would waste ammunition. But the guns challenged army discipline on a more basic level: by lending themselves to individual and improvisational fighting, they contravened the terms on which army discipline was imposed.

Under its own understanding of war, then, the Ordnance Board's verdict was correct. A repeating firearm was unsuited to battle between nineteenth-century armies. It called for a different kind of fighting force, against a different kind of enemy.

VIII

The P.A.M.C. finally went into full production in the fall of 1837. The completed mill was a handsome stone building, four stories tall with a cupola that made it appear even taller, topped by a weather vane in the shape of a rifle. Despite the association Colt's name would come to have with six-shot handguns, the first model made at the mill was a rifle with a massive cylinder of eight chambers. After a number of these rifles were produced, the machinery was retooled for a run of small .28-caliber "pocket" pistols. Later there would be rifles and pistols of different sizes, then carbines, shotguns, and even muskets, all with revolving cylinders.

One day that fall an entourage of men, led by Daniel Webster and Roswell Colt, came out from New York to tour the gun mill, "where man is engaged in forging weapons to slay his fellow man," as a reporter accompanying the party wrote. "The establishment, however, is large, and evidently well conducted." Well conducted it may have been, but between the disappointing West Point trials and the financial meltdown, the market for Colt's guns had vanished. Moreover, the guns turned out to be expensive to make, far more expensive than the company had anticipated, as Selden never tired of reminding Colt.

> You will readily perceive how great the disappointment has been to the Directors and Stockholders who instead of realizing from sales in September, find that nothing has been sold or is yet ready for sale up to this date. . . . Instead of the amount expended being in all $45,000, it has already amounted to $70,000, as I best recollect. Instead of the rifles costing as they understood from you . . . 15 or 20 dollars [to produce], the cost will probably exceed three times at sum.

Selden likewise reminded Colt that he had personally sunk $13,000 of his own money into the company and other stockholders had paid their share, yet Colt had not paid the installment he owed on his own shares of stock, some $2,000. His failure to pay was particularly egregious given the damage that his deception had done to the company in "trouble and expense."

Colt refused to accept blame. He insisted that the "improvement" he made to the design after Selden discovered his deception should have made it easier, not harder, to manufacture the guns, and therefore it was the company, not he, that bore the blame for delays. In fact, the improved design *did* streamline the fabrication of the cylinders, but Colt conveniently missed Selden's point, which was that many of the machines first had to be reconfigured to accommodate the new design.

A kind of consolation prize came to Colt in that fall of 1837 when he won the Gold Medal at the fair of the American Institute of New York "for the best specimen of many chambered cylinder rifles." The American Institute was a prominent organization of scientists and inventors, so this was a real honor; however it did nothing to secure government contracts for Colt. As a matter of history, the medal's greatest significance came in the article that heralded Colt as its recipient, in the November issue of the *Journal of the American Institute.* This is the article—as mentioned in chapter 4—that suggested Colt's inspiration for his gun was Nat Turner's insurrection:

> Mr. Colt happened to be near the scene of a sanguinary insurrection of negro slaves, in the southern district of Virginia. He was startled to think against what fearful odds the white planter must ever contend, thus surrounded by a swarming population of slaves. What defense could there be in one shot, when opposed to multitudes, even though multitudes of the unarmed? The master and his family were certain to be massacred. Was there no way, thought Mr. Colt, of enabling the planter to repose in peace?

How much of a role Nat Turner played in Colt's thinking is impossible to determine, but his motives for circulating this story in the fall of 1837 are obvious. With military contracts appearing unlikely, he saw his best opportunity for civilian sales in the south. Putting aside for the moment the cynicism of such a pitch, Colt and the *Journal* had in fact identified the real value of a repeating firearm. It was not to be found in conventional combat among armies, but in asymmetrical confrontations of one man, or several, against many.

The first ads for Colt's guns began to appear in New York papers in December of 1837. Interested buyers were encouraged to visit the Astor House, where they would find Colt himself presiding over a display of his arms and available to answer all questions about them. An article in the *New York Evening Star*, perhaps juiced with a little remuneration from Colt—such under-the-table arrangements with the press were common—extolled the guns fulsomely. "They are put up in mahogany cases with two cylinders each, ammunition flask, cap primer, and the whole equipment in the most perfect order for immediate use, and we think that independent of the immense power of the repeating rifle, that for beauty and elegance of workmanship, we have never seen superior specimens of art from any quarter of the world."

Colt intended to sell the guns at $100 wholesale and $125 retail. "These Rifles are eight times more effective and very little more expensive," claimed an early advertisement. In fact, they were two to five times more expensive than a regular rifle, making them a novelty and luxury at a time when few could afford even necessities.

No one was upset to see 1837 end, least of all Colt. He was broke. The advances he'd received from the P.A.M.C. had been spent. His pay was now based on profits, of which there were none, and Dudley Selden continued to hound him for money he did not have. Sam turned to his father for help, but Christopher, experiencing his own financial woes, had nothing to give but a word of advice: "Put your <u>trust</u> in your <u>Heavenly Father</u>, and he will guide your thoughts, and give you wisdom & friends to aid you in all good works."

IX

The Heavenly Father did really seem to smile down upon Colt and his gun mill at the start of 1838. That January, a letter arrived in Paterson from Florida, posted weeks earlier by Lieutenant Colonel William S. Harney of the US Army.

A veteran of the Black Hawk War in Illinois and Wisconsin, Harney was a merciless Indian fighter and celebrated commander of a mounted rifle regiment, the Second Dragoons. Dragoons were similar to cavalry in that they rode on horseback; unlike cavalry, they usually fought on foot. Harney's dragoons had been fighting for several years against Seminole Indians in Florida, in a conflict known as the Second Seminole War. Harney probably became acquainted with Colt's guns through some of the West Point graduates who had attended the trials the previous June. He had convinced General Thomas Jesup—the man in command of all US troops in Florida—to buy several dozen of Colt's repeating rifles for the dragoons. Harney had clearly been in contact previously with Colt and made an arrangement, which Colt had failed to keep. "I have barely time to tell you that I have been greatly disappointed in not having received the guns yet," wrote Harney. "If you have not started them yet lose no time in doing so for I wish them very much. I am still more confident that they are the only thing that will finish the infernal war."

Harney's request signaled a reprieve for Colt. A sale to the dragoons would provide the P.A.M.C. with a much-needed infusion of cash, and it would put a commission in Colt's pocket. Most important, it would open a door to the military gun market—a back door, but a door nonetheless—and allow Colt to prove his guns in field conditions.

Colt prepared at once to hand-deliver his guns to Florida. First, he needed a guarantor. As a measure of how little faith the company now had in him, neither Dudley Selden nor anyone else at the P.A.M.C. trusted Colt with his own guns. Exactly what they worried he would do with them is unclear, but they were taking no chances. He would not be permitted to leave Paterson with the rifles unless someone promised to pay their full worth should he fail to reappear. Roswell Colt, not for the last time, came to Sam's rescue. Though Roswell's own finances were under assault by the distressed economy and a lawsuit from his estranged wife's family, he agreed to indemnify Sam's shipment of guns.

On February 3, after some last-minute wrangling with Selden over terms, Colt embarked from New York aboard a Charleston-bound brig called the *Sun*. With him were ninety repeating carbines—short-barreled rifles for mounted troops—packed in ten cases, along with twenty-five thousand percussion caps. According to the terms of his contract, he'd agreed to return by March 31 with either money or unsold guns.

"My arrangements with Mr. Selden were completed for this adventure about five minutes before I embarked," Sam wrote to his father from aboard the *Sun*. He was going to Florida (or "Floridy," as he wrote it) as an agent of the company. "I am not to receive a salary for my services, neither are my expenses & that of insurance & transportation of the Rifles to be paid by the Company. . . . All the advantages that can arise out of this arrangement to me is simply that advantage of testing another market & the prospect of getting a small advance from the company in case I get more than ninety dollars & the expenses of the adventure for them."

After an "infurnal disagreeable" passage of ten days on rough seas, Colt arrived in Charleston on February 13. He spent a few days there, giving demonstrations of his guns as he waited for a ship to take him farther south, then sailed on to St. Augustine, the old colonial Spanish city on Florida's northern coast. From here he turned in to the Indian River.

The Indian River was not a river but a hundred-mile-long lagoon running north-south between the mainland and the thin barrier islands lining the east coast of central Florida. This pretty and gentle artery led right into the heart of the war with the Seminoles.

On March 3, Colt sailed into the Jupiter Inlet and swung west into the wide mouth of the Loxahatchee River. Three miles on, rising from a point between the river's north and south forks, he came to Fort Jupiter. The fort was close to the front lines of the war against the Seminoles, and was as near to battle as Colt would ever get.

Compared to later armed engagements with natives in the western United States, the Florida conflict is a nearly forgotten episode in American history. That is probably because it dragged on so tediously and supplied none of the cinema-ready scenes—cavalry charges across vast grasslands, feathered braves whooping from hillsides, wagon trains circling in the shadows of buttes. It also gave no pride to those who fought in it. It was, as many said, an "inglorious war." Little over two years old when Colt arrived in Florida, the conflict already seemed interminable to its participants.

The *Second* Seminole War was the sequel of a campaign waged against the Indians by then general Andrew Jackson in 1818. That first war had ended in 1819, when Spain sold Florida to United States. Andrew Jackson, as president, had instigated this new conflict, too. Under the terms of his Indian Removal Act of 1830, the Seminole, along with the other "civilized" tribes of southeastern woodland Indians—Cherokee, Chickasaw, Choctaw, and Creek—were invited to relocate west of the Mississippi. It was an invitation they could not refuse, as all who tried discovered. Many of the southern tribes had already resigned themselves to their fates and moved to Oklahoma. The rest would soon join them on the Trail of Tears, the long and often fatal march to Oklahoma that would commence later in the summer and fall of 1838. But the Seminoles of Florida were more intransigent than other tribes of the south. Though some had been persuaded to sign a treaty by which they agreed to give up land and move with their fellow Indians to Oklahoma, a large group, led by a young chief named Osceola, had refused to budge.

If the stated objective for the Americans was to remove the Indians, there was an unspoken corollary. General Jesup, the commander of the American war effort, came right out and admitted it in a private letter: "This is a negro war, not an Indian war."

Every Indian war in the south was a kind of "negro war." The purpose of expelling Indians from Georgia, Alabama, and Mississippi was to clear land to put in plantations where slaves would pick cotton or cut sugarcane. In Florida, the connection between Indian expulsion and slavery was more complicated. The land the American army was attempting to seize was not suitable for growing cotton. Indeed, it was "the poorest country that ever two people quarreled over," in the words of a twenty-six-year-old army surgeon named Jacob Rhett Motte. But for generations the everglades had been a destination for escaped slaves. Coming mainly from Georgia, the slaves fled into the Seminole lands and melded with the Indians. While some were taken in as slaves by Seminoles, even these were treated more or less as members of the tribe. A number of "Black Seminoles" became influential leaders and councilors. Over generations, an extraordinary mixed-race culture had evolved, one race hiding out, the other trying to stay put. For whites, the usual rationale for the Indian wars—to displace Native people to cultivate the land—made no sense. The Seminole presence was intolerable for a different reason: the refuge they offered to fleeing slaves.

The Second Seminole War was fought in scorching sun, or in gloom and damp, against an enemy "pertinaciously retreating to their hiding places," as Jacob Motte wrote, "in country rendered almost impenetrable by the wide spread morasses and everglades, the dense hammocks and fastnesses that cover its surface, in which no troops in the world could operate." Wading through cypress swamps and palmetto thickets, troops confronted quicksand, dense clouds of mosquitoes, and saw grass so sharp it cut through clothing and skin. It was all "a perfect paradise for Indians, alligators, serpents, frogs, and every other kind of loathsome reptile."

Despite casually lumping Seminoles in with reptiles, Motte and many of his fellow soldiers had a begrudging respect for the Indians' resolve and courage. The army estimated the number of Seminole warriors at fourteen hundred but it was probably more like three hundred holding out against an army of nearly nine thousand. "Their indomitable and long uncompromising spirit cannot but excite admiration in every breast," wrote Motte.

The American effort, on the other hand, struck many observers as poorly prosecuted and morally indefensible. In the early stages, General Winfield Scott had tried to use conventional battle tactics against the Seminole, moving his men through the swamps in formal marches, two abreast on jungle paths. Scott had published a military manual in 1835 that promoted the kind of European-style military formations that might have succeeded in Florida had the Indians cooperated by lining up in rows and waiting to be shot. Instead, the Seminole used the advantage of their superior knowledge of the terrain and employed guerrilla tactics to snipe from cover, then melt back into the forest. Battles generally followed a depressing script. A detachment of American soldiers would march through wilderness in search of Indians. As the Americans rounded a bend or came to a river, they would find themselves suddenly surrounded, in a shower of arrows and bullets amid harrowing war whoops. In the chaos, the Americans would fire their weapons at half-hidden and fast-moving targets; then, as they reloaded, the Indians would charge in with bow and arrow or tomahawks for slashing and scalping. The Americans had more guns but the Indians had better tactics.

One of Andrew Jackson's last acts as president had been to replace General Scott with General Jesup. Jackson believed that Jesup, a personal friend, would find a way to turn things around in Florida. Privately, Jesup had a distaste for the Seminole conflict, a "reckless waste of blood and treasure," as he described it. But Jackson was not mistaken in assuming that Jesup would do what it took to end this war. There were no more grand marches or choreographed maneuvers drawn from Scott's textbook. The American

Army was fighting a war of attrition now and borrowing Indian tactics, such as breaking into small, fast groups for quick skirmishes and running fights.

As evidence that Jesup's approach was working, a large group of Seminoles, unable to grow food or hunt and starving after two years of dodging Americans in the swamp, had come into Fort Jupiter to surrender. Now camped a mile away, they begged to be permitted to remain in Florida, with the promise that they would lay down their arms and keep south of Lake Loxahatchee, out of the Americans' way. General Jesup was not a man of tender feelings, but he was a pragmatist, and the proposal made a good deal of sense to him. On February 12—three weeks before Colt's arrival—he'd dispatched his aide-de-camp to Washington with a letter to Secretary of War Joel Roberts Poinsett, in which Jesup proposed letting peaceful Indians stay in Florida. There had still been no response as of March 3, when Colt showed up at the fort with his guns, nor by March 9, the day a board of officers from Harney's dragoons met to test Colt's guns.

The board was composed of three officers, two of whom were first-rate marksmen. The officers, according to their report, tested the rifle "in every manner that occurred to their minds." First, they fired at a "hard green Pitch Pine tree" from a hundred yards. Two of six balls that were fired struck the target and penetrated two inches into the bark and pith. When the officers moved back to a distance of two hundred yards, the balls still penetrated, digging in an inch deeper than those of the single-shot carbines used by the dragoons. The officers were unanimously convinced that "they have never seen any fire arm (in proportion to its caliber) to be compared to Colt's Rifle for force and depth of penetration." As for accuracy, the board concluded that Colt's gun was "as perfect as possible."

Next they tested celerity. The officers loaded two "receivers," or cylinders. Since each rifle cylinder had eight chambers, this totaled sixteen charges. They fired one cylinder, then put in another and fired it, then reloaded the first and fired again. When they were done, they deemed the gun's rate of fire "as great as could be desired, and even greater than most occasions will require." This was precisely what Lieutenant Colonel Harney had hoped for in Colt's repeating firearms, and why he believed they were well suited to fighting Indians in Florida.

According to the army surgeon Motte, nobody was more impressed by Colt's guns than the Seminoles, many of whom had come into the fort to watch the shooting. These were the first Native Americans to see a Colt weapon in action, and their response anticipated multiple scenes that would play out in the western United States in years to come. "The Indians exhibited considerable astonishment on witnessing the wonderful performances of this weapon, and came to the unanimous conclusion that it was 'great medicine,'" wrote Motte, "and the first day after witnessing the capabilities of this rifle they were very particular in avoiding any approach to that part of the camp where they knew it was."

Colt was still at Fort Jupiter on March 20 when Jesup's aide-de-camp returned from Washington with Secretary Poinsett's response. Made in consultation with President Van Buren, the secretary's orders were unconditional: the Indians could not stay in Florida. They must go west to Oklahoma. The blacks who lived among them were to be returned to slavery.

That night, as the Seminoles enjoyed a "grand frolic" of dancing and whiskey (provided, no doubt, by the army), General Jesup ordered his troops to surround their camp. At dawn, after the Indians' "faculties had become completely obumbrated by the plentiful libations," wrote Motte, the army moved in. Two days later, on March 22, the first group of Seminoles was loaded onto boats and shipped to St. Augustine for the start of their long journey west. They were not permitted to take their yelping and howling dogs with them. The animals were quickly silenced with bullets.

Colt remained at the fort for another week before he signed a contract with Harney and Jesup. He sold them fifty rifles plus appendages, at $125 each. This was not as many guns as Colt had hoped to sell, but the US Army was now in possession of his invention and he was in possession of $6,250.

Colt started for home on March 29. In his contract with Selden and the P.A.M.C., he had obligated himself to return to Paterson with money or guns by March 31. Dudley Selden had been fuming since early March because Colt had failed to respond to numerous letters. This was probably not Colt's fault—the mail between Florida and New York was slow—but Selden was in no mood to understand. "I shall decline all correspondence until receipt of my letters is acknowledged," Selden had written in early March, around the same time Colt was arriving at Fort Jupiter.

On March 31, Colt was drifting up the Indian River, hundreds of miles and weeks if not months from Paterson. On April 6, Roswell Colt wrote to Christopher Colt: "I have received notice from the Patent Arms Co. that they hold me responsible for $9000 for 100 rifles furnished Samuel in January which he was to return or repay by 31 March. . . . It will be ruinous to me to have to advance this money and I beg you to write to your son, calling his attention to this business."

Four days after Roswell sent that urgent letter, Sam was still south of St. Augustine. His ship had made it through the Indian River and was attempting to sail up the coast. Marooned by a powerful headwind, the ship had made no more than 150 miles in seven days. With food and water running short, the captain had put all aboard on rations. Colt decided he'd had enough of waiting for the wind to die. With two other passengers, including an army lieutenant in poor health named Seth Thornton and a crew of four sailors, he climbed into a small boat and pushed off for shore. He left the forty unsold guns on board but had the draft for $6,250 in his luggage.

About a mile from shore, as the sailors dug in with their oars, the boat slipped into the breakers. A large wave crashed over the side. The little boat capsized and everything in it plunged into the surf. When Colt caught his breath and looked around for his luggage, he saw it in the distance. It was floating away, and with it went his draft for $6,250.

PART III

SMOKE AND MIRRORS

1838–45

There is a countenance which haunts me, turn as I will. There is an hysterical laugh which will forever ring within my ears.

—Edgar Allan Poe,
"The Oblong Box,"
1844

CHAPTER NINE

Legerdemain

1838–42

The University Building, on the eastern end of Washington Square.
Colt's room was on the top floor of the near tower.

I

From the middle of the floor, Colt could reach out and nearly touch the stone walls—the room was as small as a prison cell. On rainy days, such as this one, the roof leaked and the walls dampened. But the rent was inexpensive, just $30 a year, and because the room was five stories above the street, the light was good and the air fresh. Best of all, it was located inside the New York University Building. Erected six years earlier in a Gothic style meant to emulate the English colleges of Oxford and Cambridge, the building

149

had a white marble facade, arched windows, and crenellated towers at each of its four corners. Colt's new room was at the top of the southwest tower.

If the exterior of the University Building evoked the misty past, the men who inhabited it were mainly focused on the future. They were an array of writers, artists, and, above all, scientists, some of whom were connected to New York University, while others, such as Colt, simply rented apartments on upper floors that provided, as an advertisement put it, "every comfort and accommodation for single gentlemen." In 1837, Samuel F. B. Morse, professor of painting and sculpture, had demonstrated his new electromagnetic telegraph in a room in the opposite wing of the building from Colt's. In the summer of 1840, Morse and his colleague John William Draper, professor of chemistry, climbed to the roof, constructed a glass studio, and made some of the first daguerreotype images in the United States. Morse had since moved out of the University Building, but he and Draper still taught at the school, and both would soon become friends and collaborators of Colt's.

Let us imagine Colt in his tiny chamber on a wet afternoon in mid-September: Friday, September 17, 1841, to be precise. He has just taken over the rent, two days earlier, from a man named Houghton. Colt will continue to spend nights in hotels downtown, but days will go to his work at the "Invention and Improvement Office," as a friend will later describe his tower room. He is still settling in, so the room is probably in disarray. Furniture and supplies—a bale of copper wire, plates of zinc, compounds of mercury—are bunched against the walls where they were left by the men who carried them up the steep and narrow stairs. Rain taps on the copper roof above him. The air outside is gray and thick, but even on a day such as this his little windows offer sweeping views of the city. ("You stand as it were upon an eminence," his stepmother had written to him a decade ago. "Look around.") To the north, blocked partially by the high roof of the chapel, is the future city, still rising from the fields and rocky hills of upper Manhattan. South is the dense metropolis, much of it rebuilt since the Great Fire of 1835 though still in harried flux—"confused heaps of buildings," Charles Dickens would describe it when he visited in 1842, "with here and there a spire or steeple, looking down upon the herd below; and here and there, again, a cloud of lazy smoke." The prettiest view is to the west, across Washington Square Park, a former potter's field transformed over the last fifteen years into a glade of grass, flowers, and ailanthus trees. The park is enclosed by a wooden fence and surrounded by the grandest town houses in the city. Years later, the novelist Henry James, whose father, Henry James Sr., boarded at the university shortly before Colt moved in, would describe Washington Square of the early 1840s as "the ideal of quiet and genteel retirement."

But it was not quiet and genteel retirement that brought Sam Colt to Washington Square in that autumn of 1841, and he would find none here. Indeed, his years at the University Building would be even more tumultuous than the four he'd just endured.

II

The period between Colt's "Florida venture" in the spring of 1838 and his arrival on Washington Square in the early fall of 1841 had been an eventful yet repetitive cycle of disaster, salvation, and more disaster. For four hours after getting tossed into the sea, Colt had waded in the breakers near St. Augustine, grasping the overturned boat, trying to stay afloat as he watched his luggage drift away with the $6,250. A rescuer at last reached Colt and the others with a long rope, and the stranded men dragged themselves through the surf to the beach. So difficult was the experience that Colt's fellow passenger, Lieutenant Seth Thornton, already gravely ill with "florida feaver," was not expected to survive.

The following day, Colt had returned to the beach to look for his luggage. He had been assured that it would drift in on the incoming tide. For four days he remained in St. Augustine, searching the beach. His luggage never showed up.

When he finally got back to New York in early May of 1838, he was sick, exhausted, and broke. Repairing to a room in the Astor House, he took stock of his circumstances. He owed the P.A.M.C. not only for the fifty rifles sold to Colonel Harney but also for the forty unsold. He had no money to pay for them. What he had instead was a fishy story about the ocean swallowing up $6,250. "I expect nothing but trouble from all quarters," he wrote to his father from his bed in the Astor House. "It is of vital importance to me that you come immediately. . . . Your neglecting to come here by the first conveyance would double my embarrassment."

Christopher had often rushed to his son's side in the past, but he now declined. He, too, was ill, suffering a bad cold he'd caught on a recent trip to New York. A return to the city would be "imprudent."

The news from home was gloomy. Sam's little half sister, Olive, had died while he was in Florida, and Christopher's silk business was failing. Also while in New York, Christopher had heard "some insinuations . . . touching you unfavorably." One source of these was Dudley Selden, who "did not appear to credit" the tale of the lost luggage. The only recourse Sam had was to reach out to Roswell Colt. "I trust you will be able to satisfy Mr. Colt of the truth of what you have written," wrote Christopher, sounding not at all satisfied himself.

So it was Roswell, again, who came to the rescue, despite the extremely uncomfortable position Sam had placed him in with his delayed return to New York. Negotiating on Sam's behalf with Selden and the board of the company, Roswell managed to put them off for a few months.

In late June of 1838, Colt finally got a replacement draft of $6,250 from the government. Though a kind of vindication, the money, as a practical matter, was too little, too late. Gun sales were poor, and Colt's personal finances were worsening by the day. He now owed more than $300 to his tailor, Hatfield & Pearson. He owed $320 to a man named Holmes, from whom he had borrowed in Charleston, and another $100 to a man named Irwin in St. Augustine. And then there were all those outstanding debts to the company and to Dudley Selden, who was becoming more "pugnacious," as Colt described him, by the day.

That fall, Colt calculated what he owed in total: $2,270. Half of this he could delay paying for another year; the other half was due immediately. Back he went to Roswell Colt to ask for another $1,500. This time, Roswell turned him down. "I am grieved, in my present situation, to say that it is not in my power to meet your wishes." In October, a new bill arrived for Sam, from the Astor House, for $556.

If Colt's behavior in these years gave an impression of a young man self-destructing by profligacy and prevarication, it also demonstrated his extraordinary resolve and energy. His refusal to admit defeat would appear almost delusional at times. The army's report following the West Point trials had effectively quashed his chance of doing business with the government, and Colonel Bomford of the Ordnance Department had made clear that he had no intention of buying repeating guns. Nevertheless, at the end of 1838, Colt went back to Washington. Through the winter of 1839, he traveled the windswept avenues of the capital, lodging at Gadsby's and entertaining government officials in the salons and taverns of the city. "With a little Legerdemain," he wrote to Dudley Selden, "I think I may be able to obtain an order." Legerdemain mainly involved plying politicians with prodigious amounts of alcohol, then sending the bills to Selden. Receipts from that winter show that in his three months in Washington, Colt spent $75 on about eighty-five bottles of brandy and sherry. That does not include bar bills or other types of alcohol he purchased.

Legerdemain also meant sneaking around the back of Colonel Bomford and trying to convince military commanders to buy his guns with or without approval of the Ordnance Department. On at least one occasion, it meant proposing to offer Bomford a bribe. Selden was stunned. "The suggestion," he wrote to Sam, "is dishonorable in every way." Selden was even more outraged when Colt put up some of the company's guns as collateral to secure a personal loan. "I know not what you may think of the morals of this business," wrote Selden to Colt, "but it seems to me not much better than putting your hand in a man's pocket." The treasurer's disappointment in his young cousin was almost total now. "All your promises have proved illusory."

As Selden and others lost hope in the company, Colt pushed on. He organized demonstrations of his guns at outdoor venues around Washington, inviting army officers and politicians to a winter's afternoon of shooting and drinking. Having entertained and inebriated them, Colt coaxed the numb-fingered officers to sign a petition in favor of his firearms. Some signatures were harder to collect than others. "I danced constant attendance on them," Colt wrote of his efforts upon the holdouts. "I got them one by one to ride with me a few miles in the country to the Race Course where after sundry trials and invitations to dinner I succeeded in convincing most of them of the superiority of my arms and added their signatures to the paper."

The morning before he departed Washington to return north, Colt hand-delivered the petition, with the gift of a pistol, to the home of Joel Roberts Poinsett, the secretary of war. Poinsett was a good audience for Colt. Born in South Carolina but raised in England and Connecticut, the secretary was a cosmopolitan and curious man who appreciated technological advances. A few years later, he would be one of the founders of the organization that eventually became the Smithsonian Institution. Like many prominent and educated men of his time, Poinsett was also fascinated by botany. During a diplomatic mission to Mexico, he had discovered a red-leafed plant that he introduced to America, known today as the poinsettia.

The secretary read the petition as Colt waited. He tried the gun a few times (loaded only with percussion caps) and pronounced himself "extremely pleased with its operation," as Colt reported to the P.A.M.C. board. Poinsett then enthusiastically directed Colt to submit the petition to his office the following day and assured him that the War Department would place an order.

Two days after delivering this good news to the P.A.M.C. directors, Colt wrote back to withdraw it. He had received a new communication from the secretary. Poinsett was not disposed to order Colt's guns after all. It seems that Colt's nemesis, Colonel Bomford, had dissuaded him.

Colt quickly regrouped. Rather than sell to Washington bureaucrats, he would go directly to the states and convince their legislators to purchase his guns for their militias. He seized upon a law from 1808, known as the Militia Act, which suggested to him that state militias had the right to buy whatever guns they pleased from the appropriations Congress gave them. Among those Colt tried to enlist in his efforts was Daniel Webster, the esteemed senator from Massachusetts and perhaps the greatest legal mind of the age. Webster reminded Colt that some of his relatives, the LeRoys, were investors in the P.A.M.C., so getting involved in the matter would be a conflict of interest. Furthermore, "I do not see any grounds for the opinion that the existing law gives other states the choice as to the kind of arms; nor am I certain that Congress, if applied to, would pass a law to that effect."

Webster was right, and Colt's attempts to sell directly to states would come to nothing for the moment. It speaks to Colt's perseverance, or maybe his desperation, that he ignored Daniel Webster and redoubled his efforts. His debts, meanwhile, continued to mount. He now owed $160 to a board-inghouse proprietor in Paterson named Armstrong. He owed $43.50 to a bootmaker for a pair of gators and six pairs of "calf boots," at $6.50 a pair. He still owed $400 to Dudley Selden, who threatened to sue him for nonpayment. "I shall be very reluctant to take proceedings in New Jersey to collect the same," wrote Selden in July, "but unless something is done without delay I shall consider myself bound to do it." He owed Roswell Colt $1,000 for repayment of loans. "I beg you to prepare in due time to meet it," wrote Roswell in August; "the times are such as requires all my means to meet my own engagements." He still owed large sums to the tailors Hatfield & Pearson, and he owed a small fortune to the Astor House. He even owed his stepmother $14 for shirts she had made for him. "Dear Samuel," Olivia wrote, "If you will please send the money for making your shirts you will extremely oblige me."

Between plying government officials with liquor and dodging debts, Colt somehow found time to improve his guns and file a new patent in August of 1839. He had put considerable intellectual energy into solving some of the problems of his gun. Most important, he'd redesigned the cylinder, again, shaping the mouth of the chambers "to better direct the energy of the exploding gun power in to the barrel" and lowering the likelihood of chain fire. He also simplified the method of turning the chamber between shots and made the cylinder easier to load. The industrial historian Charles R. Morris sums up the paradox of Colt pithily: "One half of Sam Colt was the buncoing fabulist, the walking bonfire of other people's money, the drinker and carouser; the other half was a truly gifted inventor."

Colt was also increasingly showing himself to be a gifted merchant, combining his natural flair for persuasion with a prescient grasp of mass marketing. He branded his guns not only with his name, but with engravings that were pressure-rolled onto the cylinders. The scenes he chose for these engravings—one showed a stagecoach holdup, men facing off with pistols, several on the ground wounded or dead—indicate how well he understood his gun's appeal by 1840. Not only did the engravings associate his revolvers with self-defense and derring-do, they verified them as authentic Colts amid the onslaught of imitation revolvers he correctly assumed was coming. Nor did he neglect the presentation of the guns. Each came in a handsome mahogany box, lined in velvet, with a beveled lid and a nameplate. An even better idea, which Colt arrived at later, would be putting some of the guns inside false books, a gimmick, but one that hinted knowingly at the future of these guns. *Law for Self Defense* was the title on the spine of one of these books. Other titles included *The Tourists Companion* and *The Common Law of Texas.*

In the spring of 1840, Colt tallied the number of guns made in Paterson since the mill went into production: 1,312 long arms and 2,700 pistols, all revolvers. The pistols were five shots with hidden triggers that dropped down from the lock only when the gun was cocked. They were single-action, meaning that pulling the trigger produced only the firing of the gun, not the double action of turning the cylinder, a feature many later revolvers would incorporate. Colt would eventually abandon the drop-down trigger as an unnecessary complication and would add a sixth chamber to his revolver cylinder, but he always believed that single-action guns, simpler to make and easier to handle, were superior.

The main difference among Colt's various pistols was size. "One for the pocket, one for the belt, and a third for the holster" is how Colt described the handguns in a letter to navy officers in 1840. Based on the model numbers, gun collectors today refer to the smallest of these pistols, a .28-caliber, as the No. 1, also known as the Baby Paterson for its diminutive size. The .31-caliber midsize, or belt, pistol was produced in two production runs, No. 2

and No. 3. (No. 4 seems to have been aborted.) The No. 5, "for the holster," was a massive .36-caliber. It would come to be known as the Texas Paterson.

Texas remained the one bright spot during these years. While Colt struggled to sell the rest of the world on his guns, Texans needed no convincing. They instinctively grasped that repeating arms were well matched to their hostile land. Oddly, it was the Texas navy, not the Texas army, that first showed serious interest. In April of 1839, 108 of the No. 5 revolvers were purchased by Texas as boarding pistols for its small fleet on the Gulf of Mexico. The purchase did not provide enough cash to make much of a difference to the company's bottom line, but for Colt it would ultimately prove critically important.

Now and then Colt's fortunes appeared to be on the brink of improvement. An angel investor arrived, a British industrialist named Richard Pullen. In return for use of the patent in Britain, Pullen promised to furnish Colt with as much as £800 a year, "as said Samuel may from time to time require for the purpose of defraying his personal expenses so that said Samuel shall be enabled to maintain his rank in society as a gentleman," according to a draft of the contract presumably composed by said Samuel himself. After handing Colt a check for $600, Pullen got cold feet, stopped payment, and abruptly withdrew the offer, leaving Colt back where he started.

So it went, like one of those forge-side water-powered hammers at the Springfield armory: up followed rapidly by down. In the late fall of 1840, the US Army conducted a series of tests at Carlisle Barracks in Pennsylvania. "When our arms were fired for celerity they astonished even ourselves," Colt exulted in a letter. "We had eight men. The day was very pleasant & their fingers nimble." But Carlisle failed to persuade anyone at Ordnance and gained Colt nothing.

Colt found an opportunity to prove his guns again in Washington in February of 1841. The popular version of this episode places it on the lawn of the White House. As the demonstration of Colt's rifles commenced, the eruption of gunfire startled President Martin Van Buren's carriage horses; the horses bolted, the president's carriage smashed into a post, and the president's coachman was launched from his seat and fatally impaled on a post of the White House fence.

That account is wrong on several key details but is based on a real event. It was not President Van Buren's horses that bolted from the sound of Colt's guns, but the horses of former president John Quincy Adams; and the incident occurred not on the White House lawn but in front of the US Capitol. On the morning of February 18, Adams, now a seventy-three-year-old congressman, arrived by carriage to watch the exhibition of Colt's "new invented instrument of destruction," as he later wrote in his journal. He was out of the carriage and safely on the ground when Colt's guns began to fire. At the first volley, Adams's horses took off at a wild gallop, his carriage careening away after them. The carriage smashed into a fence post, and Adams's coachman and footman were both "precipitated" from the carriage. The coachman, an Irishman named Jeremy Leary, was taken to a room inside the Capitol, where Adams found him in "excruciating torture." His wounds were mortal. "Your horses are gone and carriage with them," the coachman apologetically told the former president, according to a newspaper account. "Never mind the horses and carriage," responded Adams. "If you are a dying man, think of your soul."

Adams had been fond of the coachman, and the man's death left him despondent.* In his journal, he blamed the accident on "Providence," but he also seemed to hold it against Sam Colt. His revenge would come later.

After four strained and fitful years, the P.A.M.C. finally collapsed over the spring and summer of 1841. The end was as ugly as the beginning had been hopeful. The beleaguered Dudley Selden was out as treasurer now, replaced by another shareholder named John Ehlers. At first, Ehlers and Colt got along well enough, but Ehlers, like Selden, soon tired of pinched profits and empty promises. In March of 1841, Ehlers told Colt that the company was doomed unless new orders could be obtained at once. "I have done all I am willing to do & it appears to me that some of our stock holders will not & others can not give any aid to the concern to hold it together."

Soon Ehlers was an even greater antagonist than Selden had been, doubting or opposing everything Colt claimed or did while chastising him for his liberal spending. "I can not help to repeat what I told you before that you must not be so extravagant & you must draw in your horns until you make money; at present you are merely making calculations what you will make if all goes well, but that is still far from making money." After learning that the secretary of the navy, James K. Paulding, "had taken a great dislike to Mr. Colt" on account of some unspecified conduct, Ehlers suspected that Colt's efforts in Washington were hurting more than helping the company. When Colt wrote to report that he had at last secured a sale to the government of one hundred carbines, Ehlers almost scoffed: "I hope that the next mail will bring me the copy of the order, to show our directors there is no humbug in it."

* The accident occurred two days before Adams was to appear before the Supreme Court to argue the famous *Amistad* case, representing slaves who had mutinied aboard a slave ship. The former president was so agitated by the coachman's death that he asked the chief justice for an extra day or two to prepare. His gloom only began to lift, he later wrote, when he stood in court to speak on behalf of the mutinous slaves.

Matters came to a head in August of 1841, when Ehlers began placing classified ads in the *New York Evening Post* and other papers in which he offered for sale three-quarters of the right to Colt's patent. The announced sale date was September 15, 1841. If the sale went through, Colt could no longer profit from his own invention. Meanwhile, Ehlers removed more than eight hundred guns from the Paterson factory and the company's New York sales office at 155 Broadway, apparently to be held by himself as collateral against Colt's debts. Colt sought to retaliate by writing his own classified advertisement, in his own inimitable style:

Absconded

A Jerman calling himself John Ehlers, about fifty years of age, five feet eight inches high, the upper part of his head balled short locks of yellow hair on the back & sides of his head, faice round, figure stout & vulgar looking . . .

Any information that can be furnished of the mustirous movements of said individual or of the disposition he may have made of said property will be very thankfully received by the undersigned.

Colt never published the ad, but on September 2, in the Chancery of New Jersey, he pleaded for an injunction against Ehlers. On September 3, on the advice of his lawyer, Colt sent one of his brothers to deliver a legal notification to the offices of the P.A.M.C. The record of this is a brief note to Colt from his lawyer, now preserved in Colt's papers: "Enclosed you have the notice to be served upon the company. They must be compared by your brother to see that they are correct and the one served, and the one marked copy to preserve kept by him, upon which he is to make an affidavit of the manner of service."

The brother who was to perform this task was not named by the lawyer in the note to Colt, but his identity can be deduced. Sam's younger brother James was in St. Louis pursuing a career as an attorney. Sam and Chris Jr. had had a serious falling-out over money matters and were not on speaking terms. That left just one Colt brother to do the deed: John.

III

On that same drizzly Friday afternoon that Sam Colt was settling into his new room on Washington Square—September 17, 1841—John Caldwell

Colt, a thin man of thirty-one with curly brown hair and well-groomed whiskers, sat at a desk inside a narrow second-story room at the corner of Broadway and Chambers Street. The room was sparsely furnished with the desk, a table, and a couple of hard wooden chairs. A few piles of books awaited shipment. On the floor lay a large pine crate, three feet long, eighteen inches high and wide. On a table lay a tool called a half hatchet or a shingle hatchet: one side of its iron head was the blunt face of a hammer, the other a sharp blade.

For a man about to become notorious, John C. Colt left a puzzling trail. This was not for a lack of bread crumbs but rather too many, scattered too widely. Volumes would be written about John in the months he had left to live—more than would be written about Sam over his entire lifetime—but the theme of all this writing would be incoherence. He went everywhere, did everything, was all things to all people.

John's name appears rarely in Sam Colt's archives, and then only attached to a question or a rumor. This absence may reflect his black sheep status while he lived or, more likely, his exile after he died, when well-meaning heirs and executors tried to scrub his name from Sam's legacy. In truth, of the four Colt brothers, Sam and John were most alike. Both were extremely ambitious, intelligent, and restless young men who left home as soon as they could and remained in motion as long as they lived.

John's youth would be described in diverse narratives, but in all he was a playful and mischievous boy until the family began to collapse in 1819. Perhaps because he was four years older than Sam he was more deeply affected by his father's bankruptcy and his mother's death, when he was ten and eleven, respectively. He resented his father's choice of a new wife, finding Olivia to be cold and censorious, and at sixteen ran away (as related in chapter 1) to Albany. After his regrettable decision to join the Marines (as related in chapter 2), he spent a year working in New York City as a clerk, followed by a year studying mathematics at the University of Vermont. In 1831, while Sam was aboard the *Corvo*, John went west and built himself a log cabin in the Michigan wilderness. By 1833, he was back in New York City, trying to make a go of it as a manufacturer of soap—and then he was off again, always moving, seldom in contact with his family. "Do you know where John is? We would hear that he is located," Christopher had written to Sam in December of 1834. "John I am informed is not going to Texas but is in Cincinnati," wrote Christopher again in 1836.

The most stable and profitable period of John's life were the several years in the 1830s that he spent along the Ohio River, shuttling between Cincinnati and Louisville. He was in Louisville long enough to open a little business as a teacher of accounting and penmanship. Borrowing from Sam, he called himself Coult: "John Coult Accountant, teacher of Book Keeping and Professor of Penmanship."

Among the terrible ironies of John's life was that he found a true calling in accounting. In 1837, he published a book entitled *The Science of Double Entry Book-Keeping*, in which he introduced readers to a new system of recording and tracking income and expenses. The book suggests that John may have been the brainiest Colt, if not the most "singular," as his younger brother James later described him. He seemed to imagine himself as a kind of poet of numbers, to view accounting as a lofty pursuit that could bring order to the world and settle "doubts, disputes, and collisions" before they turned ugly. The strangest thing about John's book was his use of real names and situations to illustrate his concepts. Fictional profits and expenses of the Patent Arms Manufacturing Co. appear in one example, and so do the names Dudley Selden, Samuel Colt, and even John C. Colt, for whom he conjured up a fictional wife and a make-believe inheritance of nearly $20,000.

Along with his flights of fancy, John had a predilection for overwrought love affairs. There may have been a dalliance with a married woman that ended in a duel. There was definitely a relationship with a raven-haired young widow named Frances Anne that involved impassioned long gallops on horseback on the banks of the Ohio River and, one summer night, an impromptu swim. Throwing off her clothes, Frances Anne jumped into the river and raced John to the Kentucky shore, where she arose, victorious, nude, bathed in moonlight. Later, after John left for New York in April of 1839, Frances Anne killed herself with an overdose of opium.

Books brought John back to New York. He came to revise and sell his own book to a larger market, but also to establish himself as a publisher. With a partner he purchased and printed a book entitled *An Inquiry into the Origin of the Antiquities of America* by John Delafield Jr. Why John expected this book to sell is unclear, but it did not and lost he more than $1,000. The loss seems to have precipitated a moral as well as financial decline.

The question of John Colt's character prior to 1841 would be deliberated ad nauseam in the press. There were notable incidents of kindness and empathy, including one widely circulated tale of him as a boy rescuing one of his little brothers (whether Sam or James was not specified) from drowning in a river and another of his attempt to save a lamb from the butcher's knife. But there were also reports of adult criminality. He was discovered skulking through the Astor House with a set of "false keys," presumably to break into rooms and steal things. On at least one occasion, in 1839, his actions brought him to the attention of New York's district attorney. John did "feloniously and burglarously" enter a second-floor office on Nassau Street, according to court documents. A sympathetic 1842 account of John's life would blame this incident on "merry companions" who lured John "into frolics over wine," after which he "blundered" into the building. This explanation seemed to satisfy the district attorney. The record shows that Sam bailed out John for $500, and the matter soon went away.

John left New York once more, briefly, for Philadelphia, where he ran a bookstore for six months. He returned in January of 1841, and in early August arranged to rent a second-floor room in the five-story Granite Building (as it was known) on the northwest corner of Broadway and Chambers Street.

John should have been long gone from the Granite Building by that rainy Friday in September. According to his original agreement with Asa Wheeler, his six-week tenancy had expired a few days earlier. But John had asked for more time and Wheeler had obliged. That afternoon, John was at his desk, facing the wall, working on an accounting problem. The pine crate lay on the floor where John had been preparing it to ship books. The shingle hatchet that he used to build the crate was on the table. Despite the cool and damp, the window that looked over Chambers Street was open a little, and into the room wafted the usual odors of horse dung, wood and coal smoke, and human sewage. Physicians of the day believed the thick city air carried dangerous miasmas, invisible clouds of disease, that made people ill, and the weekly release of mortality statistics from the coroner's office seemed to confirm it. So far this week's dead numbered 213, including 28 fatalities by cholera *infantum*, 27 by consumption, and 17 by dropsy, as well as 5 by drowning and 2 by suicide. One more death, by murder, would bring the week's total to 214.

At about 3:15 p.m., a book printer named Samuel Adams approached the Granite Building and entered through the door on Chambers Street. Adams was stout, whiskered, and grumpy. People who saw him on his way to the Granite Building recalled that he appeared preoccupied. According to John's account—the only one we have—Adams came into John's office without knocking and sat in a chair next to the desk. John knew why Adams was there. He had hired Adams to print a new edition of his accounting book and owed him for his services. Adams was angry that John had not paid him. John, for his part, was miffed that Adams hadn't completed the job by the agreed-upon deadline. Mainly at issue was a discrepancy between the $71.15 that Adams thought John Colt owed him and the $55.80 that John thought he owed Adams—about $15. After John showed Adams an account book to prove his point, the printer became only more convinced that John was trying to dupe him. "You lie!" Adams shouted. Whereupon, as John later described it, "word followed word, until it came to blows." Adams pushed John against the wall and grabbed the cravat around his neck, choking him. John reached for the nearest weapon to defend himself—the shingle hatchet lying on the table.

If John Colt is to be believed, he was not in possession of his faculties in these seconds. "I lost all power of reason," he later claimed. Had he been able to slow time and achieve clarity, he might have considered the irony of the situation. The man who wrote a book intended to end financial conflicts was about to kill a man over a financial conflict.

In the room next door, Asa Wheeler was teaching a pupil. The two were startled by a loud sound. Later, both described it as harsh, clanging, and metallic, like clashing foils. That was the sound, apparently, of a sharp hatchet blade meeting a human skull.

Adams crumpled to the floor, blood oozing from his head. For a minute or two he breathed heavily, then stopped. John sat by the window above Chambers Street, stunned and sickened, "a horrid thrill" coming over him as he contemplated what he had done. So much blood drained from the printer's head that John worried it would seep through the floorboards and drip into the apothecary below. With a towel he mopped up as much as he could.

John remained in his room with Adams's body until darkness, waiting for the rumble of a passing omnibus to disguise his steps. Then he crept out, locking the door behind him. He hurried across Broadway to City Hall Park and turned south, passing under trees to avoid being seen in the flickering of the gas lamps. His destination was the City Hotel, he later recalled, his purpose "being to relate the circumstance to a brother."

Assuming, as we have, that Sam Colt spent the earlier part of that Friday moving into his new room at New York University, he had since made his way south to the City Hotel. For some months, he had made the hotel his residence of choice, bypassing his old favorite, the Astor House. The price of a room at the City Hotel—$2 per night—was the same as at the Astor House, so Colt wasn't motivated by economy. More likely he owed the Astor House so much money he was no longer welcome there.

That John's impulse after cleaning up Adams's blood was to find Sam at the hotel is striking. Strangely, no one, not police or prosecutors or newspaper reporters, ever posed an obvious question: Why did John go to Sam? At the least it suggests that John was in close enough contact with his brother to know where to find him that Friday evening. It also suggests he trusted his younger brother implicitly. Sam was the first person he wanted to consult at the most significant moment of his life.

Sam was in the front parlor on the ground floor of the hotel, in the company of two other men, enjoying the conviviality of a well-lit room on a damp evening. Through a window from Broadway or upon entering the hotel—his account does not make it clear—John caught Sam's eye. The sight of John, cold, wet, and wild-eyed, must have been startling to Sam or anyone else who saw him that evening. Sam briefly left his companions and went to his brother. "A few words passed between us and, seeing that he was engaged, I altered my purpose and returned as far as the park," John recalled. What words? Did John make any effort to explain his appearance? Did he mention that he had just killed a man?

John headed back up Broadway. He spent the next hour pacing in the gaslit gloom of City Hall Park. He considered going to the magistrate to confess but could not bear the shame this would bring upon his family. He thought of "firing" the Granite Building—burning it down to destroy evidence of his crime—but he knew that some residents were asleep in its rooms and did not wish to kill anyone else. At last, he went back to the building and climbed the stairs to his office. He quietly let himself in, closed his shutters, lit a candle, and began to calculate. Samuel Adams had been five feet six inches tall. The pine box was three feet long, eighteen inches wide and high.

For the next hour, John performed a ghoulish procrustean chore. He lined the inside of the box with pieces of fabric cut from an awning, then used a rope to tie Adams's body. Folding the dead man's legs and pressing his knees against his chest, John squeezed the corpse into the box. He also shoved in Adams's coat. Then he went downstairs to the privy and threw out the rest of Adams's belongings. Using the pump on Chambers Street, he filled a bucket with water and hauled it upstairs to clean the floor.

After all this was done, John left the Granite Building and went to the Washington bathhouse on Pearl Street and Broadway to wash himself and his clothing. Then he walked to his lodging house at 42 Monroe Street.

This is where the story gets strange: Waiting for John in his room was a pretty young woman of German descent named Caroline Henshaw. The same Caroline Henshaw, that is, who at sixteen—according to the biography of William Edwards and repeated in many books since—had secretly eloped with Sam Colt in Europe. Now twenty-two or so, she was living with John Colt and seven months pregnant.

IV

The rain was gone the next morning. The skies were clear, the breezes soft and warm. That Saturday, Sam Colt drafted a letter to Samuel L. Southard, the powerful US senator from New Jersey. A copy of this letter, preserved in Colt's papers at the Connecticut Historical Society, reminds us that at the very moment John Colt was trying to extricate himself from a bloody murder, Sam was trying to launch a remarkable new venture. He called it the submarine battery.

The name may have been new, but the idea was not. The submarine battery was a more sophisticated version of the device Colt had demonstrated twelve years earlier in the mill pond at Ware: an underwater mine triggered from shore by an electrical charge. Colt had revived his idea at least once since Ware Pond, in the winter of 1836, after he returned to the United States from Paris convinced that war was about to break out with France. He had made several drawings of his idea at the time—"first thorts," he titled these—but filed them away when talk of war fizzled.

Now, in 1841, there was talk of another war, this one with England. The conflict this time stemmed from a disagreement over the border of Canada. Hard as it may be now to imagine the issue sparking a major war, it was taken quite seriously at the time and placed before Americans the prospect of the world's largest navy returning to US shores for a reprisal of the War of 1812. This put Congress in a mood to spend on coastal defense and inspired Colt to dust off his adolescent scheme.

So far, his efforts to promote the submarine battery had been auspicious. Over the summer he had met with President John Tyler, who mildly endorsed the idea. More significant, Colt had received serious interest from Senator Southard, a former secretary of the navy and governor of New Jersey. Southard was serving as president pro tempore of the Senate, which placed him, that September, next in line to the presidency.* He not only approved of Colt's invention, he liked it so much that he intended to buy

---

* Upon the death of President William Harrison the previous spring, after only a month in office, Vice President John Tyler had assumed the presidency, leaving the vice presidency vacant. Because the presidential line of succession ran at the time from president to vice president to president pro tempore of the Senate, the absence of a vice president moved the pro tem up a notch. If Tyler left office for some reason, Southard would become president of the United States. Given efforts by Tyler's enemies, such as Henry Clay, to force him to resign, this possibility was not entirely abstract.

large quantities of stock in a corporation to fund it, thus enriching himself when Congress, at his urging, appropriated money for it.

What exactly would this money be appropriated *for*? Colt was cagey about his invention, so even today some aspects of it remain mysterious. Fundamentally, though, it was not hard to grasp. Like Colt's rudimentary device in Ware, the submarine battery had three main components, albeit on a much larger scale. First was a waterproofed mine filled with gunpowder. Second was a loop of waterproofed copper wire, running to and from the mine, through which electricity could flow. Third was an energy source capable of producing a charge strong enough to spark an explosion; the submarine battery would be a battery in the sense of a defense system, but it would also incorporate a battery as a source of electrical current. When all of this was put together, it would constitute a system for blowing up enemy ships.

In September of 1841, the submarine battery was still a concept waiting for money to make it a reality. With the assistance of Southard and others, Colt would get that money. What he would do with it over the next several years would amount to one of strangest chapters not only in his life but in the history of the US Navy.

Composing his letter to Senator Southard is the only action we positively know Sam Colt took that Saturday, September 18, but he may also have visited the Granite Building. This possibility is suggested by an exchange between John Colt and his neighbor later in the day.

Early that morning after the murder, John had returned to Chambers Street to dispose of Samuel Adams's body. He sealed the pine box into which he had crammed Adams, wrote an address on the lid, and dragged it down the stairs to the street. He flagged a cartman on Chambers Street and directed him to deliver the crate to a New Orleans–bound ship, the *Kalamazoo*, berthed at the bottom of Maiden Lane. The address indicated that the crate was to be shipped to St. Louis via New Orleans.

Back inside the Granite Building, John knocked on the door of his neighbor and landlord, Asa Wheeler. In a brief and awkward exchange, John asked Wheeler a few questions, apparently trying to ascertain whether Wheeler harbored any suspicions. Then he asked Wheeler if he had seen Sam at the building that morning. When Wheeler said he had not, John told him that Sam had been there and had waited over an hour to speak with him. Why John asked Wheeler about his brother, or why Sam would have waited for Wheeler in the first place, are questions that were never asked at the time and cannot be answered now. But unless John was lying to Wheeler for some reason, it seems that Sam had gone to the Granite Building that morning with something so important to communicate to Wheeler that he waited an hour before leaving.

At the least, John's exchange with Wheeler suggests that he had been in contact with his brother that morning. If so, this raises, again, an interesting if unanswerable question: What did John tell Sam about the death of Samuel Adams? Did Sam Colt know that his brother had killed a man? Did he take part in John's effort to cover it up?

V

Over the next few days, John did his best to project sangfroid. Asa Wheeler heard him singing in his room, and he seemed eager to engage Wheeler in light conversation. When Wheeler asked him about the noise he'd heard the previous Friday afternoon, John first claimed he had not been in the office that day, then immediately changed his story. "To tell you the truth, Mr. Wheeler, I upset my table, broke my ink bottle and spilled my books—hope I didn't disturb you."

On Wednesday, Wheeler read a notice in the *Evening Post* asking for information about a missing printer named Samuel Adams. He made the connection at once and walked across Broadway to City Hall to report his suspicions directly to the mayor. The mayor, Robert H. Morris, arrested John Colt on Friday, September 24, one week after the death of Adams.

The next day, following a tip from the cartman who had transported Colt's crate, Mayor Morris visited the wharf at the bottom of Maiden Lane. Unfortunately for John Colt, the *Kalamazoo* had been delayed in sailing and held in port beyond its scheduled departure. It was finally set to embark that very afternoon but was still in its berth that morning, and the pine box, though buried under other freight, was still in its hold.

The box was located and hauled to the deck. When it was pried open, an overwhelming stench wafted over the ship, forcing hardened sailors to turn away in revulsion. Inside were the decomposing remains of Samuel Adams. The penny presses would later describe the scene in vivid detail: the way Adams had been trussed up with a rope that ran from the back of his neck and around his thighs; the dizzying odor of decaying flesh; the small white worms crawling over the body; and Adams's skull, "the pieces of the bone beaten in and entirely loose among the pulpy mass, which was the brain."

VI

When John Colt lowered his hatchet on Samuel Adams's head, he ended a man's life and brought grief to that man's family and his own. He also delivered an extraordinary gift to the penny presses of New York—and to just about every newspaper in the country. That first Monday after his arrest, editors and publishers everywhere reached for the word—HORRIBLE; FRIGHTFUL; TERRIBLE; SHOCKING—that might adequately modify the next: MURDER.

The penny presses were not new to New York—they had been around for nearly a decade—nor was crime, but the way the papers covered crime was rapidly evolving in the late 1830s and early 1840s. Some of the brighter editorial lights had realized that the best way to engage readers was not simply to report crime but to scream and shout about it from city rooftops. That news should be lurid and sordid was a given; that it should be cloaked in moral outrage was genius. It was the particular genius of James Gordon Bennett, the brash forty-six-year-old Scotsman who owned and edited the *New York Herald*. In just six years he had turned the *Herald* into the best-selling paper in the country.

The summer before John Colt killed Samuel Adams, the *Herald* had demonstrated its special recipe of prurience and indignation with its coverage of the biggest crime story in New York since the 1836 murder of Helen Jewett. In this case, the body of a beautiful young "cigar girl" named Mary Rogers had been found floating near the New Jersey shore of the Hudson River. Bennett turned Rogers's death into a full-fledged moral crusade. What happened to Rogers was an "awful atrocity," proclaimed the *Herald*, demanding "vengeance from the depth of the Hudson."

By mid-September of 1841, though, the Mary Rogers story had run its course. No one had ever been caught for the murder, and apparently Rogers had died from a botched abortion rather than at the hands of lustful predator. So, with exquisite timing, this newest story fell into the laps of Bennett and his fellow newsmen, complete with a villain who engaged in human butchery.

New Yorkers made the acquaintance of John C. Colt on the morning of Monday, September 27, after he arrived at the coroner's inquest with "a wildish look," as the *Herald* put it, dressed in black and looking pale. "He is well made but very slim. He is about 5 feet 9 inches high. His hair is dark brown and curly, and he has largish whiskers. He would be good looking but for his eye, which is one of those brown colored class of eyes that cannot easily be read, and that are generally found in the faces of all scoundrels, schemers and plotters."

Neither the *Herald* nor its competitors wasted any time giving John the presumption of innocence. The depravity of his character was sealed by the next detail in the *Herald*: the accused shared his bed with a "kept" woman whom he had placed in circumstances so delicate their description required French. "She is by him *enciente*," reported the *Herald* of Caroline Henshaw, "and the period of her *accouchement* is near."

The indictment was read on Wednesday, September 29. In leg irons and handcuffs, John was escorted into a courtroom at City Hall "crowded to suffocation by respectable persons" who were eager to see him in the flesh. The papers made no mention of Sam Colt on this first day, but he was certainly present in the courtroom, as he would be at all future court proceedings. The three attorneys standing in John Colt's defense were named. One was John A. Morrill, who had lately represented Madame Restell, the notorious abortionist. Another was Robert Emmett, a stockholder of the P.A.M.C. and well-known lawyer.

The third, and lead, attorney was a surprise: Dudley Selden. Since withdrawing from the directorship of the P.A.M.C., Selden had been practicing law and occasionally dabbling in Whig Party politics. One might suppose he'd had enough of his Colt cousins after his experience with the P.A.M.C., but here he was again, out of family loyalty or personal obstinacy, in the thick of another Colt disaster.

John Colt later claimed that his concern for the reputation of his family drove him to hide his crime. The press coverage following his arrest suggests he had every reason to worry. Accounts of the murder raced from New York across the country, to Philadelphia and Boston within a day or two, and to just about every other town east of the Mississippi within a week. For the next thirteen months, the coverage, both locally and nationally, would be relentless. John was suddenly the most infamous man in America, and nearly every article would contrast his crime with the "respectable" family from which he came. Few failed to mention that the killer's brother was Samuel Colt, inventor of the patent revolver.

The rest of the Colt family learned of John's arrest from newspapers. Christopher Colt had been relaxing in the sitting room of the City Hotel in Hartford when he overheard another man read aloud an article about

John. According to local sources, the news had "completely driven reason from its throne, and made a wreck of all his earthly peace and happiness." James Colt stumbled upon an article about John in a St. Louis paper. "I cannot express to you the intense agony of my feelings at this sad moment," he immediately wrote to Sam.

James refused to believe that John was guilty of cold-blooded murder; even if he had killed Adams, he must have been "deranged" when he did so. James reminded Sam that their sister Sarah Ann had killed herself after too much time with her books. He supposed that John had lost his mind in his accounting studies. "His habit is and always has been when he undertakes to do anything to do it with all the intensity of a madman."

The field of psychology did not formally exist in 1841, but this did not stop the press from diagnosing John Colt's mental condition. Correspondents looked to the past for clues: "The family are of great respectability, and highly esteemed, but are high-spirited, and of violent passions, for which John was proverbial in his younger days." The question was whether John's actions emerged from inherent defects of character or from events in his younger life—nature, that is, or nurture. "His early history was somewhat distinguished by a course of wild and adventurous conduct," reported one paper. Another claimed that he had been a "passionate, cunning, and revengeful boy." A pamphlet, entitled *The Authentic Life of John C. Colt*, painted a more sympathetic view of John's youth. It achieved this mainly by throwing his parents under the omnibus. He had been denied affection and compassion as a child, argued the author; such treatment of a boy inevitably "stimulates the taste for liberty in his mind, sometimes even to licentiousness."

For sheer theatrics, none of the narratives of John Colt and his terrible deed matched James Gordon Bennett's daily reports. As the trial neared, Bennett and his reporters waxed Shakespearean. "Colt seemed like a man just wakened from some horrible dream," reported the *Herald* of one of the prisoner's appearances in court. He glared at the widow of his victim "like MacBeth upon the ghost of Banquo," while the poor widow of Samuel Adams "walked as if a spirit moved her," having gone stark raving mad since the murder. "Her reason is a shattered wreck, and it is probable that she will soon lie peacefully beside her husband in the quiet grave."

After so much anticipation, the opening day of John Colt's trial, on November 1, 1841, turned out to be a false start. As an enormous crowd packed the courtroom and surrounding area, John entered. Looking wretched, he smiled weakly at Sam. Then Dudley Selden stood and asked the judge for a postponement. A key witness, explained Selden, was in her "confinement" and not able to be present.

Soon after, Caroline Henshaw gave birth to a boy. For years to come, people would wonder at the name she chose for him: Samuel.

The postponement freed Sam to devote his attention to his submarine battery. As John's incarceration had been a distraction, it was also now a prod. Sam hoped to use the company's stock to raise money for John's defense. With this in mind, he went to Washington in the first week of November of 1841 and sought a meeting with the new secretary of the navy, Abel Upshur. After Colt briefed Upshur on "the whole plans and secrets of my inventions," the secretary agreed to authorize $6,000 for experiments on the submarine battery. This was far less than the $50,000 Colt had hoped for but enough to proceed.

Colt returned to New York at the end of November, then spent the next two weeks traveling—to Paterson, to Springfield, to Boston—to seek investors. In addition to the $6,000 from the government, he hoped to raise an additional $100,000 by selling 2,000 shares of stock at $50 a share. By mid-December, he had a draft of Articles of Agreement for the Submarine Battery Company and had enrolled a number of subscribers. The largest of these was Samuel Southard, with 250 shares. Roswell Colt took just 20, but Major Gibbs McNeill, a prominent army engineer, purchased 200 and George Whistler purchased 50.* Colt gave each of his brother's lawyers ten shares, worth $500, as a down payment on John's defense.

VII

On New Year's Day of 1842, a thirty-one-year-old Connecticut native named Phineas Taylor Barnum opened a museum on Broadway and Ann Street in lower Manhattan, just south of City Hall Park. P. T. Barnum had already achieved fame and notoriety in New York for his "humbugs," good-natured cons meant to entertain the public and enrich their creator. The best known of these had been a tour he arranged for Joice Heth, promoted by Barnum as a 161-year-old former slave who had been George Washington's nursemaid.

---

* McNeill and Whistler were old friends from West Point. They became brothers-in-law when Whistler married McNeill's sister. Whistler's son would grow up to be the painter James McNeill Whistler, making McNeill's sister the subject of *Whistler's Mother*.

A newspaper's portrayal of John C. Colt murdering Samuel Adams.

Miss HENSHAW, (Colt's Mistress) and THEIR CHILD.

*Caroline Henshaw with her son, Samuel Caldwell Colt. It was scandal
enough that the boy had been born out of wedlock. More shocking would have
been the news that the father was probably not John Colt, but Sam Colt.*

Barnum understood that people were willing to pay for the pleasure of believing in unbelievable things, and he saw no harm in helping them do that.

Barnum's American Museum would soon make him wealthy and internationally famous. But for a few weeks at the start of 1842, the greatest showman of the age found himself upstaged by a bigger and more bizarre spectacle than even he could produce. "At the time Adams was murdered by Colt, the excitement in New York was intense," Barnum later recalled in his autobiography. When a pamphlet published by the *New York Sun* purported to show a portrait of the dead man, Barnum hurried to buy a copy. "Like thousands of others, I desired to know how the poor man looked." Upon opening the pamphlet, Barnum instantly recognized the bulbous-nosed, sharp-chinned figure depicted in the drawing: himself. Apparently, the *Sun*, having no drawing of Adams on hand, had simply used an old likeness of Barnum. "I fancied then, as well as many times before and since, that 'humbug' did not belong exclusively to the 'show' business."

On the rainy morning of Monday, January 17, 1842, as Barnum advertised his upcoming attractions for the week—"Indian Warriors and their Squaws" was the lead act; "the Albino Lady" was another—hundreds of New Yorkers crowded around City Hall to glimpse the murderer. John Colt was already inside, having been ushered there earlier that morning. Reporters with access to City Hall observed him passing the time near the warmth of the courtroom stove, chatting with his brother Samuel and perusing the pages of the *Herald*—according to the *Herald*, anyway. The newspaper noted that Sam seemed "a good deal affected" by his brother's plight.

Finding jurors who had not already made up their minds about John Colt consumed several days. Voir dire was still underway when the *Herald* put out a special EXTRA afternoon edition on the Colt trial. The front page featured a large drawing of a gnomish naked figure curled up on a table, its face and head ghoulishly distorted. "SAMUEL ADAMS, THE PRINTER," read the headline, "BEFORE HE WAS CUT UP AND SALTED." James Gordon Bennett knew very well that Adams had not been cut up and salted, but the real portrait Bennett was after was the monster—a *cannibal*!—that the public wanted John Colt to be. Walt Whitman, attending the trial as a journalist, pointed out that the real monster in this tale was not John Colt but the hordes of New Yorkers possessed of an "unrelenting public appetite for blood."

On Thursday, January 20, with testimony set to begin, crowds clambered to gain admittance to City Hall, overflowing into the park. Inside,

John wore a blue beaver coat, with a black silk handkerchief tied around his neck. His sixty-one-year-old father, Christopher, was in the courtroom, "a venerable, fine, benevolent looking man" who appeared "as if he had been crying bitterly and long." The lawyers made their opening statements, then Asa Wheeler, the penmanship instructor who had rented John his room, was called to testify. He described the day of the murder and John's odd behavior in the aftermath. Wheeler was followed by other neighbors and the cartman who'd transported the crate with Adams's body. Then came several witnesses who claimed to know John Colt as a man of rash, yet also cold and calculating, temperament.

On Monday, January 24, the crowds were even larger than they had been the previous week. Christopher Colt was no longer in the courtroom, having gone back to Hartford in distress. The prosecution began the day by changing a crucial detail of its indictment. The murder weapon was not a half hatchet, the district attorney now claimed, but a pistol—a Colt revolver, in fact. From here, matters took a decidedly peculiar turn. "Altogether," Bennett's *Herald* would proclaim before the end of the next day, "this trial presents the most remarkable features of any trial ever known."

The prosecution first established that John Colt owned a Colt revolver. Asa Wheeler was called back to the stand to describe a conversation he'd had with John several days before the murder, in which John had offered to show him the gun. The weapon Wheeler first described to the jury sounded more like a pepperbox than a revolver, but then he updated his memory to suit the gun presented to him in the courtroom. To explain how a gun could have been fired in the middle of the afternoon without anyone hearing a shot, the prosecution asserted that the revolver had been discharged with percussion caps alone, not with a full load of powder as it would normally be.

The prosecution rested late on the morning of Tuesday, January 25, and the defense took over. The first witness Dudley Selden called to the stand was Sam Colt.

Following cues from Selden, Colt loaded one of his five-chambered revolvers with balls and caps but no powder. He lifted the gun with his right hand, put his left palm directly in front of the muzzle, and pulled the trigger. *Crack!* Then he pulled back the cock and fired again, and then three more times. He shot all five balls directly into his hand, catching each in a fist. When Selden asked Colt to fire at an open law book about fifteen feet away, the ball barely made a dent on the pages. How could such a weak projectile penetrate a man's skull?

Any spectator whose attention had not yet been roused was sure to be shocked by what came later in the day. To prove that the holes in Adams's skull were not made by a revolver, Dudley Selden had requested, that morning, that Adams's corpse be exhumed to allow doctors to examine it. Now he introduced the detached cranium into evidence. If not quite the ghost of Banquo that James Gordon Bennett had summoned in the *Herald*, Adams's skull was at least as haunting as that of Yorick. Alas, poor Adams: his still-decaying head arrived in the courtroom accompanied by a nauseating stench.

The defense proved its point. Expert witnesses were definite in their opinion that the holes in the skull could not have been made by a ball fired from a gun. But Selden and his colleagues lost the larger argument, and possibly the entire trial, by letting Adams's skull anywhere near the courtroom. For the rest of the day, the only testimony that mattered was the silent utterance of a dead man's rotting head.

After Adams's skull was removed from the courtroom, the defense tried to humanize John with the testimony of a few friends and acquaintances. One of these was a young paper manufacturer named Cyrus W. Field, with whom John had done business. Later in life, Field would team up with Samuel Morse to lead the effort to lay the first telegraph cable across the Atlantic, an achievement that had nothing to do with John Colt but would owe plenty to Sam.

Another witness, already famous that winter, was John Howard Payne, composer of the most beloved song in the country, "Home, Sweet Home." Payne told the jury that he had been friends with John for several years and held "the highest opinion" of him.

The excitement of the spectators picked up again when Caroline Henshaw entered the courtroom. With the possible exception of Samuel Adams's skull, she was the star attraction of the trial, and the newspapers gave her close attention. "She had on a dark lilac colored silk bonnet, with light lilac spotted ribbon, and a black lace veil," reported the *Herald*. "She looks to be about twenty one years of age; has fine features, a gentle, innocent, and almost infantile expression; a very beautiful and small mouth with lips like a sleeping infant's in their shape, a fine round full forehead, lightish brown hair, parted plain across the forehead, blue eyes with a very mild expression." The *Herald* also complimented her "perceptive organs": "She gave her testimony in an artless, simple, clear, and unaffected style, with great sensibility."

Under questioning, Caroline described meeting John in Philadelphia, then following him to New York and moving in with him. In the fifteen months she had known him, she had never seen him so much as lose his temper. "He was very kind and very mild, and always treated me kindly."

The defense attorney Robert Emmett shocked the courtroom once more on Thursday, January 27, by reading a long confession from John Colt. On the face of it, this was a cunning move, as it allowed the defendant to essentially testify in his own defense without subjecting himself to cross-examination. But it may have been even more ill-conceived than introducing Adams's skull into evidence. In taking the jury again through the night of Adams's murder, it exposed them, once more, to Colt's clinical and grotesque disposal of the dead man. It was those hours *after* the killing, not the act of violence itself, that turned John Colt from a run-of-the-mill hothead into a psychopath.

The trial ended on the afternoon of Saturday, January 29. Less than twelve hours later, at 2:30 a.m. on Sunday, John, Sam, and the attorneys were called to the courtroom. John stood, with Sam at his side. Just after 4:00 a.m. the jury entered and the verdict was read. John C. Colt was pronounced guilty of murder. He took the news almost impassively, according to reporters. His brother, though, appeared as if "his heart had died inside him."

VIII

On a foggy Wednesday in early March, Sam Colt boarded a steamboat on the East River and traveled up Long Island Sound to the town of Stonington, Connecticut. That afternoon he dined with William Gibbs McNeill, the former army engineer and one of Colt's Submarine Battery Company investors, and "Capt. Vanderbelt," as Colt wrote in his small pocket journal. In fact, the name of their dining companion was *Vanderbilt*, and he was generally known by the title of *commodore*, not *captain*.

At forty-seven, Cornelius Vanderbilt was already one of the richest and most powerful men in the country. That spring, Vanderbilt was on the verge of buying the "Stonington," as the rail line from Stonington to Boston (via Providence) was commonly known. One of the curious things about this meal with Vanderbilt is that McNeill, who evidently arranged it, was chief engineer of the company that owned, operated, and did not wish to sell the Stonington line. In other words, he worked for the intended victim of Vanderbilt's hostile takeover. "I'd sooner have *him* with us, than against us," McNeill had written of Vanderbilt to his bosses earlier in the year. Perhaps this meal was a part of McNeill's campaign to stay on the good side of Vanderbilt.

As for why Colt was there, we can only wonder. One possibility is that he wanted Vanderbilt as an investor in his new company and McNeill had set up this meeting so Colt could make his pitch. If that is the case, Vanderbilt evidently turned him down.

After the meal in Stonington, Colt headed down the coast to New London. The chief reason for his visit to Connecticut was to further his investigations into submarine warfare. He was looking for older residents who might recall an event that had occurred during the War of 1812, when a man named Silas Clowden Halsey created a mechanism to destroy the British warships that blockaded New London. Like David Bushnell's submarine, Halsey's vessel was designed to approach ships from the deep and attach explosives to their hulls. Also like Bushnell's, Halsey's never succeeded. Rather, it seems to have sunk, with Halsey inside it, to the bottom of Long Island Sound.

As Sam carried out his inquiries, John was never far from his mind. The small pocket journal in which he had recorded his meeting with "Vanderbelt" was a schedule book for the New York courts, so every time he opened it, he was reminded of his brother's case. Yet Sam clearly enjoyed this early-springtime interlude on the Connecticut coast. He stayed in New London with the family of Captain Abner Bassett—the same Captain Bassett on whose whaling ship he had nearly sailed a decade earlier. Bassett, his wife, and their pretty twenty-year-old daughter, Lucretia, entertained Colt and accompanied him around New London. Colt's journal is filled not with facts about submarines or explosives, his ostensible subjects, but with the names of Miss Bassett and her friends. On Friday, March 4, he recorded a visit to Fort Trumball with "Miss Perkins Miss Church & Miss Bassett," adding, "I was introduced to Miss Brandigiee Miss Camelia Perkins Miss Fanny Perkins." The following day, Colt visited another fort in the company of "Miss Chappell, Miss Church, Miss B——."

On Sunday, Colt traveled farther up the Thames River to Norwich, the town where Lydia Sigourney had been born and the home of his long-ago sweetheart Eliza Spalding. Eliza had died the previous year. It's not clear why Colt came here, but he enjoyed himself despite the foul weather. (The spelling and punctuation are all Colt's.)

Weather misty all day. Went to Norwich landing. atteneded piscopal church. after dinner walked to the old town of norwich by way of the falls of the Tames [Thames River]. rambled through the town & over the hils in an between town & landing untile 5 o'clock PM then caled on Mrs. Chappell. was introduced to her husband (fine fellow) & two of her brothers. took tea & spent the evening very pleasantly to say nothing of the whiskey just returned to hotel at 10 o'clock in a storm of rain & dark as a rat bag.

The next day, Colt returned to New London by steamboat, noting "senery on the river very beautiful." He spent the day with Miss Bassett and her friend Miss Church, then, at 10:00 p.m., boarded a steamer back to New York.

IX

Shortly after his return to the city, Colt sent a note to Professor John William Draper. He and the chemist had recently become acquainted at New York University. "Since seeing you I have met Professor Morse & he has appointed to be at the laboratory of the University at half past 2 O'Clock Tuesday Afternoon. I hope the time will suite your convenience perfectly." Thus began a brief but important collaboration, facilitated by John Draper, between Samuel Colt and Samuel F. B. Morse.

At the time, Morse, an accomplished portrait painter, was a professor of art at the university, but art was no longer his focus. Six years earlier, he had begun working on an idea to use electricity to transmit messages through wires. He was not alone in exploring electromagnetic telegraphy, as this new field was called, but he was further along than others in establishing a practical application of electricity to long-distance communication.

Morse and Colt made an odd couple. Colt was a man of little formal education on whom religious faith had no deep hold, a drinker, and the brother of an infamous murderer. Morse was a highly cultured teetotaler of extraordinary intellectual range and religious devotion. He was also a man of extreme prejudices, especially against Catholics, whom he despised. He had recently run for mayor of New York on the so-called Native American ticket, espousing an anti-immigration and anti-Catholic platform (which amounted to the same thing since most immigrants to New York at the time were Irish Catholics). Morse's loss in that election was a win for the world, keeping him out of fearmongering politics and allowing him to devote himself to the perfection of his telegraph.

For all their differences, the two Sams shared several important traits and experiences. Both were inventors with vast ambitions. Both were broke and beholden to a government that failed to understand or value what they had accomplished. Both feared that competitors would steal their ideas before they could make anything of them. And, in the spring of 1842, both were working on essentially the same problem, albeit with different goals. Colt's challenge was to create a large-scale electrical circuit he could use to trigger an explosive. Morse wanted to use an electrical circuit to send signals for his electromagnetic telegraph.

Morse devoted much of his effort to developing a practical method of turning intermittent spurts of current into usable information—the code that would come to bear his name. But he was also fixated on creating and deploying the kind of giant electrical circuit that would be needed to send his signals over long distances. For his technology to become commercially viable, it was not enough to demonstrate that he could send signals a few hundred feet, as he had already done at New York University. He needed to devise a way to send them hundreds of miles, between cities, across the nation, and, sometimes, through bodies of water.

This is where Colt came in. "During the last several months," Morse wrote to the scientist Joseph Henry in Princeton, New Jersey, "I have availed myself of the means which Mr. Samuel Colt has had at his command in experimenting with wire circuits for testing his submarine batteries. . . . The experiments were highly satisfactory."

With no electrical grid to plug into in 1842, anyone hoping to use electricity had to produce his own. Colt had probably used a simple Leyden jar to spark his mine at Ware Pond, but to blow up distant objects, he needed a powerful current. The only way to achieve this was to create a galvanic battery. Such batteries were relatively well understood by 1842. Sir Humphry Davy—of nitrous oxide fame—had been an early experimenter, as had been the Italian Alessandro Volta. Closer to home, Morse's correspondent, Joseph Henry, had done important work with galvanic batteries.

Professor Draper had worked closely with Henry and knew more than either Colt or Morse about batteries. He probably helped Colt build his. Precisely how Colt's batteries were arranged is not known. Generally, though, a galvanic cell—also called a voltaic pile, in honor of Alessandro Volta's advances—is made by layering rectangular plates of zinc and copper, alternating between one and the other, and placing the whole stack in an electrolyte-rich (salty) solution to facilitate a chemical reaction between the metals. Electrons move through the solution from zinc to copper, generating an electric current.

In his lab on Washington Square, expanded in April of 1842 to include a second room, Colt performed a number of experiments with electricity.

One evening Draper came upon him walking back and forth on Washington Square with his hand over his eyes, evidently in pain. When Draper asked what was wrong, Colt told him that he had been trying to fuse a piece of platinum using his galvanic battery when the platinum suddenly lit up with blinding brilliance. After stumbling upon a new way to create artificial light, he had stumbled into the park to relieve his eyes in the fresh air. Colt was in too much of a hurry to pause and consider the implications of his discovery, but Draper ran some experiments with battery-charged platinum in the building's chapel. He created a light so bright that it filled the chapel "with an unanticipated clearness and strength," as a university student later recalled the event.

Colt gave the first demonstration of his submarine battery on May 24, 1842. He chose a quiet location, a few miles up the Hudson River from downtown New York, near today's West Seventy-Ninth Street. Burnham's Hotel stood above the river, and Sam advised his select group of invitees, including Samuel Morse, William Gibbs McNeill, and a new friend, Commodore Matthew C. Perry—commandant of the New York Navy Yard at the time—to arrive at the hotel before 5:00 p.m. "If it succeeds you will be abundantly paid for your trouble," he wrote in a note to another guest. "Don't forget the time & be sure to be there."

Colt had purchased several thousand feet of copper wire from the firm Brown & Elton, in Waterbury, Connecticut, producers of metal hardware. Neither they nor anyone else had ever been called upon to make such lengths of copper as Colt would require of them over the next several years. There is no record of how Colt's first demonstration went, but several days later he wrote to Brown & Elton to request immediate delivery of 250 plates of "zink" for his batteries, "four & a half inches wide, twelve & a half inches long and one eighth of an inch thick." The urgent order suggests that insufficient current had been generated by the battery Colt used at Burnham's Hotel.

Colt now had just over a month to prepare for the true debut of his invention. The date he'd selected for this honored not only his country but his original experiment on Ware Pond thirteen years earlier. He promised to blow up a ship on July 4.

Independence Day, 1842, would be remembered in New York as the day fresh water came to the city. At the break of a cloudy dawn, 24 million gallons, drawn from the Croton River in northern Westchester County, gushed

through pipes into a great stone-walled reservoir at Forty-Second Street and
Fifth Avenue. This was the culmination of the greatest engineering feat since
the construction of the Erie Canal, and crowds traveled to Forty-Second
Street, the northern edge of the settled city, to taste the clean cold water
and promenade along the high stone wall that surrounded the reservoir.

From the reservoir in the morning, New Yorkers hurried south to Battery Park. The sky had cleared. Vessels of every type drifted in the harbor.
Crowds thronged the wharves and stood on nearby rooftops. Guns began
to fire at noon, first a thirteen-gun salute on Governors Island, then salutes
from several of the naval vessels in the harbor, including the American
warships *North Carolina* and *Columbia*. Yet for all the naval power on the
water, the focus of the crowd's attention was a dilapidated old gunboat
festooned with "piratical flags and death's heads."

Shortly after noon, the doomed vessel was cut loose from its moorings
and given a soft tug by another boat. It drifted a few moments, and then—
whoosh!—vanished in a rocketing chute of water. "The vessel was shattered
into fragments," reported the *Evening Post*, "some of which were thrown
two or three hundred feet in the air." The water came crashing back down,
thickened with debris. The crowd roared its approval.

After the water settled, the crowd waited for Colt to show himself.
Some were under the impression that he had triggered the explosion from
beneath the surface and expected that he "would soon make his appearance
under the water in some submarine boat or infernal machine," as the *Herald*
put it. In fact, Colt was hundreds of yards away, on the deck of the *North
Carolina*, with Samuel Morse by his side. An instant before the explosion
he had "brought the plates of his voltaic pile in contact," closing the circuit
and sending an electrical current hundreds of yards through the water to
a barrel containing hundreds of pounds of gunpowder. It was, the *Tribune*
reported, a "triumphant result."

John spent that July 4 as he had spent every day since January, in his cell
in the Tombs. The given name of the prison was the Halls of Justice and
House of Detention, but almost from the moment it had been built four
years earlier, people had started calling it the Tombs due to its ancient and
ominous appearance. Already the place seemed decrepit, cold and dark
and damp, its walls starting to crack. When Charles Dickens had toured
the Tombs in March, during a hectic and disgruntled visit to the United
States, he described it as a "dismal-fronted pile of bastard Egyptian, like
an enchanter's palace in a melodrama." In the center of the building was

an open atrium surrounded by four tiers of prison cells. "They look like furnace doors," Dickens wrote of the cell gates, "but are cold and black, as though the fires within had gone out."

Surprisingly, Dickens did not mention John Colt, the prison's best-known occupant. But another writer, Charles A. Dana—later one of the city's leading newspaper editors and publishers—went to the Tombs specifically to see the murderer. Dana found Colt living in relative comfort despite the surroundings, puffing on an "aromatic Havana" and cloaked in an "elegant dressing gown" to ward off the chill. "As the keeper swings open the door of Colt's cell the odor of sweet flowers strikes you. It is no delusion, for there they are in a delicate vase upon the center table." For his lunch, Colt received not the usual jailhouse slop but a catered meal from a nearby hotel of quail on toast and various pâtés, all washed down, claimed Dana, with cognac and coffee.

John received many visitors at his cell. Along with Sam and Caroline came his lawyers and his friends, several of whom were quite famous. John Howard Payne, the composer of "Home, Sweet Home," who had testified at John's trial, was one of these friends. Payne believed, as did many others, that John had killed Adams in the heat of a quarrel. He had made a grave mistake in not going to the police, but did not deserve to hang for bad judgment.

Through the spring and summer, John and his friends were sustained by the belief that he would be retried. But one then another appeal collapsed. The last chance came in late July, at a circuit court in Utica, New York. John lost and the case was remanded to the Court of Oyer and Terminer in New York City for his sentencing.

On September 27, Judge Kent heard a final argument from John, then condemned him to be "hanged by the neck until you be dead." The execution was set for November 18.

X

Three weeks after John Colt's sentencing, as news of his approaching execution continued to echo across the nation in newspapers such as the *Boon's Lick Times* in Missouri and the *Wetumpka Argus* in Alabama, Sam Colt summoned the New York public to another demonstration of his submarine battery. This would be his third public experiment. In late August, he'd detonated a mine under a ship on the Potomac River near Washington, to the delight of President Tyler, who watched with his cabinet and generals from the deck of a nearby steamboat. Afterward, Colt had been invited aboard the president's ship and presented a bouquet of flowers by Tyler's daughter. "Dear Father," Colt wrote later that evening, "This has been the most triumphant day of my life." He had recently turned twenty-eight.

Now, as John awaited his execution in his cell a mile to the north, Sam returned to the Battery. He promised his biggest explosion yet. He intended to blow up a three-hundred-ton brig, which he had rechristened the *Volta*.

On the afternoon of Tuesday, October 18, nearly forty thousand people pressed into Battery Park and climbed onto rooftops and trees. Among the spectators were Colt's special guests, investors, friends, and "all the Navy and Army officers in port," according to Colt. The sponsor of the event was the American Institute, the same organization that had awarded Colt a medal for his gun in 1837. The Institute's two-day exhibit would also feature an attempt by Samuel Morse to demonstrate his telegraph.

In the past, Colt had kept the mysteries of his invention to himself. Now, emboldened by his previous successes—and hoping to silence critics who muttered that he was too secretive—he gave the world a peek. A fee of fifty cents gained spectators admission to Castle Garden, a former fort and now public amphitheater, to view the "galvanic battery." Meanwhile, several newspapers carried a firsthand description of the workings of the invention. The anonymous correspondent, who signed himself simply as *C*, was evidently well informed. He described the mechanism in a single breathless sentence:

> The battery consists of a light sheet iron box filled with gun powder, and having two copper wires wound around with cotton, then varnished over with a mixture of gum shellac, alcohol and Venice turpentine, and extending through tight corks in one side of the box, having a piece of platina wire extending between them in the box amongst the gunpowder, and the two copper wires extending off from this box, which may be anchored in the channel of a river, to a large one of Grant's electricity collecting machines, electrified by a galvanic battery, which may be seven or eight miles distant from the box, and where the operator is, having one of the wires in his hand, ready to attach them to the collector the instant the signal is given to explode the box.

For all that he revealed, Colt was too much of a showman to give away everything. As in previous demonstrations, he kept his location secret from the crowd. Most assumed he was aboard the *North Carolina*, as he had been in July. In fact, he had surreptitiously boarded another vessel, a nondescript cutter.

At 3:45 p.m., the firing of a thirteen-gun salute from the *North Carolina* warned nearby vessels to back off. The crowd hushed. The autumn sun lowered over the New Jersey meadowlands, silhouetting the *Volta*. The explosion came just after 4:00 p.m.: "The whole was enveloped by a huge pile of dense mist, some two hundred feet in diameter and about eighty feet high, through which now and then were seen pieces of timber." It took a minute for the mist to settle and reveal the debris of the *Volta* floating over the water. The *Herald*, pen in cheek, claimed to know the exact number of pieces: 1,756,901.

All agreed the demonstration had been "sublime" and earned Colt generous government support—and also that something terrible and wonderful had occurred before their eyes. "On this very day, have you not witnessed a prodigy which, if we had only read of it in ancient annals, we would have placed among fabled recitals," declaimed the diplomat and politician Auguste Davezac in a speech at Tammany Hall that evening. "A ship lightly floating on the waves like a swan sporting in his own element, unconscious of coming peril, suddenly lifted from the water, shaken in its whole structure, dismembered, as by the unseen arm of some potent magician."

Colt had borrowed several of Samuel Morse's large wooden reels to unspool his insulated copper wire across the water, and the following day, October 19, he repaid the favor by lending Morse two miles of wire. Morse intended to send a telegraphic message across the harbor, from Castle Garden to Governors Island, where his partner, Leonard Gale, was to receive it. Just as Morse began to send signals, a nearby schooner discovered that its anchor was fouled by Colt's wire and cut it with a hatchet. Morse's telegraph went dead, ending his demonstration before it had properly begun. Still, for a few seconds, Morse, with Colt's help, had achieved the first-ever underwater telegraphic communication.

XI

The destruction of the *Volta* occurred one month before the date set for John Colt's execution. As riveting as the Colt case had been over the past year, it now reached whole new levels of intensity. All other options having been foreclosed, John's lawyers and advocates, including a number of new allies who had taken up his cause since the end of the trial, boarded steamboats and headed north to Albany to plead for John Colt's life. They went to see William H. Seward, the man who ran New York and controlled John's fate.

William Seward's historical destiny, still two decades ahead of him, was to be Abraham Lincoln's secretary of state, the most important member of the so-called Team of Rivals, who advised the president during the darkest hours of the Civil War. In the fall of 1842, Seward was the forty-one-year-old governor of New York, nearing the end of his four-year term and undergoing one of the greatest challenges of his political life so far.

For several months, Seward had been fielding appeals from friends and constituents to pardon John Colt. "My table groans with letters from gentlemen and ladies of acknowledged respectability and influence," he wrote to one constituent. Now John's advocates came to him in person. One group was led by Dudley Selden and included the well-known writer and editor Lewis Gaylord Clark and three surgeons. The surgeons brought with them a hatchet and a plaster cast of the skull of Samuel Adams, to prove to the governor that the wounds on Adams's skull could only have been made by Colt acting defensively.

"You can have no idea of the fatiguing weariness of the week spent in hearing every form of application for pardon to Colt, and in studying the voluminous papers submitted," Seward wrote to his wife one week before the execution date. But he had made his decision. In nearly six thousand words, reprinted in entirety by some newspapers, he restated the facts of the case, then his reasons for refusing to pardon John Colt. "A deliverance of the prisoner by Executive clemency would be an encouragement to atrocious crime," wrote Seward. "Nor does the prisoner's character or conduct recommend him to the favor which can be only sparingly yielded."

That did not end the matter. In the week before the execution, Seward continued to receive visits from people pleading for clemency for Colt. This included a committee of the New York Bar Association, numerous "wandering philanthropists," and a phrenologist who tried to prove to the governor that "certain bumps on John Colt's head indicated that society, not Colt himself, was to blame for any violence he may have committed," as Seward explained to his wife. He did not tell his wife that he had also received at least one serious death threat.

"Now that the last act is done, and only the event remains to be contemplated, I find myself suddenly sinking from a state of excitement," he wrote on Thursday, November 17, the day before the execution. "It will never be known, and cannot be conceived, how much I have heard, read, thought, and felt, on that painful subject."

Visitors to the Tombs noticed a steep decline in John Colt's physical appearance after Seward's ruling. His penknife and razors were taken from him, and two deputy sheriffs guarded his cell day and night, lest Colt try to deprive the public by killing himself.

"Colt is the all-engrossing topic," wrote the attorney and diarist George Templeton Strong on November 17. Strong had followed the Colt case like every other New Yorker and personally knew some of the participants—one of his best friends was George Anthon, the son of Reverend Henry Anthon of St. Marks in the Bowery, who had been ministering to the condemned man at Sam Colt's request. Strong was no fan of public hangings, but he thought the execution had to happen because, if it did not, New York would break out in a riot.

The writer Lydia Maria Child was disgusted by the carnival atmosphere in New York in the days before the execution: "The hearts of men were filled with murder; they gloated over the thoughts of vengeance, and were rabid to witness a fellow creature's agony." Circulars had been handed out inviting people to the execution, she told a friend. "I trust some of them are preserved for museums. Specimens should be kept, as relics of a barbarous age, for succeeding generations to wonder at."

George Templeton Strong went back to his diary at the end of the next day, Friday, November 18: "This has been a day of memorable excitement and agitation, for it has witnessed the last act of the tragedy that has thrown everybody into fits every now and then since it began with that frightful murder. And the end has been worthy of the beginning and of the extraordinary character of the whole affair from its commencement."

The morning had started cold and cloudy, then turned bright and windy—"this wild and stormy day," one newspaper described it. The first person to arrive at the Tombs, at 6:30 a.m., was Sam Colt. He stayed with his brother about fifteen minutes. By the time he left, the streets around the Tombs were filling with the kernel of a crowd that would eventually reach from the prison at Franklin Street and Centre Street all the way to Broadway. "From eight o'clock this morning the Tombs were literally besieged by a mob, blocking up every street around it," wrote Strong, "all assembled not with the hope of getting admission, but to gaze eagerly at the walls that contained the miserable prisoner and to catch what rumors they could of what was going on within them." Outside Colt's cell window, workers were preparing the gallows in the prison yard. The sound of hammers hitting nails echoed off the walls.

Sam returned to the Tombs at 11:00 a.m., accompanied by Reverend Anthon. At 11:30, the lawyers arrived, and so did the Colts' friends John

Howard Payne and Lewis Gaylord Clark. They came to witness a ceremony that began shortly before noon. That is when Sam escorted Caroline Henshaw into John's cell. According to the *Herald*, Caroline wore "a straw bonnet, green shawl, a claret colored cloak trimmed with red cord" and looked anxious and thin. As Sam and the others watched, John and Caroline stood before Anthon, who quickly married them. "It was indeed a sorry bridal, and well calculated under the circumstances, to be regarded by the spectator as a scene of horrid sublimity."

After the wedding, John asked to be left alone with Caroline. "It is now one o'clock, and Colt has just ordered a quart of hot coffee," reported a special afternoon bulletin of the *Herald*, "which has been brought in and himself and wife are drinking it."

Shortly after 1:00 p.m., Sam, with John Howard Payne and Lewis Gaylord Clark, entered the cell again to join John and Caroline, whom they found sitting chastely on the edge of the cot. John said his final goodbyes. "For a doomed man, so near his certain death," recollected Clark some years later, "I never saw a person so little agitated. He was standing in the middle of his cell, holding in his hand a cup of coffee with perfect steadiness, and pointing to a wooden box of white sugar standing on the iron water-pipe, said: 'Sam, won't you pass the sugar?'" But Clark noticed that John's eyes were "red as blood" and moved "tremulously and rapidly" in their sockets.

John asked that the door be shut so that he might spend his last hours alone. In the courtyard, workers hammered in the final nails of the gallows. On the street outside, the crowd stirred and emitted a kind of howling sound, one reporter wrote, like "an army of wild beasts." Sam Colt was observed by a reporter outside the cell, nearly overcome with emotion and crying out, "Oh, I did not think it would come to this!"

In his reminiscence, Clark recalled leaving the Tombs after visiting John for the last time. He and Payne rode in a carriage with Reverend Anthon. They went east toward the Bowery to drop off Anthon at his rectory, then continued north to Washington Square and New York University.

Sam was already back in his little room at the top of the tower when Payne and Clark arrived. They found him sitting at a table, the brim of his hat pulled down low over his eyes. His hands were on his face and tears streamed between his fingers. The three men sat in silence for a few moments. Then Sam gathered himself and asked Clark to help him write a letter to his brother James, in St. Louis.

*   *   *

Deputies checked on John shortly before 3:00 p.m. and found him pacing in his cell. At 3:55, five minutes before the time set for the execution, the sheriff, accompanied by Reverend Anthon, dressed now in a dark robe, went back to John's cell to escort him to the gallows. The sheriff turned the key and opened the door, and Anthon stepped in—then immediately jumped back. Lying on the cot, supine, was John Colt. The handle of a knife jutted from his chest. The reporter for the *Herald*—almost certainly James Gordon Bennett himself—had followed Anthon and the sheriff into the cell, and when he touched the temples of the dead man he found them still warm. "His vest was open, the blood had flowed freely, and his hands, which were placed across his belly, were very bloody; he had evidently worked and turned the knife round and round in his heart after he had stabbed himself, until he made quite a large gash."

At almost precisely the moment John's body was discovered, a great cry went up in the streets outside the Tombs. "Fire!" the crowd shouted. "Fire!" The crowd was looking up. The cupola atop the Tombs was burning. As the wind whipped the flames, they spread fast through the tower, spitting embers onto the roof of the prison below.

Lydia Maria Child was in the screaming crowd. Looking up she found the sight almost mesmerizing, "for it was exceedingly beautiful," she wrote to a friend the following day. "The fire had kindled at the very top of the cupola, the wind was high, and the flames rushed upward, as if the angry spirits below had escaped on fiery wings." She was elated by the news that John's body had been discovered and that he had been spared the horror of hanging.

The dead body, the fire, the wild crowd, the bells of fire engines racing to the Tombs—it all left James Gordon Bennett, the man who had done so much to bring this day about, speechless. Or almost speechless: "We hardly know where to begin, or how to express the feelings and thoughts which rise up in the mind in contemplating this awful—this unexampled—this stupendous—this most extraordinary and most horrible tragedy."

Inside the University Building, Sam and his companions heard footsteps on the stairs. A coachman burst into the room. "Mr. Colt! Mr. Colt! Your brother has killed himself—stabbed himself to the heart! And the Tombs are afire! You can see it burning now!"

Colt and the others climbed out through the window on the eastern side of the tower, down a short ladder to the roof of the building. Over the tops of houses and other buildings they could see south to the Tombs. They watched the flames and smoke "licking up and curling around" the burning cupola, encouraged by a wind that blew hard from the west. "There was something peculiar about the air—the atmosphere—on that day," recalled Lewis Gaylord Clark many years later. "One felt as one feels on a cold autumnal night, while watching, uncovered in the open air, the flickering of the aurora borealis in the northern sky."

"Thank God! Thank God!" exclaimed Colt, with an expression, recalled Clark, "almost of joy."

It was an odd thing to say. What Colt meant by it Clark did not presume to know. But for years after that terrible day, many people would think that Sam Colt had just pulled off the greatest legerdemain of his life.

CHAPTER TEN

In the Blood

1844–45

John Coffee Hays, the original tight-lipped,
squint-eyed Western gunfighter. "Jack" Hays
brought fame to the Texas Rangers—and to Sam Colt's gun.

I

In June, the Hill Country of south-central Texas turns oven hot. The blue-bonnets and buttercups that have speckled the grasslands through the spring wilt and fade to dusty greens and tans, and everything alive lists toward the rivers and creeks. Even in the heat, the Hill Country can be an entrancing landscape of undulating prairie covered in knee-high grass, stands of live oak and juniper casting blessed pools of shade, and fast creeks running clear over limestone. But the beauty is deceptive. This is a harsh environment—"a trap baited with grass" is how Robert Caro memorably

189

described it in his biography of Lyndon B. Johnson, whose ancestors were among the settlers lured here in the 1850s. In many ways, the Hill Country was a preview of the world many thousands of Americans would encounter in the middle of the nineteenth century, as the nation vaulted the ninety-eighth meridian, moving beyond the great deciduous forests that had defined the national frontier for centuries and into the seemingly limitless prairie and desert. This part of Texas was the southeastern portal to the high plains, where the air turned dry and the soil alkaline, and mercurial winds swept down from the north. Here a man could nearly die of thirst one day and get swept away in a flash flood the next. Far worse, in 1844, he might look up from a streambed where he'd stopped to water his horse and find himself surrounded by Comanche Indians, knowing he was about to die but not before he was thoroughly tortured first.

On June 8, 1844, fifteen Texas Rangers rode through the Hill Country, scouting for Comanche. The rangers had been on patrol for several weeks, north of San Antonio, along the upper Perdernales and Llano Rivers. They stopped to rest at a fast narrow stream, called Walker's Creek, a tributary of the Guadalupe, the big river that ran across the Hill Country from the far west before veering south to the Gulf of Mexico. One of the men heard bees and climbed to a hive in a tree to steal some honey. In some versions of this story, the man in the tree was the first to spot the Indians. In most versions, it was two rangers who had lingered back as a kind of rear guard. They galloped into camp to report that they were being followed.

Thus began the Battle of Walker's Creek, also known as Hays's Big Fight. By the time it ended an hour or so later, it would be, as one Texas historian puts it, "a defining moment, if not *the* defining moment," in the history of the Texas Rangers. It would also be a defining moment in the life of Sam Colt, even though he was thousands of miles away when it happened.

Before the summer of 1844, the Texas Rangers were known, insofar as they were known at all, as a loose outfit of freelance horsemen—"mounted volunteers," they were sometimes called—who patrolled the frontier. They had existed in some capacity or another since 1823, but not until 1836, after Texas won its independence from Mexico, did the Texas Rangers become an official budgeted entity of the Texas Republic. Even then, they continued to ride their own horses, wear their own clothing, and, usually, carry their own weapons. They ate what they could hunt, pick, or forage, drank from the rivers, made fires from the branches and trunks of oak trees, and slept in the open with saddles as pillows. They fought Mexicans as necessary in south Texas, but the primary assignment of rangers in the spring of 1844 was to flush out and engage the Comanche who came down from the high plains of the north and west.

The Texans' confrontation with the Comanche is a singular chapter in the history of white Americans' relationship with Native Americans. While it would eventually end up in the same sorry place as the rest—with Native Americans dispossessed of their land, their culture, and, in many cases, their lives—it did not follow the usual pattern of whites forcing or tricking Indians into near extinction. The Comanche refused to play the role of doomed savages; if there was to be a Trail of Tears in their future, they would be sure to inflict plenty of sorrow first.

Part of what made the Comanche so remarkable as fighters—"the best light Cavalry of the nineteenth century world," according to the Texas historian T. R. Fehrenbach—was their skill on horseback. For white Americans accustomed to the footbound Indians of the eastern forests, mounted Indians were still a new phenomenon in the 1840s. The Comanche rode small but fleet mustangs, galloping across great distances and striking out of the blue with lethal effect. They put fear in the hearts of adversaries not just because they were extraordinarily good at killing, but because they relished the preliminaries. Eastern woodland Indians had sometimes tortured male enemies who fell into their grasp but generally left women unmolested. The Comanche were far more sadistic. After cutting or burning off the genitals of their male captives, they gang-raped and mutilated any females above the age of puberty. Younger children they often took and raised as their own, though infants, as a matter of course, they killed. In hundreds of these raids innumerable Texans had been killed and otherwise brutalized. If none of this excuses the order given by President Mirabeau Lamar of the Texas Republic in 1838 to "exterminate and expunge" the Indians, it does explain the urgent need Texans felt to protect themselves.

The rangers were putting up as good a fight as anyone could against the Comanche. Along with fine horsemanship and marksmanship, the young men of the corps exhibited remarkable bravery and daring. "To speak of courage among Texas Rangers is almost a superfluity," wrote the Texas historian Walter Prescott Webb. The courage was necessary because the rangers did not have much else going for them. There are no good records of ranger mortality, but all indications are that many young men died bad deaths. By one ranger's estimate, half of them were killed every year.

The great problem the rangers faced was that they were not only out-manned in their engagements with the Indians but effectively outweaponized, even though they had the better firearms. Until 1844, the rangers carried an assortment of shotguns and flintlock rifles. These were accurate and well-made weapons, but they were cumbersome to carry, required two hands to operate, and were almost impossible to use on horseback. Rangers had to dismount to fight, turning themselves from moving targets into stationary ones. Most problematical, their guns took a long time to load. Before each shot the men had to measure out powder, pour the powder down the barrel of the gun, place a ball in the barrel, shove it down with a long iron rod, sprinkle primer into the flashpan, adjust the flint—then shoot and do it all over again. An expert rifleman in ideal conditions could possibly do all this in twenty seconds, but thirty seconds or even a minute was more likely in battlefield conditions.

The Comanche had a few guns, too, but what made them so lethal were bows and arrows. These were nearly perfect weapons for mounted fighters. Comanche braves carried twenty arrows in a quiver. While charging a target at twenty to thirty miles per hour, an agile brave could get off an entire quiver in the time it took a ranger to reload.

Even by the standards of Texas Rangers, the men on patrol that June day in the Hill Country were a remarkably tough and able group. They included Samuel Walker—a name that would later come to be closely associated with Samuel Colt—and other legendary rangers such as Robert Addison Gillespie and Mike Chevalier. They were led by perhaps the greatest ranger of them all, twenty-seven-year-old John Coffee Hays. Small, slender, and laconic, Hays was a Texan who defied the Texan stereotype of big, loud, and brash, even as he supplied the template for a new iconic American figure, the tight-lipped, squint-eyed gunslinger who would come to populate the western range in reality and imagination: cool under pressure, fearless in a fight, content to let his gun do his talking. "So far as the records show," wrote Walter Prescott Webb, "no great Ranger captain has ever been loquacious."

In addition to his other qualities, Jack Hays was fiercely protective of his men. That is why, in the early months of 1844, he'd arranged to get possession of some new equipment. Commander E. W. Moore of the Texas Navy had purchased 180 .36-caliber, five-shot Colt revolvers in 1839. Intended as boarding pistols, for ship-to-ship combat, some of these had been deployed in the Battle of Campeche in 1843, when the Texas Navy joined the Republic of Yucatán in a fight against the Mexican Navy. After Moore's squadron disbanded, Hays laid claim to a batch of the guns.

Jack Hays was probably the first person to grasp the true potential of a Colt revolver. That it had not occurred to anyone before is because no

Americans had been in the kind of fights that Hays and his men engaged in routinely. Hays understood that, despite its many imperfections—hard to load, easy to break, prone to misfire—the revolver was the most perfect tool for mounted horsemen that had ever existed, and especially for mounted Texas Rangers facing Comanche Indians. On that day in the Hill Country, Hays and his fourteen Rangers each probably carried two Paterson five-shooters. This gave each man ten rounds.

It appeared at first that just ten Comanche were on the rangers' trail, but Hays sensed an ambush and held back from a confrontation. Shortly, the Indians showed themselves in full. There were about seventy-five of them. They stood at the crest of a hill, calling down taunts in Spanish, no doubt waiting for the rangers to start firing. When the rangers paused to reload, the Comanche could attack as usual.

Holding fire, Hays led his men into a copse of trees, then into a defile, out of sight of the Indians, and around to the back of the hill. Only then did he give his order to charge. All at once, the rangers galloped up the hill behind the braves. After discharging their rifles, the rangers did not jump to the ground to reload, as they had always done. They kept coming and kept firing. "Never was a band of Indians more surprised than at this charge," wrote Andrew Jackson Sowell, an early chroniclers of the Texas Rangers.

> They expected the rangers to remain on the defensive, and to finally wear them out and exhaust their ammunition. The rangers ran close beside them and kept up a perfect fusillade with pistols. In vain the Comanches tried to turn their horses and make a stand, but such was the wild confusion of running horses, popping pistols, and yelling rangers, that they abandoned the idea of a rally and sought safety in flight. Some dropped their bows and shields in trying to dodge the flashing pistols. The pursuit lasted three miles, and many Indians were killed and wounded.

"I will never again fight Jack Hays, who has a shot for every finger on the hand," a stunned Comanche chief said after the battle, in which thirty-two Indians died. The rangers did not get through unscathed—Samuel Walker was pinned to ground by a Comanche lance and another ranger died—but the battle marked a turning point in the history of the Texas Rangers and, by extension, the history of Texas. "Every culture or subculture has had its distinctive arm: the Macedonians their eighteen-foot phalanx pike, the Romans their Spanish-short-sword," T. R. Fehrenbach would write. "In the 1840s the name of Texas became indelibly linked with the Colt's revolver."

Walter Prescott Webb suggested that the clatter of Colt's guns that day sounded far beyond the borders of Texas. "We come now to the first radical adaptation made by the American people as they moved westward from the humid region into the Plains country. The story of this adaptation is the story of the six-shooter, or revolver."

II

Many months would pass before Colt learned of the events at Walker's Creek, and many more months before he began to realize their significance to himself. At the moment, on that Saturday in June of 1844, he was in Washington, filling out forms at the new Patent Office building on F Street. Texas was probably on the periphery of his mind because it was on everybody's mind in Washington that summer. President Tyler was considering a treaty to annex the republic, and the new Democratic candidate for president, James K. Polk, had made annexation a priority in his platform. That very day, the Senate was in session debating the issue. But Colt had more pressing concerns.

Several months earlier, in April, he had completed the fourth and final public test of his submarine battery. The setting was again the Potomac River, near the armory. Congress had adjourned to witness the demonstration, and the president and his entourage were once again in attendance. So many people made their way to the river on that clear warm day that a cloud of dust, raised by traffic, filled the sky all the way back to the Capitol.

On the face of it, the demonstration went as well as Colt could have desired. The target this time was a five-hundred-ton vessel, the largest yet, rechristened the *Styx* by Colt. He triggered the detonation from an undisclosed location, probably the upper floor of a brewery several miles downriver. The vessel was blown to smithereens, the crowd applauded enthusiastically, the press was appropriately adulatory, and Colt's name was bruited, again, from one end of the country to the other. Yet his immediate purpose—to have himself awarded a substantial honorarium by Congress—had not materialized. Congress had turned substantially against him, thanks in part to John Quincy Adams, whose disdain for Colt had never recovered after the death of his coachman. The submarine battery was "unchristian," "cowardly," and "no fair and honest warfare," Adams told his fellow congressmen. All government appropriations to Colt were "the throwing of so much money into the sea."

When Samuel Southard was president pro tempore of the Senate, Colt had enjoyed the protection of a powerful and highly invested ally, but Southard was dead now, and many in Washington were starting to agree that Colt's invention was little more than a violent exercise of smoke and mirrors—"very beautiful and striking," as one critic put it, but of minimal use "in the practical application." This impression had been formalized in a seventeen-page report prepared and submitted to Congress on May 8 by Secretary of War William Wilkins. Entitled "The Secret of Colt's Submarine Battery," the report featured expert opinion from the likes of Robert Hare, professor of chemistry at the University of Pennsylvania and a pioneer in the field of galvanic detonation, and Joseph Henry, esteemed professor of physics at Princeton and the foremost American authority on electromagnetic induction.

Neither man gave Colt much credit for his invention. Robert Hare wrote that "the galvanic process employed by Mr. Colt has not the slightest claims to originality." Samuel Morse had reached out to Joseph Henry on Colt's behalf, urging the professor to render a gentle verdict, but he was only slightly less dismissive than Hare. "I do not think it in the least degree probable," wrote Henry, "that Mr. Colt has added a single essential fact to the previously existing stock of knowledge on this subject." Perhaps for Morse's sake, Henry concluded with faint praise: "I ought to say, that whatever may be the result of the investigation relative to originality of his plans, I think he deserves credit for the industry and practical skill with which he has brought them before the public."

Colt fought back in a long memo addressed to a sympathetic member of the Congressional Committee on Naval Affairs, Henry C. Murphy, of Brooklyn, New York. Recounting the history of his invention, Colt allowed that using galvanism to blow things up was not original to him. He slyly intimated, though, that if Congress knew the full range of his secrets—secrets so remarkable he could not divulge them even to the distinguished members—it would be more than willing to compensate him for his discoveries. But how could Congress evaluate the system if Colt would not fully explain it? Perhaps with some prompting from Colt, Murphy suggested a solution. Let Henry Ellsworth of the Patent Office be the judge. If Ellsworth and his associates deemed the submarine battery novel enough for a patent, that would "justify the further consideration of the government."

This explains, then, what Colt was doing in Washington, a city he had come to detest, on that same Saturday in June that Jack Hays and his rangers were fighting the Comanche in the Texas Hill Country. Colt was applying for a patent on his submarine battery. He submitted the application that morning, paid his $30 fee, then returned in the afternoon, after Ellsworth had had a chance to review it, and withdrew the application before anyone else could see it. He had $20 refunded and left $10 to pay for a place-holding caveat. The commissioner's verdict of his friend's son's invention was never in doubt. He pronounced that it contained "novelty sufficient to sustain a patent."

The patent application that Ellsworth considered that Saturday, now preserved in Colt's papers in Connecticut, divulges the secrets he did not want to share with Congress. It makes clear that the explosive device was not where Colt's claim to originality lay. Rather, it was in his method of determining the location of enemy vessels relative to the submerged "torpedoes" of the minefield, such that the "operator" could know when to detonate which mine. Colt's solution was two large convex mirrors. The first mirror would "take in the whole field of view of the channel, or harbour where the torpedoes are anchored." Images in this mirror—that is, reflections of an enemy ship passing by—would be cast onto the second mirror, which was to be a kind of viewing screen and control panel. Because the mirrors would be angled just so, the location of the passing vessel on the second mirror would correspond to sets of connecting wires; if the ship appeared at location X on the mirror, for instance, the operator would know to connect the wires that detonated the mine at location X in the water. An instant later, the ship would vanish in a puff of smoke.

Colt's system, in short, truly was smoke and mirrors.

III

While most of Sam's time since John's death in the fall of 1842 had been devoted to his submarine battery, other business interfered now and then. The P.A.M.C. was dissolved, but the former treasurer, John Ehlers, was still pursuing Colt for unpaid debts. To raise much-needed money, Colt briefly considered licensing his pistol design to a manufacturer in Massachusetts, but that deal never got off the ground. Another enterprise of Colt's, producing tinfoil waterproofed powder cartridges, remained an ongoing though not very profitable enterprise.

Along with business concerns were personal responsibilities. The most pressing of these involved Caroline Henshaw—or rather Caroline Colt, as she now called herself after that day in November of 1842 when she became the wife, then the widow, of John Colt. Of course, referring to Caroline as the widow of John Colt assumed that John Colt was dead, and that was far from a settled matter. Suspicions that he had survived his supposed suicide took root in its aftermath. Some of these were privately expressed, as in a letter by New York State assemblyman Alvah Worden to Governor

Seward (who was Worden's brother-in-law): "I cannot see enough in the circumstances detailed before the coroners duty & given out in the papers to satisfy me that Colt actually committed Self-Murder. I don't believe the body found in Colts Cell was his. It all looks to me like a got up affair."

The theory of Worden and others was that during the long interval when the newlyweds were left alone in the cell, John had slipped into Caroline's clothing, then escaped, posing as a woman. How Caroline got out after him was not explained, but somehow all of this had been made possible by the burning of the Tombs' cupola, "a part of the contrivance," in Worden's words, to distract guards and give John a chance to escape. Then another man's corpse had been placed in the cell. "There is in the minds of very many of our citizens a suspicion, not very decided perhaps, but still a suspicion, that Colt is yet alive," reported the *New-York Tribune*.

More responsible members of the press pointed out that the dead man in John's cell had positively been identified as John—as positively as possible, that is, in an era before fingerprinting and other forensic tools. As for the coincidence of the conflagration in the cupola, this was explained by the sentry posted there. He'd lit a fire in a potbellied stove to warm himself. As the moment of the hanging neared, he left his fire unattended to watch the proceedings. In the gusting wind, the stove overheated, sparks flew, and the wooden cupola ignited.

Reasonable explanations notwithstanding, the strange events of that day—the hasty marriage, John's suicide, the fire at precisely the intended moment of the execution—were too much to dismiss as mere coincidence for many New Yorkers. That Sam Colt was at the time using electricity to trigger explosives only added to the intrigue. Had he somehow sent his electrical current to the cupola and set it afire? Had he used smoke and mirrors to free his brother?

Every bit as absorbing and perplexing to future generations would be the question of Sam's relationship to Caroline. By the time William Edwards published his biography of Colt in the 1950s, it had become accepted wisdom that Sam, not John, was Caroline's lover and the father of her son. The relationship that began when Colt was in Europe to obtain his patents had continued, according to Edwards, right through the conception of the child. Edwards even claimed the existence of a marriage license that proved Sam and Caroline were man and wife.

In fact, there seems to be no hard evidence of their union, but there is plenty of circumstantial evidence—as we will see. If true, it seems that Colt, by marrying Caroline to his brother on the day of John's execution, had solved several problems at once, making Sam's son (or "neffue," as Colt would call him) a legitimate heir while freeing Sam to marry another, more appropriate, wife.

Whatever the truth of this, and however John Colt's death did or did not occur, the woman who was, or was not, his widow remained indisputably alive and in need of food and shelter, not only for herself but for her young child, little Sammy. Colt took it upon himself to find them suitable accommodations. More accurately, he enlisted his new friend, the writer Lydia Maria Child.

If Colt's friendship with Samuel Morse was unlikely, his relationship with Lydia Child was in the realm of a category error. It's hard to imagine two such dissimilar people in the same room, much less enjoying each other's company. Today Lydia Child is probably best remembered for her lilting ode to Thanksgiving, first published in 1844 and later adapted into a Christmas song ("Over the river, and through the wood / To grandfather's house we go!"), but in the early 1840s she was known far and wide for her novels, children's books, advice manuals for women, and, above all, advocacy for the abolition of slavery. In 1833, just four years after William Lloyd Garrison's highly influential speech at Park Street Church in Boston, Child had published *An Appeal in Favor of That Class of Americans Called Africans*, a book that earned her the praise of abolitionists but derision and outrage from many others. In 1840, she moved to New York from Northampton, Massachusetts, to edit the *National Anti-Slavery Standard*, a weekly that promoted abolition and other humanitarian causes.

What brought Child now into the orbit of the Colt family was her strong opposition to capital punishment, and to John Colt's execution in particular. This is just about the only opinion she shared with Sam Colt. She was a pacifist, he was an arms maker; she advocated for Native American rights, he supplied guns to Indian killers; she was an abolitionist, he was—well, it's not clear exactly what Colt thought about slavery at this time but he was no abolitionist. The only sign he ever gave of antislavery views was the $2 he paid in December of 1842 for a subscription to the *Standard.* But those $2 probably revealed more about Colt's transactional relationship with the press, and with Lydia Child, than his views on slavery.

Colt and Child may have been formally introduced by a mutual friend, perhaps Lydia Sigourney, or by a member of the New York literary world, such as Lewis Gaylord Clark. Or it may be that Colt, having read Child's essay about John in the *Standard*—in which she'd praised not only John but Sam, "who never forsook his disgraced and suffering brother"—simply decided to pay her a visit at the *Standard*'s offices on Nassau Street in Manhattan.

However much Child disagreed with Colt on important issues of the day, the very qualities that made her a crusader for all things moral and decent made her an ally to him. She clearly felt some personal warmth toward him, too. At the time they met, she was separated from her husband, David Child, and Colt, for all his foreignness, seemed to attract her as much as she believed she attracted him. "Nothing amuses me so much as the wondering respect of Samuel Colt," she wrote to a friend in December of 1842. "It is evident that he never met with such a woman before, and had no idea that God ever made such a one. How should he? His acquaintance has been among officers' wives, and other phantoms of that sort.

> He evidently considers me as interesting a curiosity as a stone from the moon. I have no doubt he would blow up any packet full of people, if I were to signify that the sight would give me especial gratification. I hint that I know of a battery better than his, to defend harbours, and protect nations; and he shows that he has a flickering perception of what my battery may be, by apologizing for his invention. "I would not make it known," quoth he, "did I not think it would put a stop to war."

Child was skeptical of Colt's claim that he was more interested in stopping war than in making money. Nonetheless, "he seems to have a very kind heart, and noble impulses." When he asked for her help in finding Caroline a place to live, she took up the challenge as a kind of calling.

It was not a simple task, she soon learned, due to the notoriety of the case. This showed no signs of dying out. On the contrary, it was fueled by stage plays, popular songs, and literary references. In 1844, for example, Edgar Allan Poe would publish a short story, "The Oblong Box," about a young man, from Chambers Street in New York, sailing north with a pine box containing salted human remains. The occupant of the box was the young man's dead wife, but no reader at the time would have missed Poe's debt to John Colt for the inspiration. (Herman Melville would later invoke the case in "Bartleby, the Scrivener," in which the narrator suppresses his urge to kill Bartleby by recalling the fate of "poor Colt.") Sam had considered sending Caroline to live with the family of a minister in a small town somewhere, but he worried that she would attract attention and be scorned. New York was impossible for her now, and other cities were too risky for a young woman with a baby and an infamous dead husband.

Child came up with a solution. She was friendly with a group of liberal-minded intellectuals, mostly self-described transcendentalists, who in 1841 had founded a commune in West Roxbury, Massachusetts, at Brook

Farm. Members and associates of Brook Farm included such prominent and soon-to-be-prominent men and women as Bronson Alcott (father of Louisa May Alcott), Charles Dana, and the early feminist writer Margaret Fuller. Ralph Waldo Emerson was a frequent visitor. Nathaniel Hawthorne lived there for a time and in 1852 would publish a roman à clef about it, *The Blithedale Romance*, in which he suggested that the little utopia was not all it was cracked up to be. (Interestingly, the protagonist of Hawthorne's best-known work, *The Scarlet Letter*, published in 1850, was a woman cruelly stigmatized for giving birth to a child out of wedlock.)

On December 1, 1842, Child wrote to her friend John Sullivan Dwight, a Unitarian minister and musician who lived at Brook Farm and ran a small school there: "My heart is very full of a project in which I need you as a kind of mediator. You know the painful tragedy of John C. Colt, and have doubtless heard of Caroline Henshaw, the woman to whom he was married a few hours before his death." Child repeated the story of the tragic relationship between John and Caroline, working her way slowly to the purpose of her letter.

> Mr. Colt's brother has been to see me, and consult with me about her. He says he believes her to be a modest, worthy girl; that she never formed any other connection than that with his unfortunate brother; and that this has had the palliation of most devoted love, and of friendless poverty. He says he feels it a duty to do more for her than feed and clothe her; that he ought, as far as possible, to throw a protecting influence around her and the child, whom he shall in all respects treat as if he were his own son.

Child sought to assure Dwight about Caroline's character. The Brook Farmers may have been open-minded, but unlike residents of some other utopian communities (notably Oneida in upstate New York), they did not extend communal living to each other's bed. These were upright New Englanders with strict rules of sexual propriety. "If she were a loose woman, I would be the last to propose such a thing. But I think she is not." Child got to her point: Brook Farm would be perfect for Caroline and her little son, and taking them in would be in keeping with the community's purported philosophy of human brotherhood. "Oh here is a rare chance to teach the world a noble lesson! Will you forgo the opportunity?"

The answer was yes, they would forgo it. Apparently, Caroline represented more charity than Dwight and his fellow Brook Farmers were willing to extend. She went, instead, to the town of Warren, Massachusetts, not far from Ware, to raise her child and become educated to be a schoolteacher. How Caroline ended up in Warren is not clear, but Lydia Child apparently had something to do with it. In the spring of 1844, newspapers around the country reported Caroline's presence in Warren. This was precisely the kind of attention Sam wished to avoid, but Caroline seemed unruffled. We know this because she wrote to Sam that spring. Her letter, though brief, speaks volumes. (The spelling is original, though some capitalization and paragraph breaks have been added.)

Warren April 23rd 1844

My Dear Samuel,

This is the 3rd letter I have written to you without ever receiving one word in reply to mine. This letter will be a short one as there's no fun in writing without answer. The little boy is well he runout from sunrise to sunset he growed a big boy. If you do not write me soon I shall think you do not care for us. I want to see you so bad I do not know what to do.

Mr. Pearl is going to take me in the school next term which is the middle of May. I shall be glad for it willnot be so much for you to pay and will benefit me very much. He will write to you soon.

I get along with my study finely and am as happy as a lark if you would write me a little oftener. I see in one of the papers that you was blowing up everything that came before you in Washington. Take good care that you do not blow yourself up. I have wrote to Mrs. Child. Your dear little namesake can say everything. He is going to school 1 May with some little girls in the house with us.

Dear Samuel I could write all day to you I feel so happy but I shall not as I have written you so often and my study is waiting for me. I know you will not feel very well when you receive this short letter but I must leave you for the present. Write me soon as you can. I do not think I am selfish for I think you could write me once in three months.

Sincerely Caroline Colt

This is the only surviving letter from Caroline. While a single letter cannot give more than a peek into a person's heart, the tone is hard to miss. Caroline did not sound like a woman grieving the death of her husband. She sounded, rather, like a woman pining for the man she loved: *I want to see you so bad I do not know what to do.*

IV

At least two notable facts about Sam Colt are revealed in personal letters he received that spring and summer of 1844. First, that he was a lax correspondent; nearly every letter begins with its author admonishing him for his failure to write back. Second, that everyone in his family looked to him for money. "I have two objects then in writing this letter to you," his cash-starved father wrote from Hartford in April; "one is to hint that you must write a letter oftener and the other that if possible you must send me three hundred dollars." Colt could be extremely tightfisted with people he owed money to, but he was also generous to a fault with family and friends, even when he had nothing to give.

No one depended on his generosity more than his brother James. Writing frequently from St. Louis, plagued by "hard times & the blue devil" and chronically ill with recurring "bilious attacks" that left him with little energy to pursue his work as an attorney, James seldom failed to mention his urgent need for funds, nor his desperate hope that Sam would win an appropriation from Congress, "for I have necessarily calculated almost upon it as you have."

James was in these years an adoring if highly strung and self-involved brother. One measure of his esteem for Sam: as early as 1844, he started to address his letters to "Col. Samuel Colt." Later, Sam would come by the rank of colonel more or less honestly. In 1844, it was entirely unearned, but James was happy to confer it and Sam was happy to take it.

James closely tracked Sam's progress in the western press. His spirits lifted when he read of Sam's demonstration on the Potomac that spring. "The news relating to the success of the experiments spread like wildfire all through this country and everybody was pleased at the results and thought Congress ought to do something in the matter at once." When James learned that the congressional appropriation had been tabled, he was devastated, not so much for Sam's sake, he readily admitted, but because he'd been counting on it. Then he seemed to realize that Sam might have his own feelings on the subject. "But never mind. For god sake don't you get discouraged if such a thing were possible."

In mid-July 1844, Colt received a letter from his half brother, William Upson Colt, now a nineteen-year-old student at Washington (later Trinity) College in Hartford. "Dear Sam," William began archly, "It is so long since I have heard directly from you that I have undertaken to provoke a letter by sending you one." William had little to report of his own tame college life—"I doubt whether a man who deals with such powerful elements as you could receive much pleasure from such productions of such a quiet genius as myself"—other than the fact that he expected to leave school $200 in debt. "Were my brother the distinguished inventor already rewarded as I trust the next Congress will reward him, I should not have the least hesitation in applying for a sufficient loan, but as it is I do no such thing." If not money, he hoped Sam might offer him some assistance in securing a government job. "Will it be possible for me to find any situation in any of the public offices through you?"

William's inquiry did provoke a response from Sam, though probably not the one he anticipated. "I would serve you," Sam wrote back, "but not in the way you desire."

What followed was less a letter than a manifesto. Scolding his half brother for considering government service, Sam expressed a set of maxims that would not have been out of place, decades later, in the works of Friedrich Nietzsche. The messy draft that survives appears to have been dashed off in a jarring fury, as if Colt were racing to get down his thoughts while careening around curves on a narrow-gauge train. (For the sake of clarity, spelling has been corrected and punctuation added.)

> To be a clerk or office holder under the pay & patronage of government is to stagnate ambition and hope. By heavens I would rather be captain of a canal boat than have the biggest office in the gift of the government. Even a secretary of state says in all his diplomatic intercourse "by direction of the President of United States I do" so and so. The very language is that of subservitude and the soul that can do it is a slave.

Colt had turned thirty two days before taking up his pen to respond to William. He was still a young man but he had been living on his own for fifteen years. Many of those years had been spent in an increasingly frustrating campaign to win government funding for his inventions. But his letter to William is more than a rant against bureaucrats and politicians. It's a roughly worded Weltanschauung:

> Why not aspire to something higher? Why not seek to be the government itself? Everything must have a head, from the government of a nation to the God of the universe and the making of a religion. There is the same wide range for talent there always has been. Select the object of your ambition uninfluenced & untrammeled, & reach its zenith of your hope or die in the attempt. Life is a thing to be enjoyed. It is the only certainty & in proportion to our achievements, so it yields its fruit to our appetites.

Make up your mind determinedly what station in life you will reach & rely upon it with proper exertion you will not be thwarted. Your great study should be man. Lose no opportunity to mingle with the mass & view nature in its most primitive state. All mankind have naturally a yielding disposition to what may appear a superior. . . . If you allow other people to govern you, you subscribe yourself inferior to them.

If by any chance William still missed the point, Sam brought it home again at the end:

Don't for the sake of your own good name think again of being a subordinate officer of government. You had better blow out your brains at once & manure an honest man's ground with your carcass than to hang your ambition on so low a peg.

All of this must be taken with a heap of salt, given that Colt had been living, or at least trying to live, in "subservitude" to the government for years. Much of the last decade of his life had been spent shuffling around Washington hat in hand. But the anger and frustration was real, and his desire to be his own master, and master of others, was sincere.

In July, Colt wrote to a friend in Washington, professing himself happy to be free of that "dull, hot & dusty" city and enjoying New York to the fullest, spending days at Coney Island eating oysters and nights at Niblo's Garden watching a risqué ballet called *Revolt of the Harem*. "This or its equivalent is my every day's business." The happy-go-lucky self-portrait was as much a fiction as his pretense to William that he would disdain a "gift of the government." Until Congress came through with an appropriation, Colt had no money for tickets to Niblo's or oyster-eating excursions to Coney Island.

His money woes only worsened through the fall and winter of 1844–45. When a friend named "Charley" Miller wrote from the Westchester County jail to explain that he was unable to pay $50 he owed Colt as he had been imprisoned for punching a man in the nose, Colt wrote back, at first humorously, then less humorously, to tell Charley he needed the money anyway. "I am most damned hard up in money matters, which embarrasses me very much, & will be more & more so until congress acts on my claims." Colt wrote again to Miller in early January of 1845, then again at the end of that month. "I would not trouble you, but I am suffering extremely for the want of it $ you must send me some at once or expect to have a submarine battery fired under your fundament before the next change of moon."

In February of 1845, having nowhere else to turn, Colt wrote to the man who had so often come to his rescue, Roswell Colt. "I am entirely out of funds at the very time I need them most to enable me to complete my business before Congress." Would Roswell lend him $200? He assured Roswell that two bills before Congress, one to compensate him for the time he'd spent on his submarine battery and another to pay for his waterproof cartridges, were sure to pass. "My prospects were never so good as now."

In fact, his prospects were never so poor. On March 19, 1845, Colt received notice that the Senate's Committee on Naval Affairs had voted against sending either bill to the floor, effectively ending Colt's dreams of congressional financing. The *Brooklyn Daily Eagle* declared the final verdict on Colt's invention: "The Secretaries of War and of the Navy, to whom the subject was referred by the last House of Representatives, have arrived at the conclusion that Colt's sub-marine battery is nothing new; that he is entitled to neither praise nor reward," and that every dollar spent on Colt's invention had been wasted.

V

Though he had no way to know it at the time, March 1845 was among the most pivotal months of Colt's life. In the very weeks he was coming to grips with the end of his submarine battery, the universe, having conspired against him for so long, began to reorient itself in his favor.

That March, he received a letter from E. W. Moore, the commander of the Texas Navy who had purchased 180 Colt revolvers for use in Texas. Moore wrote to tell Colt how useful the guns had been in Campeche. He also relayed to Colt, for the first time, news of the engagement between Jack Hays's Texas Rangers and the Comanche the previous June. Hays had told Moore "that he would not be without them"—Colt's revolvers, that is—"for any consideration." For the moment, this praise was of little practical value to Colt, but soon it would be, thanks in large part to the man who became president of the United States that March.

Colt was in Washington on March 4, 1845, but he did not attend the inauguration of James K. Polk. "My mind & time has been otherwise employed," Colt responded when a friend asked for his impressions of the event. Polk tended to inspire that kind of unenthused reaction. A sour and plodding man who had somehow beaten Henry Clay for the presidency, he thrilled no one. What he lacked in brilliance and charisma, though, he made up for in self-discipline and hard work. And if he often appeared small-minded, he was in fact consumed by a vision of the United States as capacious as any ever held by an American president. In his inaugural speech, under gray and wet skies, Polk laid out a design so grand that it seemed to come from the mind not of a technocrat but of a prophet or a madman.

He began by denouncing the national bank and abolitionists, Democratic boilerplate in the vein of Andrew Jackson. (Polk was sometimes known as Young Hickory.) He then warmed to his real subject, the territorial expansion of the United States. In February, Congress had voted to annex Texas, so this was already a foregone conclusion. But Texas, for Polk, was just a beginning. He wanted Oregon and California, too, despite the fact that Oregon was partly a British possession at the time and California was entirely a Mexican possession.

If Colt did not yet appreciate the implications of Polk's inauguration to his own future, he quickly grasped the significance of another development that March. Six days after Polk's inauguration, on March 10, 1845, Samuel F. B. Morse signed a contract with Amos Kendall, the former postmaster general of the United States, to run the business operations of Morse's telegraph. This agreement marked the launch of the American telegraph network.

Over the previous year, Morse had enjoyed the kind of success that eluded Colt. Congress had awarded him $30,000 to build an experimental telegraph line between Baltimore and Washington. On May 24, 1844, a few weeks after Colt's last demonstration on the Potomac, Morse had christened the line with a phrase from the Bible (suggested to him by Annie Ellsworth, daughter of Henry Ellsworth): "What hath God wrought." Several days later, Morse's telegraph communicated to Washington the surprising news that Polk had won the Democratic nomination at the party's convention in Baltimore. All at once, Americans, even skeptics who had tended to dismiss the telegraph as an elaborate humbug, grasped the potential of this new technology.

Morse had originally hoped that Congress would in its wisdom buy the full rights to his patent and make the telegraph a federally operated communication system, rather like the US mails. When Congress declined to act, Morse had no choice but to build out his telegraph privately. He had neither the temperament nor the acumen for such an undertaking, and he was smart enough to know it. Thus, Amos Kendall.

Kendall, at fifty-five, was the ultimate insider in antebellum Washington, the "Man to See," as the historian Bernard DeVoto has called him. A former lawyer and journalist, he had been President Jackson's postmaster general. Abolitionists could not forget that Kendall had used his powers as postmaster general to prevent antislavery literature from going south, but overall Kendall had a reputation for piety, integrity, and, despite his somewhat caved-in appearance, great energy.

Kendall's experience as postmaster general would serve Morse's telegraph well, as the post office was the system most similar to the network Morse and his partners hoped to build, with trunk lines reaching out from urban hubs and feeders branching off to smaller cities and towns. Much of the actual construction of the lines would be undertaken by subcontractors who aspired to enter the telegraph business. Among Kendall's responsibilities was granting licenses to suitable applicants.

Kendall's appointment could not have been better timed for Colt, who found himself without occupation or income and yet as prepared as any man in the country to build a telegraph line. On the morning of April 5, 1845, he left a message for Kendall at his home on Twelfth Street in Washington. "I called twice yesterday to see you on the subject of Morse's Telegraph. I have a presentation to make for purchasing the right of running a line between two southern cities." He asked Kendall to send him an answer at Mrs. Rummey's, a boardinghouse near the Capitol to which Colt had been reduced in his penury. Kendall invited him to meet the following evening.

Colt's initial proposal was to collaborate with a partner named H. H. O'Callaghan to run a line between New Orleans and New York. When O'Callaghan turned out to be unreliable, Colt turned his attention to a less ambitious but potentially more lucrative proposition: a line between New York City and the offing.

Offing is a term seldom encountered today, but it was commonly used during Colt's lifetime to mean the horizon over the ocean, as far as the eye (with the aid of a telescope) could see. In Colt's case, the offing, practically speaking, meant Coney Island. Just under ten miles from Lower Manhattan, this was the farthest eastward point Colt's telegraph could reach within a reasonable limit of time and budget. The purpose of such a line would be to send "marine intelligence" from ships that were approaching New York Harbor. As Colt would later advertise, rapid delivery of such news would be useful to those who did not want to wait until the ships anchored. What Colt did not say—he did not have to—was that the value of this early news was greatest to speculators who sought to buy or sell commodities from London or Paris or New Orleans and who could profit by knowing prices or other financial news hours or days before competitors got their hands on it.

Colt was not the first person to seek profit by speeding up the communication of marine intelligence. James Gordon Bennett's *Herald*, for example, maintained a small fleet of boats in the Narrows to intercept ships and then beat them back to the city with whatever news they carried. Colt was not even the first to attempt to do this by telegraph. *Optical* telegraphs had been in use for decades. These were semaphore links, based on the French system, in which towers were spaced ten or twenty miles apart to form a chain from the offing (the beaches of Long Island, in the case of New York) to the city. Men with telescopes read and relayed signals, communicating tower to tower with large mechanical arms they manipulated to form coded letters. The United States never had an optical telegraph comparable to the extraordinary network in France, where hundreds of towers radiated out from Paris into the countryside, but a chain of semaphore towers had stretched as far as New York to Philadelphia. Now the electric telegraph would put these other methods out of business. Not only would it transmit information at a speed many multiples faster, but it could operate at night and in foggy weather, when optical telegraphs were useless.

With Kendall acting as agent, Colt drafted a preliminary agreement with Samuel Morse and his partners on May 8, 1845. As a stipulation, he agreed to construct the line as far as Coney Island within six months. The price for the patent right would be $8,000 per year.

Two days later, Colt wrote to tell Kendall and Morse that he wanted the rights for Boston to the offing, too. If he could control marine intelligence in both New York and Boston, as he wrote to a friend, he would "hold the monopoly of all foreign news coming upon the coast."

VI

On the day Sam Colt signed the contract for rights to build the Boston-to-offing telegraph line—May 31, 1845—James Colt lay in bed in St. Louis, recovering from a bullet wound to his hip and composing a long letter to his brother. The subject was the duel in which he'd just been shot.

Prior to this, James had been in steady contact with Sam, filling frequent and lengthy epistles with news of St. Louis politics, updates on his social and professional advancement, and, always, anxious inquiries about Sam's financial prospects, with an eye to his own. In recent months, another focus of his letters had been Caroline and what to do about her. Sam had mentioned the possibility of Caroline's moving to St. Louis to become a teacher. The ever-obliging Lydia Maria Child had written to friends in St. Louis to inquire about opportunities for Caroline. James strongly discouraged the move. "If you want to save her character do not by any means permit her to come here," he wrote to Sam. "The waywardness of the western people would lead her to be very much exposed and this in no way could be prevented. . . . The whole west is made up of new settlers, adventurers and speculators, and among such people what could she expect?"

Then, as if to prove just how wayward the western people were, James got himself shot. According to newspaper accounts, the duel had been fought on May 20, in Illinois, directly across the Mississippi River from St. Louis. James had been challenged by a young man named John Barr for reasons, as the papers put it, "of a delicate nature." Barr had escaped the duel unscathed; James was not so lucky. "The ball struck the abdomen, on the right side, near the hip," according to the *St. Louis Reporter*, "and passed in front, making a slight wound, until it reached the centre, then took a course downward, passing through the muscle of the left thigh."

News of the duel must have come as a shock to Sam. Not that dueling was unusual in America in 1845; especially in the south, the practice was considered a legitimate and, in some states (though not Missouri), perfectly legal method of settling a quarrel, especially when honor was involved. But just a year earlier, James had fiercely denounced dueling in a letter to Sam. The occasion for that "dissertation" had been Sam's admission, in his own letter, that he'd served as a second in a duel, apparently near Washington. "Dueling at best is a relic of barbarism and is not American," James had written then. "My principles are opposed to dueling entirely."

How, then, had James landed in a duel? It seems that a resident of St. Louis, Mr. Wilson, had gotten it into his head that his wife intended to leave him, and that she had been encouraged to do so by James Colt, "which," wrote James, "is not true." Nonetheless, "a thousand stories were in circulation," including rumors that James had been caught in "sectual intercourse" with Mrs. Wilson. Again, not true, insisted James, but Wilson had issued a "peremptory challenge" for a duel. Negotiations between representatives (*seconds*, in dueling parlance) of Mr. Wilson and James were undertaken, compromises were reached, and tensions started to dissipate. Just then arrived in St. Louis the brother of Mrs. Wilson, twenty-one-year-old John Barr. The young man had decided that he, not Wilson, must stand for his sister's virtue. So there would be a duel after all. James consulted an exiled Hungarian nobleman who was visiting St. Louis and had ample experience with duels. The Hungarian advised him to stand perpendicularly to his opponent, with his hip thrust up to take the ball and protect his vitals.

The night before the appointed day, James crossed the river with his second and slept on the Illinois shore. At 6:00 a.m., he met John Barr in a clearing near the river. They walked off ten paces. They had three seconds to shoot. Barr's bullet hit James. James's bullet missed.

Other than to protest his innocence in the affair, James's main object in his letter was to make Sam understand that he had missed his own shot *on purpose*. Nearly half of the letter was devoted to this clarification. While his antagonist had been "pale as death and trembling," James was "cool and determined." He pointed his barrel into the air at the moment of shooting, he wanted Sam to know, out of consideration for Mrs. Wilson, the woman whose honor was at stake. In 1841, following John Colt's murder of Samuel Adams, she had been just about the only person in St. Louis who did not shun James on account of his brother's infamy. So he could not now, in good conscience, kill *her* brother.

Exactly how much truth was in James's description of the duel or his motivations is hard to say, but he seems to have been less than forthcoming. "Cool and determined" were not traits generally displayed by James Colt; his letters fairly rattle with jumpiness, and later behavior suggests a man easily unhinged. As for his insistence that he in no way encouraged Mrs. Wilson to leave her husband, this, too, seems contradicted by facts. Mrs. Wilson did leave her husband soon after the duel and remarried almost immediately—to James Colt.

VII

James Colt's name was in the press throughout the summer, as he was arrested, tried, and convicted of dueling. In July, Sam solved the problem of James's notoriety the way a man with a toothache might relieve it by poking himself in the eye. He put his own name back into the papers by committing assault and battery.

His victim was Joseph Patten, an attorney representing the Astor House. Patten had filed a "creditor's bill" to collect $1,200 that Colt owed to the hotel. Colt went to confront Patten, or Patten to confront Colt, in the reading room of the Carlton House hotel. According to one newspaper account, Patten said something derogatory about Sam's brother (presumably John, though possibly James), and Colt punched Patten, knocking him to the floor. Witnesses saw Patten get back to his feet and stagger about the room, bleeding from the face. Colt exited briefly, then returned, still enraged. "Damn you, Patten, you have got what you deserved." To which Patten responded that Colt was "a damned Coltish scoundrel."

Colt was arrested and held on bail of $500. Eventually, he would be let go and fined just $50, but in the meantime the press agreed that he had committed "a brutal and unprovoked" assault. A newspaper in New London headlined a story about the assault with a sharp reference to previous Colt family violence: "IN THE BLOOD."

The violence emanating from the Colts that summer had to be disconcerting to Amos Kendall, that pious and earnest man who was attempting to set up Samuel Morse's telegraph network. Some days Kendall must have wondered what he had signed on to in his deal with Colt. He got a grim kind of answer late in that summer of 1845 when he found Colt's name in the papers again, and his own name tragically linked to it.

The story, according to various accounts, went like this: On a late mid-August afternoon in Washington, while Amos Kendall was visiting New York on telegraph business, his twenty-two-year-old son, William Kendall, walked into a drugstore on Pennsylvania Avenue at Fourteenth Street with two other young men, William Elliot and Josiah Baily. The three had been playing tenpin at a nearby alley and entered the store as best of friends, their arms draped over one another's necks and bantering. After William Kendall ordered a soda, the banter turned suddenly harsh. Kendall teasingly called Elliot a coward; Elliot called Kendall a "damned liar." Then Baily, coming to Kendall's side, punched Elliot in the face. After the scuffle, Kendall and Baily resumed their game of tenpin. Elliot, fuming, walked down the block to a nearby bookstore. Along with books, the store sold guns, including, for $22, Colt revolvers.

An hour later, Elliot was standing on the corner of Pennsylvania and Fourteenth Street when Kendall and Baily came out of the tenpin alley and headed up the street. Elliot approached them and started firing. Several shots rang out in quick succession. Baily was hit in the arm. Kendall was hit in the chest. He was carried to his father's house on Twelfth Street, where he died.

The news of his son's death traveled to Amos Kendall part of the way by the very telegraph he was helping Samuel Morse build. It must have seemed a dark conspiracy of coincidence when he learned that the murder weapon was a rapid-firing pistol invented by the man with whom he'd just signed a deal to build another telegraph line.

Colt had ironies to contemplate, too, starting with the fact that the gun that bore his name was probably not his. Revolvers sold as Colts in 1845 were generally guns assembled by John Ehlers from leftover parts bought at auction from the liquidated P.A.M.C. They had Colt's name on them but he received not a dime from their sale.

The greater irony, one that would redound ultimately to Colt's benefit, was that the many times the name Colt appeared in newspapers in association with acts of violence, going back to John's arrest in 1841, brought notoriety to the Colt family but also something else: name recognition. Colt was a household name by the mid-1840s. This owed to the personal behavior of John, James, and Sam, and to coverage of the submarine battery. More and more, it also owed to Colt's name appearing in newspaper stories such as those about young Kendall, in which his revolvers were brandished in robberies, murders, and even duels.

VIII

The deal Colt signed with Kendall and Morse in May of 1845 required him to put up his telegraph line within six months. But it was now the start of September, and he had yet to raise a single telegraph pole. He did not seem worried. On the contrary, he was happily calculating the extraordinary profits he expected to make. In a letter to a Hartford surgeon and prospective investor, E. E. Marcy, he estimated that he would build the New York telegraph for $5,000, operate it for $3,000 a year, and bring in $15,000 a year. Of course, as John Ehlers had once warned Colt, "making calculations" was "still far from making money."

Most of Colt's calculations were based on guesswork. Other than Morse's experimental line between Baltimore and Washington, no one had completed a functioning telegraph line, much less operated one as a business. The early telegraph builders were pretty much figuring it out as they went.

They were, at first, a small group. Morse and his longtime collaborators Leonard Gale and Alfred Vail had been working on the technical development of the telegraph for years, but most came from other occupations. These included a former Maine congressman, Francis O. J. Smith, who owned a quarter of Morse's patent and took responsibility for overseeing the line between New York and Boston, and an Irish American ex–newspaper editor named Henry O'Reilly, who proposed to build a line from New York to the Great Lakes. Another was Ezra Cornell, a former machinist and plow salesman whom Morse had originally hired to dig trenches for his wires between Washington and Baltimore. Cornell would eventually become a founder of Western Union and, in 1865, the patron of Cornell University.

These telegraph pioneers shared discoveries and equipment, though they quickly began to argue over who deserved credit—and profit—for improvements. Colt and Cornell got into an argument almost immediately about which man came up with a technique to use just one wire for the telegraph by putting a battery at both ends of the line. (Alfred Vail, who was in a position to know, said that it was Colt.) The dispute with Cornell would be one small irritation in a surfeit of challenges to come, but Colt did not know that when he wrote his calculations to Marcy.

> I have all the wire insulated & prepared to put up as soon as I can get money to buy the posts & $2500 is all I will require to put the telegraph in operation. . . . Now then if you will advance me this money by installments of $500 each . . . I will pay you lawful interest & will give you as an additional inducement a premium of ten percent of the profits arising out of the enterprise until I have the means to pay off the mortgage. An early answer will much oblige.

Marcy declined to get involved. At the end of September, Colt signed a deal, instead, with a New York businessman named William Robinson. While Robinson supplied the capital and manned the office, Colt would supervise construction of the line to the offing.

Unsurprisingly, given the unprecedented nature of the endeavor and his own pie-in-the-sky tendencies, Colt had underestimated the logistical challenges and costs of putting up a telegraph. To begin, he needed many miles of good copper wire, at a cost of $50 per mile. He also needed a large supply of thirty-foot-long wooden poles ("red cedar or locust unless chestnut or white oak can be bought for a good price") and work crews to raise the poles and hang the wire. He needed batteries to supply electricity, and he needed instruments to send (the *key*) and receive (the *register*) messages, not to mention operators who could quickly learn to use the instruments. Finally, he needed a small fleet of boats, and crews for these boats, to intercept incoming ships and retrieve whatever news they might carry.

Robinson rented an office on the corner of Beaver Street and Hanover Street, behind the Merchants' Exchange on Wall Street. It had a view of the Exchange from the windows; from the roof, you could see all the way to the Narrows. The office was to function as the terminus of the telegraph line and headquarters for the New York and Offing Electro-Magnetic Telegraph Line, as Colt and Robinson called their service, as well as the Telegraphic Bulletin and Foreign News Room, where subscribers could come for the latest intelligence. It must appear obvious to businessmen, stated a company flyer, "that this mode of instantaneous communication of intelligence is with them not so much a matter of choice as of necessity, for, without availing themselves of it, they must necessarily be behind others in that which is essential to their success of the business."

Colt began constructing the line in October. He immediately confronted the greatest hurdle of the entire endeavor. To get to Brooklyn and beyond, the East River had to be crossed. No one had yet managed to successfully carry a telegraph line across a river. The problem of crossing the Hudson (North) River, on the other side of Manhattan, would so stump Morse in running his own line from New York that he would resign himself to terminating in Fort Lee, New Jersey, and transporting the intelligence to upper Manhattan by boat. In 1845 no one knew more about transmitting electricity through underwater cables than Colt, but crossing the East River was a far greater challenge than anything he had met with his submarine battery.

On October 23, 1845, with hundreds of spectators watching from the Manhattan and Brooklyn shores, Colt used a steamship to lay a six-thousand-pound lead pipe on the bottom of the East River. Inside the pipe were four copper wires, each completely insulated "so as to insure the transmission of the electro magnetic fluid," as one newspaper described the operation. The following day, the New York press was ecstatic about Colt's "perfect success" in crossing the river. What had been achieved was nothing less, according to the headline in the *Brooklyn Evening Star*, than "LIGHTENING UNDER WATER."

PART IV

YOUNG AMERICA

1846–51

Eastward I go only by force; but westward I go free.

—Henry David Thoreau

CHAPTER ELEVEN

Year of Decision

1846

War News from Mexico *by Richard Caton Woodville.*

I

In his classic history of the American west, *The Year of Decision 1846*, Bernard DeVoto described the annus mirabilis of his title as "a period when the manifold possibilities of chance were shaped to converge into the inevitable." A war in Mexico, a migration of more than two thousand Americans into the far west, a hurried exodus of some twenty thousand Mormons across the Mississippi toward some as yet unnamed promised land—these were just a few of the developments that made 1846 transformative.

Of course, as DeVoto acknowledged, no year can be isolated from those around it. The events of 1846 were astonishing, but none qualified as surprising to anyone who had been paying attention in 1845. Many of the fateful decisions DeVoto writes about had already been made before 1846 began. Congress had already decided to annex Texas and welcome the former republic as the twenty-eighth state in the union. President Polk had already decided to obtain for America, either by negotiation or by bluster, parts of the Oregon territory still under shared dominion with Britain.

Polk had made another critical decision before the year began, though he kept this one close to his vest: the United States was going to take possession of the contiguous lands between Oregon and Texas, those parts of America now within the states of California, Nevada, and Utah, along with parts of the current-day states of Arizona, Colorado, Kansas, and New Mexico—altogether more than 600 million acres that were still, at the start of 1846, in Mexican hands. This land was the bounty Polk hoped to reap for America by whipping Mexico into submission in a war he expected to begin shortly.

Not every American approved of Congress's or Polk's decisions. Henry Clay, the great statesman from Kentucky whom Polk had beaten to become president (largely because of their differing policy on the annexation of Texas), represented the views of many of his fellow Whigs when he dismissed territorial expansion as a waste of resources and effort. "It is much more important that we unite, harmonize, and improve what we have than attempt to acquire more." A young second lieutenant in the US Army named Ulysses S. Grant believed the coming war against Mexico would be the "final consumption" of "a conspiracy to acquire territory out of which slave states might be formed for the American union." Grant was echoing the concerns of abolitionists in the north, such as Lydia Maria Child, who foresaw the conquest of Mexico as a victory for slavery. Texas would enter the union as a new and large slave state, and so would other territories taken from the Mexicans. Ralph Waldo Emerson prophesied that the result would be disastrous for the country. "The United States will conquer Mexico, but it will be as the man who swallows the arsenic which brings him down in return," wrote Emerson. "Mexico will poison us." Emerson's friend Henry David Thoreau, who spent the winter of 1846 living in a small cabin on the shores of iced-over Walden Pond, protested the war and the expansion of slavery by refusing to pay his poll tax, an act of "civil disobedience," as he called it, for which he would spend a day in jail.

But even Thoreau, who would never venture farther west than Minnesota, was susceptible to the westering urge that took hold of Americans in the mid-1840s.

> When I go out of the house for a walk, uncertain as yet whither I will bend my steps, and submit myself to my instinct to decide for me, I find, strange and whimsical as it may seem, that I finally and inevitably settle southwest, toward some particular wood or meadow or deserted pasture or hill in that direction. My needle is slow to settle—varies a few degrees and does not always point due southwest, it is true . . . but it always settles between west and south-southwest. The future lies that way to me.

And so it did for the many Americans who considered Polk's expansion plans not only sensible but necessary. "It is time now for opposition to the annexation of Texas to cease," wrote the magazine editor John L. O'Sullivan, and to allow "our manifest destiny to overspread the continent allotted by Providence for the free development of our yearly multiplying millions." Manifest Destiny, first coined by O'Sullivan in the summer of 1845, was the vague but grand rationale that swept away all objections to expansion. Anyone with a good map and a decent sense of symmetry could see that the United States was meant to fill in the land between the Atlantic and the Pacific. This truth was as self-evident to O'Sullivan and his fellow expansionists as those inscribed by Thomas Jefferson in the Declaration of Independence. At the start of the new year, in an essay entitled "America in 1846: The Past—The Future," O'Sullivan once again exhorted his fellows Americans to reflect on "the great result" of America's former glories, and to welcome "the great purposes of providence, and the evident mission of our people!"

Some Americans had already started on that mission, manifesting their destinies without waiting for an invitation. In addition to the tens of thousands who had gone to Texas during the previous two decades, thousands more had been gripped by "Oregon fever" over the past several years. By the dozens, then by the hundreds, they had forded the Mississippi River, then the Missouri River, and followed the wide valley of the Platte River west. They had hauled themselves over the Rockies at South Pass, and crossed a desert—a real desert this time, immense and flat and as dry as the bones of the creatures that perished of thirst in it—only to scale the steep and dangerous Sierra Nevada. Some had gone all the way to the Willamette Valley in Oregon, where several thousand Americans were living as 1846 began. Others had split off for the Sacramento Valley in California, where as many as a thousand had already settled.

By one count, 541 wagons would make the journey west before 1846 was done. They would launch mainly from Independence, Missouri, or from Council Bluffs, Iowa, or one of the other towns along the Missouri River, as soon as the prairie grass was high enough for grazing. In the meantime, travelers made or bought the equipment they needed for the journey and for the life they anticipated when they arrived at their destination. Much of this—anvils, grinding stones, plows, scythes, ovens, trunks, furniture—would be jettisoned on the way, too heavy to drag over deserts and mountains, but at least two items would make it all the way. One of these was their Bible, and the other was their gun. They needed guns for hunting to supplement the food they carried with them. More immediately, they needed guns for protection against foes they expected to encounter on the trail.

By foes they meant mainly Indians. Few Americans had met a western Indian, but they had heard of the horrors endured by Texans in Comanche raids and had been warned of the horse tribes that haunted the valley of the Platte. Rumors floated up and down the Missouri of likely attacks, including one specific rumor regarding a group of Kansas Indians lying in wait on the western trail.

How seriously the emigrants took these threats can be seen in how they spent their money. The largest expenditure for a family going west went to its wagon and oxen ($400) and food for the trail ($120 for a family of four). Then came guns. Families spent an average of $60 or $70 on arms, powder, lead, and shot. In 1846, the guns were likely to be single-shot rifles, powerful and accurate but of limited use in the event of a large-scale Indian attack.

If the emigrants were lucky and had money, they might also carry a Colt revolver. Early guidebooks for western travelers spoke highly if somewhat fancifully of Colts. It's not clear which Colts the guide writers had in mind—whether Paterson models or those assembled later by John Ehlers—but the guns were rare and hard to acquire. Those who had them wore them proudly. While in the frontier town of Westport, Missouri (now part of Kansas City), Francis Parkman, whose memoir of his western travels in 1846 would become an American bestseller, wrote of a man named Woodworth who "paraded a revolver in his belt, which he insisted was necessary." Parkman did not have a revolver of his own but judged that "it may have been a prudent precaution, for this place seemed full of desperadoes."

For all the guns in the hands of civilians, most of the firepower in the west in 1846 belonged to the US military. Several army expeditions were either underway or soon to muster as the year began. The smallest and farthest flung of these was the third expedition of John Charles Frémont, the handsome and dashing "Pathfinder," who had spent the previous several years exploring the trans-Mississippi wilderness for the US government. That January, Frémont was in California, at Sutter's Fort, near present-day Sacramento. Already celebrated as an explorer, Frémont was now looking for a greater glory—a military triumph in the war against Mexico that he, like everyone else, believed was coming. Nearly two thousand miles east of Frémont, mustering at Fort Leavenworth, Kansas, and also preparing for that war, were General Stephen Watts Kearney and his seventeen-hundred-man Army of the West. They would soon commence the longest march ever taken by an American army, to Santa Fe, New Mexico, eight hundred miles southwest of Fort Leavenworth. But by far the largest and most obtrusive army in the west at the start of the year was camped one thousand miles south of Kearney, in Corpus Christi, Texas, under the command of General Zachary Taylor. Taylor's three thousand men had been waiting for action since the end of 1845. Known as the Army of Occupation, they were in reality an army of provocation, as they would soon reveal.

The props, then, were set. The actors were on their marks and knew their lines. All that was required was a sign to begin—a dimming of the lights, an overture in crescendo, or a comet soaring west across the American sky. Such a comet appeared on January 13, 1846, then instantly split, strangely and magnificently, into two distinct fiery balls. In retrospect, a westbound comet dividing midflight should have been read as a dark omen. At the moment, it seemed to presage only wonders.

II

As his compatriots gazed west at the start of 1846, Colt began the year still looking east, to the offing. Construction of the telegraph line between New York City and Long Island was underway but slow going. Many of the frustrations Colt encountered were the same as those that beset every telegraph pioneer. No sooner did laborers raise the wooden poles than a stiff wind came along and blew them down. Or a vandal with an ax felled one for firewood, then stole the copper wire for good measure. Even unmolested in the sky, the wires were problematic, as fragile as gossamer, susceptible to changes of temperature, expanding and contracting until they snapped. The nonconductive glass knobs over which the wires were draped cracked easily and made tempting targets for boys with rifles.

Despite delays, Colt had the line from Fulton Ferry landing in Brooklyn to Coney Island working, at least intermittently, by mid-January of 1846.

At each end of the line a young man, conversant in Morse's code of dots and dashes, operated the instruments. At Fulton Ferry, the operator was Charles Robinson, the nineteen-year-old son of Colt's partner; at the Coney Island end, it was Charles L. Chapin, just sixteen at the time, who occupied an old lighthouse with a view of the bay. ("A more desolate location one can hardly conceive of," he recalled many years later.) Chapin would get news from ships entering the lower bay, tap this into his key, and seconds later young Robinson would receive it on his register and translate the dots and dashes into plain English.

The biggest problem for Colt's telegraph was not the dozen or so miles between Brooklyn and Coney Island, which ran more or less successfully despite frequent breaks and interruptions, but the span of the East River. Almost as soon as his first attempt to cross the river had triumphantly been proclaimed the previous fall, the underwater cable was pulled up by the anchor of a ship and severed, a repeat of Samuel Morse's mishap in 1842. Colt tried to lay the cable again, but again an anchor caught it. After the cable was destroyed a third time, Colt decided to carry it *over* the river. To avoid the masts of ships, the wire was to be slung on poles 150 feet high. It would cross from the Fulton Ferry landing in Manhattan to the landing in Brooklyn, foreshadowing the great catenaries of the Brooklyn Bridge, which would one day swoop over the river there. When this effort failed, too, Colt returned to his original scheme of submerging the cable in the river, but now several miles north of Wall Street, at Hell Gate, a turbulent narrow channel where ship anchors presumably posed no threat. Finally, on April 9, 1846, the press announced that Colt had succeeded in extending the line across the river at Hell Gate.

There was no time to celebrate. With mounting expenses, few subscribers, and little incoming cash, the New York and Offing Electro-Magnetic Telegraph Line was in trouble. Worse news came from Boston. Colt had entered into an agreement with an outfit named Hudson & Smith, proprietors of a profitable semaphore telegraph business, to build a line between Boston and the offing (Hull, Massachusetts). Hudson & Smith began having second thoughts almost the moment they signed the contract with Colt. The start-up costs were too high, the profits too low, and Colt, they came to believe, not to be trusted. He overcharged them for equipment, then expensed to them "every dam glass of liquor he had drank on the road" between New York and Boston. By mid-February of 1846, they wanted out. "We are sick of it and the whole affair must be closed."

* * *

As Colt sought a buyer to take over the Boston operation, he devised a plan to save the New York line. He would incorporate it and raise capital by selling stock, as he had done with the Patent Arms Manufacturing Company and the Submarine Battery Company. He prepared a grandly visionary prospectus for investors. Not only did he propose to extend the Long Island line to Montauk, at the eastern tip of Long Island—120 miles beyond Coney Island—but he intended to run a line in New Jersey from Jersey City, just across the Hudson from downtown New York, via New Brunswick, all the way to Cape May on the Atlantic Ocean.

In May, Colt went to Albany to lobby the New York State Legislature for a charter. It was there, at the Congress Hall hotel, that the fraught correspondence of his dispirited partner, William Robinson, found him. Robinson's news was all bad. Endless problems bedeviled the line, the workers were useless, and no money was coming in to meet expenses, "which almost bothers my life out," wrote Robinson. "I would not live as I have for the last 2 months for all the telegraphs now invented or hereafter to be."

The bill to incorporate the New York and Offing Magnetic Telegraphic Association passed on May 13, 1846. That same Wednesday, in Washington, Congress voted to declare war on Mexico.

III

For all practical purposes, the war was under way well before Congress declared it. On January 13, President Polk had issued orders to General Taylor to begin marching from Corpus Christi to the Nueces Strip, a hundred-mile-wide stretch of land between the Nueces River and the Rio Grande. Traditionally, the Nueces River had marked the boundary between Texas and Mexico, but Polk wanted Mexico to cede land all the way south to the Rio Grande—the entire strip. The Mexican government had already tacitly forfeited Texas to the United States, but an American army crossing the Nueces was intolerable. Which was exactly what Polk intended it to be.

It took a month for Taylor's army of three thousand to march in its entirety from the salt-scented air of Corpus Christi to the arid scrub-oak plain a hundred miles to the south. By March, the Americans were dug in on the banks of the Rio Grande, at Fort Texas, across the river from the town of Matamoros. Now it was a matter of waiting. Second Lieutenant Ulysses S. Grant understood exactly what they were waiting for: "We were sent to provoke a fight, but it was essential that Mexico should commence it."

On April 23, 1846, Mexico finally did what Polk wanted it to do. It sent sixteen hundred troops across the Rio Grande to reclaim the Nueces Strip. The Mexicans landed both upriver and downriver of Fort Texas, in the nearly impenetrable head-high scrub oak—the *chaparral*, as the press would invariably call it—that grew north of the river. The first skirmish occurred that afternoon, when Taylor sent a company of mounted dragoons upriver to reconnoiter.

The dragoons were led by Captain Seth B. Thornton. This was the same unlucky Thornton (then a lieutenant) who had been swamped with Colt off the coast of Florida in the spring of 1838. A few months after that incident, Thornton had nearly died again when a steamship carrying him north exploded off the coast of South Carolina, killing 129 of his fellow passengers. He had survived those ordeals only to suffer this. His dragoons were ambushed in the chaparral by a vastly superior force of Mexicans. Sixteen Americans were killed or wounded. Later, Thornton would be court-martialed for leading his men into an ambush. In fact, Thornton had done his commander in chief a great favor. Polk now had his pretext for war.

By the time the Mexican War ended two years later, the electric telegraph would transmit news of its progress at lightning speed. But as the war got under way in that spring of 1846, just 120 miles of telegraph wire had been hung in America, and none south of Richmond, Virginia. Most news still came the old-fashioned way, by land and sea, so slowly that Washington did not know that fighting had broken out on the Rio Grande until nearly three weeks after it commenced. Then came a steady sequence of daily bulletins from "The Seat of War." War, it turned out, made even better newspaper copy than crime.

It was in these early days that the press minted one of the first true American military heroes since Andrew Jackson captured New Orleans in 1815. His name was Samuel Walker. Along with his glorious military exploits, all the world would soon know two facts about Samuel Walker: first, he was a Texas Ranger, and second, his weapon of choice was a Colt revolver.

A few other details came out along the way. His full name was Samuel Hamilton Walker and he was twenty-nine years old at the start of the war. Small in stature, he had soft blue eyes, light hair, thin lips, and high cheekbones, and was said to be soft-spoken, almost diffident. But his delicate features and humble manners belied extraordinary resilience. He had been badly injured while fighting under John Coffee Hays in the famous battle against the Comanche in June of 1844, when a warrior pinned him to the ground with a lance. Before that he had served in the Seminole War in Florida—where he probably first encountered Colt guns—and had fought with both the Texas Army and the Rangers against the Mexican Army. He had been imprisoned several times by the Mexicans and had once escaped by scaling the wall of the prison, though not before being subjected to beatings and other mistreatment. He was also among the Americans who had been forced to participate in Santa Anna's infamous death lottery in March of 1843, when the Mexican president ordered 176 captured Texans to choose their fate blindly from a container of beans; those who drew a white bean, such as Walker, lived; those who drew a black bean—one out of every ten prisoners—were executed by firing squad. Through it all, according to a fellow ranger, Walker was "as brave a man as ever breathed."

Like many Texas Rangers, Walker was an excellent horseman. "It is told of him that he will ride at full speed upon his horse and fish up a letter from the ground, and that he will also pick up a common sized man from the ground and place him before him on his saddle, in despite of the man's efforts to prevent it," reported one newspaper. He once saved a fellow ranger whose horse had been shot out from under him; as a Comanche warrior galloped toward the grounded ranger to finish him off, Walker "rode up with almost lightning speed, caught his friend with his right hand, and with a tremendous effort of strength swung him upon his saddle and galloped off, but not until he had shot the Indian with his pistol."

Walker seemed to have been born for battle. As a boy growing up in Maryland, he had soaked up the "chivalry and noble deeds" of Revolutionary War heroes, he later explained in a letter, and "being naturally fond of military glory, I determined to try my fortune on the field of battle on the first opportunity that presented itself." As a fellow Texan put it, "War is his element, the bivouac his delight, and the battlefield his playground."

When the war broke out near the Rio Grande in April, Walker and a group of rangers under his command answered General Taylor's call for volunteers and reported for service at Point Isabel, the army depot on the Gulf of Mexico. They came as irregulars, lacking uniforms and army training. Because they were preceded by a reputation for wild and occasional outlaw behavior, Taylor had concerns about accepting the rangers. But they also had a famously cavalier attitude toward killing and dying, making them useful for high-risk assignments.

Shortly after arriving at Point Isabel, Walker requisitioned thirty-two Paterson Colt five-shooters from the depot. These were probably leftovers from the 1839 Paterson purchase, seven years old and hard used. Or they may have been from a lot of 150 revolvers the army had purchased from John Ehlers in 1845. In either case, they had apparently been rejected by officers in the regular military units who had first dibs on them, and Walker grabbed them.

On April 28, under Taylor's orders and with his thirty-two Colts and his twenty-four rangers, Walker left Point Isabel and rode west into the chaparral to scout the enemy. This first expedition ended in disaster. Walker and his men were halfway between Point Isabel and Fort Texas, camping for the night in the chaparral, when a large force of Mexicans came upon them. Walker tried to direct a retreat, but many of his men scattered. With just a dozen rangers at his side, Walker fought hard for fifteen minutes, then fled, galloping back to Point Isabel, pursued much of the way by Mexican horsemen.

The first press reports that came north were sprinkled with insinuations of cowardice and poor leadership by a captain who "did not distinguish himself," as the *New-York Tribune* put it, "otherwise than in running." Just two days later, though, the *Tribune* dramatically revised its story. "Injustice has been done to this gallant young fellow." The newspaper's sudden change of heart was prompted by a series of remarkable do-or-die missions performed by Walker over several days at the end of April and start of May of 1846.

The first of these occurred on April 29, the morning after his flight to Point Isabel. Walker volunteered to relay to General Taylor the important intelligence that Mexicans were near Point Isabel and the depot was in imminent danger. To do this he had to somehow penetrate the Mexican forces that now held the ground between Point Isabel and Fort Texas, twenty-five miles inland. The odds of surviving this were low, but Walker insisted on trying.

Walker departed Point Isabel with six rangers under his command. They passed through lagoons near the Gulf, then rode into the chaparral north of the Rio Grande. At one point the rangers encountered a platoon of a hundred Mexican lancers. As they considered how to sneak around the lancers, Walker, according to a ranger named Nelson Lee, "coolly announced he was going *through* them." They approached the lancers slowly, pretending to be local rancheros passing by. At fifty yards' distance, Walker gave the order to charge. "Instantly the spurs were buried deep in the side of our good horses, which bound forward like the wind, and greeting them with a terrific yell, we dashed right through." Dodging and firing with their Colts, they left the Mexican lancers in their dust.

Walker accompanied General Taylor and a large part of his army back to Point Isabel on May 2. They went to reinforce the depot and resupply for the return to Fort Texas. The next morning, May 3, they woke at dawn to the low but steady thud of cannonade. The Mexicans were taking advantage of Taylor's absence, and the garrison and the five hundred men he'd left at Fort Texas were under heavy attack. Even from a distance of twenty-five miles the reverberations were dreadful. "What General Taylor's feelings were during this suspense I do not know," wrote Ulysses Grant, "but for myself, a young second-lieutenant who had never heard a hostile gun before, I felt sorry that I had enlisted."

Grant was under the impression that there "were no possible means of obtaining news from the garrison" to ascertain how the troops there were holding up under enemy fire, but he was wrong. Later that same morning, Samuel Walker volunteered to race over the twenty-five miles to Fort Texas, collect messages from Major Brown, then report back to General Taylor at Point Isabel. It was an even more suicidal mission than the first.

Again, Walker and his rangers somehow slipped through the enemy. Arriving at Fort Texas by 3:00 a.m., they established that the Americans holding the fort were in decent shape. One man was dead but the battlements had withstood the artillery fire intact, none of its cannons dismounted. Across the river, the town of Matamoros had been leveled by the Americans and many hundreds of Mexicans had been killed. Major Brown assured Walker that the garrison could hold as long as it took for General Taylor to make it back.* Walker attempted to leave the fort at 4:00 a.m. with this intelligence but was forced back inside. After daybreak, he tried again. This time he made it through the siege. When he and his men trotted into Point Isabel on the afternoon of May 5, the Americans there were stunned to see them alive.

News of Walker's daring exploits spread by steamship across the Gulf, first to New Orleans, then, within two weeks, to the northern papers. His mad dashes through enemy territory were precisely the stuff American newspaper readers craved. On one press-perfect occasion that May, Walker

---

* The fort would indeed hold, but Brown would be killed two days after meeting Walker. The fort would be renamed in his honor, as would the city that grew up around it, known today as Brownsville.

had his horse shot out from under him by a cannonball. When a Mexican lancer galloped up and raised his lance to finish him off, Walker pulled out his Colt revolver, shot the Mexican with "his unerring five-shooter," then leaped onto the man's horse and rejoined the fray. At once, a collection went up in New Orleans to buy Walker a new horse. In St. Louis, an artist named Charles Deas quickly painted *The Last Shot*, a "wild and picturesque" depiction of Walker killing the man who had come to kill him. A newspaper in New Orleans published an ode to the gallant hero of the chaparral:

> This is the tribute Freedom sends
> To thee, who art her bravest son. . . .
> Speed on—afar thy fame resounds;
> Thy praises come to every ear,
> From lips that murmur sweeter sounds,
> Than men less brave deserve to hear.

IV

The letter is undated but Colt probably wrote it in mid-July 1846. It is addressed to Mr. Levi Slamm. "Believing you may have it in your power to favour my views & that you will act with promptness," Colt informed Slamm that he was enclosing a second letter that he hoped his old friend would deliver to the president and other influential men in Washington.

Levi Slamm had been a shipmate of Colt's aboard the *Corvo*. There are no records of communication between Colt and Slamm in the years between the *Corvo* voyage and this letter, but the men had clearly stayed in touch. Slamm's trajectory had been in many ways as interesting as Colt's and arguably more successful. A locksmith by trade, he had risen in New York City politics to become a leader of the fractious pro-labor branch of the Democratic Party known as the Locofocos, so named after a kind of self-igniting match. (Another Locofoco was Henry Bangs; the party was known colloquially as Slamm, Bang & Company.) Slamm was considered by his enemies to be a "rascal" and a "bad man"—to quote a letter from one of those enemies to President Polk—but he had paid his dues and earned himself patronage from the Democrats. As the war with Mexico got under way, he was named purser of the US Navy.

Colt's letter was prompted by a report he'd read in the newspapers about the now celebrated Samuel Walker of the Texas Rangers. According to this report, Walker had been offered a captaincy in the US Army but intended to turn down the commission and remain a ranger. One explanation for Walker's refusal was that the army commission amounted to a demotion from his rank in the Texas Rangers, where he was now a lieutenant colonel. An unnamed friend suggested that another reason was Walker's conviction that army discipline suited him poorly. "As a scout, or skirmisher, he has not a superior; but as a soldier automaton, to be moved by others . . . he would never submit to it."

Walker's refusal made some sense. What made no sense at all was Colt's belief that he, a man who had never served a day in the military, much less led men into battle, was qualified to take Walker's place as captain in a mounted unit of the US Army. Having been called "colonel" for several years by his brother James, Colt was now seeking a demotion from a rank he did not hold to a rank he had no chance of obtaining.

Urging Slamm to do all he could to secure him the captaincy or, failing that, to "endeavor to cause a delay in it until I have time to make a fair show for myself," Colt purported to be driven by patriotic motives. In his enclosed letter to President Polk, though, he could not help conflating his desire to serve his country with his desire to serve himself: "My claim upon the government for this appointment is based upon the fact that I have spent the last ten years of my life without profit in perfecting military inventions."

Colt's apparently genuine hope that his letter to Polk would yield a positive response can only be explained by the fact that he was, as he hinted to Slamm, desperate. The telegraph company was foundering and the scheme to raise stock by incorporating had not panned out. The war should have been a good time to be in the news business, and it was—but not for Colt's telegraph service. Five of the city's largest newspapers, including the *Herald* and the *Sun*, had agreed that June to pool resources in gathering news of the Mexican War. A precursor of what would eventually become the Associated Press, these combined newspapers purchased a fast steamboat to intercept ships as they approached Sandy Hook in the lower bay of New York. The steamboat sped the news to Manhattan, sometimes releasing homing pigeons in advance to fly special bulletins to the city. While not as fast as Colt's telegraph, the newspapers' methods of communication were more dependable. So instead of Colt putting newspapers out of business, as he had threatened, they were putting him out of business.

Colt saw the writing on the wall for his telegraph. He likewise understood that the war with Mexico was probably his last chance to make a profit on his guns. More than a decade had passed since he filed his patent. He had less than four years before it expired.

Colt's letters to Slamm and Polk were among several he wrote that summer to solicit military commissions. Some went to federal officials in Washington, others to state militia commanders. None were taken seriously by their recipients.

Perhaps the most ludicrous of these was the one he wrote to Jonathan Drake Stevenson on July 1. A state assemblyman from New York who had recently been made a colonel by President Polk, Stevenson was organizing a regiment for an expedition to California. He was a most improbable officer himself, a "mercenary swaggerstick," as one historian has called him, who looked the part of a commander with his "vulturous nose and a hawkish brow," but who had no more military experience than Colt. Indeed, Stevenson might have been an inspiration to Colt; if a political hack from Staten Island could get himself appointed as commander of an expedition, surely Colt could acquire a brevet or two.

President Polk did not look to Colonel Stevenson to execute military operations. If all developed as Polk intended, the fighting would be done and California would be part of the United States long before Stevenson arrived in San Francisco. Rather than warriors, Stevenson and his regiment were to be settlers—an Army of Occupation that would morph into an American population. They would be a stock of tradesmen and farmers and merchants to seed the future welfare of the territory with their skills and arts. That was the idea, anyway. In reality, the men who signed up for Stevenson's regiment were a motley group of ne'er-do-wells and thugs. One volunteer summed up his reasons for joining the regiment as follows: "Roast beef and two dollars a day, plenty of whiskey, golden Jesuses, pretty Mexican girls, safe investments, quick returns."

Colt must have had his own reasons for wanting to join this expedition. He may have seen it as a chance to get his guns to California and find a market for them. Or he may, like so many others who went west in 1846, have been looking for a new beginning after years of frustration.

"In tendering you my services I by permission state that I am actuated by that sense of duty which every American owes his country in time of war," Colt wrote to Stevenson. "My whole life has been devoted to military matters, and I believe that if you will grant me a personal interview at your earliest leisure on this subject that I shall be able to convince you of my ability to render you essential service." Had Stevenson accepted his application, Colt would soon have found himself sailing to California, perhaps to settle there for the remainder of his days. But Stevenson wrote back to inform Colt that every position was filled.

At least Stevenson replied cordially. Not so General Hamilton of the New Jersey state militia. When Colt made a proposal to arm a New Jersey regiment with a "Battalion of Repeating Rifles," the general upbraided him for his presumption: "I ought not to be taxed with communications of gentlemen affecting exclusively to their own business & personal interests."

"Be kind enough to inform me if I have taxed you beyond a sheet of paper and five minutes of time," Colt wrote back. "For the sheet of paper, I return you two as near of the same quality as I have on hand, and I enclose one dime, a sum that in my judgment will compensate you for the valuable time spent in reading and answering my letter."

V

On the morning of Saturday, September 26, 1846, after mustering for weeks on Governors Island, Jonathan Drake Stevenson and his regiment of 770 men, along with assorted wives and children, sailed off in three seven-hundred-ton ships, pushed by a "spanking twelve-knot breeze," as the *Tribune* put it. The ships had not been scheduled to leave until that afternoon, but Colonel Stevenson had a number of creditors and legal problems pursuing him in New York so an early departure was deemed advisable. So abruptly did the ships sail that dozens of passengers were left stranded onshore, including a mother who had gone home to fetch medicine for her sick baby, only to find that her baby and her husband had embarked for California without her. She was seen running up and down the Battery, "making the most frantic gestures of despair and chattering like a maniac," according to the *Tribune*. "Surely this is the most ill-starred expedition of conquest ever set on foot by a Christian Government," the newspaper scoffed. "Even Mexico herself would be ashamed of an affair so impotently ridiculous."

Of Colt's feelings upon the departure of Colonel Stevenson's little armada, nothing is recorded. Probably he understood that he was lucky to be on dry land and not aboard one of those crowded California-bound tubs. But perhaps he also experienced, on that breezy autumn day, the pangs of missed opportunities. Far from Colt, but near enough for him to read about in newspapers, volumes of American history were being drafted without him. Epics were being etched into the land by human feet and hooves and wagon wheels, grooved into the prairies and salt flats, or, now that late September had come, into the plush sod of the Sacramento Valley and the Willamette Valley.

For those already at the end of the two-thousand-mile journey, it had taken about six months, each mile more grueling than the last. From the springtime prairie, they had slowly risen to the Continental Divide, following the path of the North Platte and the Sweetwater, passing rock formations jutting from the plains that would mark the way for the many millions to follow—Chimney Rock, Castle Rock, and Independence Rock (where many paused to scramble up the granite bulb and carve their names). If they were on schedule, they had made it through South Pass in July. Then had come the truly hard part: a monotonous slog through the flat desert lowlands, followed by a steep ascent into the Sierra Nevada. By this point, dissension and misery had set in, and loved ones had died of sickness or mishap or violence.*

For all the hardship and grief the travelers suffered, many recognized this journey west as the most important thing they would ever do. They kept journals and wrote letters to memorialize it. Along with reports on progress and descriptions of the landscape, nearly all the journals noted two phenomena. The first were the vast herds of buffalo and the splendid occasion for hunting these offered. The second were the mounted Indians.

Typical was a letter from an emigrant named John Craig, who traveled in 1846 with a small well-armed group of men on a "long and some what perilous Journey." He wrote to a friend of the "imense herd of Buffel I Seen what Sport we had in runing them on horse back over theas vast plains." Then he turned to the Indians.

> Neither have I time to tell you of the thousands of the red Sons and daughters, not of the forest, but of the great American desert that we seen as we traveled slowly along through thair chery country. At times those Sons of nature would through [throw] our camp or party into quite a flurry by approaching us on horse back at full Speed thundering and dashing over the plains towards us thair robes and blankets streaming in the air behind them which with thair painted faces and other indian equipage made them have quite a warlike appearance.

In later years, the Native Americans of the Plains—the Cheyenne, the Crow, the Pawnee, and especially the Sioux—would become a serious threat. For the moment, to the surprise of many white travelers, encounters with Indians were

---

* Or worse. On that same Saturday in late September that Colonel Stevenson's regiment sailed from New York, a group of emigrants known as the Donner Party rejoined the common trail to California after taking a supposed shortcut. They were now a month behind schedule and in a race to make it over the Sierras before snow began to fall. It was a race, as most American schoolchildren know, they would lose.

mostly amicable and ended not in death but in stilted attempts at conversation and shared moments of amusement. A traveler named Edwin Bryant wrote of such a meeting with a band of Sioux who were just coming back from a war party. The emigrants and the Indians engaged in a friendly shooting match.

"The Indians shoot the arrow with great accuracy and force, at long distances," wrote Bryant. "One of them handled the rifle with the skill of a marksman and hunter. The rapid repeating discharges of Colt's revolving-pistol astonished them very much. They regarded the instrument with so much awe as to be unwilling to handle it."

With these words Bryant may have recorded the first-ever meeting between the Sioux and Colt's revolver.

VI

On the same day in late September that Jonathan Drake Stevenson steamed out of New York for California, American troops in Mexico were celebrating the capture of the city of Monterrey. The Mexican War was now five months old, and the United States Army had scored a major victory. They had done this with the help of Texas Rangers under the command of Jack Hays and Samuel Walker, who gained several strategic hills early in the battle but suffered significant casualties. "Boys, place me behind that ledge of rock and give me my revolver," said ranger Robert A. Gillespie after he was mortally shot in the stomach. "I will do some executing on them yet before I die."

After taking the hills, the rangers had entered the city, shooting their way through it in house-to-house, roof-to-roof combat, precisely the kind of quick-moving and up-close fighting at which they and their revolvers excelled. When the Mexicans asked to negotiate a truce, Walker, the highest-ranking commander at the front of the battle, went to meet General Pedro de Ampudia to discuss preliminary terms on which Mexico would surrender Monterrey to the Americans.

In the days after the armistice, the American troops did what armies sometimes do after victories—they made themselves at home in the conquered city, plundering and respecting no law but their own. The rangers were the worst offenders, and General Taylor was eager to send them back to Texas, "for I regret to report that some shameful atrocities have been perpetrated by them." As the rangers departed, one American officer hoped that "all honest Mexicans were at a safe distance from their path."

*   *   *

Walker was not blamed for the disorder, nor was he sent on leave. Rather, that autumn, he was sworn in to the US Army in the position Colt had coveted and which Walker had, after hesitation, decided to accept. He was now a captain of a regiment of mounted riflemen in the US Army.

In early November, in the company of Jack Hays, Walker boarded a steamship and left Texas. Arriving in New Orleans on November 12, the two men created an enormous sensation. "They were warmly greeted by thousands, and they will pardon us for saying that we heard repeated exclamations of surprise that such brave hearts and the authors of such bold deeds were found in gentlemen so unpretending in appearance and so totally free from assumption of manner or thought."

After a short visit in New Orleans, Jack Hays returned to Texas. Walker boarded another steamship to resume his journey. He was bound for Washington, where he hoped to raise money, men, and guns for his new regiment.

Walker arrived in the nation's capital on November 22. The next evening, he was feted by more than five hundred men in the Odd Fellows Hall in an impromptu celebration. "The vast hall rang, and rang again, in response to encomiums upon the deeds of Walker and the army of General Taylor." Then the hero turned north again, to New York, where Sam Colt was waiting to meet him. No man ever rode more gallantly to another's rescue.

The draft of the first letter Colt wrote to Walker is undated. Most likely it was sent in late November of 1846, directly after Walker's arrival in New York. "I have so often heard you spoken of by gentlemen from Texas," Colt began, "that [I] feel sufficiently acquainted to trouble you with a few inquiries regarding your experience in the use of my repeating Fire Arms & your opinion as to their adoption to the military service in the war against Mexico.

> It has also occurred to me that if you think sufficiently well of my arms to urge the President & Sec of War to allow your company to be thus armed you can get them. The arms are very much improved since we first commenced their manufacture & I have no doubt that with the hints which I may get from you & others having experience in their use in the field that they can be made the most complete thing in the world.

Colt's letter was not much different from dozens of others he had written over the previous decade to solicit support from politicians or military figures. But he'd never heard back so fast, nor so courteously, as he did now. "In compliance with your request I take great pleasure in giving you my opinion of your revolving patent arms," Walker wrote on November 30.

> The pistols which you made for the Texas Navy have been in use by the Rangers for three years, and I can say with confidence that it is the only good improvement that I have seen. The Texans who have learned their value by practical experience, their confidence in them is unbounded, so much so that they are willing to engage four times their number.

Walker related the story of the rangers' first use of Colt revolvers in the fight against the Comanche in 1844. In this and other skirmishes, wrote Walker, the Colt revolver had proved decisive and had given the rangers confidence to undertake "such daring adventures."

It was a glowing review, but it contained what could be read as a veiled criticism of the gun. Or, as Colt himself read it, a proposition. "With improvements I think they can be rendered the most perfect weapon in the World for light mounted troops."

This exchange initiated one of the most remarkable relationships in the history of American manufacturing: on one hand, a brash easterner who had spent much of his life in hotels and factories and offices; on the other, a laconic westerner whose deeds spoke louder than his words and whose life had passed mostly outdoors under open sky. Between these two Sams lay a country that was about to change in ways neither could have anticipated. Yet both would have plenty to say about how it happened.

CHAPTER TWELVE

Now Is the Time

1847–48

*There would be many accounts of Samuel Walker's death in Mexico.
This print depicts one of them. Not shown is the pair of revolvers Walker
received from Colt several days before he died.*

I

The year 1847 began with a false spring. The weather was so mild in the
east that flowers peeked out months before they were due, insects appeared
in bewildered swarms, and ice melted from the rivers, to the consternation of
ice merchants, who wondered where they would get the product to fill their
icehouses for summer. In these balmy early days of January 1847, Samuel
Colt and Samuel Walker finalized a deal "for the immediate construction
of 1,000 or a larger number if hereafter determined . . . of said Colts patent
Repeating Pistols." The secretary of war, William Marcy, endorsed the
contract on January 6.

Walker had done a great deal for Colt in the weeks since they began exchanging letters in November. Most important, he had single-handedly persuaded the Ordnance Department to contravene, at least temporarily, its long-standing objection to Colt's pistols. Anecdotes that sounded like fiction but contained elements of fact circulated in the press. In one, Walker was told by an Ordnance official that Colt's revolvers were not sanctioned by army brass. "General Scott don't approve of them," said an Ordnance officer.

"Well, I do," Walker shot back, "and I have tried them—General Scott has not."

"But it will cost as much to arm one regiment with these as three with the common arm."

"Give my regiment Colt's repeaters," said Walker, "and we will undertake to whip any three regiments you have got."

Whether or not such an exchange actually took place, the opinions of the famous Captain Walker undeniably carried weight in Washington. He had achieved in a few weeks what Colt had failed to achieve in years. Colt was suddenly back in the gun business.

Walker's significance to Colt went beyond resurrecting the revolver. The Texan also changed the design of the guns. By the terms of the contract, he acted as a kind of proxy client for the government. This meant the new gun would be tailored to his personal preferences. And what Walker preferred was one of the largest and most powerful pistols ever produced. The full length was to be fifteen and a half inches from the tip of the muzzle to the back of the grip. The barrel alone was to be nine inches long. The fist-size cylinder was to hold six shots, one more than Colt's Paterson pistols, and .44-caliber balls. The whole thing would weigh more than four and a half pounds, unloaded. When Walker finally got a chance to fire one—this would be many months later, shortly before he died—he would pronounce himself delighted. "They are as effective as a common rifle [at] one hundred yards, and superior to a musket at even two hundred." Colt's own reputed assessment: "It would take a Texan to shoot it."

Walker wanted not just a more powerful gun, but a simpler gun that was easier to operate in the field. Even devotees of Paterson pistols had to admit that loading them was a chore that required essentially dismantling and reassembling them every five shots, challenging enough in calm conditions with steady fingers, nearly impossible in the heat and dust of battle. Shortly before the P.A.M.C. shut down, Colt had started to address some of these issues in his guns, and now he sought to solve them to Walker's satisfaction. In the Colt Walker, as the gun would come to be known, the cylinder would remain intact during reloading. The ramrod would be attached to the bottom of the barrel and operated by a lever, dispensing with the need for a separate tool to press the ball and powder into place. Other refinements to Colt's earlier design included better sights, making the Colt Walker easier to aim than a Paterson pistol, and an exposed trigger—the hidden drop-down trigger of the Paterson had always been more clever than practical. To address complaints that the Paterson did not hold up well under hard use, the Colt Walker would be made of the "best hammered Cast Steel," which at the time meant steel imported from Sheffield, England. (Firth & Sons would be a supplier to Colt for years to come.) Finally, the gun would be made of "parts sufficiently uniform to be interchanged, with slight or no refitting." This was not quite a stipulation for the identical machine-made parts that would later become the standard for gun and other manufacturers, but it was a step in the right direction.

In person, by letter, and by telegraph, Walker and Colt consulted over every detail of the gun through the early months of 1847. For all his celebrated modesty, Walker was not shy in expressing his demands. "The powder flasks you propose to furnish . . . I do not approve of, as I prefer it plain & substantial suited for a narrow leather strap." "In regard to the sights you must make the hind sight much finer and the front sight, of German Silver, and of different shape altogether from the model furnished, say half inch in length 1/8 of an inch at bottom tapering to 1/16." "The handle of the pistol is rather short & not quite full enough, and must be increased a little in length and thickness if it can be done without much delay."

Colt accommodated Walker's improvements without objection. Indeed, he welcomed them. Gratitude did not come naturally to Colt, but he seemed to sincerely acknowledge his debt to Walker. He was also smart enough to realize that Walker knew better than he did what worked, and what did not, in the kind of fighting Texas Rangers regularly engaged in.

No doubt Colt recognized, on some level, that Walker's value to him lay not just in influence and practical advice but in his very *being*. By attaching Colt to himself, Walker was placing Colt and his guns in the western firmament at the very moment the west was about to fundamentally change. In Colt's youth, the west had meant Kentucky and western Illinois—the frontier of Daniel Boone, forest paths, gurgling creeks, and rifles as long as men were tall. The frontier that opened in the 1840s was the west beyond trees, beyond rivers, almost beyond imagining to easterners. It was the west of open spaces, cunning yet magnificent tribes of horse Indians, and white men galloping across the range with one hand on the reins and the other—Walker and his fellow rangers were seeing to this—aiming a Colt pistol.

II

First, though, Colt had to make the guns. He had promised to deliver the first hundred within three months so that Walker could take a batch with him back to Mexico. This would have been a tall order even if Colt had a factory already spitting out pistols by the dozens. As matters stood, he had no factory, no machinery, and no men. He did not even have one of his old pistols on hand to help him fabricate the new one. (He later said he had to advertise in newspapers to acquire one, though there is no evidence of this.) Colt knew the only way he could come close to meeting Walker's deadline was to piggyback on the operations of an already thriving armory.

Within days of meeting Walker, Colt had approached Eli Whitney Jr., the twenty-seven-year-old son of the late cotton-gin inventor and gun manufacturer, to discuss having his pistols made at the Whitney Armory on the outskirts of New Haven, in Whitneyville. Eli Jr. may have lacked his father's genius for invention, but he ran a profitable armory, manufacturing serviceable if uninspired muskets by the thousands for the US Army. "Be kind enough to inform me if you have machinery suited to the manufacture of my repeating pistols," Colt had written to Whitney in December, "and if so would you like to undertake the manufacture of a few thousand for service immediately." After some initial hesitation, Whitney agreed to Colt's proposition. In return for all expenses plus a $3,000 bonus, Whitney would put his men and machines at Colt's disposal.

Along with the machines already in use at the Whitney Armory, Colt required new machines and tools. Like Eli Whitney Sr. half a century earlier, he had to make or otherwise acquire these before he could start producing guns. It was an "everlasting job," he wrote to Walker on January 18, as it began to dawn on him just how daunting and expensive this undertaking was going to be. "I shalnot save one dollar out of the contract for 1,000 but for this I care nothing."

Walker had come to share Colt's low opinion of the bureaucrats in the Ordnance Department, but he encouraged Colt to look to the future. "I repeat the assurance that I have always given that your arms would be in great demand. . . . But it is useless for me to waste any more time in argument with a set of asses to convince them of the importance of getting your arms. I flatter myself that the best argument I can use will be in the field."

*   *   *

On February 26, 1847, Walker and a hundred or so recruits boarded a train in Baltimore and started for Newport Barracks in Kentucky. Here Walker would gather horses and train his men before deploying south. "I arrived here today all safe and sound," Walker wrote on March 6, 1847. "I have a fine set of young men and all I want now is the arms. . . . There is nothing now not even a Female that gives me so many thoughts."

Walker wrote again two weeks later. "Do for heavens Sake rush things as rapidly as possible and send me some of the Pistolls immediately. I want to commence drilling my men on horse back with them. . . . Everything now is depending on you."

At the end of March, Walker and his men boarded a steamboat to begin their voyage south, via the Ohio and Mississippi. They were destined for Veracruz, a port city on the Gulf coast of Mexico, a thousand miles south of New Orleans, to join General Winfield Scott's march on Mexico City. As the men drifted downriver, the women of the town lined the shore, waving handkerchiefs until the ship passed out of sight. "They of course expect to hear a good account of us," Walker wrote to Colt from aboard the steamboat, "and I am in great hopes of receiving some of your Pistols very soon so that I may not disappoint them."

Walker posted several more letters from New Orleans urging Colt to make haste. He wrote once more, on April 28, to inform Colt he expected to leave for the "Seat of War" on May 1. "I have nothing more to write than merely to reexpress my hope that you will make some arrangement to forward my Pistols direct to Vera Cruz."

III

For all of Walker's entreaties, and all of Colt's promises, the pistols were not remotely close to completion. Colt was besieged by difficulties, frustrations, and delays. In addition to getting his machines and dies (patterns) set for milling the revolvers, he'd been stood up by suppliers. A company in Windsor Locks, Connecticut, hired to make unfinished steel cylinders was slow in sending them, and when the cylinders finally arrived in New Haven, a fifth were too brittle to drill for chambers. Colt had enough experience with metals by now to identify the problem as too much carbon in the steel. He advised the company, Slate & Brown, to "anneal" the metal—that is, to heat it gently to reduce carbon content and increase ductility, making it softer and more pliable. He also suggested that they pack it in "common wood ashes & soft wrought iron turning" to leach out some of the carbon.

At the start of June, the first batch of pistols, 220 for Walker's rifle company, was at last complete. Another month passed as an inspector put the revolvers through numerous tests. Not until June 26 were they ready for shipment.

The gun that emerged from Whitneyville was far from perfect. It was too freakishly large to endure as any kind of standard firearm. The weight made it unmanageable for anyone who lacked a horse to carry it and a strong arm to aim it, and the length made it hard to stow in standard holsters. The fist-size cylinder was so large that soldiers often made the mistake of overloading the chambers with powder and blowing the whole thing up, and the loading lever, convenient as it was, tended to pop out of its catch with every recoil. Nonetheless, the Colt Walker was a remarkable handgun, the most efficient and powerful multicharge killing machine that had ever been produced.

If you could put aside its purpose—to shoot Mexicans—the Colt Walker was also a handsome object of brushed steel and black walnut, endowed with the kind of unfussy, clean-lined elegance that modernist American designers would embrace in the next century. Each finished gun was stamped with a serial number and the name of the rifle company for which it was destined. On the cylinders was the faint depiction, made by the highly regarded New York engraver Waterman Lilly Ormsby, of the Texas Rangers' fight against the Comanche in June of 1844. Like the engravings on Paterson pistols, these would ensure the authenticity of Colt's guns, while also reminding users of a scene already fixed in Texas legend and crystallizing into American myth.

Altogether, nearly eleven hundred Colt Walkers were made at the Whitney armory. In addition to the thousand ordered by the army, Colt ran off approximately eighty-five for himself. He intended to sell some of these on the public market, but he also intended to give many away. He had adopted the practice of giving away guns while at Paterson, but with this batch he undertook a campaign of strategic largesse that was to become as crucial to his brand as the guns themselves. By putting his guns in the right hands—"influencers," as advertising professionals would later call such people—he boosted their popularity. More immediately, he bought himself leverage, for with every quid came a quo—a favor, a written endorsement, an introduction to some other powerful influencer.

In the short term, according to Colt, he made no profit on the guns. "I got 28,000 dollars for the first 1000 arms," he would recall some years later.

"They cost me about what it came to, a little more or less." But on July 13, Secretary Marcy sent orders to the Ordnance Department to contract with Colt for a thousand more pistols. This was another small order, much smaller than Colt would have preferred, but it was enough to give him the confidence he needed to plan for the future. Now he just needed a place of his own to make his guns.

IV

Colt had been thinking about building an armory since the start of the year. As far back as January, when he was hammering out the design of the Colt Walker and convincing Eli Whitney Jr. to lend him machines and men, he had solicited his father for capital to build one. For some reason, he persisted in believing that Christopher had money to spare for such a venture. "I regret my Son, that it is not in my power to assist you," wrote Christopher, now sixty-six years old and in continuing poor health. "I should be wanting in duty to myself in my present infirm state to part with the little I possess."

Colt then tried his aunt Ethelinda Selden, sister of Christopher and mother of Dudley. Of the one-eighth interest in Colt's patent right that her late husband, Joseph, had purchased back in 1835, Ethelinda had inherited half, or one-sixteenth (the other sixteenth having gone to Dudley). In a letter to Ethelinda, ostensibly about the terms for leasing her portion of the patent, Colt tried to sell her on the idea of investing in an armory. "I am perfectly satisfied that money can be made out of them should the War with Mexico continue & if you will aid in their manufacture I am certain that you will be repaid handsomely." Conversely, her share of the patent would be "not worth a farthing" unless some way could be found to make guns. "The premium in my judgement is a mere matter of moonshine to what you could realize if the business can be started & carried on as it ought to be with our own means."

George Selden, one of Dudley's brothers, responded on their mother's behalf. "My mother desires me to say in answer that under no circumstances can she engage in the manufacturing however promising the prospects may be." Others might have taken this as a definitive rejection by the Seldens. Not Colt. Instead, he wrote to Dudley to propose that *he* invest in the armory; a mere $7,000 would be sufficient to raise a suitable building in New York.

When Selden declined, Colt let the matter rest awhile, then tried again. "The more I have thought on the subject the more I am convinced that New York is of all others the place for such an establishment as I propose putting up & if you will aid me in accomplishing the object I will be exceedingly obliged." Selden again declined. Having lost some $10,000 on Colt's first gun business, and having then been paid in worthless Submarine Battery stock for John C. Colt's defense, Selden was understandably reluctant to get embroiled in another costly Colt debacle. How could he know that this scheme was the one that was going to make Colt rich?

In the end, Colt settled on a place in Hartford. A four-story brick building on Pearl Street, belonging to "Old Mr. Brinley," became available for just $250 per year. Even better, Colt found a cousin in Hartford, Elisha Colt, willing to supply him with the capital he needed to convert the former twine factory into a gun armory. The son of one of Christopher's brothers, Elisha was cashier of the Hartford Exchange Bank; within a year, he would be the bank's president. The cousins worked out a line of credit for Sam "not to exceed . . . fourteen thousand dollars." It was not much, but it was enough to get going.

The move to Pearl Street was a homecoming of sorts. The building was two blocks from the Main Street shop where Anson Chase had worked on Colt's first pistol and a short walk from the home, at 229½ Main Street, where Colt's father and stepmother still lived. Lydia Sigourney, having moved off Lord's Hill some years earlier, was nearby, as were many other familiar faces. But much had changed in Hartford since Colt's youth. The population—13,500 in the 1850 census—was nearly triple what it had been in 1820 and would double again in the next ten years. The railroad had come in 1839, passing by Lord's Hill and blanketing its once bucolic charms under smoke and ash.

Hartford grew rapidly in the 1840s for the same reason many American cities did. Immigrants from Europe, displaced by famine and war, had begun pouring into the United States in search of better lives, and many of them settled in urban areas. At the same time, steam power had improved and become a safe and affordable alternative to water power. Factories no longer had to be located next to streams or rivers. They could operate anywhere, and cities, with large pools of labor and ready transportation—turnpikes, ships, and now train lines—were the natural settings for them. A year before Colt's return to Hartford, James L. Howard & Co. had built the first big factory on Asylum Street, near Lord's Hill. Between 1848 and 1850, at least four new factories would open, including Tracy & Fales, manufacturers of railroad cars, and Woodruff & Beach, an ironworks that made boilers and other large machinery.

For his armory Colt had considered not only New York, but Boston, Northampton, and even St. Louis. Hartford made the most sense for Colt, and not because it happened to be his childhood home. No other place in America had more metal-cutting know-how than the Connecticut River Valley, and no other people knew more about making guns than Connecticut Yankees.

The first guns produced on Pearl Street were stitched together from unused Whitney parts, including cocks, springs, and cylinders that had been milled and drilled for Colt Walkers but never found a place in one of them. Adding new parts to the old, Colt made about 240 of these "transition" guns. Then he turned to the new government order for a thousand guns, to be known as dragoons because they were intended for mounted horsemen. To make these revolvers more manageable, they were about an inch and a half shorter in the barrel than the Colt Walkers, a quarter inch shorter in the cylinder, and several ounces lighter.

By September of 1847, orders were coming in from gun dealers, soldiers, and private citizens. One of the first came, indirectly, from President Polk; he wanted a pair of revolvers to give to his brother, an army officer who was "exceedingly anxious" to acquire them. Another came from William C. Fink of San Antonio, who wanted twenty-four revolvers and twenty-four rifles for "Surveyors and Officers in the Frontier Regiment." Junius Boyle of the US Navy had been ordered to Mexico and had searched in vain for a Colt revolver; he requested that one be sent as soon as possible. W. D. Lee was on his way to Veracruz and hoped to take some guns with him to sell. A newspaper publisher in Hickman, Kentucky, Jesse Leigh, desired "to be placed in possession (at the earliest possible period) of a pair of your new modelled repeating pistols, of a size not too large to be carried about one's person, yet large enough to be relied upon in any emergency." Leigh wanted Colt to know that he was a man of some influence in Hickman, and quite a fine shot, too. "Do not send me an article that will sometimes fire and sometimes fail and sometimes carry the ball directly forward, and at other times throw it to the right or left of the object. I have any quantity of such pistols on hand already."

V

Samuel Walker would be long dead before the Whitney pistols made it into the hands of his rifle company. Impediments of war and bureaucracy held up their shipment even after they passed inspection by the Ordnance Department. When they were finally sent to Veracruz, they languished at the government depot for months as Walker waited for them in vain.

Walker did finally receive a special pair meant just for him, a gift from Colt. When these reached him in the fall of 1847, he was posted with his company a hundred miles inland from Veracruz, at the town of Perote, inside an eighteenth-century Spanish-built fortress known as Perote Castle. Americans occupied the fortress and the surrounding territory, but Mexican insurgents harassed the supply lines between Veracruz and Mexico City, which had been captured by General Winfield Scott on September 14. The assignment of Walker and his men was to stop the insurgents. With his background as a Texas Ranger, Walker was exceptionally well suited to the task.

The capture of Mexico City had been an important victory, but the war was losing support in the United States. Many young American men had died for what was, it had to be admitted even by those who supported it, the conquest of a weak but sovereign nation to take its land. Making all this harder to swallow were the stories trickling north into the press of inglorious acts. A disproportionate share of these were blamed on Texas Rangers, which may have been scapegoating on the part of the regular army but was also probably deserved. Walker himself had been charged with condoning barbarity, owing to his practice of never returning from scouting expeditions with prisoners.

On the night of October 5, 1847, Walker wrote his brother to say he was heading out in the morning, under the command of General Joseph Lane, to confront Santa Anna's army of eight thousand men, at the pass at Pinar, some fifty miles west of Perote. "If I had my Revolving Pistols I should feel strong hopes for capturing him or killing him. I have written three times to different officers at Vera Cruz to forward them and two caravans have come up since they arrived at Vera Cruz, but I have no hope of getting them until Jack Hays comes up. I have also made repeated applications to go for them but without success."

At least he now had his own pair, he told his brother, even if his men did not have theirs. "There is not an officer who has seen them but what speaks in the highest terms of them and all of the Cavalry officers are determined to get them if possible."

Four days later, Walker was about fifty miles west of Perote when General Lane received intelligence that Santa Anna's army was in the town of Huamantla, on the road to Mexico City. Lane sent Walker and about sixty mounted men ahead as shock troops and scouts, following with an infantry of more than fifteen hundred.

Walker came upon Huamantla early in the afternoon. Santa Anna was nowhere to be seen, but five hundred Mexican artillerymen and *lanceros* were holding the town. Walker led a charge into the main plaza, where his mounted troops quickly overcame the entrenched Mexicans. In the calm after the battle—this according to the first versions that made it into American newspapers—the frenzied father of a fallen Mexican soldier suddenly rushed into the plaza and stabbed Walker in the back with a lance.

Many versions of the events in Huamantla would appear in the press in coming weeks, and still others would surface later from soldiers who claimed to have been present. In some, the man who killed Walker was not just a grieving and vengeful father but a "celebrated guerilla chief." In others, Walker was shot, not lanced, and killed his attacker with two bullets from his revolver before succumbing to his wounds. Several accounts suggested that he was decapitated by a cannonball, which, if true, makes the next part of the story difficult to imagine. "Although your captain has fallen," Walker reportedly told his men as he died, "never surrender, my boys." Another newspaper reported Walker's dying words as "Boys, forward, and don't flinch a foot; I know I'm dying, but don't give way," and still another as "Don't surrender, boys, the infantry will soon be here."

The infantry did come. American soldiers retrieved Walker's body and took it back to Perote. But first, enraged by the death of their gallant captain, they unleashed a reign of plunder and terror on Huamantla that would not soon be forgotten by those Mexicans who survived it. That part of the story did not make it into the American newspapers, where the death of Captain Walker was mourned for weeks to come.

VI

Three months after Walker's death, on the morning of Monday, January 24, 1848, a millwright named James Marshall was walking along the raceway of a new sawmill on the American River, in the forested foothills of the western flank of the Sierra Nevada, when a glimmer in the water caught his eye. It was "one of those rare moments," as historian H. W. Brands puts it, "that divide human existence into before and after." Marshall hurried to the cabin where his workers were eating breakfast. "Boys," he announced, "I believe I have found a gold mine."

The discovery of gold in California in January of 1848 was one of the many hard-to-believe coincidences that occurred so regularly and providentially in the United States in the early years of its existence. James K. Polk could not have timed it better if he'd planted the ore in the American River himself. Just over a week after Marshall made his discovery, on Wednesday, February 2, 1848, Mexican and American officials, ignorant of events in the Sierra Nevada, signed the Treaty of Guadalupe Hidalgo. For a bargain price of $15 million the United States took possession of more than half a million square miles of Mexico, including the largest prize of all, California. Adding this to Texas and Oregon, the United States was now half a million square miles—33 percent—larger than it had been when Polk became president three years earlier.

Most historians agree that the Civil War became inevitable the day the treaty to end the Mexican War was signed. It suddenly made pressing the future of slavery. What sort of land would this new territory be—slave, free, or some combination thereof? Heretofore, the nation had handled slavery mainly by kicking the can of worms down the road, but it now became clear that no peaceful way—no compromise, no law—could solve this issue.

The appropriation of Mexican lands also sealed the fate of Native Americans in the west. The tribes of the plains and the mountains had lived in awareness of whites to the east, but aside from their diseases and liquor, the whites had not yet presented a serious threat. That would change now.

Sam Walker was dead, but Sam Colt's time had come at last. As he wrote in a letter to an old friend that December, "Now is the time to make money."

CHAPTER THIRTEEN

Oh! This California

1848–50

*In the 1850s, Colt commissioned the famous western artist
George Catlin to integrate revolvers into a series of paintings. This lithograph,
based on one of Catlin's works, shows the artist hunting buffalo with a Colt.*

I

Not until late summer of 1848 would news of gold arrive in the east. "We have received some late and interesting intelligence from California," the *New York Herald* would inform its readers that September. "It relates to the important discovery of a very valuable gold mine." Two days later, in more fulsome detail, the *Herald* would follow up with facts "stranger than fiction," as its California correspondent acknowledged. "Were I a New Yorker, instead of a Californian, I would throw aside your paper and exclaim, 'Bennett had better fill his paper with, at least, probable tales and stories, and not such outrageous fictions of rivers, flowing with gold.'" Yet it was all true. Men were collecting gold worth $5 to $30—even $100—in a day. "Oh! this California, to what will it come at last?"

At the start of 1848 Colt had no way of knowing what was coming to California, but he spent the year preparing as if he did. The Pearl Street plant was turning out guns now, dozens a day. This was a minuscule output compared to that of large private armories such as Whitney's and Simeon North's, but even this slow start worked to Colt's advantage. After the urgency at Whitneyville, he could assemble his company with a little circumspection. "I must creep before I walk and am compelled to be mighty carful how I involve myself," he wrote to an old friend, C. B. Zabriskie.

The greatest mistake of his past, Colt believed, had been ceding control of his business to others, and he did not intend to repeat it. The new enterprise was to be a company but not a corporation; there would be no charter, no stock sale, and no one to tell him what to do. "I am working on my own hook and have sole control and management of my business," he told Zabriskie. No longer would he be "subject to the whims of a pack of dam fools and knaves styling themselves a board of directors."

Compared to the state-sanctioned, board-approved launch of the P.A.M.C. in 1836, the establishment of this new company appeared informal and improvised, Colt staffing more or less ad hoc. But in this way the armory became a kind of bodily extension of Colt himself. Almost everyone he hired to help manage the business and sell guns was related to him by blood, marriage, or long bonds of acquaintance. Along with his cousin Elisha, who would assume some management responsibilities, and his younger brother James, who would come and go over the next decade, Colt brought in his stepmother's brother, Luther P. Sargeant, as a secretary and manager. Zabriskie, an army surgeon who had done some selling for Colt back in the Paterson days, again became a kind of agent, to be paid on commission. The factory work was carried out by forty to fifty employees, many of whom Colt knew from Paterson or Whitneyville, some of whom he'd poached to Hartford with offers of better pay.

As important to Colt as the men in his direct employ were several others whose relationship with him is harder to pin down. They came, almost inevitably, from Texas. Among these was Ben McCulloch, the most celebrated Texas Ranger after Samuel Walker and John Coffee Hays. Though McCulloch had not participated in the famous Battle of Walker's Creek, he had been at just about every other major engagement in Texas. Like Walker and Hays, he was a man of action rather than words, impassive in the face of danger and a fierce and able fighter. Unlike them, McCulloch looked the part of a Texan, over six feet tall, with a prominent forehead and wide jaw.

McCulloch began corresponding with Colt in March of 1848, after receiving a gift of pistols from the Whitneyville batch. Now came the part where Colt asked for something in return: "I wish you would write the President a strong letter expressing your opinion of the value of these arms in Mexico and our frontiers, taking good care to state incidents in which you may know where their merits have been tested. Do this at once that he may have time to ponder over before I reach Washington, and have for me a copy of your letter." The tone of Colt's address in this and other such letters is striking. He seems to be not so much asking a favor as giving an order. A few days later, McCulloch did as Colt directed and wrote to Polk.

Colt's most important ally in Washington during the years after the Mexican War was a US senator from Nacogdoches named Thomas Jefferson Rusk. At forty-four, Rusk was a Texas legend, nearly as lauded as his fellow senator Sam Houston. Before entering the Senate, Rusk had been a general under Houston at the Battle of San Jacinto and, later, secretary of war of the Texas Republic. In 1838, he led a command to drive Cherokee Indians out of Texas. Unlike Houston, who had a soft spot for Indians and counted some as friends, Rusk never met an Indian he did not want to kill.

Rusk could be an intimidating man, "blunt, frank, and out-spoken," as the *New York Times* would put it. Daniel Webster considered him to possess one of the finest minds in the Senate. Despite his determination and intelligence, he was subject to fits of volatility and intemperance. "In early life he frequently gave way to ungovernable temporary spells of dissipation wherein he lost his usual command over himself," as one account described him. "While in them, his friends often feared that he would injure himself with weapons, and were careful as far as possible to keep them out of his reach." Rusk would in fact take his own life, in 1857, with a rifle shot to the head, but in 1848 he was at the height of his powers as the forceful chairman of the Senate's Committee on Military Affairs.

Rusk had thrown his support behind Colt's firearms two years earlier, when he introduced a resolution calling on the military to purchase two hundred Colt repeating rifles for the war with Mexico. Colt wrote to thank the senator for his support, and Rusk wrote back to assure Colt that he would do all he could to promote Colt's guns, "believing as I do that they are the most effective weapon of the kind that has been invented."

In the spring and summer of 1848, Rusk again pushed for a large order of Colt firearms by the Department of War. He introduced bills in the Senate to provide funds for the purchase and he sang the gun's praises. There remained numerous obstacles to Rusk's efforts, however. The greatest of these, always, was the Ordnance Department. During the operation of the P.A.M.C., the department's opposition had been personified by Colonel George Bomford. Now Bomford's even more inimical successor, Colonel George Talcott, was undermining Colt at every turn.

Colt's suspicion that Talcott was out to get him was confirmed on April 5, 1848, when the Ordnance Department reported its most up-to-date opinion of Colt's guns: they were too expensive and "peculiarly liable to the accident of simultaneous discharge from two or more chambers at once." Colonel Talcott allowed that special circumstances, such as a "bold man" encountering a superior force, might favor the Colt revolver, but then added—with a dig at Colt's now well-known association with Texas Rangers—"whoever supposes that placing a Colt's pistol in the hands of an ordinary soldier will make him a 'Jack Hays,' will be disappointed."

Rusk buoyed Colt with encouragement. "The subject of your arm is now in a fair way to come fully before the Country. The advantages which will result from its use; the popularity which it will certainly gain in the Service, will render it a very easy matter, to afford you, thro' Congress, that additional compensation to which I know you will be entitled."

But the greatest service Rusk did Colt in 1848 was to provide a rationale for his revolvers even as the conclusion of the Mexican War obviated the urgent need for them. Subduing the Mexicans, Rusk argued, solved only half the threat facing westerners. He explained himself that August in a letter to Polk, urging the president to support the adoption of Colt's guns, not just in Texas and Mexico but in California and Oregon:

> Having spent many years of my life on the frontier, and seen the effects of Indian hostilities on its defenseless inhabitants and having a large extent of frontier in the State of Texas exposed to the depredations of faithless, if not hostile Indians, I have felt it to be my duty to use my efforts to have placed upon the frontier that sort of efficiently armed force which will effectually hold the Indians in check. And being fully impressed that the Revolving Pistol is the only arm calculated to effect that object, I have so repeatedly called upon you, that I fear I may be considered annoying on again presenting the Subject. . . . If the Indians are to be held in check upon the frontier, in California and Oregon, to arm our mounted force with this arm would be the most effectual mode of doing it.

This was a remarkable declaration at the time. Beyond the special case of Texas and the Comanche, little violence had occurred on the trans-

Mississippi frontier, and Rusk would be long dead before the great battles there began. Yet he was accurately anticipating the future of the American west, both the conflict between whites and Native Americans and the part Colt's guns would play in this. In many ways, his prophecy would be self-fulfilling.

II

Official confirmation of gold finally arrived in Washington in late November of 1848, brought by an envoy from the territorial government of California. James K. Polk, who would soon be handing over the presidency to Zachary Taylor, made special mention of the discovery in his final annual message to Congress, on December 5, 1848, offering it as evidence that his expansion of the nation's borders had been worth the effort. "The accounts of the abundance of gold in that territory," wrote Polk, "are of such an extraordinary character as would scarcely command belief were they not corroborated by the authentic reports of officers in the public service."

A week later, Colt petitioned Congress to issue him a contract for more guns. Pointing out that several private armories received orders for "rifles and pistols of old-fashioned construction" from ten to fifteen thousand, and as high as thirty thousand, guns at a time, he suggested Congress direct an order of five thousand or ten thousand. Colt's petition was accompanied by seventy letters of endorsement from high-ranking military officers and other prominent men of war and politics—the harvest of all those guns Colt had handed out over the years.

Again, the Ordnance Board thwarted Colt. On December 21, Colonel Talcott sent a new review of Colt's pistols to the Capitol, reminding Congress that the board held the same objections it had expressed the last time it inspected them. "The capacity of continuous fire is an advantage which they consider as greatly overrated. In special cases such a weapon may be advantageous, but it will be found that this will be the case with individuals, not of large bodies." The board did acknowledge that Colt firearms had improved since 1841, "but they desire to re-assert here their previous opinion that these repeating arms are neither suitable, or safe for the Armament of troops."

Two days after Christmas, the Texas senators Thomas Rusk and Sam Houston called on Secretary Marcy to insist that he order Colt's pistols for the army, no matter the opinion of Colonel Talcott and the Ordnance Board. Secretary Marcy "reiterated all the prejudice shown by Col. Talcott, and said much that he would have been ashamed to place upon paper," Rusk later related to Colt. "I saw that politeness and reason were all lost upon him, and I did not measure very carefully what I said to him." As Rusk rose angrily to leave Marcy's office, the secretary called him back. He promised the senator that he intended to do what was right. Rusk responded forcefully, "I told him he ought at once to arm every soldier upon the frontier with your pistols and prevent a general Indian war."

That same afternoon, Sam Houston also wrote to Colt to describe the rancorous meeting with the secretary, albeit in more neutral terms: "No conclusion was come to on the matter." Houston had become acquainted with Colt during a visit to Hartford in March of 1848, and he now addressed him as an old friend: "When will you be here? When you do come, if you have a small pistol, or will soon have one made of choice quality, I wish you to bring it with you as I wish to purchase one."

"May you have a happy New Year," Houston ended his letter to Colt. "Get married and lie warmer Sam!"

III

Colt was no closer to marriage, but signs of romantic entanglements occasionally surfaced, if only in hints. One of these came at the start of 1849 in a letter from his old friend John Howard Payne, the celebrated lyricist of "Home, Sweet Home." "My dear Colt, A Happy New Year!—where are you?"

Since the trial of John C. Colt, when Payne had testified and otherwise lent his fame to Sam's efforts to save John from execution, the two men had stayed in touch, exchanging greetings and occasionally scratching each other's back. Payne had helped Colt with introductions to President Tyler and other useful men; Colt had lent money to the perpetually impoverished Payne. Especially in the wake of John's death, Payne felt affection and admiration for Colt, praising Sam for his fidelity as a brother and his generosity as a friend. "I have myself shared the benefits of that deep and unconquerable devotedness so rare," he wrote to Colt, "and which in you has risen in some particulars above mere chivalrousness, even to the sublimest honorific." Payne had been away from the United States for several years after John's death, serving as the American consul to Tunis, but he was back home now, and he and Colt had resumed their friendship.

What brought Payne to take up his pen at the start of 1849 was a conversation he'd recently had with Colt in Washington regarding a certain artist friend of Payne's, Miss Freeman. It seems that Colt had agreed to hire Miss

Freeman for a painting, and now Payne wanted to nail down the details of the commission. He was visiting New York, where Colt had promised to call on him. The time of their proposed meeting had come and gone but Colt had not appeared. Hence, "where are you?"

As Payne explained in his letter, he and Miss Freeman had devised a plan for her to execute the painting at limited cost to herself and Colt. She would travel to Hartford from New York and find lodging in a hotel. After several days, she would call on Lydia Sigourney, an old friend of her father's. Sigourney, being the generous poet she was, would surely offer Miss Freeman an invitation to stay with her, and Miss Freeman would accept, thus procuring free room and board while she carried out Colt's commission.

All was set, then; Payne just needed confirmation from Colt to proceed. "The fact is, I am in a very awkward position concerning this matter," Payne wrote in his cramped but meticulous hand. He'd asked Miss Freeman to delay taking on another commission in Syracuse to go to Hartford. "Pray let me know distinctly what is to be done."

At first blush, Payne's letter appears to be a thoughtful if somewhat pushy attempt to bring together two friends for their mutual benefit—Colt to get a painting he wanted, Freeman to get a commission she needed. On closer inspection, though, the lyricist's inquiry is fraught with unspoken complications and intrigues. For one thing, Miss Freeman—her full name was Anna Mary Freeman—was a beautiful twenty-three-year-old English ingenue, and Payne was desperately in love with her. She had told him she enjoyed the company of older men, but Payne, balding and sagging at fifty-seven, was not quite foolish enough to believe her. "I tried to forget that I was growing old till I got tired of the trouble," he had written to Colt several years earlier. "I am throwing off all disguises either to my own eyes or to those of other people and am beginning to feel and to show myself as I really am."

Despite his brave attempt to face facts, Payne was desperate to win Miss Freeman's affections. But alas, he was not only too old, he was too poor. His song had made him famous but not rich, and he had come home from Tunis with debts and no immediate prospects for income. "I have pawned away all my pawnable articles, and have no means left to keep off those little persecutions," he'd written to Colt. All he had to offer Miss Freeman was his good name and his prominent friends. Having sold her services to Colt, Payne now had to close the deal. He assured Colt that he could "rely on my arranging all with due regard to your dignity."

The meaning of that last phrase is brought into relief by the specific art to which Anna Mary Freeman applied herself. She was a miniaturist: she painted portraits, usually watercolor on ivory, small enough to fit in the palm of a hand. Unlike normal-size portraits on canvas, miniatures were not meant for walls and public viewing. They were to be held close to the body, in a locket or tiny oval frame, and taken out for private communion. Generally, the subject of a miniature was a cherished loved one, absent or dearly departed. But miniatures had a special currency among romantic partners, particularly partners in illicit liaisons. They were private—sometimes so private that the painter obscured or simply left out the subject's face to avoid identification lest the miniature fall into the wrong hands. Daniel Webster was said to keep a miniature of his mistress that showed only her nude torso, waist to neck.

Did Colt have a special subject in mind for Miss Freeman? Or someone to whom he intended to send a miniature of himself? Was the "dignity" Payne promised a reference to the delicacy of the commission? The questions suggest more than any facts support, but they are not baseless given other hints that occasionally surfaced from Colt's life. He was now a thirty-four-year-old bachelor, an unusual status in the middle of the nineteenth century. At least one woman was a likely romantic partner—Caroline—and there were clearly others, perhaps even "a woman in every port," as James Colt once chided Sam. Did this miniature pertain to one of them?

Whatever the facts, Colt never followed through on his offer to commission Miss Freeman. Either the opportunity or Colt's interest passed, and John Howard Payne's efforts to please his young female friend came to nothing.

A short while later, Colt upset Payne again by insulting him. Payne had abashedly asked Colt for money, and Colt abruptly suggested that Payne earn it by using his newspaper contacts and literary skills to submit positive notices of Colt's guns to newspapers. Payne was taken aback by his old friend's tone: "I must frankly own that the unconfiding style of your answer to my suggestion concerning an arrangement for Washington . . . somewhat surprised me;—still, it is no more than natural that business subjects should be treated in a merely business manner, without distinction of persons, and therefore I answer you in the same spirit." Payne told Colt that "the thing could be done, if with the trouble and the occasional sacrifice of pride."

Payne needed money more than pride, and he evidently did Colt's bidding, but their correspondence ended after that. Payne went back to Tunis to try to retrieve some money he had lost, and there he would die two years later, still famous but still impoverished, and still unloved by Miss Anna Mary Freeman.

IV

Colt may have lost an old friend in 1849, but he gained two allies who would be of incalculable value to him. The first of these was a young attorney named Edward Nicoll Dickerson. "Ned" Dickerson was the son of Philemon Dickerson, the former congressman and governor of New Jersey, and nephew of Mahlon Dickerson, who had served as secretary of the navy under President Van Buren. (Both Philemon and Mahlon had been helpful to Sam during the launch of the P.A.M.C. in 1836.) Dickerson's name began to appear in Colt's correspondence in 1848, when he was just twenty-four and embarking on his law practice. He would soon play an important role in protecting Colt's patents and become, for a while, one of Colt's closest and most trusted confidants. Eventually, he would be one of the most famous patent attorneys in the United States.

The other figure who came into Colt's life in 1849 was Elisha King Root. Colt and Root would never be particularly close; other than machines and guns, it is hard to imagine a subject they could converse about at any length. Still, their relationship was to be extraordinarily beneficial to both.

It would be more accurate to say that Root came *back* into Colt's life in 1849, like a character in a Dickens novel, some twenty years after their first chance meeting. Born in Ludlow, Massachusetts, in 1808, Root had been a bobbin boy in textile factories around New England, and then, starting at the age of fifteen, an apprentice in the machine shop of the mill in Ware. On July 4, 1829, when Root was twenty-one, he'd attended Colt's debacle on Ware Pond. He was the hero who stepped in to save fourteen-year-old Sam from the angry drenched mob.

If this really were a Dickens novel, Root would have vanished after that first episode, only to reappear, out of the blue, at the precise moment Colt needed him. That is not quite how it happened, though. The men almost certainly crossed paths between 1829 and 1849, including during Colt's Connecticut River Valley factory tour (with Pliny Lawton) in the spring of 1836. Moreover, Root was married to Colt's cousin Mathilda Colt, the sister of Elisha Colt, so he was family of a sort.

Even lacking these points of connection, Root would have been known to Colt. He had achieved a widespread reputation as the chief overseer at the Collins ax factory in Chicopee, Massachusetts, where he not only supervised the cutting of new ax blades but developed precision lathes and milling machines. A Colt company biography later described Root as "endowed with a rare and searching mind and great powers of observation." He seemed to have an almost mystical affinity for machinery. When a large and complicated machine broke down at the Collins factory, and no one could figure out how to fix it, Root pulled up a stool and stared at the machine for the better part of a day, as if in meditation. He went to supper, then came back and stared at it a while longer that night. "The next morning the silent communion was resumed. Soon the clouds broke. Without a word, Mr. Root went to his desk and dashed off a sketch . . . that produced the needed notions by a few simple contrivances."

Along with his mechanical genius, Root was considered a genuinely decent fellow, not only respected for his skill but admired for his temperament. He was straightforward, unassuming, honest, and prudent—all qualities Colt lacked but recognized as valuable. The challenge for Colt was convincing Root to leave his job. Root was content at Collinsville, supervising the entire factory for a fine annual salary of $2,000. He had been offered lucrative and important jobs in the past, by the Springfield armory and the US mint, among other suitors, but had turned them down. Colt told Root to name his salary. Better yet, Colt offered him an opportunity to reenvision machine production at a far grander and more complex scale than he'd ever find at an ax factory. Even then, Root would probably have stayed where he was had Samuel Collins himself not insisted he leave the ax factory and take up Colt's generous offer "as a matter of duty to himself and his family."

Within a few years of joining Colt, Root would be making more than $5,000 a year, every dollar of it well earned. As one early twentieth-century historian wrote, "The credit for the revolver belongs to Colt; for the way they were made, mainly to Root."

Root arrived in Hartford at a moment of critical transformation for Colt's gun business. After a year on Pearl Street, the company moved, in 1849, into larger quarters, on Grove Lane, in a building owned by a wealthy Hartford landowner named Solomon Porter. With the move, and under Root's supervision, the company upgraded its technology. A correspondent from the *Hartford Courant* described the new factory as "a museum of curious machinery, of ingeniously contrived instruments and tools," employing a kind of rudimentary assembly line, years before that term would come into usage. "Every part of the pistol passes through an almost endless variety of hands; each one with his peculiar machine, performing some particular portion of the work." Colt now employed seventy men but the number was rising and would be more than twice that in months. "He has a dozen orders for every pistol he can furnish. Thousands are ordered from every part of the country, by persons going West and to California."

Later, Colt would claim that 1849 was the first year his guns ever made a profit. Money began to flow into the armory as if a raceway gate had been lifted. As Colt's fortunes rose, so did his fame and reputation. "Probably our city has never produced a genius, the invention and mechanical qualities of whose mind have accomplished results more universally celebrated, or whose inventions have attracted so wide attention and 'made more noise in the world,' than have those of our townsman, MR. SAMUEL COLT."

V

Encomiums to Colt must always be considered with a degree of skepticism, given that Colt planted a lot of them himself. That said, he *did* display a kind of genius in these early months of 1849. A number of his decisions appear obvious in retrospect, but they were high-stakes gambles when Colt made them. These include not only his expansion of the armory, but his commitment to produce five thousand guns for the government, despite the government's failure to indicate it wanted the guns.

And there was this: at the very moment business was gathering steam in the United States and his patent was under attack by a rival gunmaker, Colt decided to leave for Europe. This was a good indication of the scope of his ambition. Going back to his efforts to obtain foreign patents in 1835, he had long cast his sights beyond American shores. But to leave America now was risky, even reckless, and certainly brave.

What made the voyage irresistible to Colt was the promise of even greater riches abroad than at home. By remarkable historical coincidence, 1848, the year the United States underwent the abrupt territorial expansion that opened a vast new domestic market for Colt, brought a year of violent revolutions against monarchs in much of Europe. The conflagration started in Sicily, swept through Italy, France, and the German states, then through Austria and Hungary and up into Sweden and Denmark, taking in nearly the entire continent before it burned out. While it raged, it created a thirst for firepower in radicals and monarchs alike. Colt's friend George Sanders summarized the situation succinctly in a letter he sent from Europe in March of 1848: "Revolutionary times in Europe. Now is the time for you to make money."

James Colt, writing to Sam in September of 1848, framed the motive for the voyage in more grandiose terms: nothing less than democracy itself called for Sam to go. "I believe that there will be an uprooting of all old party lines and a new order of things will spring up," James pronounced. It was only a matter of time before modern American political ideals replaced old-fashioned monarchial practices, and Sam's task was to supply the means. "Why has it been your destiny to invent weapons of destruction?" James rhetorically wondered. "The age calls for them. Democracy must spread over the world. . . . Cities will be burned, large armies will be equipped and blood will flow. And upon the ruin and devastation and bones of slaughtered men, will arise the morning star of progressive republicanism."

Wittingly or not, James was echoing views associated with Young America, a political movement that gained many proponents in the United States in the mid-nineteenth century. Young America took its name from youth groups that had sprung up in Europe over the previous two decades—Young Italy, Young Ireland, Young Germany, and others. A diverse collection of journalists, writers (including Nathaniel Hawthorne and Walt Whitman), politicians (most famously Stephen Douglas), and businessmen, the Young Americans did not all adhere to a rigid orthodoxy—many of them disagreed vigorously—but generally they were members of the Democratic Party, subscribers of John O'Sullivan's *Democratic Review*, anti-aristocratic, strongly nationalistic, and proponents of Manifest Destiny.

As originally conceived by O'Sullivan, Manifest Destiny covered the expansion of the United States to the Pacific. But why stop there? Why let oceans, much less other nations' sovereignty, get in the way of America? Many Young Americans supported acquiring, either by purchase or filibustering, more land, in particular the Yucatán, Nicaragua, and most immediately Cuba. Young Americans also championed the export of democratic ideals to Europe and elsewhere as a kind of ideological expansionism.

What made this all so strange is that even as Young Americans embraced revolutionaries who were attempting to overthrow suppressive regimes in Europe, many of them, in some cases unashamedly, backed the perpetuation of slavery in the United States. It was well understood that those newly acquired lands to the south were to enter the union as slave states. Young America did not simply gloss over the liberty/slavery paradox at the heart of the United States; it carried it to soaring new heights of hypocrisy.

Much as Young Americans saw no contradiction in their opinions on liberty and slavery, they happily combined the promulgation of democratic ideals with the avid pursuit of profit. As they saw it, profit *was* an ideal. "Revolutionary times," to borrow the language of Colt's friend George Sanders—himself a leading Young American—may have been something to celebrate as a political matter, but they also were an opportunity "to make money."

By the time Colt boarded the steamship *Europa* on May 2, 1849, he'd arguably missed the boat. The revolutions of 1848 had run their course and almost entirely failed. Revanchist regimes were in power, leaving behind ten thousand dead and little to show for the blood. Fortunately, for Colt, this did not mean the killing was over.

Much about ocean travel had changed since Colt's last overseas voyage, fourteen years earlier. Three times as many ships were coming and going from New York in 1849 as in 1835, and the harbor was now so busy that vessels routinely bashed into each other. The greatest change was not in the number of vessels, though, but in their size and speed. Locally operated steamboats of the sort owned by Cornelius Vanderbilt had been joined by new giant oceangoing behemoths. The age of steam had come to transatlantic travel.

The two-year-old *Europa*, built and managed by Britain's Cunard company, was one of the finest and fastest ships on the ocean. With an eighteen-hundred-horsepower engine fed by sixteen furnaces that consumed sixty tons of coal every day, and huge paddle wheels on each side that could churn over adverse swells but also through the glassy doldrums that brought sailing ships to a halt, the *Europa* cut the passage between New York and Liverpool from an average length of one month to less than two weeks. Steam was transforming the world not just by providing motive power for factories but by connecting people more efficiently. The next decade of Colt's life would not have been possible without transatlantic steamships.

Docking in Liverpool on May 14 after a passage of just twelve days, Colt traveled to London, his first stop to renew and update his patents. In early June, retracing the route he took in 1835, he crossed the Channel to Paris. The city had experienced a wild revolutionary winter and spring in 1848, followed by many more months of violence and political turmoil, including the abdication of King Louis Philippe I. France was now back in the hands of an autocratic government, firmly ruled by Louis Napoléon, nephew of Napoléon Bonaparte. Colt spent six days in Paris, then launched a whirlwind tour through Brussels, Cologne, Hanover, and Brunswick, and finally, on June 11, Berlin, "driving with lightning speed to all the objects of interest."

Colt had left several men to mind his business back home. In Washington was a nephew of former president Polk, J. Knox Walker, whose portfolio included lobbying Congress and entertaining all interested customers in Washington. The armory in Hartford was in the capable hands of Elisha Colt.

In letters to Elisha, Sam veered between the pleasures of a journey through Europe and the business of the gun company. On June 12, from

Berlin, he confessed that he had not had a chance to get around much but promised to give an account in his next letter, "if I can communicate upon paper an idea of so magnificent a city." After working his way south, probably stopping at least briefly in Prague, Colt wrote again. The date was now July 18, the eve of his thirty-fifth birthday. He was in Vienna, soon to head west on the Danube, back toward Paris.

Austria, like France, had been racked by violence and disruption in 1848, only to be restored to tranquility under a conservative government. "This town or rather city is a lovely place & I should like to spend a year here," Colt wrote of Vienna. "The operas the gardens the galleries of paintings the Palaces public buildings are all equal & in some cases surpass anything to be seen elsewhere in Europe, but I have no room to describe them." Colt applied for an Austrian patent in Vienna and became acquainted with the decorative art of Boulle, "a peculiar description of inlaid work," as Colt put it. He ordered several dozen pistol cases in the Boulle style, to be shipped home. He directed Elisha to have some pistols "put up in the most elegant style possible," so they could be submitted to the American Institute in New York, as well as to prestigious exhibitions in Boston, Philadelphia, and "other places where they award gold medals in premium for the best inventions." Europeans loved medals and tributes, Colt had discovered, and winning a few would help promote his arms and make some "noyes" on the continent.

"As yet I have received only two letters from you & I feel very anxious," Sam complained in one of his letters to Elisha. "You must write by every steamer if it be but one line to say that all is well. You must know that I am extremely anxious about every little minutia of our business."

VI

He need not have worried. In August of 1849, inspectors from the credit review agency R. G. Dun & Company (later to evolve into Dun & Bradstreet) visited Colt's armory and reported that it was "making money" and enjoyed "good credit." With a workforce of almost a hundred men, the armory was producing about a hundred revolvers a week. This was not nearly enough to keep up with the surging demand for the guns.

There were plenty of reasons for the demand, but the two that mattered most were gold and Indians. As Colt traveled through Europe, an extraordinary migration was sweeping tens of thousands of people to the far edge of the American continent. *Gold rush*, *forty-niners*, *California fever*—the familiarity of the terms diminishes the enormity of what happened in

1849, when as many as 150,000 people raced one another west. And that was just the beginning. The population of California would rise more than tenfold, from 20,000 to 260,000, between 1848 and 1852. What made this so extraordinary was not the number of people but the haste with which they came. Because the gold was likely to run out, the gold rush was quite literally a *rush*.

For the forty-niners who lived along the Atlantic seaboard and could afford the fare, the preferred method of passage to California was by sea. In the early months of 1849, collections were taken up and companies formed at practically every seaport in the east, from Maine to Georgia, from Boston to Baltimore, to buy or build ships for the voyage around the tip of South America and up the west coast. In New York, so many vessels were leaving for California that the city's bakers could not bake bread fast enough to supply them. Ships were delayed in port as they waited for the bakers to do their work.

The voyage around South America was arduous, tedious, and often dangerous, but it was easier and safer than the overland route taken by more than half the gold rush emigrants. The best argument for going by land was that it cost far less than a sea voyage ($180 to $200 per person compared to $300 to $700) and, assuming all went well, was faster (as little as three months compared to a minimum of four months). For those who intended to settle in California, and not simply scrape out some gold and come back home, it was also the best way to transport cattle and other possessions to the west.

In many respects, the emigrants of 1849 repeated the methods and routes of 1846, albeit in much larger numbers. They congregated in Missouri as the weather warmed, then set out as soon as the spring grass was ready for grazing. Most followed the path that had been established earlier in the decade, west along the Platte River, now in caravans of up to a hundred wagons, dust rising in clouds above them as they entered the treeless grasslands. As always, they were both thrilled and terrified by the possibility of an encounter with Indians. And, as always, no item was deemed more indispensable than a good gun for protection.

While several violent and lethal incidents involving Indians had occurred in years past, and others would occur in 1849, the threats remained overblown. According to one estimate, just two travelers had been killed in 1848. That number would rise to thirty-three in 1849 and forty-eight in 1850. Even if these figures are incomplete, as they probably are, they challenge the idea, popular then and persistent today, that wagon trains were in constant peril from the tribes of the plains. In fact, of an estimated ten thousand emigrants who would die on their way to California and Oregon prior to the Civil War, less than four hundred, or about 4 percent, would be killed by Indians.

For the most part, the whites had more to fear from their own guns than from the Indians. Many of the travelers were easterners and not especially gun savvy. At the first sign of an Indian they lunged for their rifles and often ended up shooting themselves. Only drowning (during the numerous river fordings) caused more accidental deaths than gun mishaps. Notably, nine-tenths of the gun accidents occurred before the emigrants reached the Rockies. This may be explained by safer gun-handling techniques learned on the trail, but it also probably reflected less skittishness in the presence of Indians.

The fear of Indians that many easterners took with them onto the trail, while exaggerated, was not irrational. Indian attacks did not have to happen often to register as a significant concern, and only a foolhardy person went west without a gun. Increasingly, if at all possible, that gun was a Colt revolver. Colts were still rare, but this was quickly changing. They were prevalent enough on the trail by 1849 that an Episcopalian newspaper felt it necessary to point out that some emigrants carried "Bibles, tracts, and religious books," as well as "Colt's revolvers and bowie knives."

If Indian attacks did not generally materialize as feared, the guns found another use. Many a western traveler, at the sight of a buffalo herd passing in the distance, jumped onto a horse and rode off in pursuit with his revolver. Bullets from smaller revolvers often failed to penetrate the thick hides of buffalo, but those from the larger-caliber pistols were powerful enough to kill, and hunting buffalo with a Colt became one of the rites of crossing the continent. So many whites would kill buffalo in coming years that the Indians who depended on the animals for food began to retaliate by killing whites. Thus, in this way and others, the guns accelerated the very threat they had been brought to meet.

By the late summer of 1849—around the same time Colt was making his way south on the Rhine—the California-bound emigrants' journeys were coming to an end. They were descending the western flank of the Sierras into the Sacramento Valley. If they had found the Indians less fierce than anticipated, the greater surprise was the violence they encountered in fellow whites who had beaten them west.

California in the summer of 1849 was rowdy and dangerous. One settler would look back on this period as a time "when the strong, with revolver and bowie knife, were law." Nowhere was this description more apt than in San Francisco. "The town was full of gamblers, thieves, and cut-throats from every quarter of the globe," an early history described the city in 1849.

In 1849, George H. Baker, of Dedham, Massachusetts, sailed to California to join the gold rush. Four years later, he returned to the west coast, this time by land. His illustrations of life on the overland trail captured both the stirring sights and numbing challenges encountered by emigrants. No guns are visible in Baker's engravings, but the constant threat of Indian attacks, perceived or real, made them as necessary to western travelers as food and oxen.

It was a mostly male world of slapped-up saloons, minimal government, and negligible law enforcement. "Every man was law to himself and by midsummer disorder reigned." The disorder was maintained by a vigilante gang known as the Regulators. The gang paraded in the streets with drums and fifes during the days and extorted money, mainly from Chinese and South American gold miners, in the evenings, "spreading terror and dismay among the people." The Regulators drew their membership largely from the motley crew that had sailed out of New York Harbor with Jonathan Drake Stevenson three years earlier, leaving behind a wailing mother and Sam Colt.

William M. Gwin, a former congressman from Mississippi who had come to California with the intention of becoming its first US senator, made a speech in San Francisco's Portsmouth Square that summer of 1849 arguing for legitimate law enforcement in the state. "Let no act of violence pass without prompt punishment. Let it not be said that Colt's revolver is the common law of California." When Gwin did in fact get elected to the Senate that December, Colt would send him a gun. Forgetting his earlier admonishment against law by Colt's revolver, Gwin would respond with a full-throated endorsement. "I will state that Colt's repeating pistols are preferred in California, over any other kind of arms. . . . The Indians in the gorges of the Sierra Nevada are terrified into honest habits, by the miners in that region being armed with these pistols."

One measure of the value Californians placed on Colt revolvers was what they were willing to pay for them. The price of nearly every product was inflated wildly in California in 1849, and especially that of guns. Rifles that cost $13 in New York sold in California for $150. A normal single-shot pistol was $5 in New York and $40 in California. Nowhere was this inflation more evident than in the price of revolvers. A large-caliber Colt that could be had for $38 in New York would set a Californian back $200, according to one eastern newspaper. Another newspaper listed the price as $250, and records indicate that men paid as much as $500 for a Colt in California.

VII

September of 1849 found Colt in Paris, promoting his pistols to the French government. One day he went to Louis Napoléon's palace at Saint-Cloud to shoot revolvers with the new French president, pausing for tea. According to Colt, Louis Napoléon shot more than a hundred rounds and was impressed with the guns.

Order had been restored in Europe by the likes of Louis Napoléon—who would soon have himself crowned emperor of France, as his uncle Napoléon Bonaparte had done half a century earlier—but several revolutionary leaders remained at large despite the best efforts of Europe's governments to capture them. Most notable of these were the Hungarian Lajos Kossuth and two Polish generals, Joseph Bem and Henryk Dembinski, who had fought under Kossuth in the Hungarian Revolution. When these men fled into Turkey, Russia and Austria demanded that the sultan of the Ottoman Empire, Abdulmejid I, hand them over. The sultan refused.

While in Paris that September, Colt cosigned a public letter of support for Kossuth and his generals, addressed to the American minister to Constantinople, Dabney S. Carr. The letter itself was not remarkable. Kossuth had become a hero in the United States, lauded in the press, beloved especially by Young America. But the ease with which Colt turned from sipping tea with Napoléon III to praising revolutionaries was breathtaking.

"Sir, your fellow citizens, Americans in Paris, are filled with indignation and amazement at the attempts now being made by the Russian and Austrian governments to destroy, in cold blood the heroes of the revolution in Hungary," began the letter to Carr. "The persons of Kossuth, Bem and Dembinski . . . are sacred on the neutral ground of Turkey by every law human and divine." The main purpose of the letter was to praise the sultan for standing up to Russia and Austria in protecting these men.

The letter bears all the marks of one of Colt's fellow signatories, George Sanders—the same George Sanders who had beckoned Colt to Europe in 1848 ("Now is the time for you to make money"). Because Sanders signed his name with an elongated *S* that is easily confused for an *L*, Colt biographers have confused him for George M. *Landers*, a rather insipid US congressman and hardware merchant from Connecticut. George N. *Sanders* was many things, but insipid was not one of them.

A native of Kentucky, Sanders was raised in a prominent family and bred horses before turning to a life of politics, journalism, and general scheming. He made a name for himself with his strong advocacy for the annexation of Texas, then stumped for James K. Polk in the election of 1844. After that, he moved east, to New York and Washington, and became an "influence man" for Hudson's Bay Company, which hired him to promote the company's interests. One historian has written of Sanders that his life comprised "a record of frustrated ambitions, misdirected energy, and fleeting notoriety." Much of that notoriety would come in 1854, when Sanders would serve as US consul to London and host a dinner party featuring a guest list of Europe's premiere revolutionaries, including Kossuth and the Italians

Giuseppe Garibaldi and Giuseppe Mazzini, along with the US minister to Britain (and future US president) James Buchanan. After losing his job in the ensuing controversy, Sanders would buy John O'Sullivan's *Democratic Review* and appoint himself its editor. He would find notoriety once again, in 1865, when he'd be accused and arrested—though finally acquitted—as a conspirator in the assassination of Abraham Lincoln.

But all of that was still very much in Sanders's future in 1849. At the moment, he was working for George Law, the owner of a steamship line and himself a conniver of the first order. (Law was one of Cornelius Vanderbilt's most formidable rivals.) Somehow Law had come into possession of fifty thousand surplus US muskets after the Mexican War, and he had given Sanders the task of selling them. For Sanders, who operated at that convenient place where political ideals and personal profit converge, an obvious customer for surplus muskets had been the revolutionaries of 1848. After the revolutions failed, a new customer was needed. Thus, the public letter to Dabney Carr. The intended audience for this letter was not the US consul to Constantinople. It was the sultan, a man who might have use for fifty thousand muskets to defend the Ottoman Empire against the insults of Austria and Russia, and who could afford, not incidentally, to buy them.

The idea of involving Colt in the musket business also apparently came from Sanders. The plan seems to have been that Colt would visit the sultan to show him his revolvers, then put in a good word for George Law's fifty thousand muskets. In other words, Colt was going to Turkey as a multipurpose salesman, both on Law's (and Sanders's) behalf and his own.

Colt's passports were stamped at Marseille on October 31, then stamped again, in Constantinople, on December 5. He probably sailed right up the Bosporus to Dolmabahçe Palace, the new riverside resident of the sultan. The visit was at least a partial success. Colt sold the Sultan fifteen thousand muskets and two hundred revolvers. The sultan gave him, as a gift, a snuff box studded with 375 diamonds. We know about the snuff box because when Colt returned home in January of 1850, he made sure a full description of it was printed in the papers.

VIII

He found his father in poor health that January. Christopher Colt was now sixty-nine years old and had been failing for some time. Even by the standards of the age, when no life was spared hardship, Christopher had endured a great deal. He had lost his first wife and five of his children by her, including, most infamously, John. Both of his children by Olivia were dead now, too, most recently William, the young man who once made the mistake of writing Sam to ask for help in getting a government job. Another son, his namesake, Chris Jr., was dissolute and ill. This left him with two healthy children. James was now a judge in St. Louis. Sam was famous and on the cusp of extraordinary wealth. Such was the tally when Christopher died on April 5, 1850.

America was seventy-four years old and halfway through the nineteenth century. During the thirty-five years of Sam Colt's life the physical size of the country had expanded by more than a million square miles of land. Counted by the census in 1850, the population was over 23 million, three times what it had been when Colt was born in 1814. More than 3 million of those counted were slaves. Exactly *how* these 3 million were to be counted in America, whether they would continue to be slaves or ever be free, now became the question that would decide all others.

CHAPTER FOURTEEN

Guns in the Crystal Palace

1851

The Crystal Palace in 1851.

I

Through the autumn of 1850 and early months of 1851, a structure rose in London's Hyde Park so unlike anything built before that to call it a building seemed a misnomer. That word implied stone, brick, wood, and, in a public edifice such as this, a certain damp and ponderous thickness. What materialized in Hyde Park had neither stone nor brick. It did have wood, but only in its flooring. Its walls—if *walls* was the word for them—were composed of a million glass panels supported by thin iron spars, giving the structure the appearance of an aviary or a giant greenhouse. A greenhouse was in fact the inspiration for Joseph Paxton, the man who designed it; he had been a gardener before he became the most famous architect in England. But it was not a greenhouse, either, this gossamer form billowing over Hyde Park. It was a kind of palace—"a fairy palace,"

271

as one London journalist described it, combining "the lightness of crystal with the abiding strength of iron." That is how it would be known thereafter: the Crystal Palace.

The Crystal Palace was enormous. Its cross-shaped footprint covered more than eighteen acres. The main hall was 1,848 feet long, more than three times the length of St. Paul's Cathedral. The edifice rose to such heights that its builders, rather than cut down a row of fully grown elms in Hyde Park, simply enclosed the trees within its frame and let them grow— just one more extraordinary sight to boggle the millions of minds that would soon arrive to attend the Great Exhibition of the Works of Industry of All Nations. It was for this event—the first-ever world's fair—that the Crystal Palace had been built.

The Crystal Palace opened on May 1, 1851, a sunny Thursday. More than twenty-five thousand visitors came that first day, including Queen Victoria and her husband, Prince Albert, who had done much to spearhead the exhibition. Under the vaulting glass ceiling were one hundred thousand man-made objects from around the world, including silk tapestries, robes of pearls, and a golden saddle. Every bit as jaw-dropping as the decorative wares were thousands of never-before-seen industrial inventions, from typewriters and sewing machines to agricultural implements and factory tools, that hinted at an enchanted future of laborsaving devices. In the center of it all was a giant glass fountain spurting twelve thousand jets of water. "I think the first impression produced on you when you get inside is of bewilderment," wrote a nineteen-year-old visitor named Charles Dodgson, who would someday be known to the world as Lewis Carroll, author of *Alice in Wonderland*. "It looks like a sort of fairyland."

Though billed as an exhibition of human achievements from all over the world, this was the world through a decidedly English looking glass. As its European neighbors ricocheted between violent revolutions and repressive regimes, Britain fairly glowed with peace, prosperity, and progress. Almost with a sense of magnanimity, then, did Britain invite the rest of the world to share in its celebration of human achievement. "Britain was the world's great manufactory; let others come and marvel" is how one historian of the Crystal Palace later explained the British attitude.

Half of the objects on display in the Crystal Palace—everything west of the transom—came from Britain and its "colonial possessions," as the catalog put it. While no other country came close to matching Britain, Europe provided the greater part of the balance, with France alone contributing

1,737 items and Austria 746. Then came the United States of America, with just 534 objects.

The relatively small contribution of the American delegation was excused by several practical challenges. Its items had much farther to travel than European items, for example, and cost more to ship. But the Americans had drawn attention to the scarcity of their displays by asking for more floor space in the Crystal Palace—some forty thousand square feet—than they needed. Nor did it help that the Russian delegation, slated to occupy the space to the immediate west, had been delayed in getting to the exhibition, leaving the Americans alone at the eastern end of the hall, surrounded by a Siberian vastness. The overwhelming first impression made by the American section was, to use the word most often applied to it by the London press, "meager." Even worse, it was banal. English journalists returned from the American section in those early days with amused reports of dental appliances, soaps, wineglasses, saltcellars, and unsavory comestibles.

The insults were delivered amid the long-standing rivalry between John Bull and Brother John—as the British and the Americans were respectively known to each other—which had been freshly stoked by the diplomatic tussle over the ownership of Oregon. While the English John Bulls treated the rivalry as good, if mean-spirited, fun, the American Brothers John, led by James Gordon Bennett of the *New York Herald*, were humorless and bellicose. After wondering why anyone would travel to London, "under its everlasting canopy of smoke," to partake of the "gigantic humbug" being perpetrated in the Crystal Palace, the *Herald* turned to jingoistic boasting: "It was about five years ago that the British became sensible of the reality of their position. It was then they became alive to the power and growing greatness of the United States. It was about that time they discovered they could not afford to go to war with us. . . . England sees her destiny under our control."

To the London press, the suggestion that Britain had anything more to fear from its former colony than bad taste was laughable. No one laughed louder than the editors of *Punch*, the London satirical magazine. *Punch* suggested that everything American be shoved into a smaller area in the Crystal Palace, thereby creating cheap lodging for people coming to see the exhibition. "By packing up American articles a little closer, by displaying COLT'S revolvers over the soap, and piling up the Cincinnati pickles on top of the Virginian honey, we shall concentrate all of American art and manufacture into a few square feet, and beds may be made up to accommodate several hundreds in the space claimed for, but not one-quarter filled by, the products of United States industry."

In that same helpful spirit, *Punch* suggested a few other items the Americans might send over to fill the wide-open spaces. "The Leg of a Multiplication Table" was one. Another was "the tremendous Wooden Style that separates the American from the English fields of literature." And most pointedly, "the Whip with which America flogs all creation—especially the coloured portion of it."

Lackluster as the American section seemed to be, one object in it found immediate acclaim. This was a statue known as *The Greek Slave* by the sculptor Hiram Powers—the same Hiram Powers whom Colt had befriended in the summer of 1833, when he passed through Cincinnati on his nitrous oxide tour. Powers had come a long way since Cincinnati. Now living in Florence, Italy, he was the most celebrated American sculptor in the world, largely on the fame of *The Greek Slave.* Whatever its merits as art, this life-size statue of a nude young woman in shackles represented a brilliant act of commerce. Powers's experience in the museum business had taught him how to seamlessly combine prurience with wholesomeness, and ogling with righteousness. Lest anyone get the idea that his sculpture represented an erotic Victorian bondage fantasy, Powers explained that his subject was meant to be a Christian Greek girl—in her hand is a tiny cross—torn from her family by Turkish infidels and about to be sold at a slave market.

Even here, at this shrine to feminine pulchritude and Christian forbearance, *Punch* found a way to tweak the Americans for their backward ways. It suggested another addition to their section. "We have the Greek Captive in dead stone—why not the Virginian slave in living ebony?"

Later, Colt would stand before *The Greek Slave* and be moved enough to send his old friend one of his new revolvers. But it was probably for the best that he was not around in the opening days of the Crystal Palace to see his guns lumped in with soaps, pickles, and hams. Colt planned to sail to England later in the year, but for the moment he left his display in the hands of Thomas Peard, a young man from Connecticut who had worked for Colt at Whitneyville and proved himself capable and personable.

Peard's mission had gotten off to a shaky start when he missed by a day or two the ship that had been chartered to take the American products to London. After finding alternate transportation across the Atlantic, he had arrived late at the Crystal Palace, carrying with him five hundred revolvers and a detailed letter of instruction from Colt.

At once set at work to procure a suitable station at the end of one of the halls if you can for the exhibition of the arms and be sure to secure a plenty of wall, table, and floor room. If you can find cases and tables suited for the exhibition of the arms, make use of them. If not, get a suitable case and table made for the purpose and arrange the arms in as showy and tasteful a manner as possible.

Allowing visitors to handle the guns was fine, Colt told Peard, but he was not to let anyone learn how they operated.

Exhibit a few specimens of the unfinished part of arms, but allow no person to take drawings of the pistols or parts. It is my wish that you do not fire any of the arms or permit them to be fired until I arrive in London.

The guns Peard took with him were samples of a new Colt model that would come to be known as the 1851 Navy. The gun had not specifically been designed for navy use; the name referred to a scene Colt engraved on the cylinder, from the Battle of Campeche in 1843, when the Texas Navy used Colt's Paterson revolvers near the Yucatán. The 1851 Navy was smaller and lighter than the Walker and Dragoon pistols, but still a formidable weapon.

Colt was extremely specific about many aspects of the display in his instructions, but he left it to Peard to figure out how to arrange the pistols for viewing. Peard chose to mount them in a kind of fanned-out symmetrical formation. Five days into the exhibit, he was pleased to inform Colt that he had received numerous compliments on his display. More interesting to Colt would have been the reaction Peard was getting to the guns themselves. Exhibition-goers were visiting the American section to see *The Greek Slave* but staying to examine Colt's revolvers. Peard was soon showing the pistols to "the most influential men in country spiced with a large sprinkling of the fair sex," as he wrote to Colt. "It is with infinite satisfaction I inform you that the Pistols command universal attention interest and praise."

Many of the English visitors had heard of Colt's revolver before the exhibition, even if they had never seen one up close. The London press often regaled readers with hair-raising stories from California and other western parts of America, and Colt's guns were regularly featured in these. "Scarcely a week passes," reported one London paper, "without some dispute, when revolvers and bowie-knives are immediately produced and someone is killed." Stories of shoot-outs were not only entertaining, they confirmed what many in Britain thought about Americans, which is that they lived under barely civilized conditions in bullet-peppered air. Colt's revolver fit perfectly into this portrait. "Caring little about the length of range, they are fond of something with which they can riddle a man's body in a second; and the nature of their warfare being almost always against barbarous tribes who engage them in woods, defiles, and mountain gorges, where a man has but little time to load, has taught them the value of such weapons."

II

That spring Colt's attention was absorbed by more pressing matters than the response to his guns in London. He was engaged in his own kind of warfare, in the defiles of New England, against the Massachusetts Arms Company, of Chicopee, Massachusetts. So far, all signs pointed to victory.

Massachusetts Arms was an outgrowth of an operation left behind by a gunmaker named Edwin Wesson. Before dying abruptly in 1849, Wesson had been attempting to make a revolver to rival Colt's, and doing so with the encouragement, Colt believed, of officials at the US Ordnance Department. Wesson had also lobbied to prevent Colt from extending his 1836 patent from its initial fourteen-year term, but Colt had prevailed and won himself an additional seven years of protection, until 1857.

Edwin Wesson's patent right had been inherited by his widow, who then sold it to Massachusetts Arms. The principal shareholders of this company were Edwin's brother, Daniel Wesson, and Horace Smith. Wesson and Smith—or Smith & Wesson, as they would be known—later became important gun manufacturers in their own right, but for the moment they were hoping to profit from a pistol that appeared to be derived from Colt's.

An 1851 letter book of Massachusetts Arms shows the company developing several arguments to defend itself against Colt's charge of patent infringement. The most promising of these hinged on two related points: first, that their revolver operated substantially differently from Colt's; and, second, that even if it *did* operate similarly, several guns had been invented *before* Colt's that used more or less the same technology, so Colt could not restrict others from using it. If Massachusetts Arms could prove either or both of these claims, it was free to make and sell as many revolvers as it pleased.

Colt's prospects of earning money from his revolver rode on the outcome of the suit he brought against Massachusetts Arms that spring. His success would halt aspiring infringers; his failure would announce open season on his patent. This would be the most important legal fight Colt ever waged, and it would have far-reaching consequences not only for himself but for American patent enforcement generally.

*   *   *

The trial commenced in Boston on the morning of June 30, 1851. On the bench was Levi Woodbury, an associate justice of the US Supreme Court.* Woodbury knew of Colt and his gun before the trial started. Along with other American notables, he had served on the committee that chose which products and innovations from the United States were sent to London for the Great Exhibition. In our own era, a judge's prior association with a plaintiff might seem to recommend his recusal, but Americans of the mid-nineteenth century were less fussy about such matters. Indeed, no one seemed to bat an eye when Colt hired a young attorney named Charles L. Woodbury to join his legal team of Edward Dickerson and the well-known Boston attorney George T. Curtis. Young Woodbury would play almost no role in the trial, but he was evidently not hired for his legal skills. He was hired because he was the son of the judge.

Colt can't be blamed for wanting to stack his deck. Massachusetts Arms was a formidable opponent, well funded, deadly serious about undercutting Colt, and apparently supported by the US Ordnance Department. To lead its defense, the company had hired Rufus Choate, a former US senator and legendary Massachusetts attorney second in reputation only to his mentor, Daniel Webster.[†]

The leading man of this trial would not be Rufus Choate, though. Nor would it be Colt himself, who would remain in the wings. Instead, it was to be Colt's attorney, Edward Dickerson. "Ned" Dickerson was still quite young—just twenty-seven—and this trial marked his debut on the national stage. He was tall, handsome, and dark haired, with a long mustache that flared out like the wings of a hawk. When he spoke, he displayed the blend of stirring oratory and mental acuity that would make him one of the most sought-after US patent attorneys of the nineteenth century.

In his long opening statement, Dickerson defined what was at stake in the trial. It was nothing less than the fate of the American inventor, "a poet in wood and steel," who devotes years of toil to his invention and

---

* In the nineteenth century, Supreme Court justices divided their time between Washington, where they met to decide cases with their fellow justices, and their own circuits, where they heard local cases. Woodbury's circuit was New England and included the District of Massachusetts.

† Choate sealed his reputation in 1846 with his extraordinary defense of accused murderer Albert Tirrell, somehow convincing a jury that his client had been sound asleep when he sliced his mistress's neck with a shaving razor—then washed his hands, then started a fire to burn the evidence, then fled—and therefore was not guilty.

then, at the very moment he might finally profit, is attacked by an outside force—a corporate predator—that tries to steal the invention from under him. Not only was this a great injustice done to the inventor, it was a threat to American ingenuity and progress.

Dickerson led the jury through Colt's difficult rise. "He was at the time a young man without means, and without many friends. He was a New England boy. He came from Ware, in Massachusetts, and had made this invention without money to put it into practical operation." No mention was made of the childhood on Lord's Hill, or of the financial and personal assistance from prominent relatives such as Roswell Colt and Dudley Selden. Such details did not fit into the fable Dickerson was spinning, an industrial-age version of David and Goliath. Regarding Colt's first attempt to manufacture and market his guns, Dickerson blamed its failure on the Seminole War. The guns were so effective, they put themselves out of business.

> The arms were taken to Florida, and Colonel Harney, that gallant and distinguished officer, who became the terror of the red man, penetrated the everglades with them, when he would not have otherwise dared to do it. When the Seminoles found men who fired eight or ten times without taking down the gun, they surrendered; and that brought the war to an end.

The suggestion that Colt's guns single-handedly won the Seminole War was only a little less far-fetched than Dickerson's next assertion, that "to these arms Texas owes her independence." In fact, Texas won her independence in the spring of 1836, two months after Colt filed his patent in Washington and nearly a year before the P.A.M.C. produced its first gun. But already Dickerson had moved on to 1847, when Samuel Walker approached Colt about starting up his gun business again. "Now he sees the golden apple ripening. Now he sees a prospect to be repaid for his time, trouble, and anxious days and nights." At which point Massachusetts Arms sweeps in to steal the fruits of his labor.

When it came to questioning witnesses, Dickerson switched from gusty generalities to surgical interrogations. He had studied science and mechanics at the College of New Jersey (later Princeton) and briefly practiced engineering before turning to law, and he showed a dexterous command of levers, bevel gears, ratchet wheels, springs, and other mechanisms inside

A Colt patent drawing from 1835, featuring one of the models made by John Pearson of Baltimore. This was not included with materials Colt submitted for his US patent application in 1836, all of which were destroyed when the Patent Office burned to the ground later in the year. The revolver's components, bottom, from left to right, include the hammer, the ratchet, the spindle, the cylinder, and the barrel.

Paterson, New Jersey, several decades after the arrival of Sam Colt and the Patent Arms Manufacturing Company. The gun mill, built in the spring of 1836, when Colt was twenty-one, is to the right, with tower and cupola.

A lithograph of Roswell L. Colt, taken from a portrait by Thomas Sully. Paterson may have been the brainchild of Alexander Hamilton, but the industrial town was owned and operated by members of the Colt family, none more important than Roswell. "The greatest of all the Colts" to some, "a scoundrel and swindler" to others, Roswell was an early supporter of his cousin Sam, loaning money, providing introductions, and, not least, withholding moral judgment.

4

As his company collapsed in 1841, Colt turned to a new scheme, the submarine battery. He proposed to blow up enemy ships, remotely, using electrically triggered explosives. This painting by Antoine Gibert depicts Colt's fourth and final demonstration, on April 13, 1844. As Congress adjourned and all of Washington crowded the banks of the Potomac River, Colt—probably standing on the top floor of the old brewery down river, left—sent a charge through a submerged cable to a mine under the *Styx*, which was promptly, reported the *New York Herald*, "all blown to the devil."

5

The Texas Rangers put Colt back in the gun business when they began using his pistols against Comanche warriors in June of 1844. While glorifying white dominance over Native Americans, this 1855 painting by Arthur Fitzwilliam Tait accurately depicts the very real edge the revolver gave to the rangers, as well as the remarkable fighting and riding skills of the Comanche.

Texas Ranger Samuel Walker. The gallant Captain Walker lived by the revolver and died, at least in one version, by the Mexican lance. Colt owed his resurrection as a gunmaker to Walker.

Thomas Jefferson Rusk, US senator from Texas. Brilliant but volatile (he would kill himself with a rifle in 1857), Rusk supplied the rationale for revolvers after the Mexican War: Indians.

8

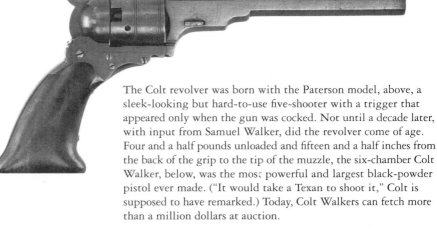

The Colt revolver was born with the Paterson model, above, a sleek-looking but hard-to-use five-shooter with a trigger that appeared only when the gun was cocked. Not until a decade later, with input from Samuel Walker, did the revolver come of age. Four and a half pounds unloaded and fifteen and a half inches from the back of the grip to the tip of the muzzle, the six-chamber Colt Walker, below, was the most powerful and largest black-powder pistol ever made. ("It would take a Texan to shoot it," Colt is supposed to have remarked.) Today, Colt Walkers can fetch more than a million dollars at auction.

9

Elisha King Root rescued Colt from a mob in 1829, then came to his aid again twenty years later. Root had one of the great mechanical minds of the nineteenth century, and he helped make Colt's Hartford armory the most advanced factory in the country. He died in 1865, but his work influenced American industry for years to come.

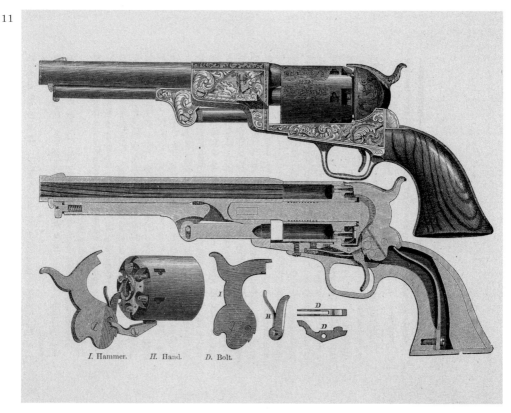

A Colt Dragoon, mid-1850s. The components at lower left illustrate how Colt revolvers operated. Pulling back—i.e., cocking—the Hammer (I) lifted a pawl, or Hand (H). This pushed up on the ratchet at the back of the cylinder, which turned the cylinder clockwise one-sixth of a full rotation. Simultaneously, the Bolt (D) dropped into a small groove on the outside of the cylinder, locking it in perfect alignment with hammer and barrel. After firing, the shooter cocked the gun again and the process repeated.

FOUR FACES OF COLT: Top left shows Colt as he and his heirs (especially his wife) wanted him to be seen: handsome and noble, firm but kind. Top right is Colt in a more solemn, if not more sinister, pose. Bottom left, probably taken after his first visit to Russia in 1854, reveals the imperious side of Colt, an ardent democrat with authoritarian tendencies. Bottom right is a rarely seen photograph, one of the so-called Imperial portraits by Mathew Brady. Though undated, this appears to have been taken near the end of Colt's life, when he was suffering from rheumatic arthritis and indulging in frequent "smiles," as he called alcoholic drinks.

Harry Love, center, and two of his fellow California rangers after killing the outlaw Joaquin Murrieta in July of 1853. This is one of the earliest-known photographs of men posing with Colt revolvers.

Young men on both sides of the Civil War stopped off in photography studios to pose with revolvers before heading off to battle. Private William Anthony Holland of the 10th Virginia Cavalry Regiment holds a Bowie knife and an 1860 Colt Army.

19

Officers were far more likely to carry revolvers than infantrymen. First Lieutenant William D. Matthews, of the 1st Kansas Colored Volunteer Infantry, favored ivory-gripped Colts.

A Union cavalryman, name unknown, with two Colt Dragoons tucked under his belt.

The Confederate "bushwhacker" William "Bloody Bill" Anderson, dead with a Colt in his hand. Anderson had six revolvers on him when he was killed by Union troops in October of 1864.

William S. Harney was the first US Army officer to use Colt's revolving guns in combat, against Seminole Indians in Florida in 1838. In 1855, he earned his nickname "The Butcher" by attacking Brulé and Oglala Sioux with Sharps rifles and Colt revolvers at Blue Water Creek in Nebraska.

Though illustrated twenty years after the fact, this depiction of the Sand Creek Massacre of 1864 vividly captures the terror revolvers brought to Indian camps. One US general explained why mounted troops needed revolvers against Native Americans: "They charge them suddenly, are in contact with them but a few minutes, and in that time must do all the execution they expect to do."

Colt is third from the left in this group portrait of nineteen illustrious American scientists and inventors. The subjects did not pose together for *Men of Progress*—painter Christian Schussele sketched each individually, then placed them in this composition. Colt looked nothing like the healthy, handsome man shown here when Schussele began the painting in 1861, and would be dead before it was completed in 1862. A revolver can be seen, faintly, to Colt's right, lying across a model just behind Cyrus H. McCormick, inventor of the mechanical reaper. Colt's friend Samuel F. B. Morse, with flowing white hair, holds court in the foreground, right of center. This painting now hangs at the National Portrait Gallery in Washington, DC, in the building that once housed the US Patent Office.

24

After Sam's death, Elizabeth Colt spent much of her life improving his image by sponsoring memorials in his honor. In her own right, she was a patron of the arts and other civic causes, as well as a doting mother. She adored Caldwell, the Colts' only child to survive into adulthood, and spoiled him. Caldwell would die in 1894, at thirty-five, under mysterious circumstances while yachting in Florida. Elizabeth lived until 1905 and left no direct descendants.

25

Samuel Caldwell Colt, the "neffue," was legally the son of John C. Colt and Caroline Henshaw. More likely, though, he was Sam's son. There's no hard proof but plenty of circumstantial evidence for this, including the fact that Colt left the young man a much larger sum than any heir besides Elizabeth and Caldwell. To Colt's dismay, young Sammy was a gentle boy who loved animals more than school. After Colt's death, Sammy became a farmer and spent his life raising animals. He was a founding member of Connecticut's first association to prevent cruelty to animals.

revolvers. "Is a lever substantially the same instrument when the fulcrum is between the power and the work, as when the work is between the fulcrum and the power?" Dickerson asked Orison Blunt, a gunsmith who testified in a deposition for the defense.

> **Blunt:** I don't know that there is any material difference in the lever, although the leverage when the fulcrum is inside is greater. . . .
>
> **Dickerson:** Is or is not the motion produced by the same principle in both, viz the cock acting as a lever?
>
> **Blunt:** They are, sir, although differently applied by another elementary power.
>
> **Dickerson:** Is not the motion in both, at the point where it leaves the cock acting as a lever, reciprocating; that is to say, moving in one direction when you cock the gun and in another when you fire it?
>
> **Blunt:** Both the same—that motion is common to all gunlocks.
>
> **Dickerson:** Is not that reciprocating motion in both guns converted into a rotary motion by precisely the same mechanical device, namely a ratchet and an escaping hand-finger or pin?

Again, it all boiled down to two questions: Was the Massachusetts Arms gun the same as Colt's, or was it something new? And were any guns invented before Colt's similar to his revolver? To the first, Dickerson's examinations elicited evidence that the method Massachusetts Arms used to turn its cylinder was essentially the same as the one patented by Colt. But this would not matter if the defense could show that similar technology had been in use before Colt made his first gun.

Rufus Choate and his fellow defense attorneys introduced five revolvers they purported to be from an earlier date than Colt's. That all had rotating cylinders was not particularly meaningful, since Colt had not claimed invention of the rotating cylinder in his patent; he had claimed a particular *method* of rotating cylinders. The salient question was how these other guns rotated and locked between shots.

Dickerson made quick work of the supposed predecessors. Regarding the oldest guns in question, by Elisha Collier and Cornelius Coolidge (which was based on Collier's patent), Dickerson cast doubt on their murky origins and operation. They may have revolved, but they did not revolve like Colt's. Collier *had* experimented, unsuccessfully, with mechanical rotation, but he had eventually resigned himself to a cylinder turned *by hand*, a very different and inelegant solution for a revolving gun.

Dickerson also introduced evidence that the three guns closer in date to

Colt's—by Adam Humbarger, David Colburn, and Benjamin F. Smith—
had arrived on the scene *after* Colt's. This argument relied on establishing
that Colt's gun was invented *before* the others—which is to say, sometime
before 1832 or 1833, the years to which the others were dated. Colt's gun,
asserted Dickerson, was first made in 1831.

To prove this, he called to the stand Anson Chase. The gunsmith was
now living in New London, Connecticut, where he still practiced his trade
and where he had been tracked down by Colt's attorneys. Chase testified,
somewhat shakily, to the 1831 date, and so did several others, swearing
they saw Colt working on a gun with Chase then.

The testimony of these men is primarily what substantiates the oft-
repeated narrative of Colt's early years of invention, leading up to his patent
in 1836. Here may be a good place to pause and wonder: Were these
witnesses remembering dates and details accurately? If we consider what
was at stake in the trial for Colt (virtually everything he had worked for)
and the lengths he and Dickerson would go to later to extend his patent (as
we shall see), it's reasonable to ask whether any testimony was contrived,
or cajoled, ex post facto, necessity being not only the mother of invention
but also, perhaps, of *recollections* about inventions. There is no proof that
anyone lied about the timing of Colt's first guns, but (as mentioned in
chapter 5) a number of documents from that period—a receipt here, a letter
there—appear to have been misdated, almost as if someone had gone back
and altered them to an earlier year.

To Dickerson's credit, before anyone could raise too many suspicions
about his client, he accused Massachusetts Arms of a blatant fraud. The
defense had introduced into evidence a gun patented by David Colburn
and made by a man named Snell in 1833. Dickerson, supplied by sources
of intelligence brought to him, as he himself put it, "by the next stroke of
the telegraph," had learned that the Colburn gun presented to the jury had
recently been fitted with new parts, and that these parts had been rusted to
make them appear as if they belonged in the original. If true, this suggested
that the defense had altered the gun to make it appear more Colt-like than
it originally was.

After Dickerson got the defense's own witnesses to admit to the rust-
ing, nothing the defense said or introduced could be counted as entirely
credible by the jury. Dickerson reminded the jury of the rust whenever
he could, even offering helpful advice to the defense on how to rust metal
in advance of future patent trials. Be sure, advised Dickerson, to put the
metal "in pickle early so that the rust may have time to change before the
trial comes on."

*   *   *

The trial sputtered though July, finally wrapping up in early August. The luck of Massachusetts Arms had long ago turned sour, and now came more bad news: Rufus Choate was sick in bed and unable to deliver the closing argument for the defense. His cocounsel R. A. Chapman stepped in with little time to prepare and gave a workmanlike summary of the evidence.

The closing argument for Colt was made by George T. Curtis. Until now, Curtis had played a secondary role to Dickerson. But he had been listening carefully.

Six years later, Curtis would enter history as one of the lawyers who argued before the Supreme Court to obtain the freedom of a slave named Dred Scott. Curtis would lose that landmark case by a vote of 7–2 (one of the dissenters being his older brother, Justice Benjamin R. Curtis), and the country would soon be on its way to war. For the moment, Curtis's reputation was based on his highly regarded work as a patent-law attorney and as the author of several books of history and biography. Curtis lacked the flash of Dickerson, but his more pedantic style gave scholarly authority to his argument.

Every man on the jury, Curtis assumed, had been following the great events at the Crystal Palace, including reports that the American section had been disparaged. Curtis took a moment to defend the reputation of American inventors.

It may be, gentlemen, that the arts and manufacturers of this country, in that stupendous exhibition of the industry of the world, which is now to be witnessed on the other side of the Atlantic, do not present a result altogether gratifying to our vanity or our pride. Nevertheless, I undertake to say, that there are now living in this country as many persons of inventive genius, whose inventions have produced a striking, important and most beneficial effect on the civilization of the age, as in any country in Christendom.

The shame of American invention was not that it lacked genius, insisted Curtis, picking up on Dickerson's opening statement; it was that it lacked fairness to the inventor, whose reward for his efforts was so often an old age of penury.

How is it that this comes to pass? How is it that this high inventive talent, which unites the facility of genius with the patience of the day laborer, which knows no defeat from the obstacles of nature, which clings to its conception with heroic tenacity, until matter has been subdued by the energy of its will to the exact condition of success—how is it that this high quality of human intellect is sometimes cheated of its rightful reward?

Curtis's depiction of an individual genius standing against corporate pirates dovetailed smoothly with the image he now painted of a lone pioneer armed with a Colt. "The traveler of the great prairies of this western continent takes it in his hand and lies down in peace, with nothing above him but the stars, while all about him prowls the savage and the wild beast." Curtis thus identified Colt the inventor with the brave men who used his invention; they were heroic individuals standing up to barbarous tribes in the defiles.

On Wednesday, August 6, Judge Woodbury gave the jury instructions. Even as he urged impartiality, he made it clear which side he favored. They must be sure not to let their sympathies bend too far in Colt's direction, he told the jurors, just "because the plaintiff stands alone, and because he has evidently been struggling for fifteen or twenty years on this subject, to do something which might confer a benefit upon his country and reward his own exertions."

Dickerson and Curtis could not have put it any better. The jury came back after a brief deliberation. They found for the plaintiff. Massachusetts Arms had infringed, and Colt's patent stood.

III

Ten days after the verdict, on Saturday, August 16, 1851, Colt boarded the steamship *Pacific* for England. He embarked a triumphant man. Massachusetts Arms had been beaten so soundly as to put all potential competitors and infringers on notice. He would have the market pretty much to himself until his patent extension expired in 1857—and the market was building fast. In 1851, just four years after reentering the revolver business with an order for a thousand pistols, Colt was expecting to produce tens of thousands of guns. He now employed three hundred men. "The demand for this arm is so great," the *Hartford Courant* predicted, "that Col. Colt will probably have one thousand men at work in a very short time."

As reward for his success, Colt had recently been appointed aide-de-camp by Connecticut's new governor, Thomas H. Seymour, giving Colt the rank of lieutenant colonel in the Connecticut state militia. After years of being saluted as colonel by his brother James, Sam could now claim the rank legitimately. For the rest of his life the world would know him as

Colonel Colt, although he would never perform a military function that was not strictly ceremonial.

The voyage from New York to Liverpool was mostly fair and smooth, and the accommodations as fine as any available on transatlantic passage. The *Pacific* had been launched in 1849, one of four ships of the Collins Line, an American steamship fleet subsidized by the US government for mail service. With vessels designed by George Steers, the best-known shipbuilder in the United States, the Collins Line was eager to compete for glory with Britain's Cunard fleet, and the results had so far been spectacular. That summer, Collins's ships had broken the record for fastest transatlantic crossing between New York and Liverpool, first in a run by the *Pacific*, and then, on the very morning Colt embarked, by the *Baltic*, returning to New York with a new record of nine days and twenty hours from Liverpool. It was the start of an extraordinary string of achievements by Americans at British expense in the late summer of 1851.

Some details of Colt's voyage are preserved in letters written by his second cousin John Colt, of Paterson, New Jersey, who sailed to England with Sam to visit the Crystal Palace and conduct business in Europe. A man of steady habits in a solid marriage, John was a different breed of Colt from either his brother Roswell or his cousin Sam. In his own quiet way, he had achieved a success almost equal to theirs, as a manufacturer of cotton textiles. His factory in Paterson produced some of the best duck cloth in the world.

John found Sam in a magnanimous mood, "as kind and attentive as possible," as he wrote to his wife. Sam had upgraded John's accommodations, offering the older man his stateroom and taking a lesser cabin for himself. Sam and John took their meals together, dining side by side at the captain's end of the table, in "pleasant company." Breakfast was at eight, lunch at noon, dinner at four, and comforts included warm saltwater baths prepared by servants. In the evening, passengers gathered in the main cabin for music.

The *Pacific* was still steaming across the Atlantic, four days off the coast of England, when fifteen yachts came together for a race around the Isle of Wight. The date was Friday, August 22. The weather was sunny and fine, a good breeze blowing from the west—a perfect morning for the Royal Regatta. A large and fashionable crowd gathered on the beach in front of Cowes Castle for the 10:00 a.m. start. The queen watched from the deck of her steamship, the *Victoria and Albert*. At a signal, the yachts cut east with the wind at their backs. Dead last was a narrow-hulled schooner called *America*.

America was the first American yacht ever to sail in the Royal Regatta. It had been funded by the New York City Yacht Club and designed by George Steers, the same man who designed the Collins Line ships. Rigged with sails of duck cloth—from John Colt's mill in Paterson, as it happened—the *America* had sailed across the Atlantic with great fanfare to challenge the British yachts. Though not officially a feature of the Great Exhibition, the race had been swept into the rivalry of it, and national pride was on the line. So it was gratifying for British spectators to see the much-ballyhooed *America* falter at the start, pushed back by a gust and calamitously tangled in a cable. Everyone agreed the *America* had no chance of catching up after that. But then, while the yachts were still within sight of the crowd at Cowes Castle, she did just that. "The *America* soon began to feel the breeze" is how one London newspaper put it, "and drew ahead softly and silently."

When the yachts came around the other side of Isle of Wight that evening, more than ten hours after the start, the *America* was in the lead. She passed the finish line just after 8:30 p.m., the winner, in an astonishing upset, of a race that would ever after be known as the America's Cup in her honor.

That race around the Isle of Wight had no real value beyond a silver trophy, but its significance on both sides of the Atlantic in 1851 was immeasurable. It confirmed what many visitors to the Great Exhibition had awakened to over the summer as they spent more time in the American section. Out of all that open space a consensus had emerged that the early dismissal of displays there was premature. Great crowds now gathered around the Americans.

N. S. Dodge, the commissioner of the US delegation at the exhibition, later explained the shift in opinion. It all began, he said, with Colt's revolvers. First, a number of officers of the British Army visited the Colt display and expressed interest in taking some of the arms with them to South Africa, where they were fighting against indigenous tribes in the so-called Kaffir war. The Duke of Wellington then came to see the display for himself and was so impressed that he returned several more times, always speaking of the guns, as Dodge recalled, "in unmeasured approbation." On the duke's heels came Prince Albert. Colt had told Thomas Peard to allow no one to shoot the guns, but Peard wisely made an exception for the queen's husband.

The press was now paying close attention, which redounded to the benefit of all American inventions, according to N. S. Dodge. Crowds that came to see the revolvers fanned out and began to look more closely at other displays, and soon these, too, were receiving praise. Charles Goodyear's "Vulcanite Court," a rubber-walled room filled with common objects made of rubber—desks, walking sticks, balloons—began to draw large and admiring crowds. The grain reaper invented by Cyrus McCormick performed astonishingly well in a public demonstration. An American locksmith named Alfred Hobbs undercut the supposed superiority of the British locksmith trade by picking a supposedly unpickable lock, then watching British locksmiths fail to pick his. All of these achievements and more contributed to a dramatic change of heart regarding American displays at the Great Exhibition. As Dodge put it, Colt's revolvers were to the US delegation "what the descent of the angel became to the waters of Bethesda."

The *Pacific* arrived in Liverpool, four days after the race around the Isle of Wight, on Tuesday, August 26, at 8:00 p.m. The voyage had taken ten days and two hours, "wharf to wharf," by John Colt's account. If not quite as fast as the *Baltic*'s westbound voyage earlier in the month, this was still extremely fast compared to transatlantic voyages just a decade earlier.

Sam and John both stayed at Long's Hotel, near Bond Street, convenient to Hyde Park and the Crystal Palace. Over the next few days they took in the theater at Covent Garden (a French opera entitled *Les Huguenots*) and toured the grounds of Richmond, site of the royal palace on the Thames. Mainly, they visited the Crystal Palace and basked in compliments, John for his now famous duck cloth sails, Sam for his guns.

In the British press Colt and his guns generally met with approval, even delight, but resentment and English chauvinism percolated through some of the coverage that September. The *Observer* pointed out that the idea of Colt's revolver was nothing new in Britain; Englishmen had conceived of such things as early as the reign of Charles I. The *Times* of London, which had ridiculed the American section in May, now graciously applauded American triumphs but voiced concerns when it came to Colt: "As for yachts, we have no doubt that by next August every vessel of the Cowes Squadron will be trimmed to the very image of the *America*; there is no doubt that our farmers will reap by machinery, and the revolver, we fear, is too attractive an embodiment of personal power to be overlooked by European mischief makers." Colt revolvers, added the *Times*, were likely "to revolutionize military tactics as completely as the original discovery of gunpowder."

The *Times* did not mean this as a compliment. It was a warning, given in the face of a nineteenth-century truism that better weapons promoted peace by making violence too costly, too horrifying, to contemplate. Colt himself subscribed to such a view. "The good people of this world are very far from being satisfied with each other," he would write to an English associate the following year, "and my arms are the best peacemakers." The *Times* suggested that this claim was specious. "In fact, while acknowledging the virtues of this ingenious instrument, we must express our suspicion that its principal effect has been hitherto to promote murder." The gun's main victims were not the foreign enemy they had been purchased to defeat but the people who purchased them. "They were, no doubt, found serviceable in 'frontier action,' but the invention cuts two ways, and we very much question whether Mr. Colt's discovery has not cost Americans more lives than Mexicans."

By the time the exhibition closed on October 11, 1851, the weather had turned cold and rainy and the roof of the Crystal Palace had sprung a few leaks—it really was just a building after all. The entire structure would now be dismantled and moved to Sydenham Hill, in south London, where it would serve as a museum until destroyed by fire in 1936.

The ephemerality of the Crystal Palace notwithstanding, the exhibition had been a transformative event, not just in England, but in the United States, where the acclaim for American products stimulated national pride. The newly enormous nation was evidently as inventive and brilliant as it was large. "Recently America has been put to the test," boasted one US publication. "But how does the race come out? As no human mind could have anticipated. The trial gives America the command of all the great interests of life."

When the exhibition prizes were announced in October, the United States won a disproportionate number. McCormick, Goodyear, and a Texan named Gail Borden who had created a dried-meat biscuit (and would later devise his more famous condensed milk) all won medals for original design. Much to the surprise of the American contingent, Colt received only honorable mention for his pistols. Some suggested this result owed more to the influence of the British gun industry than to an honest appraisal by the judges. The gold medal went to a British inventor of a repeating arm named Robert Adams.

The prize that mattered most was public opinion, however, and here Colt prevailed. In early November, *British Army Despatch* published a glowing and passionate review of Colt's guns, urging them for use in the British military, especially in its many colonial outposts. "We cannot help expressing our opinion that whoever would deny this weapon to be a valuable auxiliary in anything like irregular warfare, must be either the victim of delusion, or, what is far more difficult to remove, old-fashioned prejudice and antipathy." Another publication, the *Spirit of the Times*, called for the deployment of Colt's revolvers in South Africa. "They make one man equal, in short, to many, and strike fear into the hearts of savages."

The greatest honor of all came on November 25, when Colt delivered an address to the Institution of Civil Engineers in London. He was the first American ever invited to speak before this august body of British engineers and scientists. In attendance were also a number of prominent Americans stationed in London for various reasons, including Abbott Lawrence, the wealthy textile manufacturer and esteemed benefactor of the Lawrence Scientific School at Harvard, now serving as US minister to Great Britain. Abbott was the older brother of Samuel Lawrence, the friend of Christopher Colt's who had many years earlier delivered Sam to the *Corvo*.

Colt's talk was titled "On the Application of Machinery to the Manufacture of Revolving-Breech Firearms." He began by discussing prior examples of multifiring guns, wisely wrapping himself in the history of the revolver rather than denying it. He showed some drawings of previous attempts at repeaters that he had discovered in the Tower of London, including a fifteenth-century matchlock with a four-chambered revolving cylinder. The main point of his history lesson was not to praise his predecessors, but to point out that no one had fully succeeded until he came along.

Colt tended to tailor the story of his gun's origin to the audience he was delivering it to, and he did that now. He claimed that he invented the revolver because he lived in a country "of most extensive frontier, still inhabited by hordes of aborigines." Inspired by "the insulated position of the enterprising pioneer, and his dependence, sometimes alone, on his personal ability to protect himself and his family," he had frequently "meditated upon the inefficiency of the ordinary double-barreled gun and pistol, both involving a loss of time in reloading, which was too frequently fatal."

In fact, Colt had not developed the revolver with pioneers and aborigines in mind—they became pertinent to him only later—but he understood the appeal of this story to English imaginations. Not only did John Bull love tales of the wild American west, he was at that moment particularly interested in weapons to use against aboriginal populations in colonial outposts.

It took a while for Colt to warm to the true subject of his talk, which was not guns but machines. He wanted his audience to understand that his machines and his production methods were every bit as significant—as revolutionary—as his revolver. After chiding the English for continuing to make guns largely by hand, he introduced his audience to what would soon come to be known as the American System of manufacturing: "In America, where manual labor is scarce and expensive, it was imperative to devise means for producing these arms with greatest rapidity and economy." Machines required less labor, saved costs, and, perhaps most important of all, helped achieve uniformity. Four-fifths of the work at Colt's factory was now performed by machines, he told his audience. He had broken his gun down into the fewest possible parts (the lock had previously required seventeen components, for example, and now had just five), then replicated each of these parts by a machine dedicated to it alone.

> In fact, all the separate parts travel independently through the manufactory, arriving at last, in an almost complete condition, in the hands of the finishing workmen, by whom they are assembled, from promiscuous heaps, and formed into firearms, requiring only the polishing and fitting demanded for ornament. . . . By this system the machines become almost automatons.

When Colt was done, a few men in the audience rose to defend British industry, but most extolled Colt's revolver. At one point, Robert Adams, Colt's British rival and winner of the gold medal at the Crystal Palace, took the floor to describe the merits of his own gun, but several of his countrymen stood to say they did not think much of it in comparison to Colt's, and Adams quietly resumed his seat. Then a Mr. May stood to object that a discussion about the merits of guns was not a proper subject for the society. He urged everyone to get back to the topic advertised by the title of the speech, which was machinery. Before sitting, Mr. May shared that he was Quaker and believed that all weapons should be dispensed with, "except for protections against wild beasts."

Early the following year, Colt would be inducted into the Institution of Civil Engineers as an honorary member and awarded the organization's prestigious Telford Medal, the first American to receive this honor. Perhaps even more impressive, the ever-snide *Punch* published an ode to Colt, titled "John Bull to Colonel Colt":

> OH! Colonel Colt,
> A thunderbolt
> I'd buy—for no small trifle;
> But that can't be,
> And so let me
> Get your revolving rifle!

While singing the praises of Colt's invention—a rifle, rather than a revolver, for the sake of the rhyme—*Punch* wondered how a firearm, of all the tens of thousands of objects at an exhibition meant to promote world harmony, had come to be the most famous of all:

But Colt, alas!
To what a pass—
To what a sad condition—
Have we been brought,
Who fondly thought
The World's Great Exhibition
Would bid war cease
And endless peace
With all our neighbors send us,
Whilst its chief boon
Is found—how soon—
Your weapon to defend us.

PART V

COLTSVILLE

1852–62

There was never any more inception than there is now,
Nor any more youth or age than there is now,
And will never be any more perfection than there is now,
Nor any more heaven or hell than there is now.

—Walt Whitman,
"Song of Myself,"
1855

CHAPTER FIFTEEN

The Anthem of Bang

1852–54

Colt's London armory on the Thames.

I

From a distance, knowing what's coming, it's hard to see the 1850s as anything but a series of escalating disasters on the way to the great calamity of the Civil War. But for many Americans, the decade began as a period of confidence, even exuberance. The conflict over the future of slavery that reared up during and after the Mexican War had momentarily been tabled by the Compromise of 1850, thanks to that great triumvirate of veteran senators—Clay, Calhoun, and Webster—who found a way to horse-trade northern and southern interests. To the north went the guarantee that California would enter the Union as a free state and that the selling of slaves (though not slavery itself) would be banished in Washington. To the south went the promise that the new territories of Utah and New Mexico could choose for themselves, by voting, whether to be free states or slave. Even better for pro-slavery southerners was a new law attached to the compromise, the Fugitive Slave Act, that gave owners more power to capture runaway slaves.

Some northerners opposed the Compromise of 1850, especially the Fugitive Slave Act, as morally repugnant, but for the moment most were glad to have the union preserved so they could get on with enjoying their prosperity. The American money supply was flush with California gold, the cotton trade was booming in the south, and the newly steam-powered cities of the north were growing by the day. Amid this, the nation was experiencing a heady coming-of-age culturally. The first few years of the decade would see groundbreaking literary work from all-American but world-class writers such as Herman Melville, Nathan-iel Hawthorne, and Walt Whitman, while a loosely aligned group of artists, gathered around what would come to be called the Hudson River School, were successfully capturing the grandeur of the American landscape in paint. All in all, the news from London confirmed what many Americans already believed by the start of the 1850s: that the United States was destined to be the greatest, most innovative, most powerful nation on earth.

Sam Colt not only shared this opinion of America, he radiated it. After returning to Hartford from London in February of 1852, feeling "exalted, heroic, and invincible," as one biographer has put it, he began to think in terms farther-reaching than any other American industrialist had dared imagine. He began to envision a global empire.

Colt's most immediate aim was to open a large factory in England. He'd left the responsibility for this in the hands of Charles Manby, the secretary of the Institution of Civil Engineers. The two had become friendly during Colt's visit to London in the fall, and Manby, an engineer of sterling reputation and broad connections, had agreed to help Colt. Manby's first task was political—to acquire permission from the British government to lease a suitable factory site—after which he would undertake the practical challenge of preparing the factory to make guns. Colt appointed another man, Charles F. Dennet, an American expatriate originally from Maine, to oversee British sales.

Through the winter and spring of 1852, Colt gathered tools and machines to take with him on his return to London. He chose a dozen or so of his best Yankee workers to accompany him, apostle-like, to teach the English to use the machines to make guns. All the while, he sent numer-ous letters to Manby and Dennet urging them along. By May, Manby had obtained approval from the government to lease an old factory in the

Pimlico district of London, on the Thames River near Vauxhall Bridge. As Manby oversaw renovations, Colt sent Dennet guns from Hartford to sell as he could, reminding him not to neglect promotion: "You must keep the thing as much before the publik as possible. Have some of the arms at different shooting galleries & publik places & occasionally get a short spicey notice in the papers of some extraordinary performance by someone of her Majesty's officers with one of them."

English markets would be the focus of Colt's overseas efforts over the next several years, but they represented only a fraction of his global designs. Some of these were already taking shape, having been arranged during his continental travels of 1849 and 1851. He now had agents in France, Belgium, and Germany pursuing sales and contracts in those places, as well as envoys in Mexico, Argentina, Brazil, and Chile. His friend Lewis Carr would soon sail to China with Colt revolvers, and in 1852, Colt's friend Commodore Matthew C. Perry would take a hundred guns to Japan.

Then there was Thomas Peard, the American who had so effectively represented Colt's guns at the Crystal Palace. After the exhibition closed, Peard had boarded a ship to the south of Africa, with 215 pairs of pistols, to capitalize on the enthusiasm for revolvers among British officers who had been sent to fight the Kaffirs. No sooner did Peard get to Africa than he vanished. Reports suggested that native tribesmen had overtaken a transport carrying Colt's arms and that his representative—that would be Peard—had been roasted alive and eaten. Peard's wife and brother were understandably distraught. Colt assured them the reports were not true, though he had no way of knowing.

Happily for all, it turned out that Peard had not been eaten. In the summer of 1852 he was busy showing the pistols to British troops in the Baakens River Valley, astonishing both officers and native Africans who gathered to watch. Firing a .36-caliber Navy revolver, with a seven-and-a-half-inch barrel, he outshot British officers armed with the finest English rifles. Then he brought out a larger Dragoon pistol and began firing at an anthill on a slope about four hundred yards distant, blowing up puffs of dirt with each shot. Upon which, according to press accounts, one of the Africans exclaimed, "That's God's pistol!"

While corresponding with his overseas associates, Colt was running his Grove Lane works at capacity. With four hundred men now working overtime to meet demand, he was manufacturing a hundred guns a day and had thirty thousand in various stages of production. He hoped to soon

raise the number to fifty-five thousand. That was a significant output for
any armory, but Colt's ambitions had expanded beyond the normal scope
of armories.

That summer, he began to visit an area downriver of Hartford, along the
western bank of the Connecticut, known as the South Meadow. Most of the
land here was pasture and apple orchards. It was considered fairly worthless real estate because it was prone to heavy flooding by the Connecticut
River. As recently as the previous April the water had risen twenty-three
feet and turned the meadow into a lake. Spring flooding was most common,
but sometimes winter thaws brought flooding, too. Then the temperature
would drop, the water would freeze, and a sheet of ice would form high
above the meadow. A few winters earlier, a group of boys had been skating
over the frozen meadow when one of them fell through the ice. His body
was recovered from the branches of a tree.

Given the perennial flooding, only a fool would think to build on the
South Meadow. Colt quietly began to buy up small lots at low prices.

II

When he'd gotten his first taste of success at age twenty-one, Colt had
indulged himself in all that money could buy and soon landed himself in
debt. Now, at thirty-seven—turning thirty-eight that July—he was coming into real wealth, splendid and sustained wealth, and his indulgences
hurried to keep pace with his income. On May 17, he received a bill for
a thousand cigars. On June 14 came a bill for fourteen hundred cigars,
including a batch of "Flor de Cabanas," of which his cigar dealer wrote,
"Prince Albert himself might be glad to have them." Seven hundred more
cigars arrived on July 20.

No doubt Colt intended to give many of the cigars away as gifts, if not
to Prince Albert himself then to other worthy men, but a thousand cigars
or so a month was a staggering quantity. So was the volume of alcohol Colt
purchased during that summer of 1852, including numerous barrels of rye
whiskey and casks of brandy. Colt had always been a drinking man, but alcohol now flowed into his life in ever more prodigious amounts and varieties.

On August 9, Colt wrote to his regular purveyor of wine. The previous
order had been "tolerably good" but now he wanted "more you consider
of a superior quality." The new batch was to be sent not to Hartford, he
directed, but to Newport, Rhode Island. Later that same day, Colt wrote
to his friend and frequent business associate Lewis Carr to let him know

he was leaving for Newport that afternoon. "So you must go there at once to meet me & we will have a good time. The Miss Jarvaces etc. are there & all looks well for a merry season."

Newport counted as an indulgence, but it also provided an opportunity to mix pleasure with business. It put him in the company of important men and attractive young women of fine pedigree. If not yet the Gilded Age retreat that Edith Wharton would write about in *The Age of Innocence*, Newport had grown in recent years from a quiet seaside village into one of the fashionable "watering places" where affluent Americans decamped for a month or two of salubrious breezes and aquatics. The first giant "cottages" were already starting to rise by 1852, but social life still revolved around the grand hotels on Bellevue Avenue. Colt stayed at the grandest of them all, the Ocean House, an enormous wood-framed, gabled-roofed building that advertised "high and capacious apartments . . . gardens and meadows extending to the shore . . . large corridors and piazzas and seaside cliffs." The hotel catered to the gentry of Philadelphia, New York, and Boston, along with a large clientele of southerners who migrated to Newport each summer to escape their insufferable climates.

The Ocean House prided itself on refinement and calm, but the day before Colt arrived the atmosphere had been disturbed by a violent altercation. The incident was a tempest in a teapot but augured greater storms to come. A young Mississippian named E. M. Yerger—"a young planter from the south," as the newspapers described him—had been helping a lady to a dish in the hotel restaurant when a waiter appeared and "desired to take it from him." Yerger was a notorious hothead—he had been expelled from college for whipping a slave and would later in life shoot several men and kill another with a knife*—and now, outraged by the waiter's impudence, he pulled out a knife and cut the waiter "about the face." As the waiter staggered off, Yerger returned to his supper. The next morning, when Yerger appeared for breakfast, the waiters of the Ocean House surrounded him, intent on avenging their injured colleague. Yerger jumped to his feet and pulled out two pistols—no word on the make or model—swearing he would shoot anyone who came within five feet. A cry of "Southrons!" rang through the halls of the hotel, and other southern guests came running to Yerger's aid. Outnumbered and outgunned, the waiters withdrew. Yerger

* Byron De La Beckwith, a white supremacist who killed the civil rights activist Medgar Evers in Mississippi in 1963, was a direct descendant of Yerger's.

stormed out of the Ocean House that afternoon, accompanied by a large entourage of affronted southerners.

When southern newspapers caught wind of a rumor that the offending waiters were black—they were white, in fact—it made the outrage all the more intolerable to southern dignity. The moral of the story, as papers such as the *Richmond Dispatch* saw it, was that southerners ought to take their vacations in the south. "If Southerners would reflect upon the utterly defenseless position they place themselves in when they place themselves at Northern watering places, we are sure they would not flock thither so gregariously."

By the time Colt arrived late on the afternoon of August 9, the Ocean House had settled back into its usual calm and decorum. Regularity had resumed. What this meant, for the socially cognizant, was strict adherence to a routine of recreation and customs, "and wo to any would-be fashionable who presumes to transgress that sacred routine," warned the *New-York Tribune*. The early part of the day went to "sea bathing." The ladies went first, claiming the beach from nine till noon, wading into the water in long swimming dresses that seemed specially designed to become waterlogged and drag their victims to the bottom of the sea. At noon, the white flag over the beach came down and a red flag went up, signaling the men's turn in the surf. While the men swam—no suits for them; they went nude—the ladies ventured out on the town, "over-dressed, over-jeweled and over-silked," to shop and pay social calls. Then the men returned from the beach and passed what remained of the afternoon in such pursuits as bowling, billiards, and target shooting.

An aspiring young writer out of Princeton named Charles Godfrey Leland recalled meeting Colt at the Ocean House and visiting the shooting gallery with him—"nor did we abstain," Leland wrote, "from mint-juleps." Leland gives what may be the only surviving firsthand description of Colt's prowess with a gun, brief as it is: "I found that, in shooting, Colonel Colt could beat me *at the word*, but that I always had the best of it at a deliberate 'take your time' shot."

Evening was the most important time of day in Newport, when the sexes convened and the serious work of social climbing and courtship commenced. On many evenings the best society attended informal promenades at the corso, in the interior of Fort Adams; one portion would trot around in a circle while another portion stood on the walls and watched. Later in the evening came suppers and recitals and dances, where ingenues from Boston, New York, and Philadelphia, and belles from Charleston, Mobile, and New Orleans (those who had not been dragged off after the Yerger fracas), vied for the attention of suitable bachelors. The *Herald* described these balls as fights to the death: "Every little coterie is marshaled under a distinct banner; and though outwardly professing the most cordial and amicable relations, makes war upon another with as much petty slander, malignity, calumny and virulence."

The high point of the social season was the final costume ball at Ocean House, in early September. On the appointed day, festivities began at 9:00 p.m. with a promenade in the main room of the hotel. Then the in-house band began to play, and for the next three hours flush-faced guests danced waltzes, quadrilles, and a breathless new step from Bohemia called the polka. Supper arrived at midnight, followed by more dancing.

It was apparently at one of these dances that Colt first came to know the "Miss Jarvaces," as he referred to them in his letter to Lewis Carr, or, as the press referred to them, the "Misses Jarvis." Elizabeth Jarvis and her sister, Hetty, were regularly featured in newspaper society columns. Their father was a prominent minister and their mother was the heiress of a Rhode Island fortune, endowing the sisters with a perfect blend of respectability and money.

On the same day Colt arrived at the Ocean House that August, Elizabeth and her sister were described in the *Hartford Courant* in a special dispatch from Newport: "The two Misses Jarvis, of Middletown, Connecticut, are as lovely as ever; the bright black eyes of one and the fair complexion, mild and pleasing manner of the other possess the same power as ever, and always gather a crowd of admirers around them." Elizabeth, the eldest, was the one with the bright black eyes. Images from later years do not suggest a great beauty, but her eyes glimmer with intelligence and animation, and many men found her irresistible.

Precisely when or how Sam and Elizabeth met is not clear, but it was probably as early as 1850, when both attended the costume ball at the Ocean House. Elizabeth went as the heroine in the play of the *Enchantress*, in a Greek dress, diamond necklace, and two strings of pearls. Colt made a "splendid" appearance in "the costume of a Turkish engineer." The following year, 1851, at least one newspaper put Elizabeth and Sam together again in a small item that seemed to intimate a connection between the two of them. "The two Misses Jarvis of Middletown, Connecticut, are much admired. Their bright eyes and pleasant faces are accomplishing more mischief than they can possibly atone for by a long life of penitence. They even effect more terrible mischief upon palpitating hearts than Colt's famous revolvers."

Now, as the 1852 season wound down, Sam and Elizabeth found themselves together again at the ball. In a "dazzling scene of beauty and enchantment," reported a Boston paper, "graceful and elegant forms floated round with bewildering beauty." The paper described the usual roster of eligible young women, including this item: "The Misses Jarvis, of Connecticut, might have been mistaken for Night and Morning, so beautiful, yet so unlike were they. The one with eyes and hair black as jet, and quite as brilliant"—that would be Elizabeth—"the other with soft blue eyes, and the lightest auburn hair. Both were thronged with admirers."

As for the men, "the first in our good esteem, as the most perfect gentleman, and by all odds the handsomest man present, was Col. Colt, of revolver notoriety. To look at him one would never suppose he could recognize, much less improve upon such implements of barbarous warfare as pistols and revolvers, and such like. There is hearty good humor in the cordial grasp of his hand, and Nature's nobleman stamped upon every feature of his face."

Did Nature's nobleman make his intentions known to the young woman with the jet-black eyes? Did they dance? Did they visit the cupola at the top of the Ocean House, where courting couples sometimes went to gaze out at the sea?

Whatever they said or did that late-summer night in 1852, Colt was not ready to propose. First, he had some business to attend to abroad, including the matter of the boy he invariably called his nephew and the young woman he sometimes called his niece.

III

A month after closing the season in Newport, accompanied by tools, machines, and a group of his best mechanics from Hartford, Colt boarded the *Baltic* for England. "I shall want a first rate suite of rooms near Trafalgar Square," he had written in advance to Charles Dennet. "Trusting all will be ready on my arrival in the work shop for immediate operations."

All was not ready. Dennet had gotten the rooms—the Trafalgar Hotel for the men, the more luxurious Morley's for Colt—and Charles Manby had secured for him the factory, three stories high and three hundred feet long in a good location on the river. But the factory still required extensive additions, including an adequate steam engine to power it. As the American mechanics cooled their heels at his expense, Colt worked from an office near Trafalgar Square, at 1 Spring Gardens. From nine in the morning till eight in the evening, he labored to expedite the launch of the armory.

One November morning, while awaiting the arrival of a clerk, he took time to write a letter to his lawyer and friend Ned Dickerson. Colt grumbled that he was facing "forty thousand perplexities," but he was in feisty spirits. "Ned they say the world was not made in a minute. Damn me if I believe it would never have been made if it fell the lot for Englishmen to take the job." The idea that this industrial backwater was the world's greatest power was absurd to Colt. "Yet they say here when the lion wags his tail all of Europe trembles. Now Ned it is my humble opinion that he may wag and be damned so far as mechanic arts are concerned. His biggest flourish would not scare the youngest of the Yankee boys I brought here with me." Colt closed this very American letter by telling Dickerson about the Thanksgiving party he'd just given for about twenty Yankees. "We had a good long sitting & all went home comfortably drunk."

The factory was finally running by the start of 1853. Smoke billowed from its boiler and furnace chimneys. Workers crawled over the steep roof and painted a giant 176-foot-long sign: COLT'S PATENT FIREARMS. "It makes the bulls stare," one of Colt's American workers, Henry Alvord, proudly wrote to his brother back home. He meant the John Bulls—the English—who marveled at this brazen American self-promotion. "For the first few days it was up there was a crowd to be seen at all hours of the day viewing it."

Inside, work at first proceeded slowly. The English hands were not used to machines, much to the annoyance of their American counterparts, who derided them as dense and sluggish. As the months progressed, though, the pace picked up. By springtime, Colt had 150 employees. Journalists streamed through regularly to study the great array of American machines used for cutting, boring, and pounding. "It is so well ordered, so complete, so striking in its results, that all engaged in manufacture may learn something from it," one English newspaper observed. "It is itself one large machine, well oiled too, which takes in at one end a shapeless lump of iron and a piece of wood, and puts out at the other a beautifully finished arm."

Perhaps because they were newer to these machines than Americans, the British were better at capturing the extraordinary changes in manufacturing that would soon sweep through their empire and much of western Europe. Journalists filed long and detailed reports about the factory and the new American System. "The system of employing one machine only for one operation, and having a tool shaped for each particular part of the pistol, increases the outlay of capital on the works—but greatly promotes the accuracy of the finished article," explained one publication, the *Expositor*, that October. Because machine work required more attention than strength, women "may occupy this place with great advantage and propriety," and some of the machines were so easy to use that children could work them. When a writer from Charles Dickens's *Household Words* (possibly Dickens himself) visited the armory in 1854, he would note how "delicate-handed little girls do the work that brawny smiths do in other gun-shops." He was impressed, too, by the number of men who came to the armory from other trades. Because the machines did not take years of apprenticeship and training to master, workers could slip from one trade to another. If this could be generalized, "the working world would go more smoothly than it does."

Along with journalists came numerous luminaries to tour the armory. Lajos Kossuth visited in April and was presented with a pistol. Cornelius Vanderbilt, Colt's long-ago lunch companion, dropped by with his family while on holiday. When the famous British engineer James Nasmyth visited, he had an almost religious awakening as he absorbed the "spirit that pervaded the machines": "In those American tools there is a common-sense way of going to a point at once, that I was quite struck with; there is great simplicity, almost a Quaker-like rigidity of form, given to the machinery; no ornamentation, no rubbing away of corners, or polishing; but the precise, accurate, and correct results."

IV

During the winter and spring of 1853, Colt occasionally left his London office for a trip to Belgium. That nation had the largest gunmaking industry in Europe, concentrated in Liège, and some of its gunsmiths had realized that they could make a tidy profit from counterfeit Colts. Not only were these fakes, they were badly made fakes, wrote Colt, "the most infurnal productions I ever have looked at & better calculated to kill behind [than] before." Colt had a Belgian patent, and he intended to shut down the infringers. His agent in Belgium, John Sainthill, would then license Colt's design to some local manufacturers.

John Sainthill was given another matter to handle that spring, probably not one he'd anticipated when he signed on to work for Colt. "I sent my neffue to Brussels yesterday," Colt wrote to the Belgian in mid-March of 1853, "and directed him to call at your house when he got there, and report himself to Miss Julia, Mrs. Sainthill, or yourself."

References to the nephew and Miss Julia began showing up in Colt's letters regularly in that spring of 1853. The identity of the "neffue" is clear enough. He was Sammy, the boy born to Caroline Colt, née Henshaw, in the late fall of 1841, ostensibly the son of John C. Colt but more likely the son of Sam Colt. His full name was Samuel Caldwell Colt and he was now eleven years old, living under the care of Miss Julia. But who was *she*?

For the next several years—for the rest of Colt's life, in fact—Julia would make occasional, fleeting entrances into his correspondence. Her last name, when it first began appearing, was *Lester*, though it was soon embellished into the more English-sounding *Leicester*. It would change once more, in 1857, when she married a German nobleman named Friedrich Von Oppen and became Julia Von Oppen, or simply Madam Von Oppen. Though she debuts in Colt's correspondence in the early months of 1853, a ledger kept by Ned Dickerson in December of 1851 has brief references to her. "Rec'd of Sam Colt his check for J. Lester but had paid the same amount before and held this check to be applied." A month later: "I paid Julia Lester on order of Sam Colt—$200.00." A letter written by Julia to Sam some years later establishes that she lived in New York in 1850, taking piano lessons that were paid for by Colt, or "Uncle Sam," as she calls him, her "guardian and foster father."

According to Colt's biographer William Edwards, the identity of Julia is easily solved. She was none other than Caroline, the young German girl whom Colt secretly married in 1835—then married off to his brother on John's execution day. As Edwards tells it, Colt essentially banished Julia/Caroline (his "ward") and Sammy (his "neffue") to Europe to get them out of his way in America, where they were a distraction and an embarrassment now that he had begun courting a suitable bride.

Edwards does not reveal where he gleaned this information, other than to vaguely cite a conversation with a Colt descendent named Harold G. Colt. He may simply have deduced it. Indeed, it would make sense that the woman traveling with and caring for Colt's nephew was the boy's mother. It would be reasonable to conclude, too, that the negative attention surrounding the John Colt case had compelled Caroline to change her name. Further, it makes sense that Colt would want to send mother and child to Europe, where he could visit them regularly but where they were a safe distance from home.

Edwards's version has several problems, though, starting with a side-by-side comparison of one surviving letter from Caroline and two from Julia. Not only is the penmanship in these letters quite different, but so is the form of expression; Caroline writes in the simple, stilted fashion of someone ill at ease with language; Julia's thoughts flow off her pen exuberantly and floridly. Every indication is that the letters were written by different people.

Some evidence suggests, too, that Julia was still a young woman, not far beyond girlhood, in 1853. In a letter offering his home to Julia, for example, Sainthill mentions the possibility of acquiring tutoring or schooling for her. Even if we assume that Caroline was young at the time of John Colt's arrest in 1841, say seventeen or eighteen (press reports estimated her age as twenty-one or so), she would be in her late twenties or early thirties in 1853, well beyond girlhood and schooling. And even if we put aside the questions of written expression and age, it seems unlikely that Julia, in a personal letter to Sam—a letter she'd have no reason to expect anyone to read but the two of them—would refer to him as her "uncle" and "foster-father" if he was, in fact, her lover.

Julia and especially Sammy would remain in Colt's life to the very end, dropping more clues along the way. For the moment, in that winter of 1853, Colt was trying to find somewhere for them to live. Both had apparently been staying with him at his rooms in London, and he wished to have them removed to more permanent and, it seems, distant habitation. Sainthill, out of kindness or perhaps just an interest in pleasing Colt, had agreed to take in both the ward and the nephew. "Sammy's book education has been very much neglected," Colt wrote in preparation for the boy's journey to Brussels. "Keep a strict eye upon him without too much indulgence."

V

Colt embarked for America—again via the *Baltic*, his steamship of choice—on June 26 of 1853. During his absence his business had grown substantially. The Hartford armory now employed five hundred hands. Profits were pouring in, and Colt was becoming rich. Not Vanderbilt rich, not Astor rich, but rich enough, much to the astonishment of the accountants at R. G. Dun & Company, to finance from earnings the largest building project in Hartford's history.

What Colt was up to in the South Meadow was now clear. While his full vision had not yet been revealed, its scope was evident in the proposals he submitted to the city for infrastructure, including roads, sewers, water, and, most important, a massive two-mile-long dike on the western bank of the Connecticut River. Colt promised to undertake all the work himself, provided the city would grant him tax abatements.

Many people in Hartford found the proposal ludicrous, as it was based on the premise that Colt could hold back the Connecticut River from its natural floodplain. Whether the city should aid Colt in what might be a quixotic scheme played out loudly in Hartford's two leading newspapers. The *Hartford Times*, like Colt, was Democratic in its politics and backed Colt effusively, almost sounding at times like a company house organ. The conservative and Whig-leaning *Hartford Courant*, while admiring Colt's enterprise, took a more skeptical view of his brash plans.

As he negotiated with the city, Colt worked to pry a tract of land he coveted from Solomon Porter—the same Porter who owned the building in which Colt's current factory operated. Porter lived with his wife on elevated ground at the northern edge of the South Meadow, on a farm where he raised cattle and grew prizewinning apples. At seventy, Porter straddled Hartford's bucolic past and its industrial future. A manufacturer, a farmer, and a landlord—he held the deed to the land on which City Hall stood—he was one of the wealthiest men in the city and known to be shrewd in business, but he had never before met such a force of pure will as Colt. In a letter to the *Courant*, he accused Colt (whom he pointedly called *Mister* rather than *Colonel*) of a "grossly abusive attack," while ridiculing his hubristic "visions of an unbuilt city." Porter had been harassed by representatives of Colt, who made offers on the condition they be immediately accepted, then almost instantly changed their terms. It was not he who had behaved unreasonably, Porter insisted, "nor have I ever before heard any man blamed for declining to sell his house for a price named by a third person."

Later, stories would circulate that Colt bought up a majority of shares in a Hartford bank just for the vindictive pleasure of forcing Porter off its board of directors. Another story had it that Colt induced a local prostitute to open a bordello next to Porter's house to lower the value of his property. At the very least, Colt exerted pressure on the city (and by extension on Porter) by threatening to leave Hartford and take his business elsewhere unless his demands were met. On several occasions he went so far as to offer his South Meadow land for sale in Hartford newspapers. Porter refused to budge, and the city refused to give Colt a break on taxes.

Colt had always operated politically as an influencer, but the fight with Porter and the Common Council brought him into a more blatantly partisan role. With the Democratic *Times* carrying his water in frequent attacks on the city, Colt appealed to the public directly, first circulating a petition to the Common Council, signed by 663 citizens of "intelligence and respectability," then organizing a rally, on October 8, 1853, at which two thousand people gathered to support Colt's plan. Colt did not attend the rally himself, but the publisher of the *Times*, Alfred Burr, read aloud from a letter in which Colt warmly addressed the people of Hartford, expressing his love for the "city of my nativity" and his hope to stay in Hartford and bless the city with his business—if only the Common Council would do the right thing and grant him a tax abatement.

On Friday, October 14, in his capacity as colonel in the Connecticut state militia, Colt led the Governor's Horse Guard, sixty riders dressed in military uniform, on a ceremonial trot around Hartford. He then dismounted and addressed the men "in a handsome manner making wholesome suggestions, and expressing the kindest regard for their future prosperity," as the press reported it. He was leaving for Europe that very afternoon, he told the horsemen, and therefore regretfully resigned as their leader. Later that afternoon, the horsemen escorted Colt and his brother James to a steamboat bound for New York. The following morning, the brothers embarked on the *Baltic* to Liverpool.

VI

What James Colt was doing aboard the *Baltic* with Sam was a complicated story in itself, and the start of a longer narrative that was not going to end well for either Colt brother. Inviting James to London would prove to be one of the worst decisions Sam ever made.

Sam and James had remained close since childhood. Of the original ten Colts who had lived in the house on Lord's Hill, only Sam, James, and Chris Jr. remained alive—and the latter, long estranged from Sam and lost in dissipation, just barely. James had always been a prolific correspondent, keeping Sam apprised of his every triumph and travail in St. Louis. After years of struggling as a lawyer, he'd gotten himself named a judge, earning a respectable $3,000 a year. "You will see by the papers I am gaining a reputation," he crowed after one notable case. In another letter he announced to Sam that he was going to be asked to fill the seat of Thomas Hart Benton, the legendary senator from Missouri. When Sam expressed skepticism that James was bound for the US Senate, James assured him it was true. "[M]y personal enemies are beginning to find out that Colt will succeed in St. Louis in spite of all they can do backed by the devil himself."

When not boasting about his career, James gloated about his wife. He had been married for a few years now to "Mrs. Singleton W. Wilson," as he'd first introduced her in a letter to Sam, using the full name of her former husband—the same husband who had challenged James to a duel for cuckolding him. James's marriage to Mrs. Wilson had been a scandal in St. Louis, but he professed to be highly pleased with the results, and he wanted Sam to admire his fortunate state. "If you were to follow my example in connecting yourself with some lady whose head and heart beats with every thought and impulse of your own you too would be happier than you are now." James dangled the image of his wife before Sam, almost as if to tempt him with her charms. In one letter he described her lying in bed across the room, and in another he wrote, "I want to show you my wife and then see if you think I have been a fool." And in yet another: "My wife already knows you by daily talk as well as I do, and I am only afraid that when you are thrown into contact that she will like you a damn sight too well."

If James was petulant and narcissistic, he was also, often, ruminative and sensitive—"girlish," as he shamefully acknowledged to Sam. While Sam operated by instinct and action, James *felt*, and his letters are filled with passionate soliloquies and professions of love. Early in the mornings, hours before dawn, James sat by candlelight and wrote long letters to his brother, telling Sam that "the most pleasurable moments I spend are employed in thinking and holding communion with you." In part, James's affection sprang from gratitude for Sam's generosity. There had always been small gifts, such as the set of cricket bats and equipment Sam once sent when James was organizing a cricket team in St. Louis. There had also been a number of loans over the years, more every year now that Sam's fortunes were rising. "I've never written a letter to you that gives me so much embarrassment," James wrote in May of 1852, just before asking for additional money. By his own calculation, he owed $6,500 to Sam that May. Less than a year later, in February of 1853, the total was $12,500.

It was in a letter thanking Sam for a recent loan—"God bless you for your kindness"—that James first mentioned the plan they had discussed for James to take the helm of the London armory. James had spent much of his adult life pressing Sam to hire him, but now he hesitated. "I don't see how it is possible for me to go to Europe while I am on the bench," he'd written to Sam in March 1853, then, four days later, "The question of whether I ought to go to Europe or not I have debated a great deal."

In August, Sam had spelled out the terms of his offer: "What I want you to do in England is to take the entire charge of my business there. You will have to make all purchases & contracts & sign my name to checks in my absence. . . . For your service in London I will give you one half of the net profits of my establishment there & I guarantee that the half shall not be less than Four Thousand Dollars a year."

Difficult to discern in all of this is Sam's motive in making his offer. Was it generosity? A sense of obligation? Or was he simply looking for a way to get James to pay off the debt he owed? He must have believed that James was up to the job; it is hard to imagine he would have offered it otherwise. "I have every confidence," he wrote to James, "in your ability & integrity."

James mulled the offer over through the summer, finally deciding to accept. He resigned his judgeship at the start of fall and arrived in Hartford in late September to spend a few weeks with Luther Sargeant "to learn his way of doing the business." Then, that October of 1853, the brothers went to London.

A British journalist named Joachim Stocqueler visited Sam and James at the London armory in late 1853 or early 1854. Stocqueler found the armory to be "a model of completeness, order, and economy." He was less flattering about the Colt brothers. "Colt was extremely illiterate, and not remarkable for temperance," he recalled of Sam. "I saw him kick a panel out of his office-door in a rage, and then write to a carpenter to come and mend his 'dore.'"

Stocqueler found James "as handsome in person as the colonel, but full of prejudice against 'yellow gals.'" While out on the town with the Colts, Stocqueler witnessed an awkward encounter between James and a woman. "A negress addressed him one evening at the Argyll Rooms, where 'gravity' ought not to have been, and he shrunk from her in horror, to the infinite diversion of the northern colonel." Stocqueler left it to his readers to know that the Argyle Rooms was a club in the Trocadero section of London where wealthy men rendezvoused with high-end prostitutes. This little anecdote— James's squeamishness; Sam's mirth at his brother's expense—foretells a fraught dynamic between the Colts.

It would be a while, though, before Sam came to terms with the cost of bringing James into his business. For the moment, any apprehension either brother felt about their arrangement was swept away by extraordinary and fortuitous developments. That fall, Russia invaded the Ottoman Empire. Europe was at war.

VII

The Crimean War began with a minor quarrel between Russian Orthodox monks and Roman Catholic monks regarding access to religious sites in Jerusalem. The Holy Land was then under the rule of the Ottoman Empire, which is to say, of the sultan of Turkey, whom Colt had visited four years earlier in Constantinople. For Czar Nicholas I, the dispute was a welcome pretext to invade and annex the so-called Danubian provinces of the Ottoman Empire—modern-day Romania—then continue advancing across the Danube and deeper into the empire. In late November, a Russian convoy attacked and destroyed the Turkish fleet at the port of Sinop, on the Black Sea. The prospect of Russia expanding unchecked into Ottoman territory could not be abided by the English or the French, and before the end of 1853 both nations were preparing to join the war on the side of the Ottomans. With the uncanny timing that seemed to attend his every move in these years, Colt had opened his London armory at the very moment the market for his revolvers suddenly expanded in Europe.

At first, Colt did not have any orders from the British army. In its way, the British War Department was as stodgy as Colt considered the US Ordnance Department to be. But Colt went ahead and produced guns as fast as possible in anticipation of orders he was sure would come. "He is driving all parts of the pistol as much as though he was selling as many as he could make," wrote the American worker Henry Alvord to his brother. By January, Colt had twenty thousand guns on hand or in the works and was regularly inviting high-ranking officers to the armory to give them tours or he was in London charming and cajoling them. "I expect," Alvord wrote, "that he is trying to fife the anthem of bang into them."

Colt was confident the British would buy his guns. But if they did not, he assured his American workers, he would find other customers. On February 17, 1854, he wrote an orotund letter to Napoléon III of France: "Col. Samuel Colt, a citizen of the United States of America, has the honor to offer his most respectful felicitations to his Imperial Majesty." Colt reminded the emperor of their time together at Saint-Cloud and how much the emperor had enjoyed firing Colt's revolvers. "And in case His Majesty should desire to have a depot for the Manufacture of these Arms erected in France," Colt added, "an intimation to that effect will receive immediate attention."

The same day that Colt wrote to Napoléon III, he received a visit at the armory from Prince Albert. He greeted the prince formally, expressing how honored he was by the visit. "His Royal Highness replied that he had heard a great deal about the Colt Revolvers," reported the *British Army Despatch and Nautical Standard*, "and was anxious, by ocular demonstration, to see the manner in which they were manufactured." Colt gave the prince a tour of the entire armory, ending at the shooting gallery for an hour of pistol practice. The prince seemed to enjoy every minute of it.

Orders started coming in soon after that. On March 8, the Royal Navy requested four thousand revolvers for its Baltic fleet. Colt sent the first fifty on March 14 as a token, with a promise to send fifteen hundred more within a fortnight. Leaving the armory in his brother's hands, he then started home to America.

VIII

The America Colt left in October of 1853 was still enjoying peace and prosperity; the country to which he returned in April of 1854 seemed to be suddenly unraveling. Of course, nothing was really sudden about it. Six years had passed since the end of the Mexican War when a future conflict became practically inevitable, and another six would pass before the election of Abraham Lincoln and the start of southern secession. But 1854 was, for many, the moment of recognition.

The man who deserves most of the credit—or blame—for the events of 1854 is Stephen A. Douglas, the diminutive but fierce senator from Illinois, who would one day run for president (with Colt's support) against Abraham Lincoln. In January, while Colt still was in London, Douglas had introduced to Congress a new compromise between the north and the south meant to fine-tune some of the earlier compromises on slavery. What the Compromise of 1850 had patched up, however, the compromise of 1854 inadvertently tore apart, exposing, once again, the suppurating wound that could be covered but never healed.

Unlike the arrangement of 1850, this new compromise, known as the Kansas-Nebraska Act, did not concern western land won from Mexico in war. The land in question now was the flat prairie between the Missouri River and the Rocky Mountains. This had been acquired much earlier, in the Louisiana Purchase, and had lain more or less unpopulated by whites ever since, little more than a series of rest stops on the long road west. But as more people passed through it, more paused and poked around in the fertile soil of the river valleys and thought, Why not here? Meanwhile, powerful men back east, including Stephen Douglas—who had a financial stake in the matter—were already planning a great transcontinental railroad they hoped to run through this land on the way to California. The time had come to organize Nebraska into a US territory. This meant figuring out its disposition to slavery. It also meant confronting the Native Americans who lived and hunted there, but that was not the immediate concern of Douglas and his allies.

The south was adamant that the new territory allow slavery. A free Nebraska would disturb the carefully wrought balance of power between slave states and free states, a balance, believed southerners, on which the country had depended since the drafting of the US Constitution sixty-seven years earlier. Douglas came up with what he believed to be a clever solution: divide the territory in two, call the northern half Nebraska, the southern half Kansas, then put the question of slavery to popular sovereignty—that is, let local residents decide the issue with a vote. Presumably Nebraska would vote to be free, while Kansas, which was topographically similar to Missouri, would choose slavery. Douglas's solution had a great many problems, but the greatest was that it required repealing the long-standing ban on slavery north of the 36°30' parallel that had been established in 1820 by the Missouri Compromise.

In May of 1854, the Kansas-Nebraska Act passed through both houses of Congress and was signed into law by President Franklin Pierce. In time, it would become clear that the new law was the first in a series of Pyrrhic victories for the south that would carry the country into war and ultimately cost the south the very institution it wanted so desperately to preserve.

For many northerners, Kansas became the place to draw a line in the prairie grass and take a stand against the spread of slavery. "Come on then, Gentlemen of the Slave States," exclaimed William Seward, now a senator from New York, on May 25 in a rousing speech on the Senate floor, "since there is no escaping your challenge, I accept it in behalf of the cause of freedom. We will engage in competition for the virgin soil of Kansas, and God give the victory to the side which is stronger in numbers as it is in right."

The night after Seward's speech, a large group of antislavery whites and abolitionists stormed the city jail in Boston to demand the release of a captured fugitive slave named Anthony Burns. When federal troops sent by President Pierce violently punished the group, Boston responded with outrage. It was one thing to tolerate slavery hundreds of miles to the south; it was another to have it enforced in your own backyard. "We went to bed one night old fashioned, conservative, Compromise Union Whigs," recalled the textile manufacturer Amos Adams Lawrence, "& waked up stark mad Abolitionists."*

A newspaper in Pittsburgh excoriated the "bullies of Missouri and Arkansas" who were threatening to kill northern abolitionists who came into Kansas. The time for being "mealy-mouthed" about such insults had passed. "In this state of the case northern emigrants should remember two things. First, the whole of Kansas and Nebraska is ours, since we acquired

---

* Amos Adams Lawrence was a nephew of Samuel Lawrence, the Colt family friend.

it for a good consideration and by an irrepealable compact. Secondly, every man from the north should be provided with a good rifle and Colt's revolver."

Colt was back in Hartford that spring just in time for the flood. It began raining on Thursday, April 27, and kept raining hard for four days. By noon of Monday, May 1, the Connecticut River was nearly twenty-eight feet above low water, "the severest freshet of which we have any record," reported the *Hartford Courant*. Large sections of the city were submerged, including much of downtown Hartford, the lower floor of Colt's factory in the Porter building, and most of the South Meadow. The water rose so rapidly that men working on Colt's dike had to be rescued in boats. The dike was twenty-five feet high, making it three feet too low.

This was the exactly the kind of Icarus-like disaster that Colt's detractors had predicted for him. Even his sycophants at the *Hartford Times* acknowledged that the flood had "tested to some degree the dyke that Col. Colt is building." But as the *Times* quickly noted, the dike, though overtaken, did not wash away. It was still there when the water receded, and so was Colt's resolve. He was moving forward as planned, he announced, only now the dike would be raised to thirty-three feet. Two weeks later, he resumed buying land in the South Meadow.

On July 4, 1854, Colt invited all of Hartford to his new property to celebrate the nation's birthday. The day was oppressively hot but thousands gathered under the sun for the festivities. Shortly after 4:00 p.m., two hot-air balloons lifted off from the meadow, one operated by an American, the other by a Frenchman, each aeronaut waving his nation's flag as he ascended. Both rose to the height of nearly a mile before gradually descending and drifting east to the town of Manchester, where they landed at 5:15 p.m. or so.

Later that evening, after sunset, the meadow was even more crowded, as nearly twenty thousand people craned their necks to watch a display of fireworks provided by Colt. Afterward, everyone agreed it was the most spectacular Independence Day Hartford had ever seen.

IX

Colt's 1836 revolver patent had already been extended once after its initial fourteen-year term. That seven-year extension was not set to expire until February of 1857, but the sooner Colt had the new extension in hand, the better he could plan for the future. That is why, earlier in the year, while abroad in Europe, Colt had assigned his friend and lawyer Ned Dickerson the task of getting the patent renewed.

Colt and Dickerson were close in these years, so intimate as to seem almost romantically entangled. "You have been away so long that I begin to feel a longing to see you once more—to have another long talk and frolic together," wrote Dickerson in one of his letters to Colt. "Since you are gone I have no one to sleep with but my wife, and no one to drink with at all." Men shared beds merely to sleep in those days, so "sleep with" did not mean then what it does now, but it was a striking thing, still, for one man to write to another.

Dickerson devoted the greater part of his letters in 1854 not to personal matters but to the "patent business," as he called it. Through the winter and spring, with a cadre of lesser lawyers and agents under his command, he had worked hard to lobby Congress to vote in favor of a renewal. As for what this lobbying entailed, rumors had been flying around Washington for months, and now, in the summer of 1854, it came to this:

> Resolved, That a committee of seven members be appointed to inquire whether money has been offered to members, or other illegal or improper means used, to induce members to aid in securing the passage or defeat of a bill to extend Colt's patent for seven years.

The special committee was formed at the request of members of the House of Representatives who had come to suspect that men working for Colt—Dickerson and his underlings—had systematically cajoled, seduced, and outright bribed a number of their colleagues to vote in favor of a patent extension. Led by "Honest John" Letcher of Virginia, the committee called numerous witnesses to testify about various methods employed by "agents and lawyers" of Colt to obtain a positive outcome for him.

At the least, the investigation revealed that Dickerson had thrown numerous "costly and extravagant entertainments" in his rooms at the National Hotel, where congressmen were wined and dined and flirted with by attractive women who, sooner or later, whispered into their ears about the benefits of Colt's patent extension. (It later came out that these women had themselves been won over by gifts from Colt, including gloves sent from Paris.) When Dickerson was called to testify before the committee on July 15, he coolly admitted to hosting the dinners, but explained that it was simply his custom to share his meals with friends. "It has been the habit of my life to entertain company every day, if I can get the time."

When pressed, Dickerson further admitted that he had come to Washington with several dozen pistols to "show around." In fact, he had brought them to dispense as gifts. One small revolver had been given to a congressman for his eleven-year-old son, who was quite ill at the time. The congressman was baffled to learn that Colt's associates knew he had a sick son. They seemed to know everything about everybody.

The most serious yet hardest to prove accusation against Dickerson and Colt was that they offered money to congressmen in "contingent fees." A contingent fee was not money paid up front but rather a sum promised in advance of a vote, to be paid only if the measure passed. Not only did this arrangement support the flimsy pretense that the money was not technically a bribe, it also gave congressmen an incentive to work on Colt's behalf and promote the extension to their colleagues. Dickerson denied any knowledge of contingent fees when he testified, but in a letter earlier in the year he had plainly told Colt about his plan to use them. "If we win it will cost a large sum in contingent fees, but if we lose it will not cost a great deal."

Colt arrived in Washington on July 14 and was called before Congress on Monday, July 17, two days shy of his fortieth birthday. He began testifying at 6:00 p.m., in the cool of the evening but also, significantly, after the dinner hour. He began by reading a statement that had been prepared for him by Dickerson. This argued that Colt had been abroad all winter and therefore had nothing to do with any measures taken to secure his patent extension. "If any unlawful means have been resorted to by any person in favor of this bill, it has been done without my knowledge, consent, or approval, and I should condemn it as readily as any other person." Colt then took questions. In response to all of these he expressed ignorance and indignation, pretending to have only the vaguest idea of how much money Dickerson was given or where any of it went.

More surprising to the committee than Colt's memory lapses was that he was obviously drunk as he testified. One pro-Colt congressman, James T. Pratt of Connecticut, while conceding that Colt may have *appeared* drunk, insisted he was just ill. But even some who defended Colt did not question that he was "slightly excited." They merely pointed out that he had been called to testify *after* the dinner hour and so naturally had arrived refreshed by a few drinks.

The investigation ended with a report implicating Colt in a conspiracy to bribe members of Congress but providing no hard evidence and no clear conclusions. It was determined that the best thing to do about Colt and his patent extension, for the moment, was nothing.

X

However Congress decided on his patent, Colt continued to hold a virtual monopoly on revolvers in the United States. He also enjoyed the kind of market penetration and brand recognition that few if any other American products had ever known. If not quite staple items in American households, Colt revolvers were a staple of American newspaper coverage, featured almost daily in gripping stories of murders, suicides, accidents, adulterous affairs, robberies, and duels.

Many revolver stories began with an act of villainy by one party or another, but others featured brave and worthy gunmen who wielded the weapon to punish scoundrels. In Ottawa, Illinois, a canalboat captain named Henry Brown, armed with two revolvers and a rifle, fought off a gang of rowdies who had boarded his boat and thrown his wife's dog overboard; by the time he was done, all seven were dead. In California's Sierra Nevada, a gold prospector named Jonathan Davis single-handedly fought off eleven violent outlaws with two Colt revolvers and a Bowie knife. They died, and Davis became an American hero. In the mountains of western Virginia, a "young lady" from Kentucky, described in newspapers as "pretty, educated, and sprightly," used the gun to patrol a large tract of wooded wilderness owned by her family but claimed by a land pirate. "She always carries one of Colt's revolvers, and thus armed roams fearlessly over the mountains, following paths seldom trod save by the panther and bear." Perhaps most famously, a group of Colt-armed lawmen in California, led by a former Texas Ranger named Harry Love, pursued the bandit Joaquin Murrieta, himself a crack-shot with a Colt, finally catching and killing him in a gunfight near Fresno in July of 1853. Murrieta's captors soon made their way to a photography studio to pose with their Colt revolvers.

Across the west the revolver was now almost a required accessory, one that no self-respecting man could be seen without. When a young writer named Frederick Law Olmsted—later to achieve fame as a landscape architect and designer of Central Park in New York City—traveled through Texas in early spring of 1854, sending regular bulletins of his experiences and observations to the *New York Times*, he encountered Colt revolvers everywhere he went. "There are probably in Texas about as many revolvers as male adults, and I doubt if there are one hundred in the state of any other make."

Though more familiar by the day, the guns still had a kind of talismanic effect when displayed to Native Americans. Early in 1854, the artist and daguerreotypist Solomon Nunes Carvalho was traveling with John Frémont's fifth and final exploring expedition when a large band of Utahs "came galloping and tearing into camp," armed to the teeth with bows, arrows, and rifles, clearly intending to make trouble. Running to Frémont's tent to report the belligerent Indians, Carvalho found the Pathfinder relaxed and unconcerned. Frémont tore a page from his journal and handed it to Carvalho: "Here take this, and place it against a tree, and at a distance near enough to hit it every time, discharge your Colt's Navy six-shooters. Fire at intervals of from ten to fifteen seconds—and call the attention of the Indians to the fact that it is not necessary for white men to load their arms." Carvalho took the sheet of paper and did as instructed. He had two fully loaded Colts. First he fired one revolver, then the other. By the time he shot all dozen balls, the Indians had been "scared . . . into an acknowledgement that they were all at our mercy, and we could kill them as fast as we liked, if we were so disposed."

Unfortunately for whites, Native Americans were already starting to acquire some of the enchanted weapons themselves. In a well-reported battle in New Mexico in March of 1854, Jicarilla Apaches stole fifty horses and fifty Colt revolvers from the American dragoons. "It is to be understood that they are not so easily intimidated now," one of the news accounts reported of the Apaches, "and they say they are ready to meet the troops."

Those words captured an unmistakable shift in the attitude of western Native Americans toward whites in 1854. Previously, the western tribes had generally been restrained in their encounters with emigrants. That year, within months, various tribes separately concluded that their passivity had been a mistake. On the plains, buffalo herds were diminishing at the hands of white hunters, and Indians were starting to go hungry. The new American Bureau of Indian Affairs had coaxed some tribes to sign treaties that promised rations of beef and other annuities, but these turned out to be insufficient to sustain them. When the Indians stole food from whites, they were met with swift retribution from the US Army.

Here was another affront to the native inhabitants of the west: the army was suddenly everywhere. In 1848, the west had just eight inland forts. By 1854, there were fifty-two. The Kansas-Nebraska Act was partly to blame because it drew whites into territory on the plains they had previously avoided. The newcomers not only helped themselves to the land, they demanded that their government drive off any Indians who presumed to claim it for themselves.

Violent encounters occurred all across the west in 1854, but the most pivotal was an incident that August that came to be known as the Grattan Massacre. Near Fort Laramie, on the banks of the North Platte in eastern Wyoming, a number of Lakota Sioux from the Brulé, Oglala, and Miniconjou clans had gathered to collect their food annuity. On August 18, a Mormon emigrant came into the fort to complain that an Indian had stolen and butchered his cow. The offending Indian was a Miniconjou who was camping at the time with Brulé, under Chief Conquering Bear, down the Platte from Fort Laramie.

On August 19, with thirty men under his command, an overconfident and ill-prepared second lieutenant named John Grattan marched from Fort Laramie to the Sioux lodges. He ordered his men to set up two artillery guns at the outskirts of the camp, then made a halfhearted effort to negotiate with Conquering Bear, demanding the chief hand over the young Miniconjou. When it became clear that Conquering Bear neither could nor would do this, Grattan ordered his men to open fire. Had the guns been well aimed they would have sliced through the camp and slaughtered just about everyone in it. Because they were aimed too high, the shells flew right over the camp, though somehow in the melee the Americans managed to kill Conquering Bear. Before Grattan's men could adjust and reload the guns, the enraged Sioux attacked them. The soldiers were quickly overcome. Thirty of them, including Grattan, were killed on the spot. The thirty-first, though badly injured, made it back to the fort to recount what had happened before he, too, died of his wounds.

Inflamed and emboldened, the Sioux continued to rampage after killing Grattan's squadron. They attacked the emigrant route, which they had previously left more or less unmolested, stealing horses and robbing a stagecoach. By mid-September, according to the *New York Times*, there was "great reason to fear that at this hour at least three thousand blood-thirsty savages are engaged in the work of massacre on the far Western plains, wherever they can find a white man to murder." This was a gross exaggeration but it had some truth. The very thing white Americans had long feared had become a reality.

Many Americans understood that Grattan had stupidly provoked the Sioux and thereby created this reality, but the secretary of war, Jefferson Davis, did not share that view. Davis believed the only sensible way to respond to the massacre of Grattan and his men was to confront the Sioux with the overwhelming might of the American military, such that they would never dare to provoke it again. To carry this out, he summoned the most fierce Indian killer in the US Army, Colonel William S. Harney, former commander of the Second Dragoons and Colt's old friend from Florida. Harney was in Paris that fall, on furlough, when he received his orders from Secretary Davis. On Christmas Eve, he boarded a steamship and headed home to raise an army and acquire some Colt revolvers.

CHAPTER SIXTEEN

Emperor of the South Meadows

1854–56

*Colt's Hartford armory. The dome at the front was—and still is—
cobalt blue, speckled with gold stars, and topped by a colt rearing up on its hind legs.*

I

For a while, Crimea was everything Colt could have wished for in a war. The British Army had been slow to adopt his guns, but the Royal Navy was a constant and ardent customer. In the Battle of Alma, on September 20, 1854, British naval officers armed with Colt revolvers helped defeat Russian forces after a surprise landing on the coast of the Black Sea. Then came the Battle of Balaclava, on October 24, and the start of a yearlong siege on the Russian naval stronghold at Sevastopol. The British press demanded more revolvers for troops, and the War Department obliged. Colt would supply nearly fifteen thousand pistols to the British government in 1854 alone.

A few weeks after the Battle of Balaclava, Colt landed in St. Petersburg, Russia, accompanied by Ned Dickerson. While the men did not hide their

319

presence in the city, they left little record of it. We know something about how they passed their days from a diary kept by Andrew D. White, an attaché of the American delegation to the Russian court. White worked under the US minister to Russia, Thomas H. Seymour, the former governor of Connecticut and Colt's friend. On November 6, Colt (whom White unaccountably called "Rob" Colt in one entry) and Dickerson accompanied White and Seymour to St. Isaac's Cathedral, still under construction at the time. On November 7, the four men toured the Hermitage.

The highlight of the visit occurred on November 11. That afternoon, Colt and Dickerson were given an audience by Czar Nicholas I at the Winter Palace on the Neva River. First constructed by Peter the Great in the early eighteenth century and rebuilt numerous times since, the Winter Palace was as ostentatious a display of imperial strength as any in the world—vast, profusely gilded, and extravagantly marbled. Colt presented the czar with three gold-inlaid revolvers, lethal weapons that were also works of art.* The czar returned the favor with a diamond ring.

But Colt and the czar were not there to exchange gifts. So seriously did Nicholas take this meeting that he had made a special trip into the city from his suburban palace in Gatchina expressly to meet Colt at the Winter Palace. Exactly what they discussed is unrecorded, but we do know Nicholas was looking for some kind of miracle that autumn. He had overplayed his hand against the Ottomans and was losing the war in Crimea. For a czar who valued military strength above all else, this was an untenable humiliation. Indeed, when Nicholas died four months after meeting Colt, ostensibly of pneumonia, there would be whispers that he had killed himself in disgrace. That November, while there was still hope, he may have believed Colt's revolvers could save him.

Before returning to America, Colt stopped in London to check on his armory. The English press had gotten wind of his trip to St. Petersburg, and some papers were reporting that he'd made a secret deal to supply the Russian Army with revolvers and machinery to make guns. Such an act would have demonstrated appalling ingratitude to his British hosts, and Colt was quick to deny it. "It is not true that I have furnished arms or machinery to the Russian government or that I have contracted to furnish arms or machinery to that government," he wrote to the *London Times* that December. "The only truth, as regards me, is that I have been in Russia, as I have been in the other great states of Europe, during the last two months."

* One of these is now displayed in the Hermitage Museum in St. Petersburg. A matching revolver is in the Metropolitan Museum of Art in New York.

II

Colt was back in Hartford at the start of 1855. Pending the completion of the new factory in the South Meadow, he continued to manufacture his guns on Grove Lane. Quarters were cramped but only because business was good. In addition to civilian demand for revolvers, an order for one thousand had come in from the US War Department, to be used for "frontier service." Colt was confident that Colonel Harney—soon to be Brigadier General Harney—would ask for an additional allotment. The old Indian fighter was back from Paris now, in Washington to prepare his campaign against the Sioux.

When spring came to the South Meadow, the apple trees blossomed and the river rose as always, but the two-mile-long dike held firm. Osier willows imported from Europe had been planted along the slopes of the dike to hold the earth with their deep roots. Elm trees grew atop the dike, where the ridge had been smoothed into an attractive public road. Curious citizens ventured out from town on "a most charming afternoon drive," as the *Courant* put it, to watch Colt's new building emerge inside the dike.

The two-hundred-acre complex on the South Meadow now had a name: Coltsville. "Whether the word is sanctioned by the gentleman concerned we do not know," the *Courant* informed its readers, but either way, Colt was building an armory "such as a Titan might have dreamed of." Other structures were rising, too, including a warehouse for the tobacco Colt intended to grow and boardinghouses for workers. There was talk of other buildings soon to come, most notably a grand private residence up the hill from the armory that would represent, according to a newspaper correspondent who had been given a peek of the plans, "something quite Napoleonic in our vicinity."

Colt had already returned to Europe when his older brother Christopher Colt Jr. died, at the age of forty-three, in late May of 1855. Chris had been living at the City Hotel in Hartford with his wife and children. Newspapers gave the cause of death as bleeding from the lungs, which sounds like consumption, but that was the least of it. Years of heavy drinking had taken a toll on Chris's physical and mental health. His conduct over the previous year or so had made him a spectacle in Hartford, stirring up "a great deal of town talk," as James put it in a letter to Sam.

Sam could hardly have avoided bumping into Chris occasionally while in Hartford, but they'd had little intended contact. Chris's name seldom appears in Sam's correspondence other than in brief asides about his dissolute lifestyle and occasional references to his attempts to undermine Sam with claims that he, Chris, had contributed in some way to the development of the revolver. Years earlier, James had described their brother "agrinning" at the prospect of sharing in the profits of Sam's invention, and Chris apparently never let go of the conviction that he was due a part of Sam's success.

James Colt was in Missouri, attending to personal and political affairs, when he got the news of their brother's death. "Poor Christopher," he wrote to Sam as he started back to Hartford, "he had his faults and did many things that were wrong but there are worse people in the world than our late unfortunate brother."

As soon as James arrived in Hartford, it became evident that he was suffering his own troubles—troubles perhaps worse than those that had afflicted Chris. A friend named Harry Beach informed Sam that James was "in a very excited state & in the opinion of his friends damned near deranged—his whole conversation & acts were more like a crazy man than James Colt natural."

Later, Sam would claim that he had seen signs of instability in James for years. Certainly James had exhibited peculiar behavior in London. When Sam brought him there in the fall of 1853, it had been with the understanding that James would remain after Sam left and would run the armory in his absence. But in July of 1854, just a short time after Sam returned to America, James followed him across the Atlantic. England had not agreed with him, he explained, and he missed his wife. "This living without one's wife," he wrote to Sam from St. Louis, "is not what it is cracked up to be." (It was in this letter that James noted Sam's predilection for "a wife in every port" and his own disapproval of such habits. "God knows how you have stood it so long.")

Missing one's wife and despising English weather were hardly signs of madness, but James's natural flightiness had developed into something stranger. "This may seem ridiculous to you Sam," wrote Beach, "but in my opinion it is rather serious. He drank at times very deeply but liquor did not seem to affect him, his brain was so highly excited." More disturbing, he "broods over his imagination & has worked his brain to a fever heat making the wildest & insane speeches possible about past matters in your own family relative to quitting the world &c &c which I prefer not to repeat upon paper." Beach was referring to Sarah Ann's suicide in 1829 and John's in 1842. "I am not alone Sam when I say that nothing however desperate would surprise me with regard to him."

It's obviously impossible to confidently diagnose a man's mental condition based on a few letters written more than a century and a half ago.

But the temporary derangement described by Beach bears similarities to symptoms of what psychiatrists now call bipolar disorder. Given that bipolarity is partly hereditary, it's striking that at least four members of the Colt family suffered from serious, even fatal, mental health problems: Sarah Ann killed herself with arsenic; John, after murdering a man in anger, stabbed himself with a knife; Chris drank himself to death; and now James was "damned near deranged." By comparison, Sam, a functioning alcoholic who occasionally assaulted lawyers and doors, was a beacon of mental health.

Bipolar disorder is characterized by extreme oscillations of mood, from the heights of mania—exuberance, hyperactivity, agitation—to deep despondency. James had exhibited the latter often in the years of his correspondence with Sam, complaining of the "blue-devils" and other protracted episodes of depression. Beach's description of James as behaving "more like a crazy man than James Colt natural" is suggestive of the manic pole of the cycle. In its more acute phases, mania is an engine running at full throttle, all the time, and nothing, not even torrents of alcohol, will suppress it. Delusions of grandeur are a telltale symptom. Might this explain James's recurring assertions that he was destined to be a US senator? A less common manifestation is paranoia, and James apparently suffered this, too. "He feels (very foolishly I tell him) that everybody about you in your employ or who are in any way connected are endeavoring to prejudice you against him and anxious to make a breach between you," wrote Beach. "Those of his most intimate friends who are friendly to you have said everything to persuade him that he was foolish & too suspicious but he has got the idea firmly impressed on his brain."

James's paranoia—if paranoia it was—got a boost that summer when he received a balance sheet from the London armory. Prepared by Luther Sargeant, who had taken over the armory after James fled London, the accounting showed significant financial losses during James's brief tenure at the helm. Not only was this embarrassing, it was potentially disastrous to James's finances, for Sam had agreed to give him half of the net profits of the armory. How had the armory *lost* money during the boom years of the Crimean War? "There can be no doubt, I think, in the minds of any honorable men, but that I have been trifled with," James wrote to Sam—"trifled in a manner, the most cruelly wicked of any instance on record."

Whatever the truth regarding those supposed losses in London, the company was about to suffer much greater losses, and Sam would have no one to blame for these but himself. In his letter to the *London Times* the previous

December, he had denied making a deal to sell guns to the Russians. In fact, he'd made a substantial deal—for five thousand revolvers. He'd at least had the courtesy to manufacture the guns in Hartford, rather than in London, before sending them to St. Petersburg. The first three thousand were ready to ship by early summer. On June 5, Colt's secretary and chief aide, Milton Joslin, mailed a bill of lading to Colt in London for the revolvers plus 125 bales of cotton. Why the cotton? Joslin did not need to explain because Colt knew the answer.

The entire cargo sailed out of New York on June 22, bound for St. Petersburg via the Belgian port of Antwerp and by way of an overland route through Prussia. The Prussian leg was the tricky part. That country had closed it borders to arms during the war, precisely to prevent the transport of guns such as Colt's from going to Russia. Sometime in late July, at a checkpoint in Aix-la-Chapelle, a Prussian officer inspecting 125 bales of cotton became suspicious enough to poke into one of them until he hit something solid. Buried inside each bail was a box, and inside each box were twenty-four Colt revolvers. Both the cotton and the guns were immediately confiscated.

III

Colt was still absorbing the scope of the Prussian calamity when Brigadier General William S. Harney commenced his march on the Sioux. Commanding the largest military expedition since the Mexican War, Harney was going to avenge the deaths of Lieutenant Grattan and his men. More generally, his orders were to operate against hostile Indians who had been harassing, robbing, and, in some cases, killing travelers along the Platte River since the massacre.

After returning from Paris in January of 1855, Harney had slowly made his way across the country, from Washington to St. Louis, then to Fort Leavenworth in Kansas Territory, adding to and organizing his mostly volunteer army along the way. By midsummer he had thirteen hundred men and was ready to mobilize. Harney sent half the men up the Missouri River by steamboat to the newly constructed Fort Pierre, in Dakota territory, to await further orders. The other half he took with him to Fort Kearney, on the Platte River in Nebraska Territory.

Harney's army departed Fort Kearney on August 24, 1855. In side-by-side columns, on foot and horse, the troops marched west along the southern bank of the shallow and muddy Platte, following the path emigrants had been taking for more than a decade. Harney did not know where he would encounter Sioux, but he knew they were likely to be upriver, camped near one of the tributaries of the Platte. When he found them, he would make token gestures of peace, but nobody had any illusions of Harney's intentions. "By God," he was heard to utter as they began the march, "I'm for battle—no peace."

Though largely forgotten, Harney's campaign of 1855 was a turning point in the history of the American west. Since the Mexican War, the American military and Native Americans had skirmished numerous times in the newly acquired territories of Texas, New Mexico, California, and Oregon, as well as in those longer-held areas of the Great Plains in Nebraska Territory. But Harney's march was the first major US military campaign organized specifically to attack western tribes. It was the opening salvo in a thirty-five-year war with Plains Indians that would run through the Sioux Uprising of 1862, the Sand Creek Massacre of 1864, Little Bighorn in 1876, Wounded Knee in 1890, and countless other bloody encounters along the way.

Harney had some light artillery units under his command, but his men were divided mainly into infantry and dragoons. The infantry carried muzzle-loading, single-shot rifles adapted to fire a devilish new conical projectile called a minié ball. Invented in 1847 by the Frenchman Claude-Étienne Minié, these hollow-based bullets dramatically expanded the range of US rifles. Thus loaded, the guns of Harney's infantry were deadly accurate at four hundred yards and could kill at half a mile.

The main actors in Harney's plan would be his dragoons, those horse-mounted units who would soon evolve into the US Cavalry. They were already behaving essentially as cavalry, not just riding on horseback for transportation, that is, but *fighting* on horseback. Even traditional military leaders such as Winfield Scott, commander of the US Army, recognized that mounted units were the key to success in the west. "The great extent of our frontiers, and the peculiar character of the service devolving on the troops," Scott had written in 1850, "render it indispensable that the *cavalry* element should enter largely into the composition of the army." Many American military leaders had been impressed by the fighting prowess of mounted Texas Rangers during the Mexican War, and there is good evidence that the army's new embrace of cavalry was brought about at least in part by the influence of the rangers. One thing the rangers had proved beyond a doubt was that for mounted troops to operate effectively, they required not just horses but revolvers. Harney's dragoons were armed with Colt 1851 Navies.

*   *   *

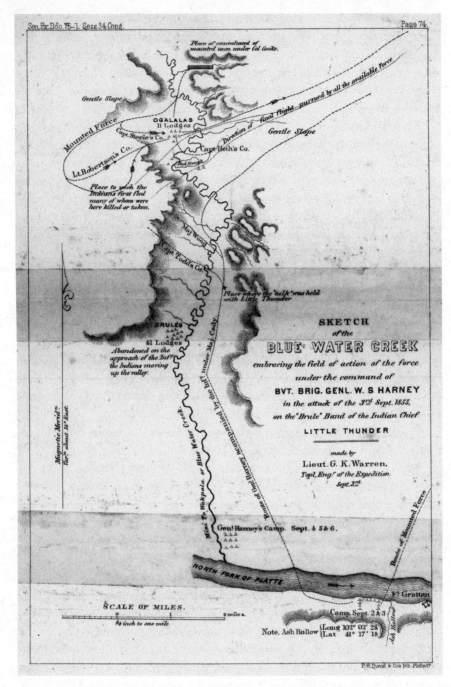

A US Army map illustrating the attack by Brigadier General William S. Harney on the Sioux in September 1855, on the Blue Water Creek in Nebraska. The man who made the map— Lieutenant G. K. Warren—privately considered the events that occurred there to be shameful.

August was too late in the season for California-bound emigrants to make the passage across the plains without risking snow in the mountains, so the soldiers had the trail along the Platte to themselves. "The weather was elegant," recalled one first lieutenant of the nine-day march. "The monotony of our marches was relieved and made fascinating to the men who had never before been on the plains by the frequent appearance of immense herds of buffalos in some instances stretching away in the horizon as far as the eye could cover." When antelope came near, the men shot several and ate the fresh meat at dinner.

On the afternoon of September 2, just beyond the confluence of the Platte's north and south tributaries, Harney's army forded the South Platte. This took them to an emigrant campsite called Ash Hollow, on a hummocky wedge of land between the South Platte and North Platte. Pawnee scouts working for Harney fanned out across the North Platte and came back to report that a band of Sioux were camped on the other side of the river, several miles north, near the banks of a creek called Blue Water. The Sioux camp was really two adjacent camps, one of Brulé Sioux and a smaller of Oglala Sioux, altogether some 250 men, women, and children. Their chief was Little Thunder, who had replaced Conquering Bear after that chief's death during the confrontation with Grattan.

Shortly before midnight on September 2, Harney ordered the infantry across the North Platte. "There are those damned red sons of bitches, who massacred the soldiers near Laramie last year, in time of peace," Harney exhorted his men from the banks of the river. "Now, by God, men, there we have them. . . . Don't spare one of those damned red sons of bitches." As the infantry crossed the river, the dragoons wheeled east around the Indian camp, then turned north to take up covert positions in the sandhills up the valley of the Blue Water.

At dawn the Brulé woke to the sight of troops amassed to their south. Under a truce flag Chief Little Thunder rode out to parley. Harney gave the chief a list of demands—such as turning over the men involved in the Grattan incident—none of which, as Harney well knew, were in Little Thunder's authority to grant. Harney let the discussion go on for a while to give his cavalry plenty of time to position itself up the valley, then told Little Thunder to return to his people and prepare for battle.

No sooner was the chief back at the camp than Harney ordered the infantry to advance and commence fire. With minié balls flying at their backs, the Brulé and Oglala fled north, on foot and horse, up the river valley—and directly into Harney's trap. "Suddenly debouching from their ambuscade," recounted an eyewitness, the mounted dragoons "charged the

Indians with sabre and revolver." The Sioux, armed only with bow and arrow and old flintlock muskets, were unable to mount a defense. Many, including women and children, ran into caves in the sandhills for protection, but the cavalry flushed them out with rifle shots, then killed or captured them with revolvers. When a large group of Indians dashed across the knee-deep Blue Water, seeking refuge in the bluffs to the east, the cavalry pursued. What followed, according to newspaper reports, was "as fine a specimen of a free fight as one could wish to see."

Colt's revolver was uniquely suited for this circumstance; it gave the quarry no opportunity for escape. As General Persifor Smith had said of Colt-armed cavalry in fights against Indians, "They charge them suddenly, are in contact with them but a few minutes, and in that time must do all the execution they expect to do, and for that purpose the revolving pistol is absolutely necessary."

The dragoons ran down the fleeing Indians for five or six miles. An Indian woman named Cokawin later recalled the scene: "As I looked around, I could see the soldiers galloping after groups of old men, women, and children who were running for their lives. Some were running across the valley, only to be met by soldiers and shot right down. It seemed as though there was no place to go." Lieutenant Colonel Philip St. George Cooke, the commander of the cavalry, put it bluntly and without apology: "There was much slaughter in the pursuit."

Eighty-six Sioux were killed, among them women and children. Seventy more women and children were taken prisoner. Harney, who lost just four men, would give a glowing account of the battle in his official report, describing the gallantry and thrill of combat on the open prairie. The impressions of a second lieutenant named Gouverneur K. Warren, attached to Harney as a member of the Corps of Topographical Engineers, were less admiring. "I was disgusted with the tales of valor in the field, for there were few who killed anything but a flying foe," wrote Warren in his journal. Mainly what he recalled of the battlefield were "wounded women and children, crying and moaning, horribly mangled by the bullets."

Following Blue Water Harney would forever be known by Plains Indians as the Butcher. He probably did not object to the epithet. Striking fear into the hearts of Native Americans was precisely what he had come to do. He did it by bringing a new kind of warfare to the west, governed by new rules of engagement. Arrive with overwhelming force. Negotiate in bad faith. Ignore distinctions between aggressors and non-aggressors, and between combatants and noncombatants. Pursue on horseback, firing revolvers at will.

IV

News from the frontier regarding Harney and his revolvers had to be heart-ening to Colt, but the three thousand confiscated Russia-bound guns con-tinued to weigh on him through the fall of 1855. Between the loss of the guns and hefty fines imposed by the Prussian government, the cost of the bungled smuggling operation was going to be as high as $100,000. So far the British press had failed to connect Colt to the Prussian seizure, and he was determined to keep it that way. "I anticipate soon further trouble before the affair is concluded," Sam wrote to James on September 15, "the particulars of which need not be explained here for not one word must be said by you or anybody else on the subject."

Relations between the brothers were strained but civil that Septem-ber. James wrote often, anxious to resolve the issue of the London armory accounting. Sam was slow to respond, much to James's annoyance—"I cannot understand why you take no notice of my letters or telegraphic dispatch"—but when he finally did, it was to make a surprising offer. Brushing aside whatever had transpired in London, he proposed that James come to Hartford to serve "at the head of the establishment during my absence." Sam's only condition was that James pledge himself fully to the business. "If you come, the change you make must be with a view of permanency and not like that to England for a few months & then to leave the business for others to learn."

Sam intended to form a corporation, he told James. It would be known as Colt's Patent Fire-Arms Manufacturing Company and capitalized at $1,250,000. Unlike the P.A.M.C., the P.F.A.M.C. would be totally con-trolled by Colt, who would own the great majority of stock. But he would allow his most trusted deputies to enjoy the benefits of growth, including quarterly dividend checks, by giving them shares. Provided that James made a commitment, Sam promised to "guarantee that your interest shall net you sufficient income," from $4,000 to $5,000 annually, "which certainly is enough to support your family handsomely and give your children the best of an education." Along with the stock, Sam pledged to throw in a new house on Wethersfield Avenue, next to the one he was building for himself.

James's odd response to this generous offer seemed to confirm that he really had come unhinged. "It is very evident to my mind and has been for some time past that you do not intend to deal justly and fairly in regard to our former business matters." He sensed a trap, as if Sam were making his offer only to evade paying him profits from London; as if, pretending to be generous, Sam were forcing him into indentured servitude. "It is time I thought you meant something when you talked a hundred times of your having done nothing for your own family yet. But no! that could not be so. . . . God forgive you for the past and that dark and cheerless future which is fast settling in upon my head and that of my wife and children."

James may have been hysterical, even paranoid, but his concerns were not irrational. If he accepted Sam's proposal, the dynamic between them would no longer be that of brother to brother but of employer to employed. Already their relationship had changed. "You don't seem to act towards me as you did before you had accumulated a large estate," James had written to Sam that fall. But the truth, as James surely grasped, is that he was already trapped. He had given up his judgeship and sold his law library to go to London. He had a wife and several children and no means to support his family in St. Louis—unless he became a US senator, which even he was coming to accept as unlikely. He also owed Sam a great deal of money.

Harder to understand than James's response was Sam's. If the initial offer to James to manage the London armory had been risky, this new offer was positively baffling. James had given numerous indications that he was not suited to running a large business enterprise. He was defensive, sometimes haughty and sometimes needy, easily distracted, frequently overwrought, and, quite possibly—if Sam's accounting of the London armory finances was correct—either financially inept or corrupt. Moreover, James did not especially want the job.

Nonetheless, on October 5, Sam sent a contract to James in which he committed to transferring five hundred shares of capital stock. James's compensation would come out of dividends, but if these ever fell below $4,000 per annum, Sam promised to make up the difference. The one condition was that James had use of the stock only so long as he remained at the company. If he quit, the capital stock reverted to Sam.

V

The new armory was finally complete and ready for operation in October of 1855. The three large buildings were connected to each other in the shape of an H. The largest building, running just inside the dike, was five hundred feet long, sixty feet wide, and four stories tall. Over it loomed an onion-shaped dome, cobalt blue and speckled with gilt stars, partly in homage to the domes of St. Petersburg and partly in homage to Colt; topping this was a weather vane in the shape of a young wild horse rearing up and lunging—the rampant colt that Sam now adopted as his logo. Altogether, the complex added up to forty-six hundred running feet of floor space, with an average width of fifty feet—more than 230,000 square feet of factory.

More impressive than the buildings were the machines inside them, some four hundred in all. Their variety—for pounding, milling, boring, filing, and otherwise shaping metal into guns—was breathtaking. A number of them had been designed and patented by Elisha Root, including a rifling machine, a new and better drop hammer, and various improvements of lathes, jigs, and gauges. Some were so innovative that they would still be in use half a century later. But as the writer Roger Burlingame contended in his 1949 history of American mass production, the true genius of Colt and Root was not their innovation; it was their selective acquisition of the finest existing technology—"the masterly combining of scattered techniques," Burlingame called it. They did not waste time making machines they could find elsewhere, and the Connecticut River Valley was abundantly prepared to meet their needs.

The industrial historian Charles Morris points out that one important reason Colt's armories in London and Hartford were "the most advanced precision-manufacturing operations in the world" at the time was because Root set the machinery up to achieve "process flow." He kept gun pieces moving along swiftly, not clogging up any one station. The longer a certain kind of machine took to perform a function, the more of that machine there were. The total number of distinct machine "operations" that components underwent on the way to becoming a revolver was 454, each so precise that "taken promiscuously from the heaps," claimed one article, the finished pieces "unite almost without manual labor."

The qualifier was important: almost. Colt and Root came close to achieving uniformity, but they did not achieve total interchangeability. Minor variances remained, and pieces still had to be hand-filed to meet tolerances and fit together. But if what came out of Colt's armory was not the final word in mass production, he and Root nonetheless achieved something so close to it, in such quantity, at such speed, as to be revolutionary.

While Coltsville was primarily an armory, it was meant to be more than that. As one newspaper put it, it was "a city within a city." America was filled with company towns long before Coltsville came along. Paterson, New Jersey, had been a kind of company town, and so were New England textile mill towns such as Ware and Lowell. Connecticut alone had Collinsville (axes), Terryville (clocks), Hazardville (gunpowder), and Whitneyville (guns), to name just a few. But Colt was up to something more elaborate than providing employment and housing. Like the founders of Brook Farm and other nineteenth-century utopias, he was trying to create a close-knit and almost self-sustaining community, with its own water supply, gasworks, parks, schools, stores, and, alongside all this, orchards and gardens and livestock. Except Colt's little utopia would have nothing in common with Brook Farm. It would not be run on communitarian or even democratic principles; it would be operated, rather, like a ship, with Colt as its captain, and his word its law.

Captain was not quite it, either. Shortly after his return from Russia, the *Hartford Courant* had nicknamed Colt the "Emperor of the South Meadows." While the paper meant this in jest, it was not far from what Colt had in mind.

By early March of 1856, twenty-three families were living in Coltsville. Housing had just been completed for twenty-four more. A grid of streets, named after notable events and figures in Hartford's history, had been laid out around the factory, and two schools had opened for the children of workers. Colt even put together a brass band—Colt's Armory Band—made up primarily of German immigrants who worked for him.

The band was on hand in early May for the dedication of Charter Oak Hall. Located just west of the armory, the building took its name from the most famous tree in the state, a giant arboreal antique near the northwest corner of the meadow, where the Royal Charter of Connecticut was supposedly hidden in 1687 by Joseph Wadsworth (one of Daniel's ancestors) to prevent the royal governor from revoking it. Charter Oak Hall was to be the center of social and cultural life in Coltsville, "reared for advancing the intellectual and aesthetic culture of mechanics." It included a library for workers and a performance space large enough to seat one thousand people. Looking around the packed auditorium on the evening of the dedication, a reporter observed "as robust, happy, and intelligent a body of artisans as ever it was the fortune of any employer to collect in any one establishment."

Meanwhile, up the hill from the armory, beyond the meadow where Colt's horses ran, a mansion was rising, the largest and most elaborate house ever built in Hartford. This house—this palace—was much too big for a single man. It needed a family. The time had come for Colt to follow Sam Houston's advice and "lie warmer."

VI

In the five or six years that had passed since Colt's first flirtations with her in Newport, Elizabeth Jarvis had transformed from a bewitching belle into a mature woman who seemed to arrive in Colt's life straight from a Lydia

Sigourney poem. Any erotic attractions she once possessed to beguile her Newport suitors had been milled and polished away, leaving a perfect vessel of Victorian wifehood. She brimmed with the Sigourneyan virtues of piety, love, and, above all, devotion. She would be so extraordinarily devoted to Colt as to seem at times to have imagined rather than known him. She later claimed, for example, that he seldom drank and never indulged in tobacco, despite the fact that at his death he would leave behind *thousands* of bottles of wine and liquor and *thousands* of cigars. Elizabeth would share just six years of her life with Sam, but in four subsequent decades she would do everything in her power to curate his image into a benevolent alter ego that bore little resemblance to the original.

Part of her effort evidently included destroying all written correspondence between them. Much about their relationship therefore remains mysterious, starting with their long courtship. Both were quite advanced in age for a first-time marriage in the mid-nineteenth century; he would soon turn forty-two; she was nearly thirty. Colt may have believed that he was too busy to settle down, but why did she wait for him at a time when waiting meant tempting spinsterhood?

Colt finally proposed by February of 1856. We know this because Lydia Sigourney wrote him a note that month to congratulate him for having won, from "the green-house of your life, a most precious Heart-flower." Other than James, perhaps no one had known Colt longer than Sigourney. So it was not surprising that she assumed an almost motherly role now that Colt was to be married, welcoming his bride into her embrace. "My sweet friend," she wrote to Elizabeth on May 29, "I am only too happy to indulge myself in saying how much I think of you and your noble life's companion, and how earnestly I pray for the happiness of both."

They were married on Thursday, June 5, in Middletown, Connecticut, downriver from Hartford and across the river from the Greek revival mansion where Elizabeth had grown up. Despite urgent national news filling the newspapers that June—more on that in a moment—the *Courant* and *Times* both featured the wedding on their front pages.

Colt gave them plenty to write about. The festivities began on June 3 with a "grand ball" for Colt's workers at Charter Oak Hall. The theme of the ball was not so much marriage as guns. Every wall and windowsill was decorated with revolvers, and the gaslit chandeliers were festooned with them. On the day of the wedding, Colt left early for Middletown by carriage. Many of his guests, including Commodore Matthew C. Perry and Colt's old shipmate Levi Slamm, followed at noon in a steamship Colt had chartered for the occasion. As thousands of well-wishers cheered from the top of the dike and the windows of the armory, the *Washington Irving* slipped into the current, loaded with the formally dressed guests and "gaily decorated with flags." In the blue onion dome above the armory a phalanx of Colt workers, armed with rifles, fired a salute into the sky.

The ceremony at the Episcopal church in Middletown was appropriately subdued—"the tremulous voice of the aged Bishop, with the clear response of the Colonel, and your own more suppressed tones" is how Lydia Sigourney later recalled the exchange of vows in a letter to Elizabeth—but the show picked up again at the reception. Guests were served from an enormous wedding cake, five feet in circumference and nearly four feet high, decorated with frosted depictions of revolvers and, in a dazzling deployment of sugar, a rampant colt. If Elizabeth had not already figured it out, this cake made it clear: she was marrying not just a man but a gun; and not just a gun but a brand.

That evening the newlyweds, accompanied by Elizabeth's sister Hetty and brother Richard, sped down to New York by express train. On Saturday, June 7, the party of four boarded the *Baltic* at its pier on the west side of Manhattan. The Armory Band and a hundred or so workers had followed the Colts to New York to give them a proper send-off, and as the band played and the crowd waved, the *Baltic* steamed away.

The nuptial send-off was all splendid and thrilling, but hovering over it was a cloud as heavy as those that would follow the *Baltic* for much of her crossing to Liverpool. In the weeks before the wedding, America had started to come apart, and so had Colt's relationship with his only surviving brother. The house, to borrow from Lincoln's famous analogy, was dividing.

Nationally, the argument over slavery had turned bitter and violent in a series of remarkable days starting on May 19, 1856. That afternoon, the abolitionist senator from Massachusetts, Charles Sumner, took the floor of the Senate to vehemently denounce the south's attempt to make Kansas a slave state and extend slavery's reach. Sumner continued his five-hour diatribe the following day, May 20, despite the flaring tempers of southern senators. On May 21, a group of eight hundred pro-slavery Missourians attacked the free soil town of Lawrence, Kansas (named after Amos Adams Lawrence), destroying two newspaper offices and a hotel, among other structures. On May 22, back in Washington, Preston Brooks, a congressman from South Carolina, entered the Senate chamber and approached a seated Charles Sumner. Telling Sumner he had come to "punish" him, Brooks proceeded to beat the senator with a cane so severely the cane snapped in half. Two days after that, on the night of May 24, in Kansas, a band of abolitionists led by John Brown, incensed by the sacking of Lawrence and the caning of Sumner, killed five pro-slavery men in what came to be known as the Pottawatomie Massacre.

It is still shocking to consider that the first blood of the Civil War was shed not in Charleston or Manassas, but five years prior to the shelling of Fort Sumter, on the floor of the US Capitol and on the plains of Kansas. "Bleeding Kansas," as Horace Greeley's *New-York Tribune* began to call the events of that spring and summer, forced both north and south to recognize the irreparable fracture between them. But the caning of Sumner, especially, inflamed the north. For many, the cane Brooks broke on Sumner's head was the straw that broke the camel's back.

Colt was in Washington immediately after Brooks's attack on Sumner. The *Washington Evening Star* announced his arrival at the Willard Hotel on May 24. James Colt was in Washington, too, also at the Willard, and here the final rupture between the brothers seems to have occurred. It is perhaps a mere coincidence that a blood feud erupted between Sam and James at the very moment blood was shed in the fight over slavery, but it may also be that the public tension brought on by events in Washington and Kansas exacerbated whatever personal animus or distrust had been developing between the brothers.

Prior to this, the Colts had given every indication that they'd worked out their differences. James had moved from St. Louis to Hartford, into the house on Wethersfield Avenue, and resumed working for the company the previous autumn. Most of the winter and spring of 1856 he'd spent in Washington on Sam's behalf, advocating for the patent extension. His primary instrument of persuasion, like Ned Dickerson's several years earlier, was the promise of money—contingent fees—to politicians who voted in Colt's favor. That Colt was still engaging in such practices after the congressional investigation suggests that the primary lesson he took from his experiences with bribery was that he could get away with it. But if the investigation gave Sam no pause, James found that it worried members of Congress. "Some members fear the accusation of bribery, however innocent they may be," he wrote to Sam that winter, "it having been so generally promulgated through the country that bribery was used and you responsible." Sam instructed James to press on anyway, reminding him to give nothing until results were in. "Be governed by your own judgement in all you do in Washington," he wrote in early May. "Take care how you promise money." To this Sam added a personal note: "Marriage fixed for 5th. I want you to be here before the momentous occasion arrives."

Then something broke. "The object of this letter is to give you notice that I withdraw from all communication with you in Europe and in this country," James wrote on June 4, the day before Sam's wedding. "I forgive you for this last act of your sublime cruelty in attack of my character."

What last act? Had James done something that required Sam to race to Washington? Had Sam simply grown frustrated by James's failure to achieve any tangible results? Or had James come to believe again that Sam was cheating him? Whatever happened in that late spring of 1856, it was another straw on another camel's back.

VII

Rain fell over the *Baltic* for much of the voyage to Liverpool. Colt's sister-in-law Hetty Jarvis suffered terrible seasickness, but between bouts of nausea she recorded the weather and other details of the voyage. On June 11, a heavy fog rolled over the ship and the *Baltic* crept into the "ice regions," as Captain Joseph Comstock stayed up all night on deck to watch for icebergs. Now and then Hetty revived enough to take promenades around the deck with her sister "Lizzie" and converse with fellow passengers, notably "Prof. Morse"—Colt's old friend Samuel Morse—who one night delivered a lecture about his telegraph. "We have the most charming people on board," wrote Hetty, "and all have been so kind and agreeable."

She saved her greatest admiration for her new brother-in-law. "The Col. is the kindest and most attentive of brothers, and a grand nurse," she wrote in the middle of her illness. A few days later: "There never was such a nice brother as the Col., so thoughtful and unselfish that I have seldom seen his equal." Her comments, written for the private consumption of her mother, and apparently sincere, are a reminder that for all the enemies Colt made through his life, including two of his own brothers, people who knew him often found him generous and warm.

Colt had long ago gotten his sea legs, but he was beset by his own stomach-churning concerns as the *Baltic* crossed the Atlantic. Even before the ship was out of New York Harbor, he was dashing off a letter to his secretary Milton Joslin, handing the envelope to a pilot to take back to shore and mail to Hartford as soon as possible. Colt would write several more letters to Joslin before the *Baltic* landed in Liverpool, with many more to follow. These make for an inventory of Colt's mind during that summer and fall of 1856. Much of their content relates to the true object of this journey, which was to close several deals in Russia. "In the hurry of leaving

I neglected to say to you that an appointment with the Russian Ambassador must be made as early as he can conveniently go to New York," he wrote to Joslin. "I shall hold myself in readiness to go to Russia at a few days' notice if it is thought best." Countless other preoccupations were gnawing at Colt: ideas and directions regarding gun production and sales, construction projects in the South Meadow, a railroad spur he wanted to extend to the armory. In one paragraph he would give Joslin picayune instructions for the Armory Band—they were to keep their uniforms and instruments in perfect order—and in the next, a directive regarding materials to be used to repair a breach in the dike or an order of guns to be sent to California.

Sooner or later, every letter came back to James, to the sad demise of their relationship but also to practical steps that had to be taken to defend the company against him. "I grieve almost to death at his consummate folly, & I cannot bring my mind to believe he is in his senses & that worse things may be heard of him."

The Colts stayed in London for several weeks, Sam working while Elizabeth and her siblings went sightseeing, joining them as time allowed. He found a few moments to write ahead to Thomas Seymour. The former Connecticut governor was still serving as US minister to Russia and had offered to play host to Colt and the Jarvis siblings for the entirety of their stay in Russia, making all the necessary arrangements for accommodations and travel. More generously, by attaching Colt to the US delegation, he had secured invitations for Sam and Elizabeth, as well as Hetty and Richard Jarvis, to attend the coronation of the new emperor, Czar Alexander II, set for September 7 (August 26 by the Russian's Julian calendar). Elizabeth and Hetty got fitted for special court dresses while in London. Colt himself planned to wear, per Seymour's recommendation, his Connecticut state militia uniform to the coronation. In his letters to Seymour he emphasized that all expenses in Russia were to be paid by him—and "money is no consideration to me in having everything done in the best possible style."

"I directed my wine merchant to forward to you a lot of wine & brandy which I intend to make as a present to you," he added in another letter. "I will take my chances upon generous natures yielding to my appetite for the beverage & will allow me the privilege of an occasional 'smile' with you from a few of the bottles."

Colt had warned Seymour that Elizabeth and Hetty would be driven "crazy by the splendor in store for them in Russia." In truth, no one enjoyed pomp and circumstance more than Colt himself, and there was enough of both awaiting him in Russia to satisfy a man for a lifetime. During their six-week stay, the Colts took part in one of the "most magnificent pageants ever witnessed in the world," as Thomas Seymour put it.

It began in St. Petersburg on August 14, when Seymour presented Colt and his party, along with Samuel Morse, to the new czar. Colt immediately sent Milton Joslin a notice of this grand honor and instructed him to have it printed in the *Courant* or the *Times*. On August 18, Colt and the others traveled by special train to Moscow with the entire diplomatic corps. The evenings leading up to the coronation were filled with balls attended by all the royalty and nobility of Europe. The morning of the coronation brought huge throngs to Moscow to view the procession of Alexander and his wife, Maria Alexandrovna. From the Red Porch of the Kremlin, the royal cortege crossed Red Square to the Dormition Cathedral, where Sam and Elizabeth witnessed the crowning of the new emperor and empress of Russia.

Dazzling as it all was, the coronation was a mixed blessing for Colt. He had come to Russia intending to conduct significant business, including nailing down an agreement to sell arms-making machinery to the Russian government. He also hoped to get assistance from the Russian minister of war in retrieving the three thousand confiscated revolvers from the Prussian government. Lastly, Colt was trying to sell one hundred thousand muskets to Russia on behalf of George Law. It's not clear whether this number included the same muskets Colt had tried to sell to the sultan seven years earlier or was a new lot, but in any event no serious work was conducted in the weeks surrounding the coronation. "This is without exception the place of all others where time is absorbed without any apparent advantage," Colt wrote to Joslin that September.

Colt sent one last dispatch to Milton Joslin, in mid-October. He wrote it aboard the *Prussian Eagle* while steaming across the Baltic Sea to begin the journey home. Composed with a heavy heart on swollen seas, the motion of the ship "so grate I can scarcely form a single letter," Colt's note was meant to be a few hasty lines but ended up being sixteen scrawled pages, including an eight-page postscript.

Joslin had sent news that James was not only refusing to turn over the important papers he held regarding Colt's patent extension, but was also bringing a lawsuit to claim money from the company. Colt was bewildered but resigned. "I never before believed the judge was capable of swearing to what he knows to be a deliberate falsehood as he has done in this case &

it more & more convinces me of his mental derangement of mind, a thing that his conduct has often heretofore given intimation of."

As the sea heaved beneath him, Colt poured out the long saga of his relationship with James, as much for his own sake, it seems, as for Joslin's. "Judge Colt was my favorite brother in his youth," Colt began. James had spent much of his early years in poor health, and when he moved to St. Louis for a better climate, "it was my good fortune to be able to assist him." Sam estimated that he had over the years advanced James $15,000. Adding to this, James had borrowed, without Sam's knowledge, large sums from the company, intending to use the money to promote his bid to become a US senator. "It has been my greatest desire to show the greatest leniency owing to the relations of blood we hold to each other, but there is a point where forbearance ceases to be a virtue," Colt wrote to Joslin. "He certainly must be quite insane."

Colt had no way of knowing as he wrote those words that Joslin himself had recently suffered some kind of mental breakdown. A few days later, in Vienna, Colt received "very unfavourable tidings" from home. According to several letters, Joslin had gotten wildly drunk, "exposing himself publicly & talking about affairs of business & private matters where he shouldn't." Exactly what "exposing himself" meant is unclear, but in any case the news was alarming enough to warrant an urgent response.

Colt wrote to Richard Hubbard, friend, lawyer, and member of the board of Colt's company: "If it be true that Mr. Joslin is behaving so badly, there is danger of the funds which must pass through his hands as Treasurer & Secretary of the Company. You and Mr. Root must at once have a meeting of the board of directors & appoint some person you can trust to fill his place until I reach home." Colt told Hubbard that he did not want anyone to know he was returning but planned to start for Hartford as soon as possible.

Though he did not mention it to Hubbard, Colt had another reason for cutting his honeymoon short, one that had nothing to do with Joslin. Elizabeth was pregnant with their first child.

CHAPTER SEVENTEEN

Fathers and Sons

1857–58

*Armsmear, Colt's first true home since his childhood,
appeared to be inspired by every place he had ever been.*

I

Elizabeth gave birth to a boy, Samuel Jarvis Colt, on February 24, 1857. In a letter to a friend, Colt joked that his son arrived "in just about the proper time after marriage," but in fact the baby was premature and weighed just four and a half pounds at birth. He quickly put on weight, though, and by mid-March appeared to be out of danger. "The Colonel," wrote Colt's father-in-law, William Jarvis, "is one of the happiest men living."

There must have been days when it really did feel that way; days when Colt climbed the stairs of the campanile at the corner of the "shanty," as he called his new mansion, to the little aerie five stories above the ground, for a few moments of solitary peace. The campanile was to be his retreat, where he could escape the clamor of business and the bustle of the house, smoke a cigar, perhaps, and tipple a "smile" or two while gazing over a realm, as one newspaper put it at the time, "more sublime than any crowned

341

king can ever behold." The vast lawn swept back from the house, down and east toward the river. Below were ranks of greenhouses where exotic flowers bloomed year-round and strawberries ripened even in February. To the south was a spring-fed pond, iced over in the winter but soon to be stocked with fish, turtles, ducks, and two pairs of swans. Farther down the slope was a deer park, where a buck and several does grazed on meadow grass, and beyond this horse pastures, orchards, a field of tobacco, and finally, more than half a mile from the house, the great H-shaped armory, its smokestacks reaching higher than the campanile, higher than the tallest church steeples in town.

That March, the *United States Magazine* published a long and admiring history of Colt and his gun, including the struggles, the setbacks, then the fateful collaboration with Captain Walker in 1847. "From that day to the present his business has been a constant success, which has resulted in the completion of the most perfect establishment for the manufacture of fire-arms that exists on this or any other continent." The proof was in the output. A decade earlier, Colt had struggled to make a hundred guns for Walker in three months. Now he made a hundred in less than a day, and in three months he could make as many as ten thousand.

From all those guns had come all this. After years of living as a bachelor in hotels and temporary flats, Colt, at forty-two, had his first true home. Later, the house would be given a name—Armsmear. *Arms* meant guns, and *mear* was an archaic term for meadow: guns in the meadow, then, or meadow of guns. Armsmear was one of the largest homes in Connecticut, second only to Iranistan, P. T. Barnum's gaudy Persian-style palace in Bridgeport. At least Barnum's residence (which would burn down later that year) had a consistent aesthetic theme and a symmetrical floor plan. Colt's mansion had neither. Though nominally designed by the Hartford architect Octavius Jordan, it appeared to arise less from a blueprint than from Colt's passport books. The numerous loggias and Roman arches evoked an Italian villa, but the spires, domes, and minarets summoned the churches of St. Petersburg and the mosques of Constantinople. The glass conservatory, with its thin iron spars and curved panes, might have been borrowed from Joseph Paxton's Crystal Palace. Even the campanile seemed to be inspired by a distant Colt memory, albeit one closer to home: the tower on Washington Square where he had worked on his submarine battery and wept the day of his brother's death.

Colt had every reason to bask in what he had achieved since those bleak days in New York. Yet, even now, as he looked over his great estate, he could not ignore the shadows on the periphery. That sudden and ominous unraveling of Joslin, for example. One day the man had been an able and trusted aide, the next a babbling drunk—and then, two weeks later, suddenly dead of unspoken causes. What had happened to Joslin?

What, for that matter, was happening to Colt? For several years he had suffered occasional bouts of "inflammatory rheumatism," or gout as his new affliction was sometimes called.* When it came on, his joints swelled and caused him great pain, sapping him of strength and immobilizing him. The illness would last for a few weeks, then go away, and he would laugh it off and get on with his work. Every episode was more painful than the last, though, and the intervals between episodes were shortening. When it struck again, rising from bed would be a chore. Climbing the stairs of the campanile would be impossible.

A few years earlier, when the illness had first made itself known, James had suggested to Sam, half seriously, that a "little attack of rheumatism will in the long run do you good." He meant that it would slow Sam down, settle him, domesticate him. James believed that Sam would be happier if he had a home and family and had for years encouraged him to marry. Perhaps Sam owed James some credit for this sound advice. The moment he took it, though, the brothers had become estranged. Now James lived in the next house down Wethersfield Avenue—the house Sam had given to him as an inducement to come to Hartford. They were near enough to call to each other across the yard, and yet they communicated by letter. "Dear Sir," James had stiffly written on February 16, responding to a suggestion from Sam that they handle their dispute with arbitration. "You will not doubt that so far as it evinces a disposition to settle all matters in controversy and to restore the amicable relations which formerly subsisted between us, it affords me sincere gratification. The reproach which a quarrel between us, the only surviving children of our parents, is calculated to beget, has not been of my seeking." James signed off this awkward note by expressing his hope "to resume our former friendly relationship." But it was much too late for that.

---

* The terms were used more or less interchangeably to describe his condition, but they denote different diseases. Gout is caused by an excess of uric acid in the bloodstream (sometimes as a result of overindulgence in alcoholic beverages and rich foods) and is usually, though not always, confined to joints of the feet. Most of Colt's symptoms sound more like those of rheumatoid arthritis, an episodic but chronic autoimmune disorder that can cause severe inflammation, and ultimately deformation, in human joints. That some of Colt's internal organs, including his stomach and brain, later became involved suggests the presence of secondary illnesses that may have been exacerbated by rheumatism.

II

"My dear Nephew, I have just been reading a letter from your new teacher who is candid enough to report to me the exact condition you are in at this late period in your education, & it has made me so sorry that I hardly know what to say to you."

It was late March of 1857. Spring was coming to the Connecticut River Valley. The ice on the pond was gone and the fields above the armory were stippled with green. Snow melted to the north and the river rose but kept its course beyond the dike. Far to the south, in Washington, America had taken a few more steps to war, first on March 4 with the inauguration of James Buchanan, a Pennsylvania Democrat with a strong tendency to accommodate the south, then two days later, on March 6, with a decision by the Supreme Court against a fugitive slave named Dred Scott. Despite the best arguments of Colt's former attorney George T. Curtis, the Court, led by Chief Justice Roger B. Taney of Maryland, ruled against Scott's quest for freedom. The Court's main argument was that Scott, as a black man, and therefore not a citizen, had no legal standing in federal court. More significantly for history, the Court revoked federal restrictions on the expansion of slavery, instantly overturning decades of precedent and practice. Colt surely understood the implications of all this to both the country and himself. He would get to these soon enough. But here, at the end of March, the matter before him was the education of the child he called his nephew.

Samuel Caldwell Colt was now fifteen. He had grown into a gentle and affectionate boy, but to Colt's great disappointment was a poor student, undisciplined and "backward," as Colt described him. This should have been no surprise. Young Sammy had been shuffled about from guardian to guardian and school to school much of his life. For a while he had lived in the town of Kent, Connecticut, attending school and boarding with a family named Fuller. In 1853, Colt had shipped him off to Europe, first to London and then to Brussels, where he was placed in the hands of a tutor named Monsieur Marzell. Now he was in Berlin, under the guidance of a strict Prussian, Dr. Schwartman.

Colt had been writing Sammy stern letters for several years on the subject of his academic performance and conduct. "I have received of late very unfavorable accounts of you, which grieves me much," Colt wrote, for example, in July of 1854, when Sammy was twelve and living in Brussels. On that occasion, the problem was not just that Sammy was falling behind in school but that he still sucked his thumbs. Colt directed Monsieur Marzell to coat the boy's hands with "some obnoxious drug that will make you sick every time you put them to your mouth." If that failed, he warned Sammy, he would advise the schoolmaster to "tie your hands behind you and keep them in that condition, night and day until you are broken of such a baby's practice."

Colt was only slightly less upset to learn that Sammy had taken up cigar smoking and wine drinking. If he ever heard another word about either, he would cut off the boy's allowance. "I have spent money enough upon you yet I am willing to spend still more, in order to give you as good an education as the best scholar in Europe or America, if you will pay attention & try to learn like other boys."

"I do not wish to be harsh with you," Colt wrote. "[I]t certainly grieves me more than it pains you."

Even accounting for stricter notions of child-rearing at the time, Colt's letters were in fact very harsh. Nearly every line between his salutations and signatures shamed the boy for his failures. On the rare occasion Colt applauded Sammy for writing a polite letter and exhibiting "the good, gen-erous spirit of a Yankee boy," he also scolded him for bad spelling and sloppy handwriting—which was rich coming from Colt, whose letters were neat and correctly spelled only because they were now copied over by an amanuensis.

For all his badgering and threatening, Colt was deeply invested in Sammy. He cared that the boy succeed and saw it as his obligation to ensure that Sammy became "as a gentleman's son should be." His mistake was in believing that he could control the natural aptitudes and interests of a fifteen-year-old with reprimands and threats. He now had nearly a thousand employees at his command, yet he had no idea how to manage an adolescent boy.

Perhaps the cruelest letter Colt wrote was the one he sent in June of 1855. As he knew, the only thing Sammy truly cared about was animals. His interest in them had apparently been sparked while living on the Fullers' farm in Kent. The Fullers had stayed in touch with Sammy, writing with updates on life at their farm and news of their animals. Colt decided to put a stop to this. The Fullers meant well, he wrote to Sammy, but "while their letters may possess some interest to a farmer's boy, who expects to earn his living by raising pigs & hens, I cannot possibly see what benefit they are to a Gentleman's Son who is seeking a refined and scientific education." He directed Sammy to compose a letter to the Fullers and explain to them that he no longer had time to think about "pigs, hens, and ponies" and ask that they write no more of animals.

If Sammy ever sent such a letter, it did nothing to improve his academic performance. Now, in the early spring of 1857, another discouraging report had arrived from the tutor in Berlin. According to Dr. Schwartman, the boy was still far behind in his studies. Colt decided to carry through on his earlier threats. Sammy would be permitted no leisure or play other than for exercise. All available time must go to schoolwork. Furthermore, "I have written Julia that she must not give you any more money or presents and I have also written the same thing to your teachers."

While his "nephew" brought Colt only frustration, his "ward" gave him something to celebrate that spring. Julia Leicester was engaged to be married, to a baron no less. The young man, Friedrich August Waldemar Von Oppen, hailed from a long line of Prussian nobility. How this match came about is unclear, but Colt, who had spent a good deal of time in Berlin, may have had a hand in arranging it. In any case, the wedding was set for May, in London.

Colt wrote in April to congratulate Baron Von Oppen and to apologize in advance that he would miss the wedding. "I have endeavored to so fix my business that I could return to London & attend the sacred ceremony, but I find it quite impossible & I must therefore finally disappoint Julia & yourself in this particular." In his place, he had asked a few American friends to be present, including Colonel Robert Campbell, the American consul in London, who would perform the civil ceremony. "Regarding little Sammy," Colt wrote to Von Oppen, "I recommend her not to take him to London with her as it would take up much of his valuable time & divert his mind from his studies. Yet if the child is very anxious to go & Julia feels she must have him with her why then I suppose I must not refuse."

Julia and Baron Von Oppen were wed on May 19, 1857, in St. George's in Hanover Square, with Sammy present. The marriage between the baron and "a ward of Col. Colt, the 'revolver' man" was announced in both English and American papers and officially registered in London and Berlin. It gave all the appearance of a propitious and regular union, except that over the entire event floated a cloud of mystery. Who exactly was this new Baroness Von Oppen?

The German marriage registration makes one thing clear: she was not Caroline Colt. Julia Leicester's age on the registration is twenty-one. If William Edwards's version of events was accurate—that is, if Sam married Caroline in 1835 when she was sixteen, then married her to his brother John in 1842, when she was twenty-two or twenty-three, Caroline would now be at least thirty-seven years old. The possibility of a thirty-seven-year-old woman passing as twenty-one is slim. For this and reasons previously mentioned, it is extremely unlikely that Julia was Caroline. But this still leaves us with the mystery: Who was she?

Baron Von Oppen's father, for one, became deeply suspicious of her origins. After the wedding, he wrote a long innuendo-laced letter to his son, demanding that not a single thaler he gave to the young man ever go to Julia. She later copied her father-in-law's diatribe and sent it to Colt:

> If Col. Colt <u>is</u> a relative of hers, <u>he</u> can make some provision for his own ward. If he is <u>no</u> relation of hers, and if she was not his ward, then she deserves to be cut out of all privileges as an inheritress of your property. She may inherit yours if you are fool enough to give it to her, but I have sworn that she shall never inherit mine!
>
> Who is she? Who were her parents? Why did every one of her guardian's compatriots turn her into ridicule and neglect her openly?
>
> Was it from real distress, or modesty, in the church vestry, or from affectation, that her hands became powerless when she took the pen to sign her marriage certificate? When I once asked her if she remembered her father, why did her face become deathly white and her lips quiver when she said: "Father died when I was very young"?
>
> Why does young Sam stare in such an idiotic manner when asked if he remembers his parents?

What did the baron's father suspect? Did he believe that Colt and Julia had been romantically engaged? Did he believe—this seems more plausible—that she was Colt's illegitimate daughter or in some other way the progeny of scandal? Whatever the baron's father's reasons, and however based in fact they were, he soon severed all ties with his son.

After the wedding, the baron and baroness returned with Sammy to Berlin. While the couple embarked on their married life, the boy resumed his studies under Dr. Schwartman. "It is my express wish that not one hours time be lost in the child's present backward condition, but that every hour which can, shall be employed in hard study and recitation of his lessons," Colt wrote to his agent in Berlin, C. F. Wappenhaus. "Should I be disappointed in this I shall be more provoked than ever to bring my neffue back with me to America."

III

Late in that summer of 1857, a financial panic hit the country like a hurricane. A hurricane, in fact, was one of its proximate causes.

Like the crash twenty years earlier, the Panic of 1857 was born of a concatenation of market forces, many of these foreign in origin. The end of the Crimean War had put a surplus of Russian wheat onto the world market, which drove down the price of American wheat. Rising interest rates in England prompted British investors to pull their capital from American markets and place it in banks at home. But the chief causes were domestic, and they were particularly western in origin. The gold rush had pumped great quantities of specie into the economy, while speculators drove up western land values and railroad stocks soared. Some historians argue that the *Dred Scott* decision, by opening the door to slavery in the west and scaring off northern investment, was the pin that pricked the bubble. The first explicit sign of collapse, however, did not come until August 24, with the failure of the New York branch of the Ohio Life Insurance and Trust Company. Three weeks later, the SS *Central America* (formerly known as the SS *George Law*, after Colt's occasional business partner) was steaming north to New York when it ran into the path of a powerful hurricane off the coast of South Carolina. The ship sank, taking 425 passengers, fifteen tons of California gold, and the already flagging spirits of the American people down with it.

Twenty years earlier, the Panic of 1837 had hurt the sales of Colt's guns. The new panic, though, probably helped. Some of the hundreds of thousands of Americans thrown out of work looked west for opportunity, and to Colt for protection.

In the past, only the most adventurous easterners, no matter how well armed, had been willing to risk the perilous journey west. Recent army activity along the Platte River, though, had created the perception that the way was safer. General Harney's well-publicized attack at Blue Water Creek in September of 1855 had temporarily quieted the Sioux. Then, in July of 1857, on the Solomon River in western Kansas, Colonel Edwin Vose Sumner, a white-bearded, thick-skulled man* who looked as if he'd been plucked from the Old Testament, added to the perception with an assault on the Cheyenne. The highlight of Sumner's campaign was a battle on the afternoon of July 29, 1857, on the north banks of the Solomon River. This would be recalled as one of the most unusual battles in the history of the western Indian Wars, mainly because Colt revolvers had no part in it. For reasons only he understood, Sumner, at the last moment, ordered his cavalry to charge with sabers rather than carbines and revolvers.

---

* His skull was truly thick. A musket ball had once bounced off it in the middle of a battle, leaving no real harm.

Normally, such a move would have been suicidal against three hundred Cheyenne warriors. But the Cheyenne had come to this battle with specific assurances from their medicine men that they were going to be magically protected against bullets—and nothing had been said about sabers. The warriors were so rattled by the glimmering steel that they turned and fled, and the battle was over almost as soon as it began. Both the Sioux and the Cheyenne would soon be back to haunt US soldiers and western travelers. But for the moment, the assaults of Harney and Sumner appeared to have foreclosed violence from Indians.

The combined effect of the financial panic in the east and the perception of a safer journey west drew Americans, including those who would not previously have dared, to try their luck on the western trail. In the spring of 1857, before the panic, the number of overland travelers had been fifty-five hundred. In the spring of 1858, it rose to seventy-five hundred, and in the spring of 1859 (driven higher by the discovery of gold in Colorado) to almost twenty thousand.

Emboldened as they were, these travelers still needed guns; and the gun they needed most was a Colt revolver. "Every man who goes into the Indian country should be armed with a rifle and revolver, and he should never, either in camp or out of it, lose sight of them." That advice came in a popular guidebook for California emigrants, by an army captain named Randolph B. Marcy. "When not on the march, they should be placed in such a position that they can be seized at an instant's warning; and when moving about outside the camp, the revolver should invariably be worn in the belt, as the person does not know at what moment he may have use for it." Marcy was clear in his gun preference: "Colt's revolving pistol is very generally admitted, both in Europe and in America, to be the most efficient arm of its kind known at the present day."

IV

Colt followed through on his threat to bring Sammy back to America. After receiving another discouraging report from Dr. Schwartman in the autumn of 1857, he sent directions to his Berlin agent, C. F. Wappenhaus, to collect the boy from the tutor and prepare to send him to New York. Wappenhaus, with veiled criticism of Dr. Schwartman—and also, perhaps, of Colt—suggested that the problem was not the boy but the methods being used to educate him. While Sammy was "certainly very careless," wrote the German agent, he was also "a good natured boy who may be easily led by kindness, but not by constant & severe reproaches." Wappenhaus offered to find another, gentler tutor in Berlin. It was too late, though. Colt had made up his mind. He ordered Wappenhaus to put Sammy on a train to Bremen, where the boy was to board a steamer to New York.

So, in November of 1857, Sammy came to live for a while at Armsmear. He passed what seems to have been a happy few weeks with Colt, Elizabeth, and their baby boy. He was there through Thanksgiving, and still there when the river closed off to shipping and snow fell that December.

Though Colt had presented the plan to bring Sammy to America as a consequence of his poor performance, it was not much of a punishment. Indeed, under the guise of discipline, Colt may have had more benign motives, even if barely aware of them himself. The infant Sammy had given the teenaged Sammy the gift of softening their father a little. In a letter sent before he brought the boy home from Germany, Colt had informed Sammy that the baby was named after the two of them and expressed the hope that should he, Colt, ever be "unfortunate"—that is, die early—"you will take as much pleasure in looking after the education & happiness of this little boy, as I now take in providing for & looking after your education & happiness." No doubt it came as news to Sammy that his uncle took any pleasure in securing his happiness, but the words were an acknowledgment that he was a valued member of the family.

Sammy would never have an opportunity to care for his half brother. On Christmas Eve 1857, after a brief illness, the baby boy died. He was buried three days later in a plot on the grounds just south of Armsmear. Despite intense cold, the full workforce of the armory turned out for the funeral. Lydia Sigourney wrote one of her pretty death poems—"Rest in thy bed, my darling / Where the bright fountain plays"—but a lesser-known Hartford poet, Lilly Waters, probably got closer to conveying the pall that fell over the Colts:

> A wail within the palace
> Hath hushed the Christmas Hymn;
> The halls so lately brilliant
> Are now with twilight dim.

V

That winter, with Sammy off to North Andover, Massachusetts, to begin schooling with a teacher named Isaac Frost, the Colts transferred their household to temporary quarters in Washington. Elizabeth did not want to go. She felt, as she wrote in a letter to Sammy, as if she were leaving her little boy all over again. But to stay in that gloomy mansion was impossible, especially with her husband absent on business.

Colt rented a large house, with room enough for servants, family, and guests. He was in the capital to launch his "Washington campaign," as he called it. His first purpose was to lobby the government to order more of his guns. His second, as always, was to do whatever he could to get Congress to extend his patent.

As Elizabeth mourned their lost son, Colt found distraction in work. He also found comfort in drink. "In looking into my wine cupboard I find I am getting short of brandy," he wrote to Luther Sargeant in early February, in a breezy letter that may have been scribbled under the influence of a "smile" or two, to borrow Colt's term for alcoholic beverages. He asked Sargeant to send a man up to the house to fill several boxes with brandy bottles, after first obtaining entry to the wine cellar from Colt's friend Richard Hubbard, "who like the ancient Peter keeps the keys of the inner gate." The brandy Colt wanted was "the A No. 1 Brand on the upper shelf of the northwest corner." Sargeant was to send this by express train. While he was at it, he might as well send a couple dozen bottles of sherry, too. "Not the very oldest of which I so rarely indulge in a single bottle but that which is in the middle west bin. Dick will point out the right article if he thinks it proper for me to make a big hole in it so soon again." Hubbard was the keeper not only of the cellar keys, apparently, but of Colt's sobriety.

Along with the brandy and sherry, Colt warmed himself that winter with a new favorite dish, stewed terrapin, as prepared by "our old negro cook." The cook served it at dinner, along with roasted duck, then again at breakfast, with hot Virginia rolls and "sundry other equally nice little things peculiar to this part of the world." Colt never tired of the dish, and between a few smiles before dinner and dinner itself, he grew rosy and fat. "These terrapins, next to pistols, are a great invention."

Colt's greatest strengths as an entrepreneur were his perseverance and tenacity. These were also his greatest weaknesses. He did not know how to concede an unwinnable fight. His patent had expired in 1857, after his first extension ran out. He'd spent four years battling to get a new extension and had been warned numerous times that future efforts would be futile. Any appetite Congress once had for considering a renewal had been soured, as his brother James had told him, by the investigation into Colt's bribery scheme in 1854. Nothing tangible had ever come of that investigation, but it scared off more timid—or scrupulous—members of

Congress from wanting anything to do with Colt and his patent. None-theless, Colt was back to lobbying as hard as he could, with the help of influential new friends.

A welcome addition to his corps of advocates was John B. Floyd, the new secretary of war under President Buchanan. That winter, Floyd wrote a glowing letter of support to Representative J. A. Stewart, chairman of the committee on patents in the House, recommending a new extension for Colt. That the secretary of war, who was in a position to order Colt's guns, was endorsing them like a paid flack struck the editors of *Scientific American* as unseemly. So, for that matter, did Colt's entire effort to extend his patent.

"It must be recollected that Col. Colt has had all the advantages which the general law can allow to a patentee," the magazine's editors wrote that April. Precisely because the revolver had during these years become "essen-tial to the public service," Colt's invention had to be publicly shared now. Moreover, it would be grossly unfair to those who had already started to manufacture revolvers on the presumption that Colt's patent was expired, "and yet Col. Colt, with a feeling unworthy [of] the citizen of an enlightened commonwealth, asks Congress to ruin these industrious men."

Colt would gladly have ruined all of his competitors, but before he could accomplish anything in Washington, he was overtaken by a painful spell of rheumatism. At the end of April, with little to show for his months away, he and Elizabeth returned to Hartford. A few weeks later, Colt was well enough to stroll the property around Armsmear every morning before breakfast, as Elizabeth wrote to Sammy, "planning some improvement almost all the time."

While recuperating, Colt sent his trusted aide, J. Deane Alden, to Washington to pick up where he had left off. Most of Colt's top aides, with the exception of Elisha Root, handled a variety of business and personal chores for their boss, but none had a broader portfolio than Alden. His responsibilities ranged from those of a senior company executive to those of a valet. Alden was the man Colt dispatched to New York to pick up fire-works for celebrations in the South Meadow, and it was Alden who oversaw the care of Colt's horses in his absence and who handled delicate tasks such as arranging Chris Colt's funeral in 1855. Alden was also Colt's scrivener, copying over most of his business and personal correspondence. Nearly all Colt's letters to cabinet members and congressmen were in Alden's hand, and so were those letters to Sammy in which Colt scolded the boy for his poor penmanship and spelling.

Like Colt, and like most of the other top men at his armory (Root, again, being the exception), Alden had obtained a ceremonial military title. He went by "Major" Alden. To give this title some brass, Colt had bestowed upon him the honor of overseeing a private militia, strictly for show, composed of Colt workers, whom Alden led on occasional marches around Hartford. Alden would surely have served under Colt in a real military escapade, so devoted was he to his boss. He had recently almost given his life to Colt in the line of duty. The previous fall, he and another Colt aide, N. E. Brace, had been steaming up the Missouri River to demonstrate some rifles at Fort Leavenworth when their ship exploded. Brace fell into the boiler and died horribly, and Alden was badly scalded by steam. Several months later, he was still recovering from his burns but insisted on going to Washington anyway to see what he could do about Colt's extension.

The good news for Colt that spring was that certain members of the patent committee in the House of Representatives were still willing to be bribed. The challenge facing Colt was that these members were wary of being found out and had raised their price. A Republican congressman from Pennsylvania named John Rufus Edie, for example, had started by asking for a contingent fee of $2,500, but hearing that another congressman was getting $4,500, now wanted $5,000. Edie's cooperation was essential because he had been appointed by the committee to write its final report. On May 12, Colt telegraphed Alden in Washington and directed him to negotiate with the congressman.

Alden went to the congressman's home at 8:00 a.m. the following morning. Finding Edie still in bed, he offered to come back later but Edie insisted he stay. The entire conversation, as related by Alden, was conducted in subtext. When Alden told the congressman that he was there to discuss the extension and that "anything which might pass between us in the course of our conversation would be strictly private on my part," Edie interrupted him to say it was of no use—"the minds of the Committee was made up, and that he saw no way that their opinion could be changed." To which Alden responded, as he later related to Colt, "If there was any way to obtain a favorable report, I should like to know it."

"I found, my dear Col., that he was very cautious," wrote Alden, "and would not give me a chance to ask him for a proposition, and it being so delicate a subject for me to act upon, that I dared not, on your account, as well as my own, propose anything to him." As Alden perceived the situation, the congressman worried that if he made a new deal with Colt and altered the report in any way to reflect well on the extension, "the other parties would expose him."

Exasperated by such dithering in the legislative branch, Colt turned his attention back to the executive—and to John B. Floyd, the secretary of war. In the year since becoming secretary under President Buchanan, Floyd had lived up to his reputation, established when he was governor of Virginia, as a man exceptionally amenable to graft. Even in the Buchanan administration, one of the most venal in American history, Floyd "presented the biggest target to graft hunters," in the words of historian James McPherson.

What Colt wanted from Floyd, besides his endorsement to Congress, was government orders for guns. The details of how he tried to obtain these are hinted at in a series of "Private & Confidential" letters Colt wrote to Floyd and to several other men in the summer and fall of 1858. Some of these were mailed with directions to tear them up after reading; others were carried directly to Floyd by Deane Alden.

In rushing back and forth to Washington to do Colt's bidding that autumn, the faithful Deane Alden nearly died—again—on his boss's account. His train violently derailed near Baltimore when it hit a horse that was standing on the tracks. One man was killed and several badly injured. Alden spent the night helping to lift a train car off the man who had been crushed to death under it, then waited for another train. He finally arrived in Washington the following day at noon, barely in time to wash up and hurry to the War Department to briefly meet with Floyd before the secretary left town.

The graft scheme had several elements, but the centerpiece was a loan by Colt to the secretary amounting to tens of thousands of dollars. Floyd's brother, Benjamin R. Floyd, was a participant in the transaction, and so was a Washington operative named R. W. Latham, the conduit through whom Colt's money ended up in Floyd's pocket. In return for the loans, the secretary was to pursue orders by the army and the navy for Colt's guns. Floyd needed a pretext for such orders. Originally, a short-lived clash between the US Army and Mormons in Utah provided this. When it became clear that the United States was not going to war with the Mormons, Latham suggested that Colt "write it in your best style, and give some 'Indean War' reasons for it." Colt did just that in a letter to Floyd a few days later.

By autumn of 1858, Colt was angry that his loans had not been reciprocated by more orders. When Latham came to ask for an additional loan for Floyd, Colt lashed out, convinced that he had given too much and received too little for his efforts. Latham reminded Colt that since March 4, 1857—the start of President Buchanan's term—he had been granted a good deal of patronage. "You have in the course of 18 months rec'd orders, which when filled and delivered amount to the exact sum of $310,816.79. In all candor is there just cause for the bitter complaints?"

VI

That October, Elizabeth sent an overdue letter to Sammy at Deacon Frost's in North Andover, gently admonishing him for failing to write more often and blaming her own lapse on a bout of illness. Elizabeth and Sammy had developed an affectionate relationship during the boy's stay at Armsmear, and she now saw it as her duty to act as his surrogate mother. For years to come, she would regularly write him, encouraging him to work harder, advising him on his comportment, sending him bits of news and clothing and money.

Before she got sick, she told Sammy, she and Colt had entertained more than half a dozen houseguests who were in town for the horse show in Springfield. One of Colt's horses, a Morgan filly named Belle, had won first prize, and several other of his horses had placed. The guests were now departed and the house was quiet, though hardly empty. They had no fewer than six servants, and Colt's niece—Chris's daughter, Isabella—had come to live with them. "We are all pretty well now and the weather is lovely, though the mornings and evenings are cool and make us think of winter."

Other than light news and the usual reminders to work harder at school, Elizabeth devoted her letter to urging Sammy to write to Julia. "She feels very badly that you neglect her & I think you cannot have forgotten all her kindness and care as she seems to think you have. Now, dear Sammy, do write her at once." Elizabeth frequently mentioned Julia to Sammy, which suggests that whatever she knew of Julia's relationship to her husband, she had decided to suspect nothing. In keeping with her own virtue, she cared for the young woman's happiness. "She does not seem to feel very well & your neglecting her makes her feel very badly."

Since marrying Baron Von Oppen in the spring of 1857, Julia had been deeply homesick for America. Though "in a position which many girls would envy," she'd written to Colt, "I want the old faces, and the English language, and above all, the hearts that I miss."

In part, the blame for her homesickness fell on her husband's family, which had spurned the young couple since their marriage. At first, the baron's father had insisted that any money he gave his son not go to Julia. Now he refused to give the young man money under any circumstances. The baron's own sister had "cut him dead" when they saw her at a reception in Berlin.

Colt had carelessly added to Julia and the baron's miseries. To help the young couple, he had offered a job to Von Oppen, to replace John Sainthill as his agent in Belgium. Von Oppen accepted at once, promising to "devote all my energies to your interest and to deserve your confidence as a man of honour." He and Julia then waited for Colt to follow up on his offer. "A most mysterious silence has been observed on your part towards us," Von Oppen wrote to Colt on June 10, after three months of waiting. "If it is not your intention to give me the situation offered, it is due to me as a gentleman to tell me so honestly at once before I insolve myself deeper into debt by waiting here all summer." Julia followed with her own letter, begging for money. At last, near the end of July, Colt responded. He advanced Von Oppen $1,000 and instructed him to report to Liège at once to begin work.

Colt's failure to respond more quickly to Julia and Von Oppen may have been explained by his illness. He was sick in the spring of 1858, then sick again that summer. Now the autumn of 1858 brought his worst attack yet. It came in late October, after the Springfield horse show.

Though in pain and unable to walk without crutches, Colt went to Washington that November to secure more gun orders from the navy and the army. On the evening of Friday, November 12, a rumor spread through Hartford that he had died in Washington. The following day this was reported in several New England newspapers, including the *Hartford Courant*. In fact, Colt was very much alive, albeit in discomfort and a foul mood. He spent part of that Saturday writing a bitter letter to Luther Sargeant—though in fact he did not write the letter himself, his elbow being too inflamed to bend; he dictated it to Deane Alden, who was faithfully at his side.

The letter charged Sargeant and others at the armory with having completely failed to carry out Colt's orders. They had not provided papers he needed in advance of his trip, then had neglected to send in a timely manner other papers and information he had requested from Washington. As a result, wrote Colt, "the whole week is lost to me and probably the whole object of my business." Henceforth, he must "have all my orders promptly executed to the very letter—without which you ought to know that my business would be very much embarrassed & much valuable time wasted."

The week may have been a waste, but the month was not a complete loss. Shortly after Colt returned to Hartford that November, Elizabeth went into her "confinement" and gave birth to a new baby, another boy. "He is a fine little fellow, with a pretty head covered with little brown curls,"

Elizabeth wrote to Sammy, "plump & healthy & only cries just enough to let us know now & then that there is such a little creature here."

The day after the birth was Thanksgiving. Colt celebrated by donating fifty live turkeys to his workers, then lent the men guns to shoot their dinner in an old-fashioned turkey shoot. He had failed to accomplish much in Washington, but events would soon deliver him a bounty almost beyond imagining.

CHAPTER EIGHTEEN

I Am Loth to Close

1859–62

An unknown Union soldier.

I

Before war came and disrupted every pursuit but itself, Colt embarked on a number of enterprises that had nothing to do with guns. He now owned nearly three hundred acres of land in and around Hartford, from the fields and orchards of the South Meadow to a hundred or so acres of pasture and woodland across the river in East Hartford, and he was determined to put this land to profitable use. He sold produce from his greenhouses, thousands of strawberries, tomatoes, cucumbers, and other fruits and vegetables.

He invested in chicken farming in his coops across the river, and in trout farming in his ponds. He grew tobacco that was said to be some of Connecticut's finest.

By far his most ambitious agricultural effort was harvesting some fifty tons of willow twigs from the osiers he had planted on the dike to hold its soil. He imported an entire village's worth of German willow workers, then built them cottages that looked as if they had been lifted from the Prussian countryside—Potsdam Village, he called this quaint settlement—complete with a beer hall, coffee garden, and Dutch windmill. Then he built a factory where these workers turned the willow twigs into wicker furniture and baskets. For a while, the Colt Willow-Ware Manufacturing Company was the largest American wicker furniture business outside of New York City.

As Colt cultivated his acreage in Hartford, he invested in enterprises farther afield. He purchased land in Wayne County, Virginia (now West Virginia), along the Big Sandy River, where he intended to use a new technology to extract oil from shale rock. He bought fourteen thousand acres around the town of Lamar, Texas, that were ripe for development. Most significantly, he bought shares in a silver mine in Tubac, Arizona, sixty miles south of Tucson, on land that had been annexed from Mexico in the Gadsden purchase of 1854. Starting with an initial investment of $20,000—$10,000 in cash, $10,000 in guns—Colt accumulated a majority of stock in the Sonora Exploring and Mining Company, then got himself named president of the board of directors. He dispatched the ever-willing Deane Alden to Tubac to look after his interests there, though mainly what Alden did was try to keep out of the way of Apache Indians.

Colt's sundry pursuits in these years can be explained as a wealthy man's natural inclination to diversify his assets. He would never give up fighting for the renewal of his patent extension, but others were now making revolvers, including formidable rivals such as Smith & Wesson, Remington, and the Starr Arms Company. Still others were filing patents for rapid-firing guns that used entirely different technologies from Colt's, made possible by newly developed metal cartridges that contained primer, powder, and bullet all in one. The Spencer repeater could fit seven of these into a magazine in the butt of the rifle. The Henry held as many as sixteen in a tube above the barrel. Colt's monopoly on multishot firearms was over. It only made sense to spread his wealth into other fields.

But was there more to it than this? Were these other ventures evidence of a desire to contribute more to the world than instruments of destruction? It's natural to look for signs of reflection and remorse in a man nearing his end. Was Colt hoping to trade revolvers and rifles for strawberries and wicker, for oil and silver?

Probably not. The most likely explanation for his many labors in these final years is that he could not help himself. As it is the function of a boiler to convert water into steam, it was the nature of Colt to convert his time (his waking hours) and space (his property) into profit—to "improve every minute," as his Yankee mantra went. He could not ride from his house to his armory without stopping off at his fishpond to consider how to tweak his trout population, or walk across his back lawn without deciding the time had come to drill an artesian well or plant a thousand dwarf pear trees. He had a weakness for drink and was sick much of the time now, but he was metabolically wired for productivity.

Most of Colt's efforts lost rather than made money. Even if he'd wanted to put guns behind him, he could not afford to do so. Guns had made him rich, and they would make him richer now than ever. He was singularly blessed and cursed in these last years of his life. The richer he grew, the sicker he became.

II

In the second week of January 1859 the temperature plunged lower than anyone in Hartford could recall. According to the *Courant*, it was twenty-one below zero on the morning of Tuesday, January 11, and rose to a high of six below. A thick slab of ice formed on the river, shutting down water travel but bringing out skaters in droves—"quite an animated spectacle," reported the *Courant*, presenting "scenes of nightly sport."

The most festive day that winter came on Wednesday, February 2, after another deep freeze. All of Hartford took to the ice, four or five thousand skaters by some counts, of every age, class, and race. Colt's Armory Band was on hand to provide musical entertainment, and so was Colt's uniformed regiment, led by Deane Alden—just before his departure for Arizona—glissading through its marching drills. The nearby Woodruff & Beach iron foundry lit off a cannon a few times to splinter the freezing air, and some wild young men in sleighs whipped their horses onto the river and dashed recklessly through the crowds. In the afternoon, accompanied by Colt's band, many of the skaters began to dance quadrilles on the ice.

A few days later, Elizabeth wrote to Sammy. She had been riding in a sleigh with her parents and sister while her baby, "a large plump little boy," rested in the house under the care of nurses and servants. "It is now snowing very hard and there is every prospect of fine sleighing again." She invited Sammy to come to Hartford to enjoy the snow and celebrate his seventeenth birthday,* on the condition that "you will give me your serious promise to study <u>harder</u>."

Colt was away in Washington when Sammy visited Armsmear in late February. He had been there since early in the month, having missed the winter frolics in Hartford. This was just as well, as cold weather aggravated his joints. He had no time for recreation in any case. "I am very sorry, my dear young nephew, that I cannot be at home to enjoy your visit," he wrote, "but this [is] only one of the many pleasures I must deprive myself of in doing the duty I owe to business that leads to feeding the multitude of men & their families you see employed in & surrounding my workshops." Like all of Colt's letters to Sammy, this one extolled the value of hard work and responsibility. His tone toward the boy had softened but his message had become more grandiose.

> Were I to neglect my duties in providing employment for this industrial class of worthy people, they not having the faculty to do so, for themselves so well as I do, would necessarily become in a little while unemployed, indolent & destitute of the ordinary comforts of life, and in lieu of being the center of pride & envy of the less favored of their profession, they would be like a vessel at sea without rudder, or compass to guide it.
>
> You see what you should remember in this picture, that the superior must control the inferior intellect, & the obligations of each to the other is mutual, and must naturally hold its relative position.

The idea that people have certain roles to play relative to one another and are obligated to play them to the best of their abilities was not original to Colt. Many societies, from medieval feudal systems to Indian caste systems, have supposed a natural human hierarchy. Colt's view was arguably more meritocratic than aristocratic—he always emphasized that Sammy had to *earn* his position, or at least *prepare* for it, rather than simply assume it—but it was also extraordinarily patronizing toward people Colt considered his inferiors. And in the context of the year 1859, it raised, again, questions about Colt's view of that most unavoidable subject in America at the time: slavery.

---

* According to press reports of the trial of John C. Colt, Caroline Henshaw gave birth to Sammy in November or early December of 1841, but for some reason his birthday was celebrated in February.

Though Colt does not mention slavery in his letter to Sammy, his argument echoes a defense of the institution made by Alexander H. Stephens of Georgia, who would several years later become vice president of the Confederacy: "There is a hierarchy among human beings which is based on natural differences, and these differences have been ordained by God." As Stephens and many of his fellow southern slaveholders saw it, "subordination to the superior race" was the natural condition of blacks.

The best way to judge Colt's views of slavery and race is by the political choices he made before the Civil War. In these years every American was forced to take a position on what would be the greatest moral and physical conflict in the country's history. The positions Colt took tell us all we need know.

As 1859 began, the great majority of Americans fell into one of three political camps, each defined by its stand on slavery. The first of these included virtually the entire slaveholding south, under the tent of the southern Democratic Party. Southern Democrats believed adamantly that slavery was constitutionally and morally permissible, and that the *Dred Scott* decision had incontrovertibly legitimized its existence and its *expansion* into western territories, if not into *all* of America.

The second camp, directly opposed to the first, was made up of Republicans. The Republican Party, formed from the scraps of the old Whig Party in the wake of Bleeding Kansas, held that slavery must be contained, whatever the *Dred Scott* decision said. As a whole, Republicans did not insist on abolishing slavery where it already existed, but the abolitionist wing was in ascendance in the party. Republicans were pejoratively known by their political rivals as *Black* Republicans, for their presumed alliance with abolitionists and African Americans.

Colt was in the third camp, which tried to split the difference. These were northern Democrats, which is to say Douglas Democrats, for when the time came they would gather around the presidential candidacy of Stephen A. Douglas, the Illinois senator. Douglas's view was that slavery should be allowed to continue where it was and, further, to spread into US territories, so long as it was approved by popular sovereignty. On this last point Douglas differed from southern Democrats, who held that slavery should be permitted *everywhere*, whether the local population wanted it or not. The most charitable view of Douglas Democrats is that they were moderates who wanted to preserve the union and avoid civil war. The more cynical view is that they were willing to pay any moral cost to avoid disrupting a national economy that served them well.

As time would tell, their position was not tenable by 1859. The reasons for this had been laid out in 1858 by two Republican politicians who would themselves soon run for the presidency. First, in June of 1858, the lesser known of these men, Abraham Lincoln, had stood in the chamber of the Illinois House of Representatives in Springfield to kick off his run for the Senate against Stephen A. Douglas. "A house divided against itself cannot stand," he told his audience. It almost sounded as if he proposed to repair the divide, but that was not his point: "I believe this government cannot endure, permanently half *slave* and half *free*. . . . I do not expect the house to fall. But I do expect it will cease to be divided. It will become all one thing, or all the other." In other words, America, in the aftermath of *Dred Scott*, could be either a slave republic or a free republic, but it could no longer be both; it had to choose.

A few months after Lincoln spoke, William Seward, the senator from New York—and former governor who in 1842 had refused to commute John Colt's death sentence—delivered an address in Rochester, New York, that painted the issue in even starker terms: the division between pro-slavery and antislavery forces represented an "irrepressible conflict," Seward declared. "I know, and you know, that a revolution has begun. I know, and all the world knows, that revolutions never go backward."

Later, for political reasons, both Lincoln and Seward would walk their views back a little. But their 1858 speeches spoke for themselves and set the ground for what followed.

Events in the autumn of 1859 put flesh—and blood—onto Lincoln's and Seward's language. On the night of October 16, the abolitionist firebrand John Brown, accompanied by twenty-one men, including three of his sons and five African Americans, made a daring but ill-conceived raid on the federal armory at Harpers Ferry, Virginia. The plan was to capture guns from the armory, then move into the countryside of Virginia, distributing the guns to slaves and fomenting a great insurrection that would sweep across the entire south. Brown's men were well armed even before they arrived at Harpers Ferry. Several carried Colt revolvers. Brown's own personal arm was a Colt that had been purchased for him in Hartford in 1857.

None of Brown's preparations was close to sufficient, and none of his assumptions—that scores of slaves would join him, for instance—came to pass. Within thirty-six hours of the attack, most of Brown's raiding party had been killed or arrested by troops under the command of Robert E. Lee. Brown himself was quickly tried for treason and sentenced to hang.

Brown's raid gave another polarizing jolt to the country. The hysteria in the south was predictable, for Brown's vision of total insurrection had been every slaveholder's nightmare since Nat Turner's rebellion almost thirty years earlier. More surprising was the response in the north. Many northerners, including abolitionists, had maintained pacifist views even through the violence of Bleeding Kansas, on the hope that slavery could be terminated by political or moral suasion. "Old Brown" put an end to this illusion. He did not make violence seem attractive, but he made it seem inevitable and justifiable. The abolitionist William Lloyd Garrison at first condemned Brown's use of force, but then changed his mind and applauded it. The poet Henry Wadsworth Longfellow, who had expressed an aversion to violence in his famous 1845 poem "The Arsenal at Springfield," wrote of Brown's raid, "This will be a great day in our history; the date of a new Revolution."

No one made a greater leap than Colt's old friend Lydia Maria Child. "In this enlightened age, all despotism *ought* to come to an end by the agency of moral and rational minds," she wrote in a letter to the governor of Virginia. "But if they resist such agencies, it is the order of Providence that they *must* come to an end by violence." She had once argued with Colt about the value of weapons of destruction. Now she seemed to acknowledge that he had the better side of the argument. "I want to shoot the accursed institution from all quarters of the globe," Child later wrote of slavery. "I think, from this time till I die, I shall stop firing only long enough to load my guns."

If John Brown got much of the credit for changing attitudes about violence among northerners, some of it probably went to Sam Colt, too. Several twenty-first-century scholars have suggested that by marketing his revolvers so expertly, Colt helped prime the American public for gun violence. The number of guns per capita in the United States in 1859 compared to, say, 1839 is hard to quantify—no reliable statistics exist—but without question both guns and acts of violence by firearms had markedly increased. Guns were prevalent in the years before the war not only in the west and south, which had always been more violent, but in the north. In Washington, by one estimate, a third of congressmen went into the Capitol each day armed, and many of those who did so were northerners. In New York City, George Templeton Strong noted a correlation between the rise in crime and the rise in gun ownership. "Most of my friends are investing in revolvers and carry them about at night, and if I expect to have to do a great deal of late night street-walking of Broadway, I think I should make the like provision."

III

In November, a clerk at Harpers Ferry named W. S. Downer wrote to Colt. Downer had discovered in the "plunder" from Brown's raid the barrel of a Colt pistol left by one of the raiders, bearing the address "Sam'l Colt New York City." He wondered how much it would cost to get a stock, frame, and lock to go with it. Colt wrote back to propose that Downer send him the barrel and any other mementos he'd collected from Brown's raid, and in return Colt would furnish him with a brand-new revolver. A week later, Downer sent a container of items left behind by Brown and his men, including a powder flask, a pocket inkstand, and a bullet from one of Brown's guns that Downer had scraped out of a piece of oak. Where these relics went after they came into Colt's possession is unknown, but he clearly attached value to them.

Of more immediate practical value to Colt was the effect Brown's raid had on his sales. The State of Virginia immediately ordered four cases of Colt revolvers, to be used against anyone attempting to rescue Brown before he could be executed, and that was just the start of it. The south developed an insatiable appetite for guns after Harpers Ferry. Given that just 3 percent of firearms in America were manufactured in the south before the start of the Civil War, southerners had to go north to get these guns. Within a month of Brown's raid, Governor Henry Wise of Virginia contacted Colt—or it may have been the other way around—to propose that he build an armory in Richmond. Colt ordered an aide, William Hartley, to Richmond to let the governor know "we will do everything in our power to carry out his designs." Colt also moved fast to capitalize on the emerging market in the Deep South.

The man he put in charge of southern sales was a New Yorker named Amos Colt. Amos was a cousin of some sort, distantly related and a few years younger than Sam. An English journalist who befriended Amos in 1860 would describe him as having "a thin, keen, nervous, sharp, hard-looking face, a moustache, shaven chin and curly black hair." When he began working for Sam, he was still recovering from an accident involving a Colt shotgun that had splashed his face with backfire.

How well Sam knew Amos before hiring him is not clear, but evidently not well enough to completely trust him with so delicate an assignment. Colt wrote to Hartley in January 1860, concerned that his distant cousin was "not quite the man for this kind of business with the governors and political officials of the Southern States." Hartley wrote back from Washington to reassure Sam that "Colt is fully competent to do all that is required of him . . . and is very shrewd." Hartley mentioned that Amos was still a little bitter about the "spit" that had blown into his face from Colt's gun, and who could blame him? "It deserves consideration that his face is tattooed with little specks."

Amos went to Richmond that January and from there launched a long state-to-state sales tour that would take him to the Carolinas, Georgia, Alabama, Mississippi, and Louisiana, then north through Arkansas, Tennessee, and Kentucky, and finally back again to the Carolinas, all the while promoting Colt's guns and doing his best to undermine rivals. He spread the word "in a quiet way," as he informed Sam, that Sharps's rifle company, a competitor of Colt's, was in cahoots with abolitionists.

It was dangerous to be a Yankee in the south after John Brown's raid, even a Yankee with guns to sell. Many northerners were forcibly driven out of the south in these months. Some were tarred and feathered, and a number were lynched. On at least one occasion, in Charleston, Amos became a target. He was publicly accused by a southerner named St. Clair Morgan of being a correspondent for the *New-York Tribune*, Horace Greeley's abolitionist-leaning newspaper. When Amos tried to correct this misapprehension, Morgan slapped him across the face with a pair of gloves. At which point, according to the *Chicago Tribune*, Amos "gave him a most deserved thrashing." Amos then waited in his hotel room, a loaded revolver on his lap, for Morgan and his friends to respond. Morgan thought better of it and slipped out of town to make trouble elsewhere.

It did not hurt Amos's sales pitch, or chances of survival, that he was an excellent shot. In the spring of 1859, he'd given a demonstration near his home in northern Manhattan, shooting forty bottles consecutively tossed into the air, shattering every one. In the spring of 1860, he was in a shooting match in New Orleans with a man Bernard, considered one of the best shots in Louisiana.

> The weapons were shotguns, Mr. Colt using his revolving shotgun. They first shot at bottles thrown in the air and then at two billiard balls, one thrown to the right and one to the left, Mr. Colt accomplishing the feat of hitting both balls before they commenced to descend. The next feat was to hit a five cent piece also thrown in the air. It is needless to say that Mr. Colt beat his adversary and was eminently successful.

Amos did well with sales but took an increasingly dim view of the future Confederacy. "Hog and Hominy is the fare," he wrote to Sam in March of

1860, from a rooming house in Jackson, Mississippi. "The hog predominates." He informed Sam that a remarkable "military spirit" resounded across the south and noted that southern men were, on the whole, good riders. "They are too damn lazy to walk. I do not now blame the Englishmen for his love of country. I am disgusted with mine—particularly this end of it."

IV

The winter of 1860 found Colt ill and housebound again. He was in the care of Dr. John Franklin Gray, a homeopathic physician from New York. He also sought relief from a "medical and animal electrician" named P. Pound, who used electricity, or magnetism, to cure illness. Pound's field, commonly known as mesmerism, was in vogue, though even then suspected of being pseudoscience. The treatments of Gray and Pound probably did nothing to help Colt, but they were no more useless than conventional nineteenth-century medicine, itself just barely scientific.

"It is unfortunate for him at this time to be confined," wrote William Jarvis, Colt's father-in-law, to a nephew in Ohio that January. "His orders are immense, and his works are driven to their full extent." The war was still sixteen months away but the armory was producing hundreds of arms daily to feed the appetite of the south. Jarvis informed his nephew that Colt, to fill domestic orders, had called back thousands of arms he'd sent to London for the European trade.

William Jarvis's weekly letters to his Ohio nephew seldom failed to mention his son-in-law, and they add key details about Colt in the years of his marriage to Elizabeth. They also provide a window into the political views of northern Democrats such as Jarvis and Colt. While it's unfair to put Jarvis's words into Colt's mouth, the men were in close agreement in their politics. When Jarvis assured his Ohio nephew that "the Hartford people are not all Abolitionists and that there are a good many of them who are not disposed to make a martyr and saint of an incendiary," he was including Colt among the "good many" who reviled John Brown. In one letter, Jarvis enclosed five copies of an "admirable sermon on the beauties of Abolitionism" that had been printed by Colt. Jarvis was being sarcastic; to him, nothing was beautiful about the "miserable fanatics," and the sermon he sent was doubtlessly *opposed* to abolition. He informed his nephew that Colt had taken it upon himself to distribute a thousand copies of the sermon.

Though his rhetoric was not as vitriolic as Jarvis's, Colt would spend much of 1860 doing everything in his power to defeat "Black Republicans." On January 11, for example, he wrote to Philo Calhoun, a former mayor of Bridgeport and a Democratic leader in the state. Calhoun was planning a large pro-south meeting of manufacturers in Meriden, Connecticut, to assure southern slave owners that the manufacturers of Connecticut were their allies, not their enemies. "I fully agree with you," Colt wrote, "as to the great importance to all lovers of the union that the most energetic measures should be taken with the least possible delay to neutralize the bad influence which our fanatical countrymen at the North have produced upon our southern Friends & Brothers." It was feckless, though, to make propositions that were not definite and biting. "There is nothing which can have the least effect now upon the minds of intelligent southern Gentlemen except the adoption by Congress of such laws as will put an end to this infernal slavery agitation in the north & to effect this end it is our duty as employers to make the stomach of these Black Republican Devils feel the vacuum." What Colt meant by those words he soon made clear.

On Monday, March 5, 1860, Abraham Lincoln came to Hartford. This was exactly a week after Lincoln's famous campaign-launching speech at Cooper Union in New York, and he was whistle-stopping his way through New England in advance of the Republican National Convention, to be held in mid-May in Chicago. He spoke to an overflow crowd that evening before the Republican Club at Hartford's City Hall. "The speech of Mr. Lincoln," the *Courant* informed its readers the following day, "was the most convincing and clearest speech we ever heard made. He carried the judgement, the conscience and the good will of his audience right straight along, from beginning to end." The *Courant* particularly admired Lincoln's way of injecting humor into his serious oration, "so as to keep everybody good natured and smiling."

Colt was not among the amused. A few days after Lincoln's visit, he began to take action against Republican workers at his armory. By March 15, sixty-six men had been discharged, fifty-six of these Republican. When he was accused by the Republican workers of bias and un-Americanism, Colt insisted in a letter to the *Hartford Times* that he had never hired or fired an employee for his political affiliation. He was only letting these men go now, he claimed, because demand for his guns was slow. In fact, though, he was executing the very policy he had recommended in his letter to Philo Calhoun back in January, making the stomachs of "Black Republicans" feel the "vacuum" by letting them go hungry.

V

Colt's health improved as the weather warmed. Lifting his spirits was a new addition to the family, a daughter born in late February, named after her mother and sharing her mother's dark eyes. She was "a noble, beautiful child," wrote Henry Barnard, "full of love and intelligence, and a queenly little form." Colt adored Lizzie, as she was called, and so did everyone else. She was baptized on May 13 with holy water that had been brought all the way from the river Jordan by Thomas Seymour.

Now Colt had an infant daughter and a thriving toddler son, Caldwell—everyone called him Collie. Sammy, meanwhile, was living in Boston with the family of a prominent educator named John Dudley Philbrick. "His improvement is constant, though not rapid," wrote Philbrick that May. "He is more agreeable in the family than he was a year ago, and his teachers speak of him with more favor."

Spring brought letters from Deane Alden. He drew a mixed picture of Colt's investment in Tubac. The silver mine was promising but the operation was plagued by troubles, from insufficient capital to spotty deliveries of machinery. The nearest railroad depot was in Texarkana, Texas, more than a thousand miles away. The closest transportation was the overland Butterfield stagecoach, which ran through Tucson on the dangerous route to San Francisco.

The greatest trouble at the mine came from Apaches. The Indians frequently came down from the hills to raid Tubac. Usually sneaking into the town at night, they would run off with cattle, mules, and horses. Alden estimated that the company had already lost $4,000 or $5,000 in damages. "The country is alive with Apaches," he wrote. "It was only a few days since they killed two of our wood choppers and drove off thirty head of the company's cattle—the bodies of the wood choppers were literally filled with arrows & and their heads nearly severed from their bodies, with the axes they had been to work with."

The whites in the area were only slightly less fearsome than the Indians. The borderland region south of the Gila River attracted desperadoes who were welcome nowhere else. Among these were members of the San Francisco Regulators, those former New Yorkers who had gone west with Jonathan Drake Stevenson in 1846. Too unsavory even for San Francisco, they had found their way to this "paradise of devils," as one writer put it at the time. Duels were common. One took place in 1859, in the town of Mesilla, between a man named M. A. Otero and a Judge Watts. As the local newspaper described it, the shooters exchanged shots at fifteen paces with Colt revolvers. "After the second shot," the *Arizonian* reported, "Mr. Otero lighted his *cigarito* and enjoyed his smoke, while Judge Watts amused himself by whistling." Then the men resumed their shooting. Neither died, but many others did. In 1860, it was reported, Tucson's graveyard held the remains of forty-seven white men. Only two of these had died of natural causes.

All of which made Arizona a risky place to mine silver but a good place to sell revolvers. "I am noticing in the newspaper occasionally complimentary notices of the Sharp & Burnside Rifles & Carbines, anecdotes of their use upon Grizzly Bears, Indians, Mexicans, etc.," wrote Colt. He urged Alden to correct this. "When there is or can be made a good story of the use of a Colt's Revolving Rifle, Carbine, Shotgun or Pistol for publication in the *Arizonian*, the opportunity should not be lost & in the event of such notices being published you must always send me one hundred copies."

Colt decided to cut his losses in the Sonora Exploring and Mining Company. In the spring of 1860 he sold his stock and summoned Alden home to Hartford. For Alden, the end of this venture could not have come soon enough.

If Colt made no profit on the silver from Tubac, he did get some use from it. Later that spring, he introduced a new standard revolver, the 1860 Army, made of "silver elastic steel," as Colt's promotional literature described it. Created at Colt's armory under the supervision of Elisha Root, the steel was supposedly an alloy with a small amount of silver, to make it stronger and lighter. "It possesses all the qualities of the most refined cutlery steel without the brittleness," the *Hartford Times* reported. "Tests by hydraulic pressure and gunpowder explosion in closely sealed tubes have proved it at least three times stronger and tougher than the best cast steel heretofore made." It's unlikely that a sprinkle of silver did much for the gunmetal, other than add a gleam of good publicity, but Colt had without question created a lighter gun without sacrificing strength. While the old holster pistol weighed 4.2 pounds, these news guns came in under 3.

The 1860 Army, alongside the 1851 Navy, would be one of the most popular guns of the American west in years to come. Its .44-caliber, eight-inch barrel gave it more accuracy than the previous seven-and-a-half-inch barrel but no less power. Because the gun had a larger cylinder and more kick, Colt also added a slightly longer grip for a firmer hold.

On May 19, a board of four army officers met in Washington to compare the new Colt model to the old. They were impressed. "The superiority of Colt's Revolvers, as an arm for cavalry service," the board reported, "is now finally confirmed." With a few small modifications, they deemed that the new gun will "make the most superior cavalry arm we have ever had, and they recommend the adoption of this New Model, and its issue to all the mounted troops."

Stephen Douglas passed through Hartford on Monday, July 16, 1860, on a campaign tour of New England. He was running as one of two Democratic candidates for president, the so-called "fire-eaters" of the Deep South having nominated their own candidate, John C. Breckinridge of Kentucky. The split in the Democratic Party pretty well assured victory to the Republican candidate, namely, as of May 18, Douglas's old debate foe Abraham Lincoln. Though Douglas had little chance of victory, he campaigned that summer as if the future of the United States depended on the outcome of the election, which, of course, it did.

Colt invited Douglas to stay at Armsmear on his swing through Hartford, but the candidate chose to stay at the United States Hotel on Main Street. Colt's friend Richard Hubbard, accompanied by Colt's Armory Band, led a greeting committee to the depot to welcome Douglas's train. Colt himself later visited Douglas at the hotel. As he wrote to his friend Augustus George Hazard (owner of a gunpowder company that bore his name), Colt was keenly aware of "the unfortunate predicament our party is at present in," but was also firmly committed to the Little Giant. "We agree that our flag is nailed to the mast for Douglas & union & shall there wave."

By coincidence, Deane Alden quietly returned to Hartford by steamboat the same day Douglas arrived in town. He had left Tubac at the right time—within a year, Apaches would butcher most of the men at the mines—and thus appeared to have escaped his destiny of dying in Colt's service. Unfortunately, he'd caught yellow fever while traveling home from Arizona. He checked in to the United States Hotel, the same hotel where Douglas and his wife were passing the night, and got into bed. Alden was well-liked in Hartford, and his illness was noted with concern in the newspapers. "We trust, however, that a change of climate and the comforts of home may speedily work beneficial results." He died a month later, in the middle of August.

Colt left Hartford two days after Alden's funeral, to join his family. Elizabeth and the children had been spending the summer in the town of Old Saybrook, on the Connecticut shore. On August 20, they all boarded a small side-wheel steamboat Colt had chartered, crew included, and embarked on a pleasure cruise of the New England coast. Despite Alden's death and his own declining health, these last weeks of the summer of 1860 would be among the finest of Colt's life. Aboard the steamboat were friends and family, including the Jarvises. Colt also brought along twenty or so members of the Armory Band, to provide entertainment, and numerous servants—altogether more than fifty passengers. Trailing the steamboat was a small sailing yacht, for fishing.

From Old Saybrook they steamed up the coast, fishing during the day, anchoring at night. Every evening they drifted into a new harbor—New London, Newport, New Bedford—as the band played on deck and fireworks exploded in the air above the ship. One evening they steamed over to Edgartown, on Martha's Vineyard, causing a stir as they visited the Methodist revival in Wesleyan Grove. "His babies and servants are in the party and one or two particular friends," wrote a newspaper correspondent in a dispatch from Edgartown. "They are having a capital time and the Colonel's beautiful children seem to thrive on the salt water."

Six weeks after they returned to Hartford, the Colts' daughter, Lizzie, became ill. "For one short week I watched my beautiful baby fade like a fair flower at the cold breath of Autumn," Elizabeth wrote to Sammy in Boston, "and then the gentle eyes closed on us forever." On October 17, at eight months of age, the girl died.

Sam was more undone by the child's death than Elizabeth. She'd always thought of her husband as a tower of strength, but now, between his grief and his illness, he completely collapsed. "Your uncle loved that little one so devotedly, that being not very well at the time, her death seemed to prostrate him entirely," Elizabeth later wrote to Sammy.

Lizzie was laid out in an open casket and the funeral was delayed, apparently to give Colt time to regain his composure. When the day came, though, Colt could not get out of bed. The girl's body, covered in flowers, was carried to him for a final farewell.

From a window of his room he watched the funeral, a small service behind the house, to the south. The sun set as his daughter was lowered into the ground next to her brother. When Elizabeth returned to the house after the burial, she found Sam in his room, Lizzie's portrait on his lap, "convulsed with such grief as one seldom sees." He told his wife that when he died, he wanted a funeral like the one his daughter had had—small and intimate. Elizabeth gave him a book of poetry to soothe him. But the poetry, she later acknowledged, did not help.

He did not leave the house for a month. At night, he was nursed by either Elizabeth or her sister, Hetty, his pain "racking, excruciating," as Elizabeth recalled. The Boston papers reported he had "gout in the stomach" and was expected to die. It was said, falsely, that nine doctors had rushed to Armsmear to attend to his final throes. Rumors of his death repeatedly raced through town. "His influence & importance are so great in Hartford," wrote William Jarvis, "that it is not strange that great anxiety should be felt for his recovery."

Colt was still in bed on Tuesday, November 6, when Abraham Lincoln was elected the sixteenth president of the United States.

VI

The months between Lincoln's election in November of 1860 and his inauguration in March of 1861 were unnerving, in part because they were so normal. In much of the country, life continued as if nothing had changed. Meanwhile, good people of both the north and the south endeavored to stop the coming war. Abraham Lincoln tried to mollify southerners with assurances that he did not intend to interfere with slavery where it already existed. William Seward, whose "irrepressible conflict" had become a battle cry in both north and south, floated a conciliatory plan to make New Mexico a slave state. A few brave southerners sounded the alarm that secession was regional suicide. Stephen Douglas, who had done so much to bring about the conflict in his attempts to find a compromise to avoid it, now urgently spoke out against secession and called upon his friends in the south to accept Lincoln's victory. ("I am with him," he would say of his old foe shortly before dying in June of 1861.) But all appeals fell on deaf ears in the south, where Lincoln's election was considered a virtual declaration of war.

The demand for guns had picked up in the south following John Brown's raid, and now it increased almost exponentially. By the time the war began, the best-armed troops in the nation would be southern state militias, which had been stockpiling guns since late 1859. Ironically, the south was assisted in arming itself by the very government from which it would soon secede. The Buchanan administration was sympathetic to the south and included a number of southern officials. None of these was more useful to the future Confederacy than Colt's confidant John B. Floyd, the secretary of war. Floyd had latitude in deciding how government arms were distributed. Under the pretense of arming state militias per the 1808 Militia Act, he spent his last year in office shipping guns and artillery to southern states. He would resign in December of 1860 under suspicion of corruption, but not before attempting to transfer 125 cannons from Pittsburgh to Mississippi and Texas. Later, Floyd would serve as a general in the Confederate Army.

Even as their militias stockpiled US government guns, southerners continued to procure weapons from private armories such as Colt's—especially Colt's. In 1860, Colt sold $61,000 worth of guns just to Alabama, Virginia, Georgia, and Mississippi. This number does not include all the guns he sold to the Carolinas, Louisiana, and Texas. He may have been sincerely disappointed by Douglas's loss to Lincoln, but Lincoln's victory had a silver lining far more valuable to Colt than any actual silver he could have hoped to mine in Arizona. War jitters were causing financial woes across the north, but not in Coltsville. As William Jarvis wrote to his nephew at the end of 1860, "Every kind of business, except the manufacture of fire arms, has nearly ceased."

Colt was quite ill in the final months of 1860 but he insisted on seeing his managers every day. They came up the carriage path from the armory to the house—Root, Sargeant, and others—to report on progress. "He will know all the details of his immense business from day to day," wrote Jarvis, "and give minute directions in regard to it." On November 15, Colt rode in a carriage, his first time out of the house since Lizzie's death a month earlier. He was still sick, though, and soon back in bed. "The Col. does not improve in health very fast; and I think it is the consequence of overtasking his brain while he is so feeble," wrote Jarvis. Finally, on December 19, Jarvis wrote to report good news: "The Col. I am happy to say is better."

The following day, South Carolina became the first state to secede from the union.

Five more states joined South Carolina in January of 1861. A sixth, Texas, declared its intention to secede on February 2. Representatives from these states convened in Montgomery, Alabama, to create a government for the Confederate States of America.

All that winter and spring orders came into Colt's armory from across the south—from Marietta, Georgia, and Mobile, Alabama; from Lexington, Kentucky, and Charlottesville, Virginia; and from Governor John W. Ellis himself in Raleigh, North Carolina. "In order to prevent seizure it would be well to pack in casks, do not put my name upon them," Governor Ellis advised Colt. Understanding that every gun that went south would eventually point north, the US government and local officials in northern states had started to crack down on shipments to the south. "In case of seizure," wrote Ellis, "advise me at once as I am resolved to retaliate."

One letter came from James Ewell Brown Stuart, known as Jeb, a US Army lieutenant and future hero and martyr of the Confederate Army. Stuart had become acquainted with Colt's guns while fighting Indians under General Harney in the West. Writing now from St. Louis, he requested "one pistol (of army ball and navy size late pattern)," plus fixtures and cartridges. "You will do me a favor by packing this in such a box as to elude the scrutiny of mob search on the road."

Colt's old friend Ben McCulloch, the Texas Ranger, wrote to request as many as two thousand army pistols for immediate delivery. For the sake of appearances, he claimed in his letter that the pistols were to be used "against the Indians." They were to be billed, though, to the Confederate States of America.

On January 16, 1861, the *New York Times*, without mentioning Colt by name, called him out as a traitor. Southerners had "bargained with Northern people for weapons for destroying the people of the North," warned the *Times*. At first, the gun manufacturers may have failed to take seriously the south's intention to go to war with the north. "But, unfortunately for the credit of these persons, they have not ceased to respond to such orders even since the deeply malignant purposes of the South have been placed beyond all question; and it is well known that several prominent factories of arms are at this moment working under the utmost pressure to furnish Southern traitors with the implements of treasonable warfare."

One cold day in the middle of January, Colt went for a stroll in the warmth of his greenhouses behind Armsmear, which now added up to nearly half a mile in length. The walking made his arthritic feet sore, but otherwise he was improved enough by January 20 to travel with his family—Elizabeth, Hetty, and two-year-old Collie—to New York on a shopping trip. They stayed at the St. Nicholas on Broadway and Broome Street, which had supplanted the Astor House as the finest hotel in the city. On January 28, Colt went into Mason Brothers booksellers on Mercer Street and purchased a three-volume biography of Andrew Jackson, bound in "full calf" leather, for $15.

The family returned to Hartford, on February 3, just long enough to announce that they were going to Cuba for the winter. The hasty plan had evidently been made on the advice of Colt's New York physician, Dr. Gray. It was a busy time for Colt to leave the armory, but it made sense for him to repair his health and gather his strength before the war began, as everyone now knew it soon would.

On February 18, 1861—the same day Jefferson Davis was appointed the first president of the Confederate States of America—the Colts arrived in Havana. "We have had a long but pleasant passage," Colt wrote back to his office in Hartford, "and I have been improving ever since we got into warm weather, the third day out, since when the thermometer has been at 70 degrees and above."

The voyage to Cuba was dictated by Colt's illness, the change of weather being considered beneficial to his health. But it was a striking place to visit on the eve of the Civil War. Slavery was as entrenched on the island as in the American south. After the war, much of the south's leadership would flee to Havana to lick its wounds at the Hotel Cubano. The Cubano is where Colt went and family went directly upon arriving in Havana.

They had gone to Cuba so Colt could rest, but no sooner did they land on the island than he began sending letters back to the armory. War was near—the war Colt had been waiting for, in a sense, since 1835—and he wanted to be ready. "Run the armory night and day with double sets of hands until we get 5,000 or 10,000 ahead of each kind. I had rather have an accumulation of our arms than to have money lying idle, and we cannot have too many on hand to meet the exigencies of the time."

"Make hay," Colt wrote, "while the sun shines."

VII

Abraham Lincoln was inaugurated under gray skies and the watchful eyes of army sharpshooters posted on the roof of the Capitol. The date was March 4, 1861. Confederate assassins were rumored to be at large in Washington. "I am loth to close," said Lincoln near the end of his address, as if by continuing to speak a while longer he might delay what was coming.

That same day a package arrived at the home of Howell Cobb in Macon, Georgia. Cobb had been a governor of Georgia and secretary of the treasury under President Buchanan. Since early February he had been president of the Provisional Congress of the Confederate States in Montgomery, Alabama. Cobb's son wrote his father to tell him that the package contained two gifts from Sam Colt. "Yours is a large horseman's pistol (revolver) in a fine case," wrote young Cobb. The other, for Cobb's wife, was a fine ivory-handled revolver. "Mother's is a book. On the back it has 'Colt on the Constitution, Higher Law and Irrepressible Conflict. Dedicated by the Author to Mrs. Howell Cobb.'"

Colt sometimes presented his guns inside cases made to appear as leather-bound books.
This one—Colt on the Constitution, Higher Law & Irrepressible Conflict, dated January 1, 1861—
is a duplicate of the volume he sent to the wife of Howell Cobb, president of the Provisional Congress
of the Confederate States, shortly before the outbreak of the Civil War. The title
is a play on a line from William Seward's 1858 speech.

That Colt sent such a gift suggests that he was still courting the south at this late date, even following the first wave of secession—indeed, he was going directly to the government of the Confederacy.

From Havana, the Colts went inland to the sulfur springs in Madruga. By the third week of March, Colt felt much improved. He no longer needed crutches and could get by with just his cane. "The daily rent here is now a little over $80 and the daily heat here now is a little over 80 degrees," he wrote to his managers in Hartford. "I still keep on my flannels and most of my thick clothes, preparing to take them off while I am taking sulfur baths daily." The only complaint came from the ladies and Collie, who were "very much opposed to the vermin of this country."

"I was able to walk to the bath some 250 yards distant without my crutch this morning," Colt wrote on March 23. He spent the afternoon watching cockfights, "the famous sport of this country." He reiterated his directive to move at full speed at the armory, then: "It is getting too dark to see & the flies and mosquitoes are biting me horribly so I must close."

The family arrived back in Hartford on Saturday, March 30, 1861. Colt appeared to be in fine health. He went to church that Sunday and spent Monday in the armory. After no more than a week at home, he left again, for New York. What business took him there is unclear, but once he arrived, he seemed to wait for events to unfold, poised to move accordingly. On April 9, he wrote to headquarters, responding to a letter that had been forwarded to him by a man named Mark Cooper in Georgia. Cooper had urged Colt to open an armory in that state. "I may leave here for the south before returning to Hartford," Colt informed his aides, apparently meaning he might go to Georgia. Given his health and the state of the country, such a move was highly unlikely, but Colt was foreclosing no possibilities.

Three days later, on April 12, 1861, South Carolina artillery, under the command of General P. G. T. Beauregard, opened fire on Fort Sumter in Charleston's harbor. The war had begun. There would be no more going to Georgia.

"It is gathered from reliable sources that you are manufacturing and shipping arms South," began a letter mailed to Colt on April 15, the day President Lincoln declared an insurrection and called up seventy-five thousand Union militiamen for service. "Now Sir, I am able to inform you that if you fulfill any more orders or ship further supplies South from this date, your establishment will be most thoroughly cleaned out. Yours with respect due a traitor." The letter was postmarked Springfield, Massachusetts, and signed by a group calling itself the Vigilance Committee.

Was Colt a traitor, as this letter charged? His sales to the south were clearly opportunistic, but so were the sales of numerous other northern manufacturers that did business with the south right up until Fort Sumter— were they all traitors? The city of New York contained so many merchants who intended to continue trading with the south that Mayor Fernando Wood seriously considered declaring New York "a free city of itself" and flouting federal restrictions.

What made Colt stand out, and why he was accused of treason while others were not, was the aggressiveness of his approach, the volume of his sales, and the fact that he was selling guns. Some gunmakers, notably Remington, had denounced sales to the south after the first states seceded; Colt did not. Perhaps it is no more fair to blame a gun manufacturer for selling guns for war than it is to blame an umbrella manufacturer for profiting from rain. But rain has no moral dimension, and war always does. Certainly this war did. Any Colt guns that went south would be used not to kill some foreign adversary but fellow Americans, including thousands of young men from New England.

Colt had continued to ship guns south through early April. As late as April 16, Ben McCulloch wrote to Colt from New Orleans to inform him that the guns he'd ordered had arrived. "I am off for Texas," added McCulloch, "where I would be delighted to see you."

April 18 appears to have marked the end of Colt's dealings with the south. That day, a letter arrived in Hartford from the Navy Department of the Confederate States of America. "Can you furnish this Department with 200 Navy revolvers? If so, send them at once by express." On the reverse of the letter were written the words "Not sent." The record shows no sales or discussions of sales to Confederate states or southerners after that. On April 19, a week after the bombardment of Fort Sumter, the *Hartford Courant* reported that Colt had sworn off southern sales. The *Chicago Tribune* responded to this news with wry applause: "This is patriotism at the eleventh hour. Better late than never."

Colt was still in New York on Saturday, April 20. From his window in the St. Nicholas Hotel, he could watch the extraordinary transformation that came over Broadway in the days after Fort Sumter. The entire city was marching and mobilizing, rallying to Lincoln's call for volunteers. New York had been the friendliest of northern cities to the Confederacy, but now crowds gathered at newspaper offices and in parks to cheer on the Union and condemn the Confederacy. That Saturday, a meeting in Union Square, a few blocks north of the St. Nicholas, drew an estimated one hundred thousand men.

Returning to Hartford on April 22, Colt found his own city in war's thrall. "The buildings of the town are flying the red, white and blue," reported the *Courant*. "The American flag is visible at all points. Union cockades are worn by all parties, at all times, and in all places." Already three companies of volunteers, 244 men in each, had mustered and started for a rendezvous in New Haven, and more regiments were forming by the hour. That evening, as troops from southern Massachusetts marched through town to the train depot, people ran out to greet them with cheese and crackers. The Massachusetts men then boarded a train for Baltimore. (When these same Massachusetts men arrived in Baltimore, they would be violently attacked by a mob of pro-secession Marylanders and become the first Union troops to shed blood in the Civil War.)

Orders flooded into the armory from small towns and cities in the north, from St. Johnsbury, Vermont ("We are raising a company here and shall probably wish to supply them with each a revolver"), and from Laconia, New Hampshire ("The citizens of this town want to know if they can be furnished with the Army pattern of Colt's Revolver . . . to present to the volunteers here"). A letter from Fitchburg, Massachusetts, inquired at what price Colt could provide "one hundred thirty Revolvers Navy size of a very plain finish," and one from Champaign, Illinois, requested "by express One Dozen Colt's six-inch revolvers with directions to collect on delivery."

Everyone, it seemed, wanted revolvers. The government would supply a limited number to officers and cavalry, but volunteers sought them as sidearms. On their way to war, many of these young men stopped off at photography studios to pose for a carte de visite, holding a Colt revolver at their side or across their chest. Most of these volunteers would soon be handed government muskets and told to form ranks and shoot on orders. They would kill or be killed from too great a range for a revolver to be useful. But the revolver stood for something. It was a weapon of *self*-defense, an assertion of individual identity in a war that would turn hundreds of thousands of these young men into rancid meat.

VIII

The months on both sides of Fort Sumter brought Colt's personal qualities, bad and good, into stark relief. If the weeks before the war highlighted his less savory traits of duplicity and opportunism, the weeks after called upon his remarkable drive and determination. Before the end of April, he decided to double the size of his armory. This was to accommodate demand not just for his own revolving guns but for huge orders of standard government muskets he expected to receive from the War Department. He assured Washington that he could produce as many as one hundred thousand muskets in 1861, and an indefinite number after that. Many Americans that April assumed that the war was going to be brief and bloodless. Colt knew better and prepared accordingly.

Whatever cure had relieved his sickness in Cuba had stopped working, and his health was rapidly declining that spring. Still, Colt drove himself to meet all demands and opportunities. "He has not yet learned prudence, and I fear he never will," William Jarvis wrote that April as Colt ordered the armory to run twenty hours a day. "If he thinks his business needs his attention, he will give it at whatever risk to his health and comfort." Of the war, wrote Jarvis, "I am sorry for it, as it will only be increasing his labors, which now are ten times greater than any man ought to perform. But work he will, with all his might, so long as the breath of life is in him."

One of the first government orders Colt met was an urgent request by the War Department for revolvers. Unlike the Confederacy, which had been arming for well over a year, the US government had done little to prepare for war and found itself flat-footed. In those early days, before troops could be amassed to defend it, no place was more vulnerable than the nation's capital. Rumors of an imminent Confederate strike on Washington whipped through the northern press. It was said that an army of five thousand men was preparing to attack from Virginia, led by none other than Ben McCulloch, the Texas Ranger who had been buying guns from Colt just a few weeks earlier. But even as northern newspapers sounded the alarm, at least one southern newspaper reported that McCulloch was no longer in Virginia. He had arrived by ship in New Orleans, having "succeeded in his mission to purchase 1000 Colt's revolvers, and 1000 repeating rifles for the use of the State."

A new daughter, Henrietta Selden Colt, called Hetty, was born to Elizabeth on May 26. Joyous as the occasion was, Colt did not have much time to devote to domestic life. Along with rapidly expanding his armory and workforce, he was starting his own small army, the fighting version of the ceremonial force that Deane Alden had led. Financed and armed by Colt for $50,000, the regiment had several hundred men, organized into companies of one hundred each, "of fine appearance and splendidly drilled and equipped," as William Jarvis put it, with Colt-manufactured weapons. Among the regiment's volunteers was Sammy Colt, now nineteen, who came from Boston to join. Commissioned as a first lieutenant, he was assigned to recruit for the regiment. Amos Colt came, too, with a lieutenant's commission. Through May and much of June, the regiment drilled on the meadow, ate at the armory dining hall, and slept in barracks on the armory grounds.

In June, to maintain the elite appearance of his regiment, Colt imposed a height requirement of five feet seven inches for all recruits. This was impolitic, to say the least, as Colt immediately alienated every man in Connecticut five feet six and under. His lordly presumptions did not sit well with the Republican governor, who by the third week of June was no longer interested in supporting Colt's private army. The state revoked Colt's commission and those of everyone else in the company. This was just as well for Colt, as his health was continuing to decline and he was in no position to lead men to war.

William Jarvis continued to marvel at Colt's tremendous work ethic. Though generally finding his son-in-law's habits "imprudent" given his health, Jarvis also realized that work was the essence of Colt, the thing to which he had given most of his life and would give all of it. "He is without exception the hardest working man that I know of," Jarvis wrote on June 19. "He generally rises at 5 or 6 o'clock and takes a ride across the river to see his garden, farm, brick-making etc. on that side; returns, gets his breakfast, and goes to his armory, where he remains often till 7 or 8 o'clock. He must love work for its own sake, I think, and it really seems that the more he has to do, the more he enjoys himself, and is in better health and sprits."

But in fact Colt's health continued to fail that summer. In mid-July, he went north to seek the cooler weather and curative powers of the springs in St. Catharines in Canada. In letters from St. Catharines, Colt made light of his condition, but he would not have left Hartford unless it was dire.

He was still in Canada on July 21, 1861, when thirty-five thousand Union soldiers, having marched from Washington to Manassas, Virginia, confronted a Confederate force of twenty thousand men under General Beauregard. After a day of fierce fighting, the northern troops fled back to Washington and the south declared victory. The First Battle of Bull Run, as the engagement would be called in the north, was a stunning correction to a common impression, still held by most northerners until that July, that the war would be quickly and gallantly won.

One day late that fall a long letter arrived in Hartford from Lisbon, Portugal. "Was many years since we have met, but I trust you have not forgotten an old friend who has always remembered you with much respect and regard." The letter came from John L. O'Sullivan, the former editor of the *United States Magazine and Democratic Review* and the man who had coined the term Manifest Destiny in 1845. Colt owed John O'Sullivan a great deal, for it had been Manifest Destiny in large part that had made Colt rich. O'Sullivan's rhetoric had also done much to bring about the Civil War, so it was ironic and even a little unseemly that he should be thousands of miles from his country when it came apart.

The war was not what brought O'Sullivan to Colt now. He had fallen on hard times since his glory days and was now living in Europe, nearly destitute. He was writing in hopes that he might cash in on some of Colt's goodwill and fortune, supposing correctly "that in the midst of the general depression the peculiar nature of your manufacture could at least secure you from suffering with the times."

He quickly got to his pitch: "I have understood that you use elegantly and worthily the great wealth yielded by your great invention & your years of patient perseverance, and that you are a liberal purchaser of works of art." O'Sullivan had made himself into something of an art connoisseur or, more accurately, an art dealer, and he had quite a deal for Colt. Enclosed with the letter was a long list of paintings, included several Rubenses and a van Dyke. "Now it is not often that an opportunity can occur for an American to get such a collection of genuine pictures," O'Sullivan wrote. He asked Colt to make him an offer. "I will only say that I am very much in want of money, and should not therefor be likely to be unreasonable on the score of prices."

There is no evidence that Colt ever responded to O'Sullivan or purchased any of his paintings. In all likelihood, by the time this letter got into Colt's hand, if it ever did, it was too late for him to do anything about it.

IX

Colt's health had shown signs of improvement after he returned home from St. Catharines. He worked as hard as ever, devoting his energies to opening the new wing of the armory and adding more worker housing, aiming to complete both projects by the end of November despite constant rain. He now employed fifteen hundred men at the armory, five hundred more than at the start of the war, and carried by far the largest payroll in Hartford, more than $80,000 a month. Before the end of 1861, the armory would produce at least 70,000 revolvers. The following year, it would produce more than 110,000.

As if he needed more work to occupy himself, Colt also started enlarging Armsmear that fall, "though I should think it was large enough already," wrote William Jarvis. If nothing else, this new undertaking suggests that Colt was thinking of the future, expecting his family to grow and imagining himself alive for years to come. "Those were very happy weeks," Elizabeth later recalled of the period between Thanksgiving and Christmas, "the children bright and well, with almost every earthly wish gratified, how could we dream of the fearful storm so soon to burst upon us?"

When he became ill at Christmas, it seemed at first to be a relatively minor spell of rheumatism. Jarvis blamed it on a draft that came into the house from the opening that had been made in the back wall during the renovation. Despite cold and damp weather, Colt was well enough on New Year's Day to welcome to the house an elderly man who had been a friend of his grandfather's, and he seemed to revive as he reminisced with his guest and proudly showed off his children. That night, though, a fierce windstorm passed through Hartford, blowing off roofs, tearing off store signs, sweeping away army tents, rattling windows, and howling through cracks.

In the first few days of 1862 Colt felt well enough to occasionally laugh and play with his children. On the morning of Saturday, January 4, he got up and tried to work, but when Elizabeth returned from an outing, she found him back in bed and, more ominously, paging through a Bible that had been given to him many years earlier by his father. Colt had never been a pious man or given to poetry, but, according to Elizabeth, he'd glued a poem inside the Bible the previous summer, while in St. Catharines. It was a religious poem by an English cleric, James Augustus Page, titled "What! Leave my Church of England!" ("Oh! bid me leave all else on earth, / The near and dear I've known, / But not my Church of England, / My father's and my own.")

Elizabeth's description of Colt's final days bears many of the hallmarks of *ars moriendi*, "the good death," as the historian Drew Gilpin Faust describes the ritualistic narratives that Americans tended to tell themselves about the dying of loved ones in the mid-nineteenth century. "Peaceful acceptance of God's will" was a critical step in preparing oneself for salvation, and this was done, ideally, in the company of loving family. The carefully wrought account Elizabeth later gave includes these soothing elements, but it leaves no doubt that Colt died no more tamely than he lived.

On Sunday, January 5, "the disease went to his brain," as William Jarvis put it to his nephew. "He talked incessantly all the afternoon & till 2 O'clock Monday morning, making poetry, and singing to airs that he was familiar with, but finally went to sleep and rested till morning, and seemed quite rational when he awoke." Soon, though, he was back in the grip of delirium. "His brain has been overworked till its functions have given out," Jarvis surmised. "It is in fact too active for his physical powers of endurance."

The week that followed sounds harrowing for all involved. "I believe he was conscious of the change as soon as I was," wrote Elizabeth. "He had the most perfect consciousness that he was losing control over his mind." In his hours of clarity, "he looked off into the great unknown future with a calm serenity and peace." Then the delirium would set in again, and Colt would resume "talking almost uninterruptedly and incoherently."

In New York, a rumor later circulated that before Sam died, he was visited at his deathbed by John C. Colt. Having escaped from the Tombs in 1842, it was said, John had been living in Texas and had somehow heard about his brother's final illness and had made the journey, in impossible time, to say farewell. According to a report in the press, James Colt was also at Sam's deathbed when John showed up and "was so suddenly brought into contact with the resurrected suicide that he lost his sense in a convulsion, and fell to the ground injuring himself severely." In fact, John did not appear, nor did James.

"Beautifully and touchingly he told me that death was very near," Elizabeth recalled of her final conversation with Sam. "Then he bade me a last farewell, calling me his faithful loving wife, asking me to carry out all his plans so far as I might. Then reason again gave way, and as he said himself, 'It is all over now.'" At nine in the morning of January 10, 1862, at the age of forty-seven, with Elizabeth at his side, Sam Colt died his good death.

Legatees and Legacies

1862–PRESENT

The ruins of Colt's armory, February 1864.

All but Death, can be Adjusted.

—Emily Dickinson

I

Within hours of Colt's death, news of it had traveled by telegraph to the major cities of the east and as far west as Cincinnati, Ohio, and Janesville, Wisconsin, where it made the afternoon papers amid dispatches from the war. By the end of the following week, obituaries of Colt had appeared in papers all over the country. Much of the southern press simply noted his demise in a tart line or two—"Revolver Colt died at Hartford" is all the

Natchez Daily Courier had to say about it—but some northern papers, such as the *New York Times*, which had criticized Colt for furnishing guns to the south only a year earlier, devoted long and flattering columns to him.

In Hartford, it had been widely known that Colt was ill, but still his death was met with shock. His loss would "leave an irreparable gap in our city," the *Courant* predicted. The newspaper did not suggest that Colt had been a good man, only that he had been a great one. "Colt's life was intense; his mind ever on the strain; his brain teeming with plans, and hopes, and enterprises." There had been luck, too, the *Courant* pointed out. Colt's fortune was inversely bound to the misfortune of others—the war with Mexico, the Crimean War, and now "our own sad Insurrection." But Colt had made the most of what life gave him. "He died a middle-aged man; but he had really *lived* far longer than those who vegetate to more protracted periods."

The funeral was scheduled for 3:00 p.m. on January 14, a cold Tuesday. By 2:00 p.m., the sidewalks on both sides of Main Street were filled by people walking south from downtown toward Wethersfield Avenue to join the crowd already gathering in front of Armsmear. Meanwhile, hundreds of Colt workers, accompanied by the brass band, marched up the hill from the armory to the house, passing the frozen lake, the deer park, and the greenhouses. When they reached the house, they filed quietly through a door in the north wing and shuffled into the parlor, where Colt lay in an open metal casket appearing, according to the papers, "very natural." The workers then passed through the library on the south side of the house and out onto the back lawn, forming two columns that ran from the house to the grave site. At 3:00 p.m., all the church bells in Hartford began to chime in remembrance of Colt. The pallbearers, led by Thomas Seymour and Elisha Root, lifted Colt's body and carried it out of the house and down the path through the gauntlet of workers. At the center of the crowd around the grave site sat Elizabeth and her family. Lydia Sigourney was nearby, and she had a poem:

> There's mourning in the princely halls
> So late with gladness gay—
> A tear within the heart of love
> That will not dry away;
> A sense of loss on all around,
> A sigh of grief and pain—
> "The like of him we lose to day,
> We ne'er shall see again."

More than forty years had passed since Sigourney looked out her window to watch the Colt family come and go and saw the curly-haired boy running through her downstairs hall on Lord's Hill. She had been one of the few constants in Colt's life, and in some ways their visages occupied opposite sides of the same American coin. She sold pious feelings, he sold guns; he ministered to dark human impulses and needs, she to lofty and pretty aspirations. Sigourney was seventy now but still a one-woman poetry factory, churning out more or less interchangeable verses on demand.

When Colt was a boy, death had seemed to stalk his family, and now it was at it again: six days after his funeral, on January 20, his daughter Hetty, eight months old, died of diphtheria. Sigourney went back to her desk to write another eulogy, and Elizabeth back to the grave site behind the house to bury another child. "My heart aches for Lizzie," wrote William Jarvis, "but the babe we cannot weep for—she blooms in a brighter, better land, and will taste none of the bitterness of this earth." Elizabeth was pregnant with a fifth child even as she buried her fourth. That baby, a girl, would be stillborn, and Elizabeth would become gravely ill with complications. She bore her afflictions "with wonderful composure and resignation," wrote Jarvis later in that bleak winter of 1862.

II

Many families were suffering afflictions that winter. The great bloodbaths of the war—Shiloh, Antietam, Gettysburg—remained unfought, but thousands of young American men had already perished. Before it was done, 620,000 would die, nearly as many Americans as in all other US wars combined. The magnitude of these fatalities, as Drew Gilpin Faust shows, disrupted nineteenth-century ideals of the Good Death. Here was the wholesale slaughter of young men who were left to rot until they could be thrown into graves. This was a reality more suited to the circumspect verse of Emily Dickinson than to the anodyne rhymes of Lydia Sigourney. For Dickinson, whose fetal slumbers had been disturbed by the vibrations of Sam Colt's cannonade in the summer of 1830, sentiment was suspect and heaven was chilly. The only good thing that could be said of dying was that it "annuls the power to kill."

The Civil War was the world's first truly industrial war. The south had gone into it better prepared psychologically, filled with a self-righteous zeal that helped carry it through its first improbable victories, but chivalry and umbrage were no match for machinery and manpower. McCormick's

reaper produced abundant grain, Morse's telegraph provided better communications, and northern railroads offered better transportation—all critical
advantages to the north. Yankee boot makers, too, having adopted from
armories the machines they needed for mass production, gave the Union
an advantage. By the end of the war, southern soldiers were often barefoot,
while northern soldiers were shod in boots that fit.

The north also produced many more guns. Given the Civil War's moder-
nity, it may seem anachronistic that most of these guns were muzzle-loading,
single-shot muskets. But they were cheap to make, simple to use, and well
suited to the conventional battle tactics favored by commanders on both
sides of the conflict, which is to say ranks of infantry aiming and shooting
in sync to lay steady fire. Part of what would make this war so bloody was
that the muskets, while mechanically similar to earlier models, were rifled,
rather than smoothbore, and shot minié balls, giving them much greater
accuracy and range. Musket-armed soldiers during the American Revolution
or the War of 1812 had been lucky to hit the enemy across 75 yards. These
new muskets were accurate and deadly at 250 yards.

To infantry units, Colt's revolver was a sideshow through most of the
war, a desirable but inessential accoutrement carried by officers and cavalry.
Still, by one estimate—likely on the low end—the company sold nearly
112,000 revolvers in 1862, or 40,000 more than it had sold in 1861, and
another 137,000 in 1863. The revolver found its true wartime niche in the
internecine struggles of the trans-Mississippi west, where pro-Confederate
bushwhackers and antislavery jayhawkers had been shooting at one another
almost continuously since the summer of Bloody Kansas. At times these
irregular troops joined Confederate and Union armies, but mainly they
followed their own whims. They specialized in fast-moving, horse-mounted
guerrilla warfare, with no front lines, no long-term strategy, no rules of
engagement, and no objectives other than to kill the enemy.

The most notorious of the pro-Confederate bushwhackers was William
Quantrill, leader of a gang that terrorized Missouri and eastern Kansas
through much of the war. Quantrill operated more like a terrorist than a
soldier. In the words of the generally equanimous Civil War historian James
McPherson, Quantrill and his gang were "some of the most psychopathic
killers in American history." Their principal arm was the Colt 1851 Navy.
"Quantrill required results in pistol-firing," wrote an early biographer, "and
the guerrilla understood this art much better than any other soldier." Every
guerrilla carried at least two revolvers, and most carried between four and
eight, tucked against their bodies or in saddle holsters on their horses. Thus
armed, they would wait in ambush beside a road. When a Union patrol

drew near, they would charge out of the brush, revolvers crackling, puffs of black smoke darkening the air, bullets swarming. Before the Union troops could get off a shot, the whole affair would be over. The bushwhackers would strip valuables from the fallen soldiers—including more revolvers if any were to be had—and mutilate the corpses, then slip back into the woods or fields from which they had come.

Quantrill did not limit his violence to soldiers and jayhawkers. Sudden attacks on farms and towns were meant to flush out abolitionists and provoke fear among Union-supporting civilians. "No more terrifying object ever came down a street than a mounted guerrilla wild for blood," wrote one of Quantrill's early biographers, "the bridle-reins between his teeth or over the saddle-horn, the horse running recklessly, the rider yelling like a Comanche, his long unkempt hair flying wildly beyond the brim of his broad hat, and firing both to the right and left with deadly accuracy."

In his most infamous attack, on August 21, 1863, Quantrill led more than four hundred revolver-wielding fighters across the western border of Missouri to Lawrence, Kansas, the town founded by abolitionist Amos Adams Lawrence and previously been raided by bushwhackers in 1856. Quantrill's orders were simple: "Kill every male and burn every house." Before his men were done, they had slaughtered nearly two hundred males, including boys as young as ten.

A year after the Lawrence massacre, on September 27, 1864, another gang of bushwhackers, led by former Quantrill lieutenant William "Bloody Bill" Anderson, and including the brothers Frank and Jesse James, performed an equally terrifying raid on Centralia, Missouri. Revolvers were again the featured weapon.

Anderson's gang came to destroy the tracks of the North Missouri Railroad that ran through Centralia, but more generally to wreak sorrow and fear. They began their raid by pillaging local stores and houses. When a train appeared on the horizon, some galloped out to meet it with their revolvers, shooting at its engine and windows until it halted. Among the passengers on the train were twenty-three uniformed but unarmed Union soldiers returning home for furlough. Anderson ordered the soldiers off the train. Saving one to hold as a hostage, he forced the others to strip and stand in a line along the tracks. Then he gave his men the signal to open fire. As the other passengers watched in horror, Anderson's men emptied their revolvers into the Union soldiers, killing all. Then Anderson lit the train on fire, instructed the engineer to open the throttle full, and sent it chuffing and blazing down the tracks to the next town, like a messenger from hell.

That same afternoon, Anderson and his men were back at their camp a mile and a half to the south of Centralia when over the ridge came 115 Union soldiers under the command of Major Andrew Vern Emen Johnston. The soldiers rode horses but carried standard-issue rifled muskets, requiring them to dismount to fight. "Not a damned revolver in the crowd!" Anderson mirthfully observed before ordering his men to charge. Under normal circumstances, a volley from 115 muskets would have been sufficient to slow 80 galloping bushwhackers. But because the soldiers were firing downhill, they committed the easy error of aiming too high; a few of Anderson's men fell but most kept charging.

In an instant, the entire problem of single-shot firearms came to a grisly head. The Union soldiers desperately tried to reload as Anderson's men, shrieking and spurring their horses, thundered up the slope—and then the bushwhackers were upon them. The soldiers tried to defend themselves with their fixed bayonets, but these were no match for men on horseback with Colts. All 115 soldiers were slaughtered. Jesse James used his Colt Navy to claim the honor of putting the first bullet into Major Johnston.

Afterward, Anderson's men scalped and otherwise abused the Union soldiers, torturing those who had not yet died, mutilating those already gone. They sliced off ears and heads. They severed one man's penis and shoved it into his mouth. Whatever natural line had been assumed to exist between civilized whites and native savages—a line that had for decades been alleged to justify the poor treatment of Native Americans—had been not just crossed but erased.

If any doubt remained of this, it was underscored two months later, in the fall of 1864, in the rolling prairie of southeastern Colorado. Colonel John M. Chivington, a towering and booming Methodist minister who hated Indians more than the devil, led about eight hundred Colorado Volunteers armed with artillery, rifles, and .44 Colt 1860 Army revolvers to a Cheyenne and Arapaho village on the banks of Sand Creek. Chivington had come to seek retribution for a series of raids perpetrated by Cheyenne on emigrants. Possibly some of the men in the village had been involved in these raids, but most of the five hundred or so Cheyenne and Arapaho were peaceful and intent on staying so.

Chivington's army attacked at dawn. Startled from sleep, the Indians lunged for what weapons they had, but the American cavalry was already upon them, galloping into the village from several directions. For two hours the Americans killed mostly unarmed Indians, taking no mercy on women or children. According to later reports, Chivington had made a

The Sand Creek Massacre of 1864.

special point of telling his men to target children. "Kill and scalp all, big and little; nits make lice." When women pleaded for mercy, they were shot at point-blank range. When a six-year-old girl approached the soldiers with a white flag, she was shot and killed. Infants were shot in the arms of their mothers, and at least one fetus was cut from her dead mother's uterus. Chivington, who seemed incapable of grasping what he had done, would gloat that his troops killed four or five hundred Indians that morning, but the number was probably closer to two hundred. Later, Congress would investigate and conclude that Chivington's army had exercised barbarity "such as never before disgraced the acts of men claiming to be civilized."

A common element of the atrocities perpetrated by the bushwhack-ers and Chivington's army was Colt revolvers. To blame Sand Creek, or American savagery more generally, on revolvers would be simplistic and reductive—many factors drove such violence in the west in 1864—but certainly the guns made the killing easier and quicker, facilitating rash conduct and quickening bloodlust. It gave targets no time to flee and shooters no time to second-guess themselves or consult their consciences before pulling the trigger.

Years earlier, in making his argument for Colt revolvers, Senator Thomas Rusk had predicted a general Indian war in the west. Though neither Rusk nor Colt was around to see it, this prediction came to pass. As Native Americans realized that their survival was at stake, they fought to keep their land and avenge encroachments. The US Army continued to attack with revolvers, among other firearms, but in the end it was a different industrial technology that defeated Native Americans on the plains. The transcontinental railroad, completed in 1869, brought whites west in ceaseless droves. These newcomers very quickly finished off the buffalo, then claimed the land where the buffalo had roamed. The Indians could stand up to guns, but they could not endure starvation.

No doubt all of this would have happened without Colt's invention, but possibly on different terms. At the least, the Indians would have held the upper hand a while longer, and whites would have taken a while longer to get a foothold, and perhaps with more negotiation and less killing.

III

Two years after Colt's death, on February 5, 1864, his armory burned to the ground. The fire began shortly after the start of the workday, in an attic room, whipped through the riverfront section of the building, and soon consumed the entire original structure. Confederate agents were suspected, but no evidence of arson ever came to light, and the factory, its yellow-pine floors soaked by oil from years of lubricating machinery, was highly susceptible to accidental fire. However the blaze started, it burned so hot that the steel parts of machines melted together. "Our admiration is especially excited," a correspondent from *Harper's Weekly* wrote after visiting the ruins, "as we glance at the confused debris of what was once the most magnificent and elaborate machinery in the country."

Elizabeth watched the fire from a window of Armsmear, bursting into tears when the blue dome toppled into the burning pile. Two days later, fully composed, she walked through the charred rubble to the remains of her husband's office. Elizabeth had inherited enough wealth from Sam—at least $5 million—that she might easily have decided to take the insurance money and let the armory close or run at a reduced size. She apparently never considered this option. In part to serve the memory of Sam and in part for the sake of the workers, she rebuilt the armory exactly as it had been, blue dome and all.

The business of gunmaking was never Elizabeth's real interest, though. She left this to Elisha Root, who took over as president of the company after Colt's death; and when Root died in 1865, she put her brother Richard Jarvis in charge. Elizabeth devoted her energies to memorializing her husband. This was not merely a sentimental gesture of adoration, but a pragmatic recognition that the reputations of both the company and the family depended in part on the legacy of the man whose name they bore.

Sam would have admired her extraordinary efforts. First, she hired Henry Barnard, a prominent educator in Hartford, to write a four-hundred-page hagiography of her husband. She then hired Charles Loring Elliott, one of the leading portrait painters of the day, to paint a larger-than-life portrait of Sam, drawn from likenesses made during his lifetime. Elliott improved upon the original, removing a good thirty pounds from his subject's waist and putting him in trim and robust health.

Most significant, Elizabeth built a church in Hartford in Sam's honor. Conceived a month after the armory fire and financed entirely by Elizabeth, the Church of the Good Shepherd was designed by the architect Edward Tuckerman Potter, whose work would include Mark Twain's house in Hartford among other showcase projects. Built of Portland brownstone and light Ohio sandstone, with a steep slate roof and a tall narrow steeple, the church appeared at a distance to be a fine example of Gothic Revival ecclesiastical architecture. On closer inspection, its singular details became apparent. Under Elizabeth's direction, Potter had incorporated Colt revolvers, and parts of revolvers, into the church facade. Downward-aiming pistols were carved into stone columns as ornamental braces for capitals. Revolver cylinders decorated the walls. Crosses were festooned by the barrels and grips of pistols.

Elizabeth believed unquestioningly in two things, her religion and her dead husband, and the Church of the Good Shepherd was her most explicit attempt to reconcile the two. It was perhaps easier to do this in the nineteenth century, when developments in firearms and the advancement of white Christian civilization were far from mutually exclusive objectives. Like the young missionaries aboard the *Corvo*, revolvers were heralds to the heathen; by taming the heathen—the savage, the barbarian—they allowed Christianity to flourish. "The more, then, arms are perfected," wrote Henry Barnard, "the stronger is civilization against outer barbarians." Elizabeth never doubted that guns and God were compatible.

As she aged, Elizabeth became Hartford's leading philanthropist and a paragon of civic virtue. She carried on many of the traditions begun under her husband in Coltsville, such as financing the Armory Band and lending the grounds for balloon ascensions and fireworks on the Fourth of July. She also branched out into the kind of good works Colt would have had nothing to do with, such as donating heavily to the Episcopal Women's Auxiliary to help emancipated slaves and fund Indian schools. She was patron to a number of significant American artists, most notably her friend Frederic Church, one of the painters of the Hudson River School. Later, she gave nearly her entire collection of art, along with a valuable collection of Colt guns, to the Wadsworth Atheneum, where they remain today.

The only surviving child of Sam and Elizabeth, Caldwell Hart Colt—Collie, as he had been called as a child—grew into a handsome young man who enjoyed all of the trappings, and traps, that great wealth can bestow. After an indulged and mischief-filled childhood, he attended St. Paul's School and later Yale, where he spent college more absorbed by "hunting and good dogs . . . and the Yale-Harvard contests in boating," as the *New York Times* put it, than by his studies. In November of 1879, when he turned twenty-one and came into his majority—and an inheritance of no less than $2 million—his mother threw him "one of the most brilliant parties which has ever been given in Hartford," according to the *Courant*.

Endowed with his father's taste for pleasure but none of his passion for work, Caldwell was the template for a generation of Gilded Age wastrels to follow. He was given a position at the company as vice president but never took an active role in the business, preferring to pass his time in Newport or aboard yachts. He made a name for himself as a sailor after purchasing the *Dauntless*, a sleek schooner previously owned and raced by James Gordon Bennett Jr., and captaining the vessel through numerous regattas. He would die in January of 1894, age thirty-five, under mysterious circumstances while wintering in Florida. The official cause was tonsillitis, but there were rumors that he was killed by a jealous husband.

After Elizabeth and Caldwell, the best-compensated legatee of Colt's estate was Samuel Caldwell Colt. For all of his disappointment in Sammy, Sam had clearly loved the young man he called his nephew. He did not grant him the lavish riches of Caldwell, but he left him enough to live on comfortably. Sammy seems to have spent his inheritance sensibly, though probably not in ways that Colt would have approved of. In 1862, at the age of twenty, he put schooling behind him forever and returned to the town of Kent, Connecticut, to the Fullers' farm, where he took up a life of farming and animal husbandry. He and Elizabeth remained close for years after Colt's death. She occasionally visited him in Kent, and when he married in December 1863, she hosted the wedding at Armsmear.

Sammy was known to be gentle and decent. When somebody lit his barn on fire in 1870, the *Courant* was mystified, for "Mr. Colt is not a man who makes enemies." The following year, he became a founding member of an association to prevent cruelty to animals. He spent his life in Connecticut, happily married to his wife, Mary, and raising six children. When he died in 1915 at age seventy-three, the *Courant* would refer to him as a "favorite nephew" of Samuel Colt, but his children and grandchildren evidently knew the truth. In 1987, the *Courant* would publish a profile of a grandson of Samuel C. Colt named Harold G. Colt Jr. At seventy and never married, Harold Colt had spent much of his life traveling the world on what remained of his grandfather's inheritance. "It frees you to do exactly what you want to do, which I like," he said of the money. He told the *Courant* that he was the great-grandson, and last surviving direct descendant, of Samuel Colt, inventor of the revolver. Harold Colt died in 1995.

Other than bequests to Elizabeth, Caldwell, and Sammy, which were generous and definite, Colt's will is a document more reflective of pique than beneficence. He revised it several times before he died, generally to punish those who had offended him. A bequest to Hartford for the endowment of a scientific school in the South Meadow was withdrawn when the city refused to accommodate one of his applications for a tax break. He wrote his brother Christopher out of his will for various offenses, then revoked a bequest to James "for his late unbrotherly conduct."

How James Colt supported himself in the years just after Sam's death is not clear, as he no longer had his job as a judge and had given up his legal career to work for his brother. In January of 1862, shortly after Sam's death, he sent a terse letter to Elisha Root seeking employment at the armory. Root does not seem to have responded favorably, and James never returned to the Colt company. In 1865, he sued Colt's estate, claiming that he was owed residuary shares of stock that Sam had failed to cancel when he revoked the main part of James's inheritance. He won $300,000, enough to make him a wealthy man who never needed to work again. He moved back to Hartford and lived there until his death in 1878.

When a newspaper in Oskaloosa, Kansas, learned of James Colt's death, it recalled the history of the Colt family, especially the infamy of John and the fame of Samuel, "one of the most successful inventors of the age," but also "one of the worst men of his day." The Colt family, the newspaper concluded, "will long be remembered for its union of genius and crime."

Tales of appearances by John C. Colt persisted through the nineteenth century. In one of these, an old acquaintance of John's named Samuel Everett was riding at twilight through the Santa Clara Valley in California when he stopped at a ranch, hoping to find a bed for the night. The owner of the ranch gave his name as Don Carlos Juan Brewster, but Everett swore it was none other than John Colt. "He was richly dressed, including silver bells. A woman, a golden-haired beauty, naturally, stood on the portico with two beautiful children." In 1875, the *Boston Post* reported another story about John Colt that raced around New York City for a time. This one featured a man in Paris who confessed to being John just before dying.

The fate of Caroline Colt, née Henshaw, remains one of the enduring mysteries of Colt's life. Her name appears now and then in Colt's correspondence through the early 1850s, then disappears. There are no records of her after that. William Edwards's claim that Caroline Colt changed her name and became Julia Leicester would do much to solve the mystery of both their lives, if only it were true.

As for Julia, we know something of what became of her from various odd mentions in newspapers. After moving to London with her husband, Friedrich Von Oppen, who took over Colt's English sales office in 1862, she tried her hand at literature. A novel she published in 1872, entitled *No Fatherland*, told the story of a young American girl who falls into a romance with the son of Czar Nicholas, then marries a Spaniard, then gives birth to twins—at which point the book's reviewers lost the thread of the convoluted plot. In six hundred laborious pages, the narrative trudged through an international set of characters who spoke "a most bewildering jargon," according to one reviewer, of English blended with German blended with French. "It may seem a strong thing to say," wrote another reviewer, "but we believe it to be true, that 'No Fatherland' is the silliest story that ever was published."

Following *No Fatherland*, Julia fell out of sight for a while, but in 1886 several American newspapers ran a story about the Baroness Von Oppen, "an elderly Russian lady, who has been a resident in England since her divorce from her husband several years ago." While traveling with her French maid on a train from New York to Philadelphia, the baroness had lost her jewels, valued at $13,000. "Strange as the story appears, the character of Baroness Von Oppen precludes the possibility of doubt as to its truthfulness," stated the *Chicago Tribune*, a sentence that seemed to suggest that there was in fact plenty of doubt. The following year, she surfaced again, this time in the *Springfield Republican*. "Madam von Oppen presents her compliments to the postmaster of Springfield, Mass.," began the article, "and hopes he will kindly tell her if there is any person there who can recollect her as Miss Leicester, when she resided with Mr. and Mrs. Warriner in 1850." Julia had mentioned the Warriners in a letter she wrote to Colt in 1857. It seems that she had lived in Springfield with a couple by that name in 1850 and 1851. "Madam von Oppen was a young girl in those days. . . . Then she went to the continent with some friends and then got married in Germany. . . . Is there a living soul in Springfield who cares to see Julia Leicester that was?"

IV

The Colt armory that rose from the ashes of the fire soon retained its former glory as the most advanced factory in the country. After Elisha Root died in 1865 at the age of fifty-seven, his influence continued to spread. "Like a mother, a superintendent may be judged, in some measure, by the children he rears, and few superintendents can show such a family," the *American Machinist* would state of Root in 1914. An extraordinary number of nineteenth-century American industries were connected to the Colt armory by one or two degrees of separation, as men who began careers there moved to other important manufacturing companies in New England and New York.

One former Colt employee, Andrew R. Arnold, took his knowledge to Lebbeus B. Miller, who later applied armory techniques as superintendent of the Singer Manufacturing Company, the world's largest producer of sewing machines. George A. Fairchild moved from the Colt armory to the Weed Sewing Machine Company, which despite its name was best known for making bicycles for the Pope Manufacturing Company, the world's leading bike manufacturer. There Fairchild and Albert A. Pope applied machinery to the mass production of bicycles and for a time produced more of them than any other factory. When the bicycle fad began to decline near the end of the century, Albert Pope would turn his attention to a new fad. He became the first man to apply machine-based mass production to the building of automobiles.

The American System of manufacturing was a mixed blessing for workers. Much as armies turned men into interchangeable parts, factories threatened to turn workers into automatons, condemning them to repetitive, soul-crushing labor (which would be taken to extremes later by scientific-management experts such as Frederick Taylor). But the system raised the American standard of living by supplying affordable mass-produced goods while providing jobs and fueling an extraordinary economy. And if Colt's methods of manufacturing made people automatons, the gun itself endowed them (much as mass-produced automobiles would in the twentieth century) with the sensation of autonomy. Long before Hollywood began to make westerns in the early twentieth century and put revolvers into the hands of actors, the six-shooter was as much an expression of American individualism and personal agency as it was a weapon. Unlike a rifle, a revolver was worn close to the body, almost as an extension of the body, and it gave the individual who wore it the power to defend himself or herself (women began to carry revolvers after the Civil War) against malefactors, protecting the weak against the strong and the one against the many. "God made man," went a popular western saying, "but Colt made them equal." There was no better weapon for the lone man on the range or, for that matter, the Lone Ranger. The actor who played the hero of the 1950s television show carried a pair of Colt .45s.

Yet the revolver was a double-edged sword. As it gave protection to the good and vulnerable, it also enabled dark tendencies in the postwar nation. Thousands of young men came out of the Civil War hardened to violence, proficient with firearms, and facing limited prospects. All seemed to have a revolver, either a memento from the war or newly acquired. At least four hundred thousand of the guns had been produced by Colt's company by the end of the war, and they were everywhere now. In the south and west, the once-rare sight of a man walking down the street with a revolver in his belt or holster became commonplace—and so did revolver-facilitated transgressions. The James brothers used revolvers to virtually invent the new crime of daylight bank robberies: two or three men would enter a bank during business hours, wave their revolvers and demand money, then take off before the alarm could be sounded. It was the brothers' ability to fire multiple rounds that made such robberies successful.

All over the American west, in boomtowns that rose with mining strikes or near cattle routes—or alongside the new railroad tracks that spidered across the plains after the Civil War—outlaws carried Colt revolvers and drew them with frequency. The Dalton Gang never traveled without Colts at their sides, nor did John Wesley Hardin, Pat Garrett, Wyatt Earp, Doc Holliday, or Butch Cassidy and the Sundance Kid. Perhaps the most famous and skilled Colt-slinger of them all was James Butler Hickok, better known as Wild Bill, who began his gun-fighting career in Kansas as a free-soil jayhawker and killed no fewer—and possibly many more—than seven men with his prized Colt 1851 Navies, before he was killed himself in Deadwood, South Dakota, by a bullet fired from a Colt 1873 "Peacemaker."

Shortly before her death in 1905, Elizabeth moved the remains of Sam and their children to nearby Cedar Hill Cemetery. To replace the tomb near Armsmear she commissioned one more monument to her husband, a giant statue of Colt standing high on a granite pedestal. At his feet was another statue, of his boyhood self carving a gun out of wood. It was not for lack of effort by Elizabeth to turn her husband into a noble hero that he was nothing of the sort.

That said, it is not fair to charge Colt, as some scholars have, as an accessory to the crime of making America a gun-packed nation. According to these scholars, early gun manufacturers, including Oliver Winchester and Eliphalet Remington, but first and foremost Sam Colt, essentially created their own market with aggressive sales techniques. This argument draws on a popular idea that America was never *essentially* a gun culture, and that an affinity for guns was somehow lodged in the national psyche through the machinations of businessmen such as Colt.

While Colt *was* a master salesman, this view gives him too much credit and too much blame. As we have seen, he was often behind, not ahead, of the curve when it came to realizing the potential of his gun in the American west. Certainly he coaxed and expanded the market, sometimes cynically so, but he did not create the conditions that made his revolvers popular. John L. O'Sullivan and James K. Polk did that. Gold did that. American ambition and desire did that. Just as it is wishful thinking to believe that slavery and Indian expulsion were incidental to American history, it is willful blindness to downplay the appetite for guns that emerged in the United States in the middle of the nineteenth century, regardless of Colt.

The Colt revolver was the first widely used multishot weapon, but it was by no means the last. As mentioned earlier, other multishot guns, such as Henry's and Spencer's, were coming to market by the time Colt died, and many more, faster and deadlier, soon appeared. During the Civil War, an American named Richard Jordan Gatling invented a hand-cranked six-barrel revolving gun that looked like a giant pepperbox pistol but could fire two hundred shots per minute. Like many other gunmakers, including Colt, Gatling justified his invention by contending that it would *save* lives, allowing armies to reduce their numbers by more or less the same rate his gun increased celerity of fire. After the war, Gatling sold his patent to the Colt company, which made his guns through the nineteenth century, before they were outmatched by the invention of Hiram Maxim, a machine gun that could spew as many as six hundred bullets in a minute. In 1893, in South Africa, fifty British police officers armed with four Maxims and two other machine guns mowed down three thousand African troops in two hours. No one was any longer under the illusion that rapid-fire guns were going to save lives. Many wars, acts of terrorism, and psychopathic rampages since have further complicated the legacy of rapid-firing guns, perhaps most poignantly the 2012 massacre of schoolchildren and teachers at Sandy Hook Elementary School in Newtown, Connecticut, just an hour's drive west of Hartford on Interstate 84. The shooter killed twenty-six children and teachers with a type of rapid-firing rifle, known as the AR-15, that had been developed from a patent once owned by the Colt company. In 2019, Colt Manufacturing Comany LLC, the successor to the business Sam Colt incorporated in 1855, announced that it would no longer supply the AR-15 to the civilian market.

Which brings us back to the present, back to unavoidable questions about the legacy of Sam Colt, and back, perhaps, to our battle-ready positions. It would be naive to believe that the story of Colt and his six-shooter will significantly change anyone's opinion about guns, but it should at least remind us of how much we owe, for better and for worse, to one gun in particular.

Acknowledgments

In the course of researching and writing *Revolver*, I accumulated more debts than I can ever repay. First, my thanks to Conor Fitzgerald. This book was born of a brief conversation I had with Conor in the spring of 2016. Since then, Conor has been extraordinarily generous with his wide knowledge of historical firearms, among other subjects, making himself available to answer every question that came into my mind, or sending me to someone who could help. A thousand thanks to Conor for his innumerable acts of kindness.

It was Conor who put me in touch with R. L. "Larry" Wilson, one of the world's leading authorities on nineteenth-century Colt guns. I met Larry only months before he died, but in the time I knew him he lavished me with books (including some of his own), letters, and other materials, and inspired me with his infectious enthusiasm for all things Colt. I suspect that Larry would not entirely agree with my view of Sam Colt, whom he unabashedly adored, but I am sure he would have approved of my not sharing *his* view, because he pointedly told me so. I will be forever grateful to Larry for his early encouragement and assistance.

My thanks to Professor Jonathan Obert of Amherst College, who shared some of his research with me—and whom I enjoyed bumping into occasionally at the Connecticut Historical Society—and to Margaret Dakin, of the Amherst College Archives, who unearthed some great material regarding Colt's 1830 cannon escapade in Amherst. My lunches with Professor Glenn Corbett of John Jay College of Criminal Justice were happy occasions to discuss my thoughts and discoveries about Colt, and to hear Glenn's. Among his many pursuits and interests, Glenn is writing a book about Roswell Colt, and he added to my knowledge of the Colt clan. Professor Christian Rojas of Barnard College helped me brush up on chemistry, and Dr. Steven Magid of the Hospital for Special Surgery helped me attempt to diagnose Colt's illness on the basis of a few very old clues. Michael Miscione, the former Manhattan Borough Historian and history sleuth extraordinaire, helped me locate the site of Colt's 1832 nitrous oxide demonstration. Julie Bullock of the Ware Historical Society guided me through an enjoyable and enlightening visit to her town. Bruce Balistrieri of the Paterson Museum led me on a sweaty but fascinating traipse through woods and weeds to the ruins of Colt's first factory on the Passaic River. Jim Griffin drove me around Hartford (with Larry Wilson riding shotgun) on my first tour of Colt historical sites. Willie Granston kindly shared with me his terrific master's thesis on Elizabeth Colt. Deirdre O'Regan, of the National Maritime Historical Society, set me straight on a few questions about nineteenth-century sea voyages. Firearms scholar Charles Pate prevented me from committing numerous mistakes in my treatment of Colt's guns. My thanks to all, and also to Alex MacKenzie, Paul Davies, John Ross, Greg Martin, Albert Birchaux, Anne Lee, and Carrie Brown. None of the above is responsible for any errors or faults in this book, but it is better because of them.

I could not have written *Revolver* without the resources and assistance of numerous public archives. I am especially indebted to the excellent staff of the Connecticut Historical Society in Hartford, where I spent many fruitful and delightful hours poring over Colt's correspondence. I also passed some excellent days across town at the Connecticut State Library and had the pleasure of meeting Dave Corrigan of the Connecticut State Museum, who showed me a number of treasures I would have otherwise overlooked. (It was Dave who emailed me scans of the remarkable letters Colt wrote to his "neffue" Sammy; the day I received those was a very good day.) These archives, and all those I mention in my source notes and bibliography, are national treasures, and I'm glad for the time I was privileged to spend with their collections.

The magnificent Kris Dahl made this book possible, as she has all of my previous books; I am fortunate to have her as my agent. It has also been my good fortune to write three of my books for Colin Harrison, my editor at Scribner. Colin has an almost preternatural ability to grasp what a writer means to express even before the writer realizes it himself, and he knows exactly what to say, and what not to say, to guide a writer home. I am also grateful to Sarah Goldberg, associate editor at Scribner, for so ably shepherding *Revolver* through the stages between raw manuscript and finished book, and to production editor Kathleen Rizzo for making it the most polished book it could be. Any lapses in *Revolver* are not for lack of effort by all at Scribner to prevent me from committing them.

I owe a very large and special debt of gratitude to my friend Constance Rosenblum, who has read all of my books in draft and improved every one of them with her incisive queries and comments, not to mention her unerring eye for typos, bad prose, and nonsense. To my wife, Ann Varney, and my sons, Jackson and Will—thank you for putting up with me and Sam Colt these last few years, and for pretty much everything else you do to make life good. And, finally, to Nancy Rasenberger, for giving me the gift of her curiosity and love of history—thanks, Mom.

A Note on Sources

Material in *Revolver* has been largely drawn from collections of Colt's letters and documents, primarily those in the Samuel Colt Papers at the Connecticut Historical Society. Other archives with abundant Colt material include the Colt Family Papers at the University of Rhode Island, the Jarvis-Robinson Family Papers at Yale University, the Samuel Colt Correspondence at the Wadsworth Atheneum, and, especially, the Colt's Patent Fire Arms Manufacturing Company Records at the Connecticut State Library and the Colt Collection at the Connecticut State Museum.

For additional primary source material I have consulted archives at Old Sturbridge Village, the Young Men's Library Association of Ware, the Historical Society of Pennsylvania, the Presbyterian Historical Society, and the New Jersey Historical Society, among other archives. I have also benefited greatly from online newspaper archives accessed at the New York Public Library, the Library of Congress, and Newspapers.com. Alongside primary source material, I have drawn on a wealth of American history covering the years between the War of 1812 and the Civil War, including the work of many wonderful writers and scholars cited in the source notes and bibliography.

In the interest of keeping this already hefty book a manageable size, I have placed my extensive notes and bibliography, in searchable form, online at **jimrasenberger.com**. Readers will also find there additional images, links to online material, new facts and errata that come to my attention, and various digressions down rabbit holes that did not make it into the book but are interesting (at least to me) nonetheless.

Because websites, like people, do not always last, the Waterman Research Center of the Connecticut Historical Society (**chs.org**), founded in 1825, has graciously agreed to retain a copy of the notes and bibliography in perpetuity and will supply these upon request.

Illustration and Photograph Credits

293 Courtesy of the Connecticut State Library, PG 460, Colt Firearms
Industry Collection

319 Public domain, with thanks to R. L. Wilson

326 Courtesy of the Nebraska State Historical Society

341 The Wadsworth Atheneum Museum of Art, Elizabeth Hart Jarvis
Colt Collection, 1905.53

359 Courtesy of the Library of Congress, Prints and Photographs Division

378 The Autry Museum

387 Courtesy of the Connecticut State Library, PG 460, Colt Firearms
Industry Collection

393 History Colorado, Accession #89.451.4825

Insert

1. Courtesy of the Museum of Connecticut History
2. Courtesy of the Connecticut State Library, PG 460, Colt Firearms
Industry Collection
3. Courtesy of the New York Public Library
4. Courtesy of Greg Martin
5. The Milwaukee Art Museum
6. Courtesy of the Library of Congress, Prints and Photographs Division
7. Courtesy of the Library of Congress, Prints and Photographs Division
8. The Wadsworth Atheneum Museum of Art, Elizabeth Hart Jarvis
Colt Collection, 1905.1005
9. The Wadsworth Atheneum Museum of Art, Elizabeth Hart Jarvis
Colt Collection, 1905.988
10. Courtesy of the Connecticut State Library, PG 460, Colt Firearms
Industry Collection
11. The Wadsworth Atheneum Museum of Art, Elizabeth Hart Jarvis
Colt Collection
12. Courtesy of the Connecticut State Library, PG 460, Colt Firearms
Industry Collection
13. Courtesy of Albert Brichaux
14. The Wadsworth Atheneum Museum of Art
15. The New-York Historical Society
16. The Nelson-Atkins Museum of Art
17. Courtesy of the Library of Congress, Prints and Photographs Division
18. Kansas State Historical Society
19. Courtesy of the Library of Congress, Prints and Photographs Division
20. Public domain; Wikimedia Commons
21. Courtesy of the Library of Congress, Prints and Photographs Division

22. History Colorado, Accession #75.64.1
23. Courtesy of the National Portrait Gallery, Smithsonian Institution
24. The Wadsworth Atheneum Museum of Art, Elizabeth Hart Jarvis Colt Collection, 1905.9
25. Courtesy of the Museum of Connecticut History

Index

Numbers in italics refer to pages with illustrations.

About the Author

Jim Rasenberger is the author of three previous books—*The Brilliant Disaster*; *America, 1908*; and *High Steel*—and has contributed to the *New York Times*, *Vanity Fair*, *Smithsonian*, and other publications. He is a native of Washington, DC, and lives in New York City.